Letters to Her

Letters to Henrietta

ISABELLA BIRD

EDITED BY KAY CHUBBUCK

JOHN MURRAY
Albemarle Street, London

First published in 2002
by John Murray (Publishers) Ltd,
50 Albemarle Street, London W1S 4BD

A catalogue record for this book is available from the British Library

ISBN 0-7195-6047 0

Typeset in 12/12.5 Monotype Bembo by Servis Filmsetting Ltd, Manchester

Printed and bound in Great Britain by Butler and Tanner Ltd,
Frome and London

Contents

Illustrations   vii
Maps   ix

Introduction by Kay Chubbuck   1

PART ONE: THE FIRST WORLD TOUR, 1872–3

The Sea   31
Australia   33
Hawaii   56
Colorado   143

PART TWO: THE SECOND WORLD TOUR, 1878–9

Japan & the Way Thither   203
China   206
The Malay Peninsula   235

Chronology   307
Notes on People and Places   313
Bibliography   346
Acknowledgements   350
Index   351

Illustrations

(*between pages 180 and 181*)

1. Isabella Bird in San Francisco, 1873
2. Isabella at the height of her fame, c. 1899
3. Tobermory, Isle of Mull, 1885
4. Isabella on her wedding day, 1881
5. Henrietta Bird
6. John Bishop
7. Suburban house, Melbourne
8. Collins Street, Melbourne
9. An Australian bottle tree
10. King William Charles Lunalilo of Hawaii
11. Picnic on Coconut Island, Hawaii
12. Letter to Henrietta, June 6, 1873
13. Hawaiian palms
14. Sketch of Kilauea, 1873
15. Griff Evans's ranch, Estes Park, Colorado
16. Isabella wearing her Bloomer Suit in Colorado
17. Isabella with camera, China, 1895
18. The cover of *Unbeaten Tracks in Japan*
19. Ceremonial entrance at Nikko
20. The Ainu of Hokkaido
21. Buddhist monk, Japan
22. 'Divinity in Wen-Shu-Yuan Temple, Chengtu'
23. 'Rock Temple, Li-Fan Ting'
24. English missionaries in Chinese dress
25. English children in Fujian
26. 'The Street of Tsa-ku-Lao'
27. 'The Bridge at Mien-Chuh'
28. Captured tiger, Malaya Peninsula
29. Isabella's first elephant ride in Perak
30. British administrators, Penang
31. Hugh Low, Resident of Perak
32. The daughter of Sir Harry Parkes, Tokyo

List of Illustrations and Acknowledgements

Grateful acknowledgement is made to the following for permission to reproduce photographs: 1 and 11, Lyman House Memorial Museum, Hilo; 3, Aberdeen University; 10, The Hawaiian Historical Society; 13, Pres. by A. S. Waley, Royal Geographical Society, London; 15, City of Greeley Museums, Colorado, Permanent Collection; 25, Mrs I. L. Bishop, Royal Geographical Society, London; 28, Royal Geographical Society, London; 30, H. Clifford, Royal Geographic Society, London. All the other photographs are from the John Murray Archives.

Maps

Isabella's Round-the-World Tours   x–xi
The Hawaiian Islands   xii

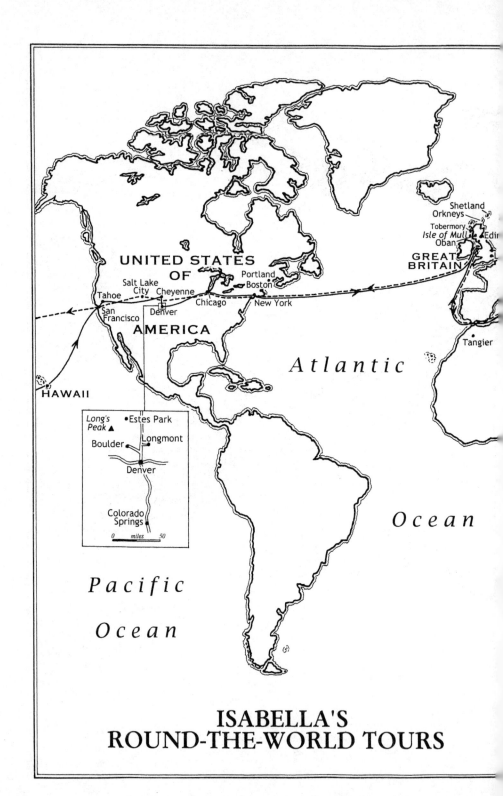

Shetland
Orkneys
Tobermory
Isle of Mull
Oban
Edir

UNITED STATES
OF

Salt Lake
City
Cheyenne
Tahoe
Denver
San
Francisco
AMERICA
Portland
Boston
Chicago
New York

GREAT
BRITAIN

Tangier

Atlantic

HAWAII

Ocean

Long's
Peak ▲
Boulder
Denver
Colorado
Springs
Estes Park
Longmont

0   miles   50

Pacific

Ocean

**ISABELLA'S
ROUND-THE-WORLD TOURS**

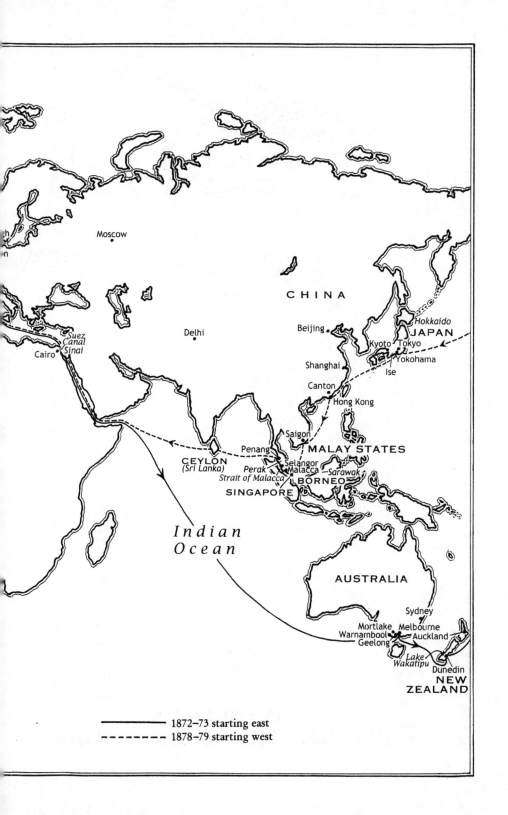

Moscow

CHINA

Hokkaido
JAPAN

Suez
Canal
Sinai

Cairo

Delhi

Beijing

Kyoto Tokyo
Yokohama
Ise

Shanghai

Canton

Hong Kong

Saigon

Penang

MALAY STATES

CEYLON
(Sri Lanka)

Perak
Strait of Malacca

Selangor
Malacca — Sarawak
BORNEO

SINGAPORE

*Indian
Ocean*

AUSTRALIA

Sydney

Mortlake Melbourne
Warnambool — Auckland
Geelong

*Lake
Wakatipu* Dunedin

NEW
ZEALAND

——————— 1872–73 starting east
- - - - - - - - 1878–79 starting west

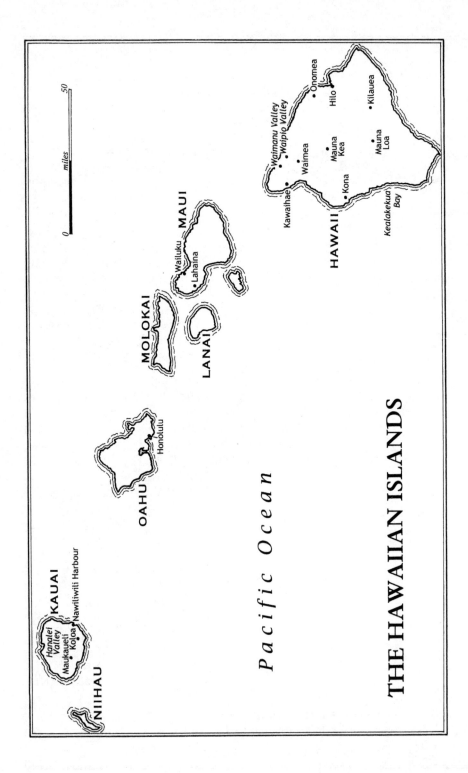

THE HAWAIIAN ISLANDS

Pacific Ocean

NIIHAU

KAUAI
Hanalei Valley
Maukaueti
Koloa
Nawiliwiti Harbour

OAHU
Honolulu

MOLOKAI

LANAI

MAUI
Wailuku
Lahaina

HAWAII
Kawaihae
Waimea
Kona
Kealakekua Bay
Mauna Kea
Mauna Loa
Kilauea
Hilo
Onomea
Waimanu Valley
Waipio Valley

miles
0   50

Introduction

Let us begin with an image, two-dimensional, black and white, dating from approximately 1899. In it, the subject is at the height of her fame. She stands proud – about four feet, eleven inches – clad in a loose-fitting gown of Chinese silk. The fabric is cut in the Manchu style, embroidered with butterflies, an exotic dress. When we look at the face, we see that the gaze is constructed: it is confident and imperious. It projects her reputation. She is the first female fellow of the Royal Geographical Society. She has dined with the Prime Minister, William Gladstone, and has been presented to the Queen. She is the author of a number of best-selling books, including *The Hawaiian Archipelago, The Golden Chersonese, Unbeaten Tracks in Japan* and *A Lady's Life in the Rocky Mountains*. This photograph will be circulated and reproduced. It is part of the currency of her literary fashion.

Now let us look at another image, dating from 1873. Here, we see a woman less assured, her mouth slightly open, showing her teeth (which were about to be removed). This woman seems expectant, breathless; she has none of the rigidity of the woman before. Nor does she seem to share her pretension: her dress is modest and forgettable, typical for an unmarried woman of her time. She, too, has written books: *Aspects of Religion in the United States* and *An Englishwoman in America*. In fact, this woman is in America now. Her photo has been snapped in San Francisco and it will be sent to friends she has made in Hawaii. Once they die, it will rest undisturbed in an archive on what is now called the Big Island for one hundred years.

Both these women are Isabella Bird, the invalid whose exploits of physical endurance were to make her the heroine of Victorian travel. Both faces – the one confident, the other anxious; the one professional, the other dilettante – articulate the truth of her complex personality. After all, Isabella was forty before she found her vocation. She was middle-aged, middle-class, living with her maiden sister on the Isle of Mull. She had been raised in an environment that preached virtues of self-abnegation. She believed in discipline, sacrifice and hard work. She undertook every journey for a cause – for health, for empire, for good deeds – yet despite herself, she really enjoyed them. Isabella thus found the juncture between who she was and who she thought she ought to be immensely uncomfortable.

Isabella's guilt about her journeys meant that she jealously guarded her reputation. This makes it difficult to distinguish conclusively between what is genuine and what is contrived, to write a fully accurate introduction. For example, Isabella's first biographer was hand-picked; she was given explicit instructions about what to write.[1] It was Isabella, too, who organised her letters before she died, cutting out sections from some, destroying others entirely. Another friend, Ella Blackie, upheld Victorian convention by crossing out passages with a thick black pen.[2] As a result, the image we have is artificial, but it is no less true by virtue of its artifice. It may be as polished as the studio portrait, but we can counter it with fragments of the more natural Isabella, of the woman who paused for the photo in San Francisco, who must have known on some level that she was making pleasure trips. It is this Isabella that I have tried to resurrect. I have used the letters printed in this volume – never before published in their original state – to explore a complex of truths and half-truths, unanswered questions, false leads and occasional loose ends.

Let us consider what remains. Aside from photos of the traveller, we have:

- two small scientific sketches of plants;
- hundreds of letters – some torn, some smudged, some cut, some missing;
- packets of photographs, uncatalogued, from her journeys;
- glass plates (her photographic negatives from the Yangtze);
- travel books and articles written after 1849;
- honours given to her by the King of Hawaii;
- the handwritten record of a purse embroidered by the murdered Queen of Korea (as well as a large paisley shawl, some Manchu jewellery, and her 'American lady's mountain dress'), offered to Christie's in 1913;
- a Japanese gilt and lacquer toilet table, sold by her publisher at auction in 1928;

1 See Anna Stoddart, *The Life of Isabella Bird (Mrs. Bishop)* (London: John Murray, 1906), 350, as well as unpublished correspondence between Stoddart and John Murray IV in John Murray Archives (JMA). Most disturbing in this interchange is Stoddart's insistence on publishing anecdotes about Isabella that Murray had proved false.

2 For Isabella's organisation of her manuscripts, see Elizabeth Kerr's letter to John Murray IV, 14 September 1912; and Stoddart's correspondence with John and Hallam Murray from 1905 (JMA). See also Isabella Bird's letter to Ella Blackie, 28 February 1888, in the John Stuart Blackie Collection (JSB) of the National Library of Scotland, Edinburgh. MS 2637 ff. 151. For Ella Blackie's omissions, see Isabella's letters in the same archive.

- the watch of Warren Hasting, first British Governor of India, now in the possession of John Murray;
- her will, with a brief catalogue of her property;
- and the biography written by Anna Stoddart, containing reflections by those who knew her and quotations from documents long since destroyed.

How do we reconstruct the 'real' Isabella from these odds and ends? How do we recreate a sense of what she was really like? The task of a biographer is to map and name, to presume the subject to be a finite structure. But real lives rarely, if ever, lend themselves to closure. And when a writer like Isabella has a propensity to invent, it becomes difficult to separate reality from fiction, or, more accurately, to find the friction where the two combine. (Of course, hardly any individual, when writing about herself, writes 'the truth'. It is difficult to resist the urge to embellish, to ignore, to misrepresent. It is hard to avoid writing about how things might have been, rather than how they were. Isabella was no different.)

I. What We Know

Certainly some facts are indisputable. We know that Isabella was born at Boroughbridge Hall in North Yorkshire on October 15, 1831. Some years later, maybe three, her mother gave birth to her sister, Henrietta. There had been boys, in her father's first marriage and in this one, but they died.[3] Isabella and Henrietta were the only living children.

Other things we know: the family was religious. Isabella's mother taught Sunday School; her father was a preacher. (So zealous was Edward Bird that he was stoned out of his Birmingham church; it was not the first time the severity of his views had cost him his post.)[4] Through her father, Isabella was related to William Wilberforce, 'the Liberator'. She had ties to the Evangelical novelist Charles Kingsley; and her second cousins were the Archbishop of Canterbury and the Bishop of Winchester. As for the women in the Bird family, they were godly, too. Isabella's Aunt Mary was a missionary in India; Aunt Henrietta had refused a clerical suitor on doctrinal grounds; Aunts Rebecca and Catherine took tea without sugar long after the emancipation of slaves in the Caribbean deprived this gesture of its power.[5]

3 Stoddart 6, 8–9.
4 Stoddart 21.
5 Stoddart 2–4, 23, 15. Also see Dorothy Middleton, *Victorian Lady Travellers* (Chicago: Academy Chicago Publishers, 1993), 20.

In terms of education, Isabella was home schooled. Her letters illustrate her knowledge of the Bible and Milton, as well as the fashionable literature of the period: she quotes the poems of Tennyson and Arnold; she praises the novels of Trollope and Dickens. We know, too, that Isabella loved hymns. She liked to knit, sketch and paint in watercolours. More unusually, she knew Latin and Greek. She had studied natural history, mathematics and chemistry. She had a passion for microscopes.

That Isabella wanted to be a writer is also sure. Her first article was published when she was seventeen. By her early twenties, she was a regular contributor to religious journals: *Good Words*, *The Leisure Hour*, *The Family Treasury*, *The Sunday Magazine*. Later, in the 1860s when the family moved to Scotland, Isabella supplemented her articles with charitable crusades. She helped crofters emigrate to Canada; she founded a training centre for medical missionaries. She established a shelter for itinerant cabmen and did her best to help Thomas Guthrie with his 'ragged schools'.[6] But it is here that the bounds between reality and fiction blur, for it was not Isabella's philanthropy that made her famous but her travels.

II. What We Assume

Officially, the reason Isabella gave for her journeys was that she travelled for her health. For such a religious woman, travelling for pleasure was absurd, and Isabella did indeed suffer from a physical complaint that eluded doctors' ability to cure. In childhood, this disease had weakened her physique; at eighteen, she had undergone an operation on her spine to remove a 'fibrous tumour'. Then, in her twenties, continued pain in her back (along with 'some sorrow' that was possibly a broken heart)[7] had compelled Isabella to try a change of scene. Her father chose the destination of North America. There, Isabella was temporarily cured, and her adventures became the subject of two books. But with her father's death, such travelling ceased; and by her thirties, Isabella had not one doctor but three scrambling to diagnose her.

Isabella's symptoms were diverse. She had carbuncles on her spine,

6 Stoddart 51–63, 67–68. See also Isabella Bird, 'A Visit to Dr. Guthrie's Edinburgh Ragged Schools', *The Leisure Hour* 10 (1861): 247–251; and *Notes on Old Edinburgh* (Edinburgh: Edmonston & Douglas, 1869).

7 Stoddart writes that Isabella's first trip, to America in the summer of 1854, was spurred by 'some sorrow, over which she brooded in the early fifties' (28). Olive Checkland interprets this as unrequited love in *Isabella Bird and 'A Woman's Right to Do What She Can Do Well'* (Aberdeen: Scottish Cultural Society, 1996), 3.

lesions on her legs. She suffered from fevers, headaches, rashes, nausea, rheumatism, chest pains, muscle spasms and hair loss. She was troubled by abscesses on her feet and aching in her jaw; she was beset by 'neuralgia, pain in my bones, pricking like pins and needles in my limbs, excruciating nervousness, exhaustion, inflamed eyes, sore throat, swelling of the glands behind each ear, stupidity'.[8] Often, she spent the whole day in bed but could not sleep: nightmares alternated with insomnia. The depression she experienced as a result of these symptoms was severe.

Yet the strangest aspect of Isabella's illness was that her complaints vanished when she travelled abroad. For this reason, her doctors prescribed a long sea voyage – the first in this volume – to Australia, New Zealand, Hawaii and Colorado in 1872–3. Unfortunately, Isabella remained ill in the Antipodes, but she improved dramatically in Hawaii. There, she scaled mountains, swam beneath waterfalls, and rode through gulches laced with monkeypod and mango trees, ferns and wild flowers. Her good health continued in Colorado; but back at home in Edinburgh her illness returned. This made another trip essential. For this adventure, in 1878–9, Isabella visited Japan, China, Singapore, Malaya, Ceylon, Egypt and the Holy Land. She fell ill only on the voyage home. The travelogues that Isabella wrote about these journeys – namely *The Hawaiian Archipelago*, *A Lady's Life in the Rocky Mountains*, *Unbeaten Tracks in Japan* and *The Golden Chersonese* – made her notable. They sold briskly to a Victorian reading public that was astonished by her ability to play 'the Invalid at Home and the Samson Abroad'.[9]

Physiologically, what was wrong? In her perceptive biography, Olive Checkland theorises that Isabella's ailments were, at least partly, medically induced. In Scotland Isabella underwent a number of operations (including one to remove her teeth); wore an uncomfortable steel brace at the back of her neck; and was bled regularly, both by incisions and by leeches.[10] In terms of drugs, she took laudanum (or opium) and chlorodyne (containing opium and cannabis), which can cause nausea, loss of appetite and constipation.[11] She drank quantities of alcohol to soothe

---

8 Letter from Isabella to Henrietta Bird, 8 November 1872 (JMA).
9 'Mrs. Bishop', *Edinburgh Medical Journal* XVI (1904): 383.
10 Stoddart 68–70, 74. See also Isabella Bird, 'Under Chloroform: A Psychological Fragment', *Murray's Magazine* 3 (1887): 327–330. Bruce Haley describes blood letting as the most frequent (and dangerous) 'cure' for nineteenth-century neurasthenic fevers. In this way, 'a disease which began as neurosis might pass into an acute stage which was mainly physiological and could be fatal'. See *The Healthy Body and Victorian Culture* (Cambridge, Mass: Harvard University Press, 1978), 32.
11 Checkland 32.

her nerves,[12] and ingested high levels of potassium bromide. This last is not dangerous in small doses, but in excess it can result in psychological derangement. This seems to have happened to Isabella. As she noted in one letter, she was 'taking bromide three times a day', but it made her 'more nervous than I have ever been and I cannot remember anything or read a book. These last few days I have felt shaking all over and oppressed with undefined terror.' She then came down with a rash, one of the principal symptoms of a bromide overdose.[13]

Ironically, bromide would have had no effect on Isabella's illness, which seems to have been carbunculosis. A staphylococcus skin infection that results in large, infectious knobs on the back and spine, carbunculosis can be accompanied by fever, fatigue, inflammation and malaise; and it can only be cured by surgical draining of the boils. So contagious is this infection that it can create lesions and abscesses all over the body – which Isabella had – as well as spread to other people.[14] It may also have been responsible for Isabella's heart pains, muscle spasms, night sweats and joint aches through a complication called endocarditis.[15] Today, carbunculosis is fairly rare, as it is aggravated by the poor hygiene more endemic in Victorian Scotland than in the modern age. Often, though, no direct cause can be found,[16] and Isabella may well have experienced a psychosomatic outbreak.

For whatever was amiss, it seems sure that Isabella's illness originated in her mind. She was, in Victorian terms, a 'neurasthenic': a woman bedevilled by physiological symptoms that arose principally from psychological problems. Why else would she experience such vitality abroad, only to 'put off my swagger with my spurs'[17] and relapse into invalidism as soon as she returned to Scotland? No ordinary patient would have felt 'less pain on a mud floor or in a wet tent, riding a horse, a mule, an elephant, a yak or even a cow than she did on a padded

---

12 For Isabella's drinking, see her letters from Australia printed in this volume. In one memorable line, she relates that she has taken 'wine at 11, lunch and beer at one, wine at 4, dinner and beer at 6, tea wine and bed at 9'. In the same letter, she writes that she is having 'wine 4 times a day' (letter from Isabella to Henrietta Bird, 13 October 1872, JMA). Later, in 1887, when a friend asked Isabella to advocate temperance at a meeting, Isabella declined, as 'to speak [on] total abstinence is hardly honest'. She informed her friend that she was obliged to drink wine 'for weakness of the heart caused by rheumatism' and did 'not regard the taking of wine, or beer, in moderation . . . as wrong'. Cited in Stoddart 184.

13 Checkland 31.

14 See 'Carbunculosis', *Medical Encyclopedia*, U.S. National Library of Medicine, 16 May 2001; 24 May 2001. <http://www.nlm.nih.gov/medlineplus/ency/article/000825.htm>.

15 See 'Endocarditis', *Medical Encyclopedia*, U.S. National Library of Medicine, 16 May 2001; 24 May 2001. <http://www.nlm.nih.gov/medlineplus/ency/article/001098.htm>. Isabella herself noted that the carbuncles had caused 'my heart . . . to be much affected'. Letter from Isabella Bird to John Murray III, 24 October 1888 (JMA).

16 See 'Carbunculosis'. *Medical Encyclopedia*, U.S. National Library of Medicine, 16 May 2001; 24 May 2001. <http://www.nlm.nih.gov/medlineplus/ency/article/000825.htm>.

17 Letter from Isabella Bird to Ella Blackie, 23 December 1873 (JSB) MS 2631 ff. 83.

Victorian sofa'.[18] Nor would any ordinary patient have been able to declare that 'the only prudent thing for me, with my present state of dangerous health, would be to go East *at once*',[19] where she could sleep on a hard, flea-ridden mat and happily slurp sea-slugs, horse cooked in bear grease, and other local delicacies out of a communal pot. Indeed, the popularity of Isabella's travelogues – in some ways, it was a brilliant marketing move – was the 'puzzle' caused by 'the frail lady who could not raise her head from the pillow without support, yet could climb 'Mauna Loa, "the Matterhorn of the Pacific" . . . and . . . round up wild cattle in the Rockies'.[20]

Did Isabella suspect that her problem was psychological? I think so, yes.[21] I also suspect that this deeply religious woman feared being 'found out', that she worried her malady was not quite *comme il faut*. We see this anxiety in the letters she wrote to Lucinda Severance, a friend she had made during her romps through Hawaii. Like the photo Lucinda was to preserve, these letters have not been altered and nothing has been crossed out. Instead, the image conveyed is of Isabella in the raw, paranoid that another friend from Hilo, Hattie Coan, has come to Scotland for the express purpose of authenticating her illness. Desperate to prove that she was 'no impostor and adventuress' to her Hawaiian friends, Isabella spent Hattie's sojourn moaning in bed and 'found it a relief when she was gone'. Most damaging are the pains Isabella then took to acquire Hattie's letters. She had to know what was in them.[22] These are not the actions of a secure or happy individual, but then, neither was her illness.

III. *What We Assume About Isabella's Relationship with Henrietta*

What was it about Isabella's upbringing that could have caused such scars? What was so stressful as to inspire a debilitating illness? To say that her complaint derived solely from the strictness of her religion would be simplistic; and as for her upbringing, the Birds seem to have enjoyed an idyllic closeness. Isabella's father took the child on rides about the

---

18 Cecily Palser Haverly, Introduction to *This Grand Beyond: The Travels of Isabella Bird Bishop* by Isabella Bird (London: Century Publishing, 1984), 9.

19 Letter from Isabella Bird to John Murray IV, 24 August 1888 (JMA).

20 Pat Barr, *A Curious Life for a Lady: The Story of Isabella Bird* (London: John Murray, 1970), 180.

21 I have based this assumption on Isabella's own words. For example, she wrote to her publisher from Korea that 'I suffer from fatigue of a social kind, and that part of *ordinary* life, the *attempt*, often fruitless, to make things "fit in," which produces attacks of nervous exhaustion and partial failure of the heart.' On another occasion, she wrote that her malady derived from 'severe prostration of the nervous system' as opposed to 'any constitutional tendency'. In yet a third, she complained that she had 'constitutional depression'. See Isabella Bird's letters to John Murray IV, 16 October 1886 and 19 October 1896 (JMA), as well as Barr 185.

22 Letters from Isabella Bird to Lucinda Severance, 8 December 1874 and 1 May 1875. Luther Severance Collection (LSC) at the Lyman House Memorial Museum, Hilo, Hawaii.

parish when she was small. He supported her first travels, both financially and emotionally, and when he died they were collaborating on a study of Evangelicalism in America.[23] As for her mother, Isabella remembered her as an absorbing teacher: 'We sat spellbound when she explained things.'[24] And then there was Henrietta.

'Hennie', as she is often called, occupies a privileged place in this collection. It was to Henrietta that most of these letters were inscribed, Henrietta to whom Isabella dedicated her first books. Throughout, Isabella encourages us to view their relationship in passionately affectionate terms, addressing her sister as 'My Darling', 'My Ownest', 'My Dearest Pet' and herself 'Its Being', 'Its All' and 'Its Poor Suffering Little Pet'. Through such endearments, Isabella portrays Henrietta as an adoring but passive 'It'. 'My heart yearns over my good sweet little thing.' 'My sweetest thing, it does not know how I care for it.'

Henrietta herself never speaks. In Isabella's letters, we are not told what Henrietta thought, nor if she reciprocated with similar endearments. Few people have ever read her words. Her diaries, employed by Anna Stoddart, are lost; we have only one letter and a handful of postscripts (which, to confound matters, are written in Greek).[25] Henrietta's poems – printed privately in a tiny, cornflower-blue volume lettered in gilt – have a circulation apparently limited to Scotland. Her articles, published anonymously, have long since disappeared.

As a result, what we know about Henrietta is what we have been told. Like the idealised Victorian 'angel of the hearth', Henrietta is presented to us as devotedly good and pure, a woman without desires, who lived entirely for other people. Anna Stoddart writes that Henrietta was 'less complex of character, less powerful mentally, less courageous physically'; while Pat Barr tells us that her 'function in life was that of lodestar to Isabella's wanderings, fire-keeper for Isabella's return'.[26] We know that it was Henrietta who moved the sisters from Edinburgh to the remote Isle of Mull, Henrietta who 'brought light into dark homes and comfort to sorrow-stricken hearts'. Indeed, so saintly was this younger Bird that the islanders called her 'The Blessed One'. A clock commemorating her philanthropy (erected by Isabella) stands in the centre of Tobermory on Mull.

The only photograph we have of the younger sister supports this pose.

---

23 Edward's death meant that the volumes were published separately. See *The Revival in America by an English Eye-Witness* [by Edward Bird], edited and introduced by Isabella Bird (London: Seeley, 1858); and *Aspects of Religion in the United States* (London: Sampson Low, 1859).
24 Cited in Stoddart 12.
25 For Henrietta's diaries, see Stoddart 123. For postscripts in Greek, see Dora Bird's letter to John Stuart Blackie, n.d. (JSB) MS 2626 f.260v. For Henrietta's only known surviving letter (to Ella Blackie), see (JSB) MS 2642 ff.19.
26 Barr 20.

In it, Henrietta seems sweet and demure. There is a dreamy look in her eyes and a giant cross round her neck. More than anything, it is this cross that commands our attention. It is tangible proof that Henrietta excelled in 'spiritual attainment, in the dignity of steadfast faith, the serenity of a soul ennobled by constant dwelling in the presence of the Most High'.[27] This photo seems to confirm that Henrietta really did wish for nothing more than to be the passive recipient of Isabella's letters, that she was happy in her 'dreary little drawing room', 'content with the traditionally feminine role of waiting and watching'.[28] But was this true?

Experience should teach us that real people cannot be equated with fictional types; we should be wary of an image so obviously informed by the sentimental literature of the period. Isabella and Henrietta were not the devoted sisters of Victorian paper dolls; they did not step out of a Kate Greenaway illustration. It is therefore important that we resist regarding their relationship in such polarising terms, and instead recognize that the real Henrietta Bird was more complex.

After all, let us consider what we know. According to John Stuart Blackie, who taught the younger sister at the University of Edinburgh, she was no meek alternative to the more dashing Isabella. Instead,

- Henrietta was a classical scholar who excelled at translations of Greek and Latin manuscripts;
- she had studied astronomy, botany, chemistry, philosophy;
- she was widely read in English literature;
- she was an accomplished artist, both in charcoal and watercolours;
- she was a regular contributor to literary magazines;
- she was a gifted poet and a skilled mathematician;
- she gave 'daily astronomical talks' about the stars and the solar system when visiting friends;
- she travelled extensively in the British Isles;
- and she wrote 'long, hearty and quaint letters' (which seem not to have been preserved).[29]

No shrinking violet, this Henrietta was forthright with a 'cordial firm grasp' and a 'composed and intelligent countenance'. She had no patience with small talk (neither did Isabella) but excelled when speaking on topics of 'real interest', which she 'pursued with intelligent zest and frankest statement of opinion'. This Henrietta had a lively mind: 'If

27 Stoddart 123.
28 Barr 51–52.
29 For Henrietta's accomplishments, see John Stuart Blackie's 'Biographical Sketch' in *Hymns and Poems of the Late Henrietta A. Bird*, ed. Isabella Bird (Edinburgh: James Taylor, 1881); and Stoddart 122–142. Isabella also discusses Henrietta's scholarship in a letter to Ella Blackie, 28 November 1899 (JSB) MS 2640 f.243.

one sought to trace on different days the subject which had been occupying her, one might find that she had been clearing up to herself some point in history or in biography, collating the statements of different authorities, and noting the substance of their views; or she might have been at her "Euclid", or following some other department of mathematical study, or working hard at a knotty problem in natural philosophy; or perhaps . . . studying her Greek Testament, and feasting on its spiritual truths.'[30] 'One had to notice her wisdom, the extent of her knowledge, the accuracy of her perceptions, the felicity of her expressions.'[31] Even Anna Stoddart (who admitted to John Murray that she neither liked nor understood the younger Bird) wrote that 'there was an inspiration in Henrietta as true and almost as powerful as in Isabella'. 'I have vexed memories,' Stoddart recalled, 'of hours spent in answering question after question upon books of history and literature'.[32]

How could such an intelligent woman have been content in the role of passive muse? Henrietta's own words indicate that she was not. The one letter we have – written to Ella Blackie when Isabella was in Hawaii – tellingly counters her older sister's adventures on the Big Island with her own in Orkney and Shetland. There, Henrietta 'had no worries' and 'let all bothers stand over, & had "no cares beyond today"'. It was her 'ambition to get beyond the parallel of 60°', to travel about on 'shaggy ponies' and in carts. Tired of the same 'asphyxiating civilization' as Isabella, Henrietta deplored having to return at the end of her journey to her old routine. Instead, she exhilarates in the traveller's life.[33]

And why not? Henrietta loved the outdoors, and was ready for her own adventures. She spent much of her time walking, riding and in boats; and it seems to have been this passion for nature (more than a desire for isolation) that had inspired her move to the west of Scotland. Moreover, Isabella admits in her book on Hawaii that Henrietta had wanted to take part in her journeys but Isabella refused. Later, in 1878, when Isabella was ordered abroad once more, Henrietta fell conveniently ill. Was the pretext that a voyage might benefit her, too? Whatever the case, she was not allowed to go. Instead, Isabella needed Henrietta to stay at home performing the charitable work to which they had both been raised. It seems that Isabella saw her sister as a surrogate self, a *doppelgänger* that enabled her to revel 'with impunity' in her travels.[34]

30 Blackie v–vi.
31 Unsigned obituary from *The Christian Monthly*, cited in Stoddart 130. This obituary appears to have been written by Blackie as well, as much of the content appears in his 'Biographical Sketch'.
32 Stoddart 65, 133.
33 Letter from Henrietta Bird to Ella Blackie, 10 September 1873 (JSB) MS 2642 ff.19.
34 Dea Birkett, *Spinsters Abroad: Victorian Lady Explorers* (Oxford: Basil Blackwell, 1989), 95.

Isabella also seems to have loved Henrietta better from afar. Certainly, the sisters did not experience the constancy of companionship that the intimacy of Isabella's endearments might suggest. Instead, Isabella seems to have spent as little time as possible with Henrietta. Until 1866 they lived together in the same house, but immediately after their mother's death the sisters separated for more than six months.[35] Given their professed closeness, it is odd that they did not cling together in this loss. For the next fourteen years, the sisters' time together was punctuated by long periods of separation. For every four months passed together, several more months were spent apart. (They did, however, regroup to weep over each other before Isabella's grand departures.) For example, at the time when Isabella set sail on the *St David* in 1871 – for the voyage that would eventually extend to Australia, New Zealand, Hawaii and Colorado – she had been touring the Highlands while Henrietta maintained a separate residence in Edinburgh. After Isabella's return in December of 1873, she spent maybe five months with Henrietta while she revised her letters for *The Hawaiian Archipelago*. She then left for London, Houghton, Salisbury and the Continent. Henrietta stayed behind in Mull. In all, during Henrietta's lifetime, Isabella was overseas for more than four years, in addition to the time they spent apart in the British Isles.[36]

Such circumstances make us question the authenticity of Isabella's endearments. Is it love they express, or guilt? The implication of all the impersonal pronouns bandied about is that the sisters formed 'a mutually absorbed and absorbing "It"', nestled in their cottage in a paradigm of bliss.[37] More likely, the Bird sisters experienced a rivalry that their evangelical background made impossible for them to articulate. Raised in the tenets of the strict Clapham Sect, Isabella would not have been able to say she didn't like her sister. She would not have been able to express any feelings of being threatened, overshadowed or annoyed. Any such emotions would have to be suppressed – and she would have learnt from her parents to internalise them early on. As a result, it seems no coincidence that Isabella developed her 'disease' at the same time as her

---

35 Stoddart 64.
36 Stoddart 28–109. In these pages, Stoddart relates that Isabella was away for seven months on her first journey to North America in 1854; twelve months on her second from 1857–8; about a month on her third in 1872; eighteen on her tour to Australia, New Zealand, Hawaii and North America in 1872–3; two months to Switzerland in 1874; and nearly fourteen on her tour to North America, Japan, China, Singapore, Malaya, Ceylon, Egypt and the Holy Land in 1878–9. In this tabulation, I have discounted Stoddart's claim that Isabella took a short trip to Portland, Maine, on the steamer *St David* in 1866, as we know from Isabella's letters that her first experience with this ship was in 1872. It seems clear that the unnamed sailor interviewed by Stoddart has made a mistake about the date, as he was remembering it after a lapse of thirteen years.
37 Barr 186.

sister's birth. Nor is it strange that one of the earliest stories that Anna Stoddart presents about their childhood has Isabella protesting against a visitor's admiration of 'the lovely little Henrietta', while calling attention to herself.[38]

How must such feelings have affected Henrietta? Like Isabella's illness, her religion seems to have been her refuge. It was an escape, more than the habit of childhood. John Stuart Blackie points out that 'the circumstances which seemed most to influence the development of her Christian character were the repeated long periods of loneliness while her sister was obliged to travel in distant lands . . . During the long periods of loneliness while her sister was away, she fell back on the companionship of God, and seemed to walk meekly before him, trusting him with her cares.'[39] Henrietta's poetry supports this perspective. With such titles as 'Increase My Faith', 'Divine Guidance' and 'Ye Would Not Have', Henrietta's verses are suffused with melancholy and desperation, a young woman turning to God in her affliction because there is nothing else.[40] We may therefore interpret her self-effacement (e.g. her role as 'The Blessed One' in *Tobermory*) as a protective shield for a woman who was treated throughout her adult life as if she did not matter. Rejected by her sister as a companion and equal, and prevented from taking part in her adventures, Henrietta came to excel at self-abnegation, in the only sphere that she had ever been taught to value. In so doing, she took on the mantle of a Dorothy Wordsworth or an Alice James – a woman writer eclipsed and destroyed by the successes of her more fortunate sibling.

It is, however, possible that Henrietta had her say. If the 'genuine' voice of Isabella speaks from these letters, then perhaps it is the more scholarly Henrietta who speaks through her books? After all, Isabella's books and her letters are not carbon copies (which is the point of publishing her correspondence here). It was Isabella's routine when she returned home to excise a mass of personal detail, while adding in its place intellectual gravitas. In many ways, these changes are enlightening, yet Isabella herself insisted she changed nothing. 'I am printing my letters literally without alterations,' she wrote to John Murray about *The Hawaiian Archipelago*, and 'as to the letters, I have relied solely on my own opinion concerning them, which is to publish them *as they were*

38 Stoddart 9, 12.
39 Blackie x.
40 A typical poem is 'For Everything Give Thanks': 'Give thanks for everything! / In the winter and the frost, / When the buds of hope are withering, / And thy dearest dreams are cross'd, / Let faith take up the strain . . . / For the broken spells, and the kindly pain . . . / Give thanks for everything.' See Blackie 1–2.

written.' 'There were fragments of Hawaiian history scattered throughout them, as well as botany, which I have extracted and thrown into a chapter at the conclusion.' Yet on comparing these letters with Isabella's published work, we must realise this is false. There is nothing in Isabella's 'on the spot' observations like the 'scholarly enthusiasm' she attributes to them, nor are there many passages that would be 'most interesting to scientific people'.[41] The ethnography, geography, politics and history that appear in *The Hawaiian Archipelago* are simply not there. Instead, Isabella's letters are better. More passionate. More personal. More wry.

Was it Henrietta who encouraged Isabella to edit her work? To add statistics? To bolster her descriptions with facts? (Letters from John Murray indicate that he did not.) By all reports, Henrietta seems to have been more academic than her sister, so it may have been Henrietta who encouraged Isabella to produce these more scholarly works. We do know from Isabella that Henrietta had some effect on her writing, for as she commented in a 'circular' letter from the Persian Gulf:

> One thing out of many which made my letters to her what they were was the singular amount of her accumulated knowledge of countries, of their geography, products, government, ethnology, religions and botany. She always read and took notes of the best travels, comparing them with naturalists and other books on the same subjects. It made her mind so responsive to all one could tell her and gave her *stores*. She could supply so much to fill me in or correct the outlines. She *informed*. While you except Ella . . . I am quite sure you know nothing of Persia![42]

Similarly, when Isabella was writing up *The Golden Chersonese* shortly after her sister's death – indeed, the very title was Henrietta's idea[43] – Isabella wrote several times to John Murray begging for articles on Chinese secret societies and Malayan politics, Blue Books on British residents and transportation – information which, for her previous accounts, Henrietta seems to have supplied.

Henrietta's erudition even opens up the possibility that some of Isabella's work – particularly 'Australia Felix', *The Hawaiian Archipelago* and *Unbeaten Tracks in Japan*[44] – may have been products of both Bird

---

41 See Isabella Bird's letters to John Murray III, 17 June 1874 and 13 December 1873 (JMA).
42 'Circular' letter from Isabella Bird, 24 December 1889 (JMA).
43 Stoddart 160.
44 I have discounted *A Lady's Life in the Rocky Mountains*, as Isabella seems to have followed her letters quite closely when compiling it, while nonetheless omitting the more dramatic passages about Jim Nugent (Rocky Mountain Jim). This work is also remarkably free from her usual disquisitions on history, geography, politics and botany.

sisters, compiled in the time they spent together. In this way, their composition – though not their relationship – might have approximated that of the Victorian aunt and niece who penned poems under the pseudonym 'Michael Field'. Isabella, after all, seems to have worked best when she was with Henrietta, though she generally departed once the work was done.[45] 'The things I am interested in are her interests,' Isabella remarked. 'She was my intellect, the inspiration of all my literary work.'[46] Or, as Henrietta complained about *Unbeaten Tracks in Japan*, 'I long very much for a single week of stillness and pure air, but such longings must be stifled for some time to come . . . "She" is toiling to finish her book.'[47] What Henrietta meant by her quotation marks can only be surmised.

IV. What We Assume about Isabella's Relationship with Men

Unfortunately, Henrietta died of typhoid in 1880, less than a year after Isabella's return from the second voyage chronicled in this volume. (Isabella, incidentally, had been suffering from typhoid, too, but she had recovered and was travelling with friends about the British Isles.) As was to be expected, Isabella fell apart in the months following Henrietta's death. 'She was everything to me,' she wrote to John Murray, 'my home and fireside, my most intimate and congenial friend.' So distraught was Isabella that she couldn't open the parcel of books that had arrived: copies of *Unbeaten Tracks in Japan*. Those letters had been 're-written in our last happy summer in the little cottage at Tobermory, which her early death has consecrated to me for evermore'.[48] Without Henrietta, Isabella felt miserable and abandoned. So what did she do? She married her sister's doctor.

Isabella's wedding is among the stranger stories of her life. In a photograph taken for the event in 1881, we see her dressed in a bridal gown of black braided serge with a matching black jacket and hat. Cloaked in these garments of deepest despair, Isabella regards us with defiance from behind the balustrade of her bow. Her expression seems more likely to make men wither than advance. In this way, Isabella's photo plays on our expectations. It gives us not her joy in becoming the bride of John

45 Stoddart writes that Isabella's 'immediate work' upon returning from Hawaii, when she was with Henrietta in Mull, 'was the revision of her letters, the excision of a mass of personal detail, the verification and correction of her statistics' (81). Likewise, Stoddart notes that the sisters shared a flat, this time in Edinburgh, in the winter of 1875–6 when Isabella was developing her 'Australia Felix' articles. They were together again in 1879–80 while Isabella wrote up *Unbeaten Tracks in Japan*.
46 Letter from Isabella Bird to John Murray III, 16 June 1880 (JMA).
47 Letter from Henrietta Bird to Mary MacDiarmid, cited in Stoddart 115.
48 Letter from Isabella Bird to John Murray III, 29 June 1880 (JMA). See also Stoddart 135, 138.

Bishop, but rather her sorrow over the sister her husband has failed to save.

For whom did Isabella create this pose? What did she intend this image to represent? To some extent, it seems like a visual embodiment of the 'abnormal' feelings Isabella had for Henrietta, while Olive Checkland has theorised that it expresses Isabella's guilt over marrying the man her sister seems to have adored.[49] At the same time, this image gives us the rationale that Isabella is getting married *for* her sister: she claimed it was Henrietta's dying wish. Both sisters knew John Bishop was in love with Isabella; it was only 'the affection and companionship of my sister that made me reluctantly decide against marrying. It is all changed now.'[50] According to Isabella, she accepted John Bishop only to make good this deathbed wish. She staggered to the altar 'drunk with loss', 'half-blinded with tears, shrinking from all congratulations'.[51] Their ceremony took place, significantly, beside the 'ancestral vault'.[52]

Yet something about the morbidity of this affair – its intensity, its glamour, its ostentation – makes Isabella's misery seem false. Being wed in weeds rather than lace, announcing the event on mourning stationery rather than with cards, ultimately invites us to produce a counter-reading of the code. It asks us to interpret Isabella's despair as an elation that she found inappropriate. After all, at fifty, Isabella had surely contemplated marriage before. (She had even previously accepted John Bishop, but had shelved the idea for reasons unknown.)[53] In just the short selection printed in this volume, we meet:

- Mr Cameron, 'the fiend', a married man from Melbourne who Isabella appears to have known – and maybe loved – before;
- Mr Wilson from Waimea, who proposes to Isabella with a letter, and who humorously compares her knitting needles to his mother's;
- Lunalilo, the Hawaiian king, who writes poetry to Isabella and teaches her to dance the polka on a missionary veranda;
- the dashing Captain Ross from the Princeville Plantation, who inquires after meeting Isabella if she is engaged;

49 Checkland 87–91.
50 See Isabella's letters to Ella Blackie (n.d. 1880, JSB, MS 2633 f.326) and to John Murray III (9 January 1881, JMA). Stoddart goes further in telling us that their wedding was without love: 'The "spark from heaven" had not yet kindled her heart', although Isabella 'reverenced and admired him more than any man living' (146).
51 Letter from Isabella Bird to Ella Blackie, cited in Barr 189.
52 Stoddart 146.
53 See Isabella Bird's letters to John Murray III, 27 July and 29 August 1877 (JMA). It is Isabella's hasty rejection of John Bishop after having accepted him – in conjunction with her sister's movements at this time – that has led Olive Checkland to theorise that Henrietta was in love with her doctor. See Checkland 87–91.

- Colonel Heath, a Confederate officer and amateur sculptor, who proposes to Isabella despite her distaste;
- 'Rocky Mountain Jim', the desperado, whose wild passions and chequered past cause Isabella to fear he will shoot her when she rejects him;
- and the quiet Dr John, who woos Isabella over a microscope fitted with slides of the 'Atlantic ooze'. Dubbed 'Mr Bird' because of his devotion, he declares, rather mournfully, that 'I have only one rival in Isabella's heart and that is the High Table Lands of Central Asia.'[54]

For a woman of over forty at the end of the nineteenth century, this list is extensive. It also provides what may be yet another motive for Isabella's travels, in addition to her illness and her claustrophobic relationship with her sister. Did Isabella make her initial jaunts about the world – in 1854, 1857 and 1872 – in search of a spouse? Was her spinsterhood – with its attendant feelings of being unused and unwanted – connected to her health?

If so, Isabella could not have chosen better locations. Australia, New Zealand, Hawaii and Colorado suffered from a dearth of marriageable women in precisely the years that Isabella visited. It would have been difficult for Isabella to be unaware of this detail: British newspapers and magazines were loud in their complaints about the colonies' staggering superfluity of men, and they pleaded with English ladies to go out and join them. Meanwhile, the census of 1862 had revealed that one million more unmarried women than men were living in the British Isles. Emigration seemed to pose a solution equitable for all. The result was that government-sponsored schemes proliferated – such as the Female Middle-Class Emigration Society, the British Ladies Female Emigrant Society, and the Caroline Chisholm Family Colonisation Loan Society – which stressed the importance of women and children as 'God's police'. One organisation was even founded specifically to assist 'distressed gentlewomen, daughters and widows of clergymen' (like Isabella) in their search for overseas husbands. 'The object of emigration was to save England's daughters from loneliness, from poverty and from despair.'[55] In the words of one journalist, these spinsters had a duty to relocate to the colonies, 'where English women are a scarce commodity, and where they might find husbands'.[56]

---

54 See Stoddart 96, 149; and Constance Gordon Cumming's letter to Lucinda Severance, 1 March 1882 (LSC).
55 Rita Kranidis, *The Victorian Spinster and Colonial Emigration* (New York: St. Martin's, 1999), 20, 24.
56 William R. Greg, 'Why Are Women Redundant?' Cited in Elaine Showalter, *Sexual Anarchy: Gender and Culture at the Fin-de-Siècle* (New York: Viking, 1990), 19. See also James Hammerton, *Emigrant Gentlewomen* (London: Croom Helm, 1979) and Charlotte Erickson, *Leaving England: Essays on British Emigration* (Ithaca: Cornell University Press, 1994).

New England in particular was the destination favoured by the daughters of the well-to-do. Not surprisingly, it was the location chosen by Isabella's father. On sending his daughter to Massachusetts in the mid-1850s, Edward Bird might well have hoped that Isabella would settle down with a young Evangelical in a religious community. Accordingly, Isabella was supplied with introductions on her 1854 voyage that 'procured her influential social privileges in Boston'. Isabella, however, had spent too much money travelling to Chicago, so she was unable to stay long. She returned home in April of the following year. Significantly, when Edward Bird sent his daughter back to Boston in 1857, she arrived at exactly the same point in the season when she had left off. On this second voyage, Isabella left her friends only during the lazy summer months to journey south and west. She then returned to Boston for the season of 1858. Isabella, however, was now twenty-six and she did not procure a husband.[57]

If one of the reasons that Isabella went abroad was this search for a spouse, then why in the 1870s did she play so hard to get? In the nineteenth century, women over the age of forty were expected to make do with what was available. This was certainly not true of Isabella. The letters printed in this volume illustrate that she was flattered by men's advances (as she wrote to Henrietta, 'What I might have said if it had not been for *you* I dont know')[58] but she balked at the actuality of marriage. Were Isabella truly eager to be wed, this would not have been her reaction to American men's proposals.

Part of it had to do with class. As Isabella informed John Murray before her trip to Japan, she was technically a 'de Byrd', a member of 'that very old Warwickshire family . . . connected with several families of the English nobility'.[59] Such lineage (whether real or imagined) meant that Isabella desired an aristocratic match; a rugged backwoodsman simply would not do. By contrast, the hunters, trappers and retired soldiers she encountered in Colorado and Hawaii would have assumed that Isabella was less genteel: the majority of unwed female immigrants to these regions were labourers.[60] (With regards to the proposal of Mr Wilson, for example, Isabella wondered 'whether I should lecture him on difference in social position, but I did not for I have suspected that he was encouraged to propose by my saying . . . I must go home and work for my living.')[61] So particular was Isabella that even John Bishop

57 Stoddart 35–45.
58 Letter from Isabella to Henrietta Bird, 6 March 1873.
59 Letter from Isabella Bird to John Murray III, 24 February 1878 (JMA).
60 Kranidis 30.
61 Letter from Isabella to Henrietta Bird, 6 March 1873 (JMA).

– a dignified surgeon from Sheffield then in practice with the famous Sir Joseph Lister – had trouble meeting her expectations. As Isabella confided to her close friend Ella Blackie on the eve of her marriage, 'I assume that my social position by birth and my literary position are too firmly established to be shaken by this match.'[62]

Another reason for Isabella's hesitation may have been her proclivity for morbidity. The same impulse that goaded her toward a black wedding made her desire a dangerous man. Deep down, she did not want a steady doctor, quiet farmer or Presbyterian clergyman. Rather, she was attracted to figures who appeared desperate or dissolute. In her youth, someone Isabella refers to as 'that hideous whisky fiend' had 'cross[ed] my path';[63] in Colorado, her passions were enflamed by Jim Nugent, a trapper known as 'Rocky Mountain Jim'. The first time they met, he was sitting astride his horse with a 'shocking' collection of knives, spurs, revolvers and axes, with an old beaver pelt dangling its four dead paws over the saddle. 'Desperado was written in large letters all over him.'[64] Camping together beneath the stars with his dog on Long's Peak, Jim recited poetry to Isabella and spun yarns about his murderous deeds. Clearly, she was titillated. Like many a daughter of a Victorian preacher, the prospect of sin was tantalising. Thus, she 'dreamed that as we were sitting by the fire, Mr. Nugent came in with his revolver in his hand and shot me'.[65] On another occasion, she said she quivered at the sight of 'a revolver at half cock lying on the table when he came in and I found my hand verging towards it. He has never come here armed before and yesterday he had 2 revolvers in his belt.'[66] As Isabella herself admitted of this strange attraction, 'I cannot but think of Mr Wilson on Hawaii and his quiet undemonstrative un-annoying ways and comparing him with this dark tempestuous, terrible character, wondering how it is that the last is so fascinating.'[67]

Unfortunately, most of the stories Isabella tells about Jim in *A Lady's Life in the Rocky Mountains* are false, but she appears to have believed them. Other travellers to Colorado were not so gullible. George Kingsley – uncle of the African explorer Mary Kingsley – quipped that Jim was called 'the Mountainous One' because of 'the extraordinary altitude of his lies'. 'Some said that he was a defrocked Canadian priest, others that he was an expelled Canadian Schoolmaster. Others that he

62 Letter from Isabella Bird to Ella Blackie, n.d. 1880 (JSB) MS 2633 f.326.
63 Letter from Isabella to Henrietta Bird, 19 November 1873 (JMA).
64 Isabella Bird, *A Lady's Life in the Rocky Mountains* (London: John Murray, 1879), 78–9.
65 Letter from Isabella to Henrietta Bird, 20 November 1873 (JMA).
66 Letter from Isabella to Henrietta Bird, 21 November 1873 (JMA).
67 Letter from Isabella to Henrietta Bird, 19 November 1873 (JMA)

was both.'[68] More recently, James Pickering in his study *This Blue Hollow* has attempted to show conclusively that Jim's past was neither violent nor notable. According to Pickering, the reason we remember Jim is because of Isabella, not because of any fame he genuinely possessed as an outlaw. Instead, as Isabella herself notes in *A Lady's Life*, Jim had 'an obvious desire to act and speak in character, and sustain his reputation as a desperado'. His appearance must have helped. If one side of his face showed 'large gray-blue eyes . . . a handsome aquiline nose and a very handsome mouth',[69] the other had been ripped off by a grizzly bear.

Of course, readers will be disappointed if they are expecting an affair that exists outside Isabella's imagination; she was not the type of woman to indulge in the indiscretions of other lady travellers. She was no Lady Jane Digby (an ancestor of Pamela Harriman) who took a desert sheik for her lover. Instead, at the crucial moment, Isabella's Evangelicalism kicked in, and she rejected Jim when he declared his love for her on a snowy afternoon in the Rocky Mountains. Rather than staying and trying to save him (though she was tempted), Isabella returned to Henrietta on the Isle of Mull. She devoted the next several years to her charitable work; she wrote scholarly books about her travels; and she bought a microscope to assist her botanical explorations. It does appear that Isabella corresponded with Jim for a time, but this was cut short by his murder in 1874 over a land dispute with the hotelier at Estes Park. Isabella was horrified by Jim's death, but not to the point that she didn't get over it. She met John Bishop; she went to Japan. When she returned, her sister died and she got married. The story of her marriage belongs to another place, but suffice to say the result was tragic. After a long, lingering illness, John Bishop died, and it was in the blind panic of this latest grief that Isabella really started to fantasise about Jim Nugent.

No one can say that Isabella grieved in a 'normal' way. If the death of Henrietta had prompted her to marry the man who had failed to save her, the loss of John Bishop found Isabella trying to contact Jim's ghost. Transferring her emotions from one dead man to another, Isabella quickly became obsessed with the notion that she had seen Jim's spirit twelve years before (something she had never mentioned at the time). Now she claimed that this apparition had materialised at the exact moment of the trapper's death, as she reclined on a sofa in a health spa in Switzerland. In great detail, Isabella recounted that she had awakened

---

68 George Kingsley, *Notes on Sport and Travel* (London: Macmillan, 1900), 179.
69 *A Lady's Life in the Rocky Mountains* 79.

at dawn to see Jim standing before her. His eyes were 'fixed on me, and when I looked at him he very slowly but distinctly said, "I have come as I promised." '[70]

Published in 1886 in *Phantasms of the Living* – a two-volume work chronicling the paranormal – Isabella's account was later changed and embellished with each retelling. John Murray wrote out a second version she had told him; yet a third was published by Anna Stoddart in her biography.[71] Each variation has its own particulars, but the most striking aspects are these: the hour Isabella chose, six in the morning, *would have been correct* had Colorado been eight hours ahead of Interlaken rather than behind. (Jim had died at two in the afternoon.) This implies a degree of fabrication. Secondly, Isabella wrote a letter to Lucinda Severance, her Hawaiian friend, shortly after Jim Nugent's death. In it, Isabella makes no mention of his ghost, but she does say she has visited a castle in Switzerland where 'an apparition has been seen flitting around the galleries of the guardroom . . . a very handsome old man, with long curled white hair, a French gray evening coat and short pants'.[72] In time, it seems, this spectre and Jim's death became fused in her imagination, and literally came back to haunt her in the agonies she suffered over her husband's death. Deprived of the people she had loved most in life, Isabella was forced to fall back in her loneliness on a relationship that never truly was. Sadly, she seems not even to have grasped that Jim was hardly the romantic figure of her fantasy. As a Colorado journalist wrote during her lifetime, 'Ask the natives whether he was not a desperate murderer and you will get a good laugh.'[73]

V. What We Assume about Isabella's Relationship with Empire

Before concluding, there is one last image of Isabella that I would like to explore: a photograph taken in Swatow, China, in 1895, during a journey that was to be chronicled in *The Yangtze Valley and Beyond*. This is a photo of Isabella as Imperial Ethnographer, a part she plays from her pith helmet down to her sensible shoes. She is 'FRGS, FSRGS, Hon. Member of the Oriental Society of Pekin' – accolades she was to have

---

70 Isabella Bird, 'The Visitation of Mountain Jim' in *Phantasms of the Living*, eds. Edmund Gurney, Frederick Myers and Frank Podmore, 2 vols (London: Society for Psychical Research, 1886), vol 1:531–532.

71 See letters from John Murray IV to Anna Stoddart, 24 July, 3 August and 20 August 1905; and from Hallam Murray to Anna Stoddart, 29 September 1905 (JMA). See also Stoddart 83–84.

72 Letter from Isabella Bird to Lucinda Severance, 9 November 1874 (LSC). Jim died on 7 September.

73 Cited in James Pickering, 'Isabella Bird's Desperado: The Life and Death of Rocky Mountain Jim' in *This Blue Hollow: Estes Park, the Early Years, 1859–1915* (Niwot, Colorado: University of Colorado Press, 1999), 80.

engraved on her tombstone. In this photograph she is busily engaged in cataloguing the people she has met on this voyage. Yet rather than being dignified and reserved – as would befit an emissary of empire – Isabella's attitude appears a little absurd. Her camera on its tripod is taller than she is; I suspect she had to stand on that box in order to be able to snap her picture.

In the final years of Isabella's life, photography became her ultimate pose. She could no longer claim that she travelled for health, having out-lived sister, husband and most of her friends – not to mention the plu-rality of her doctors. Nor was Isabella still travelling to escape; little remained to be left behind. Instead, she began to journey 'for Empire'. She strove to expand the bounds of human knowledge. Her glass plates from the Yangtze – her photographic negatives – went straight into the vaults of the Royal Geographical Society. She published a book called *Chinese Pictures*, and another, with a smaller circulation, from Persia and Kurdistan. These last tours – the ones not covered in this volume – were occupied principally in visiting governments, hospitals and missions. Once home, Isabella took on the mantle of the Traveller Extraordinaire. She spoke to the members of the House of Commons, and she advised the Prime Minister, William Gladstone, on the issue of Armenian Christians. 'I would only do that which is . . . *very well worth doing*,' Isabella wrote, 'and which would enable me to bring back a rich cargo of knowledge.'[74] Her concerns are reflected by the literal weight of her tomes. Gone is the spry woman who scrambled up the slopes of Hawaii's volcanoes. Instead, with success, Isabella became stiff and tedious.

Marianne North, a painter and fellow traveller, remembered meeting Isabella in these years. The occasion was a London geographical *soirée*, and in a back parlour, Isabella was holding court. She was perched 'in a big armchair' as though on a throne, with 'gold-embroidered slippers, and a footstool to show them on, a petticoat all over gold and silver Japanese embroidered wheels, and a ribbon and order across her shoul-ders, given to her by the King of the Sandwich Islands'. She had an annoying habit of talking 'rather as if she were reciting from one of her books'.[75] Likewise, when Robert Browning was introduced to Isabella at the height of her fame, she had the audacity to cut the poet to the quick. He remarked politely that everyone in London was reading her books. She replied acidly that she could not say the same for his!

It is a shame that this appears to be the enduring image of Isabella, for in her younger years she was less choleric. In the letters published in this

74 Letter from Isabella Bird to John Murray III, 18 March 1886 (JMA).
75 Cited in Middleton 19.

volume, we meet an Isabella who was both kind and enthusiastic. These missives show Isabella for who she was: a keen observer, a shrewd judge of character. It is perhaps not surprising that Isabella's vision of the British Empire was also more clear-sighted in these years. For example, in 1878–9, in her travels in East Asia, Isabella was astounded by the incompetence of British administrators, and she did not shy from expressing her rebuke – at least to her sister. No blind supporter of British imperialism, she saw many of these bureaucrats as drunkards, gamblers, fops and misfits – and she recorded their deeds in words, having not yet discovered the merits of a camera. Governor Pope-Hennessy of Hong Kong, she wrote, needed to be recalled because he had insulted too many influential men. William Maxwell, Assistant Resident of Larut, in the Straits Settlements, Isabella found ineffective for a different cause. Maxwell was 'too hard on the Chinese . . . He rules the Chinese rigidly and hates them' and 'I fear the hatred is returned.'[76] As for Bloomfield Douglas, British Resident of Selangor, Isabella told John Murray that he was

> the most fiendish human being I have ever seen . . .The mis-government of the state was gross and brutal. I saw scenes in which the Resident was the chief actor of the most brutal description and heard more than I saw. It was a rule of fraud, hypocrisy and violence. But as guest of the S[tate of] S[elangor] government I 'ate salt' with this man and would not under any circumstances print my opinion.[77]

She didn't. Instead, Isabella destroyed her letters to Henrietta describing her stay with Douglas. Today, we know they existed only via Isabella's business correspondence. With great anxiety, she asked Murray – on more than one occasion – *'whether Mr. Bloomfield Douglas, the Resident, has resigned'*.[78] She feared Douglas would file charges of libel if she printed what she saw. She feared, too, public censure.

Ironically, fear seems to have been the dominant motif for this coura-geous traveller. Abroad, Isabella might be healthy, liberal and free think-ing. Once home, she cringed at the notion of what other people thought. About *The Golden Chersonese*, which recorded these adventures in Hong Kong and Malaya, Isabella complained, 'All the critics will fall foul of it . . . The officials who think themselves not appreciated will revenge themselves.' 'One may criticise as much as one likes when one

76 Letter from Isabella to Henrietta Bird, 13 February 1879 (JMA).
77 Letter from Isabella Bird to John Murray III, 16 November 1882 (JMA). I am indebted to John Gullick for pointing out Isabella's omission of this critique. See 'Syers and the Selangor Police, 1875–97'. *Journal of the Malaysian Branch of the Royal Asiatic Society* 51 (1978), 53.
78 Letter from Isabella Bird to John Murray III, 16 November 1882 (JMA).

criticises yellow or brown–skinned men, but when people write on British officials and methods in any but the most eulogistic language they raise quite a storm.'[79] As a result, Isabella heavily edited her opinions when she came to shape her letters for publication. She did not retain sentences saying that the goal of empire should be 'to train the Rajas to rule Perak justly by themselves'. Nor did she admit in her books that 'we know [very little] of the great problems of the east'. 'Our ignorance' is 'loud and boastful'. 'I am daily more and more humiliated by our culpable ignorance and by our assumptions of knowledge.'[80] Such trepidation, expressed to Henrietta, rarely made it into Isabella's books. Without Henrietta, she seems not to have expressed these feelings at all.

Was Isabella right to be afraid? What would have happened had she published her reservations? Certainly, the nineteenth century was not so liberal as ours. At the time Isabella visited Malaya, Joseph Conrad had not yet written such unsympathetic works about imperialism as *Heart of Darkness*, *Nostromo* and *Lord Jim*. But it would be wrong to say that imperialism was immune from criticism. In terms of the Protected Malay States, Sir Peter Benson Maxwell, former chief justice of the settlement, had published *Our Malay Conquests* in 1878, the year of Isabella's travels. It lacerated the very concept of having colonies. Likewise, Emily Innes – whose husband plays a bit part in *The Golden Chersonese* – was so intensely offended by British imperialism in Malaya, by both its administrators and its supporters (which she took Isabella to be), that she published a muckraking rebuttal in 1881 called *The Chersonese with the Gilding Off*.

More light-heartedly, Hugh Clifford – a conservative travel writer, equally famous in his day – prodded the fitness of administrators with a photograph taken in Penang in 1891. In it, four British officers are just settling down to some 'serious' business. One is spreading a tea-towel over his knees, wearing sunglasses, judge's robes and a beef-eater's hat. Another carries a Malay spear and a woman's parasol – conflicting images of 'savagery' and 'civilisation' – while wearing the pith helmet of the archetypal explorer. A third, holding a whip and grinning at the camera, is costumed in a mishmash of Scottish kilt and an officer's decorated jacket. The last has donned an admiral's hat. Through the mock dignity of these men, we are told that the British Empire is nothing more than a lark. In this way, Clifford's photograph – like those taken by Isabella – represents an imperial ethnographic. It, too, presents a snapshot of a bygone time; it, too, codifies the manners and customs of a particular populace. Yet it does so with an abandon that Isabella feared to express.

79 Letter from Isabella Bird to John Murray III, n.d. April 1883 (JMA).
80 Letter from Isabella to Henrietta Bird, 13 February 1879 (JMA).

In the end, all I have been able to do in this introduction is to adumbrate a small section of Isabella's complexity. In so doing, I have tried to follow Wallace Stevens' dicta 'to find, not to impose' when presenting her character. I have been motivated to do so because I feel that those writers (generally women) who have been attracted to Isabella in the past have too often been beguiled by the will-o'-the-wisps of her myth. We want her to be that phoenix who rises from her sickbed to climb Mauna Loa. We want her to be a symbol of our own empowerment, to exemplify the best qualities of a Feminist Movement in which she did not participate and in which she may not have believed. Through our scholarship, Isabella Bird has become mythic – and in the process many enthusiasts have become trapped in that myth.

A better reaction would be to step back and recognise that Isabella was a complex woman whose agenda on her journeys was neither static nor simplistic. There is no one right answer as to why she left home at the age of forty to embark on a lifetime of overseas adventures. Nor is there any single response as to why Isabella chose the destinations that she did. We do not know her 'true' feelings about Henrietta, nor do we know whether she was really in love with Rocky Mountain Jim. Instead, Isabella's life, like all lives, was ambiguous. It did not possess the clarity of a fictional romance, and stories about her that seem too good to be true generally are.

Rather, we should recognise that Isabella herself fashioned the lens through which she wanted us to view her. It was Isabella who edited and destroyed her letters. It was Isabella who styled her books, like her photographs, to capture images of herself as she wished to be – and not as she was. The letters printed here in their original state would be edited by Isabella for her travelogues in order to form the package most suitable for Victorian consumption, yet the very process of editing is, at heart, intrinsically flawed. With each cut, an author can fashion a new identity. A different cut would create someone else. This is true even for the editing I have performed in this volume. The traveller in these selections is not – and cannot be – the 'total' Isabella. The letters I have chosen may not be the ones that you, the reader, might have selected. Likewise, each one of the seven book-length biographies (in English) presents Isabella in a different light. Which is true? Which is accurate? Which is real? Quite frankly, not one is. Together, they all are.

As such, I have not tried to tell the 'truth' about Isabella in this volume, nor do I mean to 'set the record straight' by publishing these manuscripts for the first time. Instead, I have simply presented Isabella as I myself most like her to be: complex, contradictory and many-sided.

My favourite letters are those she wrote from Hawaii and Malaysia, when she discusses volcanoes and tigers and riverboat journeys, when she goes on elephant treks through the rain forest and sits down to dinner with a party of monkeys like some equatorial Alice. In these letters, Isabella is on fire with her own descriptions. She was not concerned about her public face; indeed, she had not yet become famous. Rather, she was intoxicated by the novelty of her experiences, and she poured out her adventures to her sister by candlelight, trying to cram every event she could on to each page. Isabella's average letter from Hawaii takes up about ten small sheets of paper and reaches a length of nearly twenty thousand words. As the freshness wore off, her observations were condensed, explaining why she wrote so much more about her first voyage around the world than her second.

In editing these missives, I have tried to keep things as close as possible to the original manuscripts while also presenting them for a general readership. For this reason, a paragraph format has been added, and for purposes of space certain sections have been omitted or summarised. Explanations of unusual words are given in footnotes, while omissions are marked by ellipses in square brackets. The letters are followed by a chronology, and an appendix listing the people and places that appear in her manuscripts.

Otherwise, these are the words as Isabella wrote them. The images spill over one another, the narrative is loosely organised, the dates are sometimes jumbled, making her writing both immediate and alive. In these letters, Isabella uses words that no one else ever used, ones she and Henrietta invented that became their own language. In these letters, too, Isabella is carefree. She is less interested in how things might have been than how they really were. The result is that this collection provides a fascinating study of the private life of a woman who was to become one of the foremost travel writers of her time. This is Isabella as Henrietta knew her. Enjoy.

Kay Chubbuck
Princeton University
November 16, 2001

PUBLISHER'S NOTE

Isabella Bird's letters to Henrietta were written by candlelight and often in haste. Her handwriting is not always legible, which makes it difficult to discern the exact placement of punctuation marks. In fact, Isabella often dismissed punctuation altogether in the excitement of recording her experiences in far off places. While we have not added punctuation that is missing, we have adopted British style in printing what remains. This policy departs from academic practice but in our view is clearer for general readers. For the same reason – readability – paragraphs have been added to what was originally unbroken text.

To
MY SISTER
to whom these letters were originally written,
they are now affectionately
dedicated

PART ONE
THE FIRST WORLD TOUR
1872–3

The Sea

In the autumn of 1871, as Isabella neared her fortieth birthday, she became dreadfully depressed. She suffered from fevers, headaches and insomnia; she had carbuncles all over her back. In an effort to assuage her pains, Isabella's doctors prescribed a sea voyage, persuading her to engage a berth on the steamer *St David* bound for New York. Once it returned, the *St David* was chartered to go up the Mediterranean, visiting ports in Italy, Algeria, Spain and Portugal. In all, Isabella spent nearly six months at sea, and since she was happy, her health improved. No letters to Henrietta survive from this voyage, but the following to Isabella's close friend Ella Blackie* has been quoted extensively in biographies of Bird. It is the only known manuscript to have been preserved from this tour.

St David Island Harbour Maine U.S.
2:30 p.m. March 24/1872

My darling one

At last comes a visible response to your two delightful letters, one of which welcomed me at great wicked whirling overwhelming N.Y. the other at this staid quiet puritan town. Thanks for all the little details so interesting from you and as you give them, for the faithful account of Hennie, and for the love so precious, whether I am near or far away.

Hennie has written to me how you could not believe I had perpetuated such a 'stroke of genius' as introducing 47 hours at home into the heart of my sea life! It must have been equally hard to believe that after encountering the fury of an Atlantic storm for 7 days in coming home I should brave the risk again. But at last I am in love, and desperately in love, and the old sea god has so stolen my heart and penetrated my soul that I seriously fear that hereafter though I must be elsewhere in body I must be with him in spirit. I am not joking. My two friends on board this ship have several times told me that I had so imbibed the spirit of the sea, that they thought after a time on land I should crave for it again and now beginning the 5th month of my sea life I feel that there is a danger of it being so. It is a perfect infatuation. It is to me like living in a new world so free, so fresh, so vital, so careless, so unfettered, so full

---

* See Ella Blackie, under Professor John Stuart Blackie, in Notes on People and Places, p. 316.

of interest that one grudges being asleep and instead of carrying cares and worries and thoughts of the morrow to bed with one to keep one awake, one falls asleep at once, to awake to another day in which one knows that there can be nothing to annoy one. No door bells, no 'please ma'ams', no dirt, no servants, no bills no demands of any kind, no vain attempts to overtake all one knows one should do. Above all no nervousness, and no conventionalities. No dressing. If my clothes drop into rags, they can be pinned together, and at meals Robinas* scarlet cloak hides all defects. It sounds a hideously selfish life, but in the inevitable intimate association of people in all circumstances for 4 months of almost entire isolation, human relations spring up and human interests, and in some instances warm feelings of regard, which have a tendency to keep selfishness in a degree under.

I cannot tell you how much I like my life. This last 3 months my enjoyment of it has been growing till it is now difficult for me to imagine any pleasure in any other life except at home. I am often in tempestuous spirits and except on one evening always in excellent spirits. I feel like 'a viking wild', and without effort keep the whole of my messmates in good spirits and good humour during our present singular circumstances! It is a strange new experience and I think it has taught me some useful lessons. I think I am entirely unrecognisable, at least I hardly recognise my own identity. It seems a brief resurrection of the girl of 21.

It seems strange to say so, but you will understand me and not repeat it, but I never could have believed I was the kind of woman who would influence men. But manners and speech have undergone a gradual but entire transformation, refined tastes are being developed, and I know that I have the good will of all the ships company, and the warmest and most respectful regard of 2 or 3. I leave Hennie to read you as she *must* my Portland letters which sound like a feeble echo of the travels of Parry† or Kaul. I fear I am not really much better. I have strength enough for my sea life, for its grand excitements, and blissful quiet, but I fear a week of warm rooms, and seeing friends, and the usual demands of land life would destroy me again. Hennie will tell you when to write.

Believe always in a love which even Neptune has not stolen away. I have your likeness with me and am always more satisfied with it. Love to the dear Pro. [. . .] Accept my warm love unchilled by *fifty* degrees of frost, a frozen ship and a frozen sea!

ILBird

---

* See Robina, p. 339.
† See Rear Admiral Sir William Parry, p. 337.

Australia

After this adventure on the *St David*, Isabella returned home. She helped Henrietta move out of their flat in Edinburgh and into Tobermory's Strongarbh Cottage on the Isle of Mull. Unwilling to remain without a place of her own – or to accompany her sister to Tobermory – Isabella decided to embark on another journey. She departed on July 11, 1872 and this time she went to Australia, whose climate, her doctors promised, would provide lasting benefits to her health. Now, Australia in 1872 was not a known health resort, but it had acquired a reputation as a friendly place for a spinster to find a spouse. Her destination, Victoria, had become popular after the 1850 Gold Rush; yet there were still more men than women in the colony. Such details encourage us to believe that Isabella's doctors had diagnosed her 'disease' as loneliness (at least in part). She was sent to stay with two potential matchmakers: a childhood friend named Fanny Puckle;* and an old colleague of her father's, named Mr Cameron,† now preaching in Melbourne's Presbyterian Church.

Australia, unfortunately, did nothing for Isabella's health. This was largely because of a chill she caught on the voyage out: it was so severe that the captain of her steamer, the *Ben Nevis*,‡ thought she might die. Isabella's recovery was exceedingly slow, and she arrived in Melbourne feeling dull and uncomfortable. To make herself feel better, she dosed herself with alcohol (as a sedative) and so much bromide that she contracted a rash and some of her hair fell out. It was hot, she complained, and there were too many flies. She left for New Zealand as soon as she could. The following letters, printed for the first time, are the ones she wrote to her sister.

Chalmers Manse§ *Melbourne Oct 13. 1872*

My own darling

I must be in a bad way when I find it difficult to start a letter to it,¶ but I am so dreadfully depressed. I was a little better for the first four days after leaving the ship but my spirits are worse than ever. I want you

---

* See Fanny Puckle, p. 338.
† See Mr Cameron, p. 318.
‡ See the *Ben Nevis*, p. 315.
§ See Chalmers Manse, p. 319.
¶ Throughout her letters, Isabella refers to her sister and herself as 'it', as in 'its pet', 'its ownest', and 'its thing'. As Patt Barr noted in her 1970 biography, the presumption of this pronoun is that the sisters formed 'a mutually exclusive and excluding' unit. Each sister in presumably one half of the whole, both covered by the same word.

to ask Dr Moir and Dr Grainger Stewart[*] if they think it is any use going on, if I had not better get leisurely back in March. You see the place is an entire failure for I am much worse than before I left in Nov. and this climate (on this high hill in good weather with country air and quiet) which Dr Handfield Jones[†] thought so big and stimulating that he urged it above every other for one or two years certainly does not suit me. I cannot get any sleep though I sleep with my windows open and hear no sounds and take bromide 3 times a day and I am more nervous than I have ever been and cannot remember anything or read a book. These last 2 days I have felt shaking all over and oppressed with undefined terror. The *loneliness* of a long voyage and these uninteresting regions is killing. A man might get on, but not a woman, for it is not safe for her to go away from the beaten track as it is in America. It is a sickening disappointment and then having no place to be takes away all repose from the thought of getting back. And I was so much better and came here conscientiously as the best thing. I often think how you would remember the broad stately teak finished poop of the Ben Nevis as looking so much nicer and more promising than the lean desolate deck of the St David and how differently it turned out. On one the cow jumped over the moon on the other it died in a ditch.

Thus I am thinking that it will be going back to Edinburgh and mailing with the house and beginning a dil[‡] winter, patiently because it is hoping that I am getting well. If the house be not taken and Hutcheson would paint it properly and repaper the bedrooms I want it taken on again. I will pay the rent out of my own savings. If I had your room I could get on. One could have the window open at night now and I would rather drag on there than try any other plans. Had there been a telegraph I intended to have telegraphed on arriving here. My soul would die in dark street rooms and if we left Edinburgh I know not whither we should go. I have thought over it every day. Houses and situations are so profusely dismal and with this tendency to depress it is so dangerous to put oneself in depressing circumstances. We have not money enough to get a house in a good situation and the wc's of flats are so objectionable. It seems to me that for me cheerfulness indoors and a window to look out from are more important than facilities for getting out easily. If I had your room I never need be confined to bed. The winter in Athol Cres. with all the ease of getting out was the dullest we

---

[*] See Sir Thomas Grainger Stewart, p. 342.
[†] See Dr Charles Handfield Jones, p. 326.
[‡] Used by Isabella to indicate when something is particularly dull, 'dil' also conjures up an atmosphere of suffocation, frustration and boredom.

spent in Edinburgh. But I am writing as if there were no more sea and as if I were getting back, when the shortest distance is 15 000 miles. [. . .]

On Monday morning as I heard that the Ben Nevis was going to load at Geelong I had to go to Sandridge Pier with a parcel. Mr Cameron took me to the Station in a conveyance, which is the only grotesque thing in Melbourne. 8 people sit back to back in a car with 2 wheels with a hood over it. You have bars to put your feet against and straps to get up with and hold on by. It runs as easily as a Hansom and the fare is 3d. anywhere. The hood is covered with a fringed white tablecloth. It is more like the Belencian tartan than anything else. I found the captain on board so I got my mattress sewn up and my thing done at once and he escorted me nearly to Melbourne. He has taken a great deal of trouble to get information accurately about rates and to arrange my passage to New Zealand. He said he was very anxious to be of service to any friend of Mr Dunlop[*] for 'he is the most honourable and energetic man of business in Glasgow'! The ship looked splendid without those barrels, but I was well pleased to think that I should never look upon her again. I saw the old Great Britain which has just made the quickest passage out ever made. We beat every ship which sailed from any British port between June 20th and July 11. And the crack London clippers, the Wimmera and See. which passed the last net before we did, only came in yesterday and the day before. I have asked everyone what they saw in the tropics, and no-one has seen anything that I did not see, except thunderstorms.

The Mackinzies[†] came before I left. She is a timid gentle looking girl very elegant but as tall as Bessie.[‡] He is a very bright intelligent looking young man. They go for a month to Dunedin next week. They live opposite this gate and called since I came but she seemed so terrified. I cant think Mrs Cameron in a state to warrant this constant anxiety. Except that she did lose the use of her limbs for 13 weeks she had no symptoms that I have not had; constant pain at the back of her head and neck, numbness and pricking in her arms and feet, 'bubblings' in her head which unite with great nervous prostration after nangarenes.[§] But she is partly recovered and it seems so sad to see the children never free from care if the danger really is exaggerated. The doctor certainly said she was in danger of paralysis but Dr Moir has said it in a brutal way to me *several* times.

---

[*] See Nathaniel Dunlop, p. 323.
[†] The daughter and son-in-law of Mr Cameron.
[‡] See Elizabeth Ker, p. 329.
[§] Nangarenes, or, alternatively, nangings, is a term used by Isabella to describe headaches or annoyances. She also uses a verb form, 'nanged', meaning to be frustrated or overwhelmed.

I think (but it must not be said) that the fiend[*] hates Melbourne so thoroughly that if anything made it clear to him that he should leave it he would and it would be such a sad thing for him to return and have no place. He says if he had known a tenth part of what he now knows he never would have come. Certainly from what he says the state of the Presbyterian church of Victoria in every respect is as low as it can be. I don't see how he can have any pleasure. He works as hard as he did at Birmingham bereaving his soul of ease. The mere visiting of the sick is enough for one man scattered as they are. Then he has no associates. The Bishop Dr Cairns[†] and Mr Balfour[‡] are the only people he likes and of course their intercourse must be mainly about work. He is what people call 'getting on' wonderfully. Mr Budd says he has more influence than anyone in Victoria except the Bishop but it seems as if no-one could fight single handed against the low tone which is described. I had no pleasure in being at his house except in seeing his domestic happiness and unselfishness for I never saw him alone to have any talk for 10 minutes. As soon as he came into the drawing room the bell always rang and somebody wanted him and even on Sunday afternoon he had to go and see sick people. The Cairns delight in him. Mrs Cairns says that owing to his talent and good feeling everything which might have been difficult is smoothed over and that though very independent he acts to Dr Cairns like a son. She says party spirit has been entirely snubbed by him. She said that all the miserable and pitiable work which went on with Mr Dykes[§] would never have been if his wife had lived, that she was so unworldly and precious. She was nursed in their house for 5 months. Mr McIntosh should be very careful not to spread any report of the fiend not getting on with Dr Cairns for the *harmony and mutual regard are perfect* and if such a thing came back again as it may Dr Cairns would be very angry and hurt.

Mrs Budd came for me Monday afternoon with a two-horse carriage like the Otters[¶] and brought me here 7 miles from Melbourne, passing through St Kilda. It is buried in greenery at least a mile from Hobsons Bay. Mr Budd[||] is son of old Mrs Pucklestrom's sister, 1st commissioner of education and chief inspector of schools, one of the oldest colonists and held in universal respect, very lively, able, odd and with that peculiar culture only given by an English university. There are two sons one

[*] Mr Cameron.
[†] See Dr Adam Cairns, p. 318.
[‡] See James Balfour, p. 314.
[§] See Mr Dykes, p. 324.
[¶] See Admiral Otter, p. 336.
[||] See Richard Hale Budd, p. 317.

daughter a niece and wife, all very clean very practical very kind and very philanthropic. I came to them for 3 days and am staying nine, and they insist on my coming back to them from Mortlake. They live in an old fashioned house gradually enlarged with a most beautiful drawing room and a large garden and grounds. It is blazing weather dry as a bone a hot sun and a blue sky which glitters as we never see it but the house is quite cool and owing to the previous heavy rains and nocturnal showers all Brighton is one green bower. It is an old place and the native trees except on the commons have been replaced by the fairer growths of England and other lands. The commons have huge hideous gum trees on them and the wattle an acacia with clusters of yellow balls and then beyond Brighton there are ten miles of heath and thick tea tree scrub now masses of white blossom. Brighton is endless natural woods soft with great woodsides and grass and clover and fields with green trees and verandah'd one-floored houses buried in imported trees passion flowers oleanders wisteria roses and all kinds of creepers. [. . .] Of course, green must look nice in such a brilliant atmosphere but I cannot find that I admire anything as a whole only admit that it is so much better than I expected. The other side of Melbourne is hideous.

The Yarra outside of Melbourne is much like the Ouse near St Neots, high and wooded on one side and the other an expanse of flowery meadows with cows feeding in them. Elms and great weeping willows dipping into the water. The weather is splendid and the sunsets – how unlike the tropics flaming combinations of crimson green orange and violet. The air in the morning is heavy with the scent of orange blossoms, but there is little twilight and it is dark before seven.

They have taken me on a long drive each day. I get most dreadfully tired. I have wine at 11, lunch and beer at one, wine at 4 taken out if we are driving, dinner and beer at 6, tea wine and bed at 9, but I get very little strength and feel always dragging and so *dil*. Visiting should be a very unselfish process for one must take interest altogether in things external to one's self but to enjoy it one is required to be young, strong and in good spirits. [. . .] Oh oh oh how I wish I were back with *It* and Emily* and Bessie. This is too miserable.

Oct 22. On Sunday evening a hot wind came on. I could not think what made me feel so on edge and choked in the night. It was very bad but early this morning it went round to the south and became a gale.

At 12 today we drove to Melbourne with all my things to the

---

* See Emily Clayton, p. 320.

Warrnambool Steamer. Such a one for passengers I never saw. Not much longer than the Chiefton,[*] filthy and cumbered up with all sorts of cargo up to the bulwarks. The Captain said it was far too stormy to sail. If we got to Warrnambool the open boats in which people land would be swamped in the surf, perhaps the gale would moderate by tomorrow morning. So leaving my luggage we came back having had a most fatiguing drive of 14 miles for nothing. There was a 'dust storm' – it did not come quite up to us but for 2 hours it darkened the whole south shutting out of view as with a heavy brown fog all the near hills. It is the brickbuilders at Sydney. Though not in it, while in Melbourne and on the way home we were smothered in dust, hair eyes nose ears mouth filled. The commons and woodsides which were so green look as if a fiery breath had passed over them and the grasses and the oaks look greyer and uglier than ever. I think the Australian colonies must be more prosaic than any others. Such hideous country, such hideous leafage and the golden calf the one deity.

Mr Budd went into Melbourne on Sat morning for my letters. I felt sick with fear till they came and then they were the one excitement and sole pleasure that I have had since leaving home. I never seemed to take in the first letters though I read them over and over again. These are the most delightful letters that could have been delivered. They took me 4 hours to read, and the only amazing thing in them was its leaving the rat hole[†] and going to England. There was not a single thing in them in which I did not take interest. [. . .] I delight in my darling and the only treasure I have is in knowing that it has something it can like.

Mount Shadwell Mortlake Victoria Oct 27. I have been here for 3 days and seem to have been here for months. Fanny Puckle sends her love, and you are to be told that my visit long looked for is one complete satisfaction that it makes her ten years younger and is nearly as good as going to England! I am liking it. You see it is like being among my own people. We can talk over things for a quarter of a century. It is so odd to hear her speak of *them*[‡] and Fred. S. and Mohawk[§] and William Layton and all the people and things of Hunts. I forgot how much I had ridden with her when I had the money and how much I had seen of her after her widowhood.

---

[*] See the *Chiefton*, p. 320.
[†] 'Rat hole' is another term coined by Isabella and Henrietta, referring to their home, regardless of location. The sisters are presumably the 'rats' who remain snug within. Later in her travels, 'rat hole' implies anywhere Isabella is happy and feels at home.
[‡] Presumably Isabella's parents, Edward and Dora Bird, both deceased.
[§] See Mohawk, p. 335.

Lucinda always said Fred* was the flower of the family and I think he is. He is 6 ft 3 a fine handsome genial honourable gentlemanly Englishman and very intelligent and well informed. Fanny has all her old brightness originality and intellectuality but happy prosperous living circumstances and maternity have so softened and improved her character that she is now most attractive. She hardly looks any older. She has 3 uncommonly charming ladylike poetical childlike girls at home the eldest nearly 13 – delightful children to whom she is a most tender and wise mother and a boy of 14 away at school. Fred Puckle is an excellent husband father and master and I hear is greatly respected as a man and magistrate. He is magistrate of a district as large as Yorkshire. [. . .] The house is a square stone one and has no verandah in a beautiful garden. It is on the top of a hill so steep on one side that there is only just room for the carriage sweep. Behind there is a green expanse of 60 acres and then a round green hill as green as the Cuillin Hills [in Skye] dotted over on one side with blackwood trees and about 600 feet high. The hill this house stands on is over 200 feet. From the grass township road to the garden gate there is no road but you drive up the slope of a hill through the thickest grass dense with white clover. From the windows one looks over a vast plain of grass generally bright green but here and there stained red with sorrel or whitened with clover blossoms. A small wooden house here and there post and rail fences and herds of fat sleepy gorged red and black cattle only break the monotony. At a great distance the plain becomes dotted over with trees of shapeless aspect which thicken into the grey hideousness of the Australian bush along the hard horizontal line. This horizon is broken by singular protuberances which rise out of the plain like islands.

There have been 3 hot winds in the 3 weeks since I came. Being spring and not summer of course they are only moderate. When they come in hot weather I cant see how they are borne specially at horrible Melbourne. They last one 2 or 3 days. On the 3rd day as on last Monday all creation seems discoloured and gasping the sky darkens with brown clouds, then suddenly the wind changes, you draw a long breath the windows and doors are thrown open in 2 hours the mercury falls from 70 to 50 degrees and there should be torrents of rain followed by a cool bright day but the last hot wind went round without a drop which is the presage of a long drought. Dr Handfield Jones and others may think this climate so valuable but it would destroy me and the old residents say that no doctor who has lived here would dream of *sending people here* for

---

* See Fred Puckle under Fanny Puckle, p. 338.

several months, except for the winter in the earliest stage of consumption.

I am sleeping better here and eating well. There is everything you can think of exquisitely served and I have wine 4 times a day and beef tea at night but I don't get stronger. Yet on the cold blue day on which I came I drove the 35 miles from Warrnambool at a stretch without being really worse. A horse has been produced twice for me to ride on the grass, but after getting ready I have been too nervous to get on. I intend to try tomorrow if the wind changes. I could go alone on one quite well. One gets no exercise if one does not ride for the country is too hideous for driving. The gum trees are a growth which depresses you. Their colour is that of town grown willows smothered with dust. The wattle or acacia, a small evergreen tree, is such an abominable tree that if the ground is broken near its roots the smell is like that of a bad drain and a weed about here the 'stinkweed' fills the air with a smell like a combination of Pincher and Wiggie* at their worst. There is not a native tree that I have yet seen which is not ugly. Happily our fairer growths make immense strides.

I have taken my passage to Dunedin for Nov. 20th by the Albion, a steamer nearly as large as the *St David* and very like her. The Californian steamers are hated here. The newspapers are always at them and everyone abuses them for irregularity and all sorts of evils. But I think it is very much because New Zealand has secured Auckland as the terminus of this route. If I hear a good account of them from Mr Fox and others, I think I shall go by that route by the steamer leaving for St Frisco about Jan 23. I should reach California then before the end of February in its spring, and perhaps be able to spend a few weeks among those Colorado hills on which and all through the region of the Rocky Mountains all people say the elixir of life can be drunk. If my back gets well enough I seriously think that a servants place would be the best thing. Manual labour, a rough life and freedom from conventionalities added to novelty would be a good thing. I thought of going for a month to the Sandwich Islands but I fear I must give up any idea of anything in a hot climate and I must do what will seem the most cheerful things.

This is a very cheerful house. They are happy, healthy prosperous and have enough occupation. Fanny takes as much interest in one as Meg and my being here is such a pleasure to her. The children too are so nice. Then Fred and Fanny are so very good tempered and lively and there is so much intellectuality and culture all the newest books and magazines

---

* Pincher and Wiggie were the Birds' dogs.

reviews and papers in addition to a very good standard library. [. . .] I have also been at church. Hymns ancient and modern were sung. All who I care for most whether dead or living seemed to come up with the service and were Presbyterians with the psalm 'Pray for the peace of Jerusalem.' It was a very rustic congregation brought in about 20 waggons. On alternate Sundays Fred officiates! He and Fanny teach a Sunday School in the afternoon. There are no neighbours, consequently no nangarenes.

I don't know how I shall write the journal letter. After getting back to Brighton that evening* I knitted and went to bed very early, break-fasted the next morning at 7 and at 8 drove with Mr Budd to the Station and by train to Melbourne. It was a cool splendid morning. The *Edwina* was more ludicrously horrible than anything I have ever seen. The two good steamers on the same route were laid up and they were loading it beyond the bounds of safety. The accommodation for passengers on deck was in the middle of the ship under the bridge and the engine and funnel aloft this a very good plan for preventing one feeling the screw and nearly the whole ship was piled not only to the bulwarks but *much above them* with boxes planks chains orange boxes and empty hen coops. When all seemed full a waggonette was lowered on lashed on the top of a double tier of chimney cans and a horse in a box was wedged in so that his head filled up the saloon door and people had to go on the bridge up a trap. Then they piled the front of the bridge with orange boxes and still not 1/2 the cargo was on board. Then people called out that she was loaded 18 inches above her load line and would go down in the sea, so they threw off the hawsers. No standing room on the bridge the saloon full of luggage bundles and people clamorous for berths 95 wretches having to be stowed away where there was scant accommodation for 35. There 'noblerising' had begun with great vigour. I could not be on deck partly because there was no space for my camp stool, but I sat on my cushions and plaid bundle on the floor and knitted, wondering all the time at the singular type of preposterous and bottomless ugliness which is growing up.

Nearly all the passengers were Scotch and spent the day and night in drinking whisky. At one dinner was served. The food was very good but served cold and waited on grotesquely and the carver sat on the end of a trunk. After dinner I went to bed. I had secured a berth in a den intended for 4 and 6 adults 2 bags and a baby occupied it two on the floor. The floor settees tables were all covered with people. My berth

* i.e. after the Warrnambool steamer failed to embark due to stormy weather on October 22.

was only 18 inches wide. All the people were horribly sick. I was not actually so because I had laid down so early as it was not rough but so hot and close that one could not sleep. At daybreak a gale sprang up and some hen coops and all the loose hampers went overboard. Happily we were just on the bar. With every wave a chorus of cries rose from the ladies until on the top of one huge broken surf we were carried down the reef and into smooth water. When I got up a lighter was alongside into which as in the Highlands people crates boxes waggon horse were put but a gentleman came off for me with a nice boat belonging to the Customs and said Mr Puckle was on the pier.

Such was the heap and cumber that no luggage could be got at. I had to climb over boxes, the top of the boiler and uneven piles of wood to get to the gangway and there just as in the Highlands were some crooked steps and a boat rising and falling. Such a wind it seemed as if it would blow the boat out of the sea. And such a place. An inlet with low sand hills all round which were being blown away in drifts, a scraggy wooden jetty, a narrow opening to the sea which looked quite black and great walls of surf coming in one behind the other. The Captain said if the gale had come on 1/2 an hour sooner we should have had to put back owing to the overload on the steamer.

Fred Puckle met me on the pier and through clouds of sand we drove in a waggonette to the hotel in the main street of Warrnambool where a bright parlour a beautiful breakfast and good fire awaited us. A gentleman from Mortlake breakfasted and drove with us. Warrnambool seemed to have only one wide long sandy bumpy street like Kingussie [in Scotland] or some such obsolete spray place. It looked gone to sleep with age but is only 20 years old and has an immense trade. I went to bed till 12 and then we started in an American waggon with two mad horses harnessed very far from it. We got in in a stable as large as St Thomas church[*] and as soon as each man let go each horse's head each wild animal rattled shook himself and went off at a full gallop cantered into a succession of jumps before it slowed down into a furious trot. We came 35 miles in 4 hours including 2 stoppages of 20 minutes each and they galloped up this grotty hill as if they were only just going out. When we were just out of Warrnambool we got into the bush and drove through it for 30 miles along a beautiful road except for 4 miles, which was unmade and uncleared, and worse than the worst corduroy road.[†]

I liked seeing the country for once and the cold was refreshing but

---

[*] See St Thomas's Church, p. 340.
[†] A track laid transversely with tree trunks.

anything more depressing and hideous could not be imagined though the grass was bright green. It is nearly perfectly level the road generally straight with post and rail fences or 'brush fences' composed of logs and branches heaped one on another on each side and sometimes running through the brush. The forests which cover the whole country are these gum trees with their white aged looking stems and their thin grey foliage. There is no undergrowth except now and then a few scrubby wattle trees, and no variety the whole way, except that there were 3 or 4 yet uglier and greyer she oaks and 5 or 6 stumpy bottlebrush trees. There are no young trees the cattle destroy them all. Add to this hide-ousness that every third tree is dead, that one often goes through acres of dead trees and once we drove through a mile of them all holding high their white gigantic arms as if in remonstrance and looking blasted and desolate. They say that dead trees are a feature of every Australian land-scape. Even on the commons close to Melbourne there are quantities of them.

In all this expanse of dreariness we passed about 6 cabins on clearings and two bush inns the last neat ground floor things with four trim little front rooms each opening on the verandah and 4 clean little back rooms with beds. You might have liked to see me in front of one of these while Fred and his companion were inside with the reins in one hand and a tumbler of brandy and water in the other and the green Australian bush all round. Four miles from Mortlake the country is more fenced the trees are fewer and you see the grassy top of Mt Shadwell above them. Then we suddenly came out on the grass road which goes into Mortlake and galloping up the hill Fanny met us.

Oct. 29 It is a castle of indolence. I seem to get nothing done. Yesterday and today there has been a westerly gale which came in on Sunday night with a roll of thunder which shook the house. It is *bitterly* cold. We have large fires and I sleep in my shawl. It has been too blus-tering either for riding or driving and today I walked briskly down to the village and could not get warm. I am having the luxury of being cold to the bone. I should never care how cold it was but I wish I had my polarion. I am liking being here very well, that is liking the people, but it is just the same as visiting them in England. They both are so very nice and they delight in having me. I am making my stay a fortnight at least and shall be sorry to leave them for it is a kind of oasis among my dreary wanderings. Fred is such a nice man and they are so happy and suited to each other. Fanny lets me into her soul. They are really uncom-monly nice. If the climate agreed with me I could I think get on with them for 3 months. Fanny often kisses me saying 'Dear old bleached face how delightful it is to have you.' She doesn't think me much altered! We three 'crack' ceaselessly about Hunts and the old days. [. . .] How I pity that hothouse child* and all town children when I see the sweet ways and innocent interests of these. I think it is one of the saddest things in after life to have been brought up in a town and to have such hard and unwholesome memories.

Nov. 3 Sunday A hot wind again, the 3rd Sunday since I landed and a horrible glare for the grass in some places is beginning to get bare and brown. Fred Puckle conducted the service this morning and read most beautifully. The waggon gave some bad jolts on stones in the grass in coming back and made my head very bad.

I left four days ago to hold lunches in different parts of the district riding one horse and leading another with a valise on it. The day we left I had the great griffin saddled and rode 4 miles with Fannys eldest child with me on a pony. It did not hurt me for the long springy action of a superb horse on grass is so different from the pounding of a hired brute on stony roads. I rode again yesterday but the sun was very hot and the horse though he did not quite run away galloped with great leaps and almost pulled me down his neck and was fractious the whole way. I was not hurt but exhausted and afraid of being hurt. I cant hold the reins in my left hand and my right and back feel very weak when a horse begins to pull. When I stopped him I felt as if I should fall off with exhaustion. I think I could ride *slowly* a good way on a cool day. [. . .]

This last week I have made a white twilled calico tunic for Fanny and have bound a two yards square carriage cover. Also made a new tunic for my white alpaca dress. I am staying for 3 weeks. There is a want of variety partly because the roads generally are too bad for pleasant driving and I cannot ride so far as the nearest 'station'. I am getting impatient to leave Victoria for 'ills I know not of'.

You never remembered my birthday even to send me a card nor did Emily. I remember yours is next Tuesday but can send nothing except care for it. If we both live I hope we shall be settled at this time next year. I have hated my life since July 11th. I have seen nothing worth seeing and no interesting people. The dilness generally is something frightful. The noise made by the bluebottle flies on every warm day is so tedious. There are about 40 in my room now, though I shut the

---

* Presumably Isabella herself: she greatly regretted the time her family spent in Birmingham, and later claimed, not entirely accurately, to have suffered from being brought up in the cities rather than the countryside.

window when the wind changed at daybreak. How I should like the mercury at zero. North and east winds are both bad here. The east seems to crackle up ones skin and sting ones eyes, and the north is *terrible*. The south though cool has not the elixir in it that our north has the west is very pleasant. The southern lights look very strange. [. . .] My sweetest thing it does not know how I care for it, or how pleased I am when it thinks any of my ways nice or how I wish to make its life happier. Thank Meg for my note and introductions. Make *comments*. I dont know that you can take such interest in people you have not seen as I can. I delighted in the rat hole letters. But I dont think it should be *expected or desired* that I should live solely on the interests of other people! No doctor must expect me to be away another winter nor to *live* without a *house* nor to be a mere pulp.

Nov 5. This is my great things birthday.*

Mortlake Nov 8. 1872

My Pet

The last letters were finished on Tuesday night this is Friday. We already knew of the election of General Grant[†] on Wednesday!

I hope there will be letters at Dunedin for me but the paper today in reference to the mail contract says that the Californian mail service is so uncertain that all important correspondence to and from New Zealand is sent via Suez. I had a letter from Mrs Slater yesterday forwarded from Dunedin a very nice one. No one can imagine what it is to get a letter. I should welcome one from anybody in whom I felt the least interest. I suppose that none of my relations will trouble themselves to write. Except the Sumners[‡] I dont think any one of them cares whether I am well or ill happy or miserable living or dead. One cant believe that people care for one if they never show it.

The Puckles want me to stay over the new year. I would willingly do so but that I find the heat and this climate disagree so dreadfully with me. People keep saying that the heat so early in the season and the hot winds are unprecedented and today I saw a meteorological report for ten years from which it seems that this is true. There have been 8 hot winds in the 5 weeks since I have been in Victoria! The last began at 6 on last Sunday morning and continued with only an imperfect respite for 7

* This must be Henrietta's birthday.
† See General Ulysses S. Grant, p. 325.
‡ See John Bird Sumner and Charles Richard Sumner, p. 342.

hours till 4 on Thursday (yesterday) afternoon. Wednesday and yesterday it was awful. Leaves and flowers hung limp and whitish looking, the
very bluebottles which are like an Egyptian plague were silent and
torpid, the servants and children looked white and damp, the 'daisy lan-
guished', the clouds were black and rainless, the air felt like air which
had been first burned then breathed. One could not eat. I saw that 'bread
enough and to spare' could not make up to me for a climate so fearful.
I was never too hot but my life seemed extinguished. Neuralgia in my
head pain in my bones pricking like pins and needles in my limbs excruciating nervousness exhaustion inflamed eyes sore throat swollen glands
below each ear stupidity. So it would be madness to stay. Indeed if there
were a steamer I would go at once. I never thought I could be so
destroyed by heat. I have kept wishing for a bath of laudanum.

Yesterday we were to go for the night to a squatters station Keilambete
12 miles off and really did set off at 3.30 as there was no sun and any
change seemed as if it would be for the better. Mr Puckle rode and F.
and I drove. In 1/2 an hour the wind changed and one breathed. It was
wonderful and there have been some showers and tonight we are glad
to sit by a fire! My beautiful umbrella fell out and the wheels went over
it cutting the silk in 3 places. The cloak Bessie gave me let the water
through nearly all over and I got wet to the skin but it was pleasant the
last 4 miles were along a bush road in which the everlasting gums were
broken here and there by the bright green of box and blackwood trees.
It was so odd to see through these uncivilised looking trees a large one-
floored red brick house with a verandah all round and 2 large pretty cot-
tages near it but no road by which to drive up only a field with grass and
clover knee deep which it seemed a shame to drive through. Then a gate
then a lovely flower garden English orchard croquet ground and a group
of well drilled croquet players. From the verandah we looked across grass
and trees to one of the green protuberances Mt Neroot. [. . .]

Yesterday was cool and in the afternoon I performed the feat of riding
with Fred, a stroll on horseback of about 4 miles. He is so truly gentle
and considerate and did not seem as if he found riding slowly at all
irksome! We only took 2 easy canters. Such riding seems to suit me very
well but I feel very weak even on horseback. Today has been really cold
blowing and pouring as at Oban. I went to church in my Rob Roy
shawl.

I am grieving to think that before another Sunday I shall have left.
The howl is something frightful. I must ask them to say nothing more.
Most gladly was I to stay here. Were I to consult my comfort and pleas-
ure merely [I would not leave] for I hate the thought of going among

people who dont care for me but it would be wrong, for the heat may come on any day with increased violence and it would nearly kill me. But it tears my heart to leave them when they howl so. They both delight in me and are so completely companionable. They say I add years to their lives and prevent them yearning for home and fit in. I like him so very much he is a true *gentleman* with that fine feeling and consideration for others without which no-one can be so. She is a constant amusement to him. They laugh at each other so pleasantly. They seem to me just what an English gentleman and lady should be shedding a refining influence over their servants and the village. [. . .] I do wish it were right to stay. I shall feel so lonely when I leave them.

Camperdown Inn. Nov 14. 7.30 am. I am sitting by a roaring wood fire on a brilliant morning waiting for breakfast. Mr P. and I left Mortlake at 4.30 yesterday afternoon in an open buggy, i.e. a gig on 4 large wheels drawn by 2 splendid horses which brought us the 26 miles here by 7.30. It is very kind of Mr Puckle to have brought me as far as the good road for the bush road down 8 miles of which we came yesterday would have been killing in what cajolingly is called the 'coach'. He has also remained here till the morning to see me off comfortably for Geelong where I sleep.

Geelong Nov. 15. 12. I am going by the 2 p.m. train to Melbourne. I very nearly up to the last night gave up all my arrangements and remained at Mortlake the howl grew so tremendous and Mr Puckle declared over and over again that the heat had quite broken up and that it would now be cold till after Xmas and the very day before I left it was so cold and fresh that going seemed aimless. But on the morning of the day I left F. said he found heat was brewing and it is *brewed* with every symptom of a hot wind tomorrow 89° in the shade! Awesome. Heat can be endured but a hot wind is death. I am now glad that I kept to my resolution and took the coach journey when I did though I dread the week in the neighbourhood of Melbourne. It is a most terrible climate, though from the absence of any climactic diseases no-one could call it an unhealthy one. You are shivering one hour broiled the next or as yesterday on the coach cold and hot together 3 petticoats my wincey dress and tartan shawl (which I never put on without thinking of it) with a sun whose fierceness dizzied one not me only but the coachman and an old colonist who shared the box seat with me.

You never saw such an object as I am. I have got the prickly heat in my face and in addition my nose and lips and one ear are *blistered* so that

I have not been able to wash my face. I dislike going a visit looking so hideous. The letters too are becoming a great toil. I am always so tired and then there is nothing to say for there are no adventures and you could not possibly be interested in people whom I only visit for a few days. The day before I left Mortlake I proposed to Fanny to begin to ride again for it is so bad for her never to do anything but potter about the garden or potter down to the village driving an old horse and I even offered to ride a big strong horse which had never had a woman on him and actually got her out with Fred. I liked that ride better than anything since I left home. It was so bright and cold and we rode solely on grass in the bush about 7 miles altogether and very slowly and that horse trotted which tires me much less than cantering except that I cannot go fast and have no strength in my arms. I am now as much at home in riding and driving as I ever was and have no feeling of being nervous. I believe on a good horse riding slowly in cool weather I could travel 20 miles a day more easily than in any other way for one can change ones position and the mere being on a good spirited horse is inspiring.

Fanny enjoyed it very much. The last time we rode together was from Graffham, I on Mohawk. Her marriage is not a romantic one but it is a singularly happy one. I think her life is almost the easiest that I know. Her first child was quite unwelcome to them both. I went to see him this morning at the grammar school here, a nice gentlemanly boy, but not at all good looking. Her children are quite delightful. She is teaching them herself. Fred is a remarkably nice man. Meg would say 'Now Is. that's the kind of man I could have married.'

I liked the drive to Camperdown in the cold gold eve even especially along the bush road. On a dead gaunt gum tree 2 white yellow crested cockatoos were squawking at each other and instantly the figure of my old Bessie rose before me! There were such quantities of green and scarlet parrots and green parroquets, but they look out of place amidst the hideous foliage.

Now every lady says without exception that I have seen the most beautiful part of Victoria so what must the rest be? Camperdown is a straggling wooden village with a crater now a dead lake behind it and a wooded rise. The inn was very comfortable but I could not sleep partly because an old cow lay under my window coughing and partly because of the noise made by 'larrikins', that is youthful rogues who I fear infest every town and village here. At first when people said of a man that he was a larrikin I thought it meant a member of some lodge or society so called. I dont think the Australians are behind the Americans in inventing words.

I am writing *Nov 16* from Mr Macbains* Scotstown barrack. The carriage in which I came from Geelong was stuffed and lined with cloth just like our own first class and the heat was tremendous. [. . .] Mrs Macbain met me with a most luxurious carriage and brought me to this pretty place 5 miles from Melbourne a large house with grounds and a pretty view over fields and wooded country to the Dandenong hills. It is the prettiest view I have seen. The rooms are large and cool. Mr Macbain is a man of great wealth and a prominent member of the Legislative Assembly. He is an elder of Chalmers Church and he called and after him his wife to ask me to visit them so I came until Tuesday. [. . .] I daresay I shall be a little sorry to leave Victoria. It seems a familiar region and New Zealand has not a familiar face. Had it not been for the great dread of the summer heat I would have remained at Mortlake. They want me to go back at the end of March when they said the weather is settled and delightful but I dont much think of it.

It is this day year that the well-fated and youth giving voyage in the much beloved St David began. 'All are scattered now and fled.' I have been thinking that it is unfair to charge too much of my present bad health to the Australian climate for from the day we sailed [on the Ben Nevis] I grew meaner and meaner, and then my illness was such a very bad one and the shaking sore mouth hindering me from taking any solid food for 31 days. I cant do without so much drink which I know must be bad, and yet I do need it for when my face is flushed drink makes it pale. I grew so very stout in the Ben Nevis which remains such an inconvenience. I believe that travelling, that is going on on on day after day riding or driving would do me good but I see no way of managing it. I like the open air and the country and irregular hours eating when one is hungry. [. . .]

Sunday afternoon. Another beautifully cool still day. Yesterday afternoon Mrs Macbain drove me to call on Mrs Balfour and Mrs Cairns. Mrs Cairns is a *very nice person* and Dr Cairns the most jovial spirit that I have seen for a long time, the height of joviality and so handsome. He said Edinburgh was 'the most delightful place in the whole world'. Really this side of Melbourne is very pretty the view from this house is far prettier than anything I have seen because it has been rendered more English. The Macbains are very pleasant people and very kind. They went to Chalmers Church this morning but the carriage dropped their

---

* See Sir James MacBain, p. 333.

niece and me at a Baptist church in Collins St to hear the fiend preach. It was such a comfortable cheery airy church with a welcoming manner and good hearty singing. I *thoroughly* enjoyed the service partly doubtless because of the coolness and the comfortable seat. I dont know when I have heard such an admirable sermon so vigorous powerful poignant telling. I think possibly the demon may lack gentleness and have a tendency to sarcasm in preaching, but it was just the style I should like always to hear. You know his manner was short and his voice destroyed before he left home but now his manner is excellent quiet yet emphatic and from the necessity of adapting his voice to a church too large for him he has so changed it as to have got back the deep melodious tone he had 20 years ago.

I saw him at the carriage door and he said his wife was not so well. I should not wonder that he goes to the vacant charge at Dunedin. Mr Macbain says that the getting on of Dr Cairns and him is something perfectly marvellous that the mutual liking and respect are so great. I think the fiend is probably a better man for having come here. I suppose he is immensely respected [. . .] Mr Macbain considers him 'superhuman in the pulpit, full of magnetic influence but out of it less than other men'. He says that the public putting forward by him of strangely anti Sabbatarian views helped the current setting in that direction. At present it is like a continual Sunday here. The fiend is thought much too rigid in general – he wont travel by train on Sunday or accept any evening engagement to preach which involves the use of a car or omnibus. Poor wretch! He should never have left home. I grieve to think that I shall never see him again. With all his faults he has neither egotism nor self-seeking, and is singularly truthful and upright. I know his soul and know how much he is suffering from strain and anxiety.

Monday 18th. A hot wind. Every chink closed! Yesterday evening I went with Mr Macbain to the South Yarra Church and heard an excellent useful, though uncouth sermon on 'Work then today in my vineyard.' I think I am stronger for I hate my life somewhat less and feel more energy for doing things so long as it is cool. The first blaze of heat takes away any idea of going anywhere or doing anything.

Will you write a *polite* note to Captain McPetrie at Aitkens and Tilburns in the last week of January asking him to send my trunk mattress and chair to the addresses on them and to let you know what is to pay for them. You may thank him for his attention and kindness during my illness for he meant to show both as far as he knew how. That voyage was most horrible. Though I am deliberately forgetting the details I can never forget the misery of it. It seems years since I left home, such a vagueness, caused partly by it being summer here. My face has got well and the sunburn which remains looks robust. My hair is *nearly all gone*. I had so much fever in the Ben Nevis that it became dry and rusty and fell out in patches. I look so old being so very stout. I wonder what *it* is doing, what is being done, anything? It seems 10 years since I left, and I daresay it does not appear as many weeks to it. I wonder how my ferns and my kangaroo vine are doing? I think something must have happened to the Californian mail and *perhaps* the letters are lost which will be distracting. The infrequent mail is a great disadvantage.

Nov. 19. Two dreadful days a hot wind combined with thunder and rain. I entirely fail to be able to swallow food! Yesterday afternoon I walked to call on Mrs Griffin. The air was baking. Her cottage is very elegant. At 7 we drove into the Assembly! Members and audience are all mixed together and I dont think there were 20 of the last though the subject was most important the establishment of a sustenation fund. The fiend spoke vigorously and well. The other speakers were very low in their tone and squabbled very much the Moderation was low and squabbled. It seemed so odd. The fiend is not liked it appears by his brethren. He is the only man of influence now Dr Cairns has retired and worries what he proposes, and they say he is bad tempered and domineering and 'rides roughshod over the Assembly'! There is something so very moderate and low toned about it. I was interested however with the discussion though I thought most of it all but Mr Cameron and Mr McKechan in the very worst taste. I saw Mr Campbell Mrs Mairs* brother in law. He gave me a most pressing invitation to Geelong.

The fiend came to me in the lobby afterwards. He looks ill and his hands small and white. His wife has been much worse. It is horrible to see him and not to see him. I think he likes me as much as ever as I like him. We drove back at ten. The horses kept taking fright at the lightening. Mrs Macbain is a very stout complacent looking easy person without an idea beyond her house. I should perish of dilness if I stayed longer. [. . . Yet] the steamer I am going in is a very small one with a ladies cabin like the Clansman. It will be odious to be crowded up for a week. I detest going to N.Z. I hope I shall like it better when there. I care for it so but I seem to belong to no-one.

---

* See Mrs Mair, p. 333.

Nov 22. Mrs McCallums Pawlett St. Fitzroy [Melbourne]. This is Friday and I have had no time to write since I came here on Tuesday afternoon. I am feeling somewhat better and for the last two nights have slept well. I have been having beer and ranging to and fro all day. This seems to suit me so infinitely better than a sedentary life when I do company and sew and write letters.

I was quite uneasy about myself the day I came here and the day before. My nerves were in a shocking state, and I could eat literally nothing. On Tuesday I went to the Legislative Assembly and to the Legislative Council where the Wifes sister bill was passed without a division also the secular education bill in consequence of which the Roman Catholics appointed a day of fasting and humiliation throughout Victoria. The halls are splendid and the Parliamentary library. On returning almost at once the fiend came and after a time we went to the Presbyterian Assembly. On Thursday I shopped for Fanny and myself for 3 hours then into the Assembly to dine at Malcolms then with Sarah for 2 hours to the Assembly. On Thursday I went to a costly photographer to be taken for Emily but though I had spent 3/4 of an hour in trying to do my hair he said it would not do so I had to let it down and comb it out and the photos are the worst of the many failures. The artist kept asking me if I could not look less sad and I thought I could not unless I were by my own fireside in Castle Terrace* with it. They look insane and suicidal. I then called on Mrs Cameron who looks very well and says nothing would induce her to leave Melbourne. [. . .]

On Friday I went to Richmond to see the Veritys and Todds [. . .] then back when Mr Hugh McCallum came then the fiend. In the evening Mrs Budd and I went in to the Assembly where there was a great debate as to what part the Church should take about the religious education of the people. I was more and more annoyed each time I went to the Assembly by the lowness and secularity and vulgarity of the tone. The only interesting evening was the discussion on Home Missions or rather on the state of religion, but a truly doleful account was given. The men who spoke seemed like low English dissenters. No interest seemed taken in the proceedings. I dont think there were 14 people at any time, not even when a sustenation fund was launched this being the last year of state aid. Mr Fraser made one of the lowest speeches about money that could be made. The fiend 'dissented and protested against a decision in his own name and that of those who might adhere to him' which sounded like Dr Bigg. The tone of the Ch. Assembly seemed much

---

* The flat in Edinburgh that Isabella and Henrietta had just given up.

higher but I can judge better when I have been once or twice again. I think that the Church of England in Victoria is full of vigour and activity going rapidly ahead and though the Scotch are numerically in the majority it is ahead of every other denomination by 80 000 and is getting into the bush by means of 'licensed lay leaders'. The Bishop is undoubtedly the leading man in the colony, and people say he is not only Bishop of the Anglican Church in Melbourne but is truly Bishop of Victoria. He called 3 times on me and sent his carriage twice.

You will notice that I express different opinions both of things and people as time goes on. One opinion or rather a first impression deepening into an opinion I never change is regarding the extreme civility of the people. It is everywhere. As to hospitality it is unbounded. I suppose the dearness of things at home and the idea of keeping up appearances are killing hospitality. Another thing I notice is how completely this is 'England in the Pacific'. Yesterday Sat. we went in carriages a party of 18 on a picnic to the Black Rock 8 miles off. I hate that sort of thing and wearied very much even though I took the body of a dress to make. We dined in a great jungle of tea trees above the seashore. It was pretty and peculiar but tedious.

I have seen a good deal of the fiend this last week. I dont think he is unhappy now I have seen more of him though anxious about his life. He doesnt want anything said about any idea of his being obliged to leave Melbourne. I should be very much surprised if he were to leave partly because his wife who has great influence with him is determined to remain and partly because he is getting on here so wonderfully. The Bishop said that in a year or two he would be the leading man in Melbourne. And he has quite filled the church. I fear his wife dislikes me very much. He seemed so much more natural away from home and besides any other reasons for disliking me so excellent a woman probably only likes her own kind. At first she was kinder and more cordial than I expected but before I left I saw a difference and she made it obvious that she did not expect me back again. There was no apparent reason for I never saw him so she could not think I took him up. When I asked her on Wednesday about seeing him to wish him goodbye she replied very curiously that he and I could make any arrangements we pleased that she never spoke of me! She looks lovely! She disliked me at Oban first for being a literary woman and doubtless has always thought me a bad companion for him. I *think* she now thinks that I am influencing him to get him to go home. While on the contrary I urge him very much to put aside all idea of it. He is just the same, only that he has given up all affectionate demonstrations. He asked a great deal about

53

you. He says what is doubtless true that the amount of work which he must get through every day prevents him from indulging in sentiment. I cannot but think that Mrs C. is getting better. It would be so lamentable to leave Melbourne.

Monday. Another cool day now that I have only 2 days more a hot wind would hardly signify. They say I have not felt a real hot wind yet. The weather they say is quite exceptional. So cloudy and so much rain. It doesnt agree with people who have been long here and they call it muggy but it is far drier than we would have it and I think it pleasant. In addition to the Puckles entreating me to come back when the summer is over the Budds propose a grand waggon and camping out expedition among the mountains which divide from Gipps Land and many other things but it would keep me too long away. I should like to have seen that scenery which must have peculiarities of its own. But I have no wish to linger in these regions. This has been the dullest 4 months I ever spent there is so little novelty and what there is, is so hideous.

Wednesday 27. The weather has become awful. I am so thankful that I go away tomorrow. Incessant rain darkness thunder heat steam. I hardly know how to get through today. I have lost my gold pen finally I fear as it is not at the McCallums. This is weather such as could not be imagined. Everyone is aghast at the prospect of fever. It has been raining on and off for a month and now the heat without sun is so serious. I have had to toil so with my clothes and to alter all my packing. Miss Knowles has *absolutely destroyed* all my best clothes. The only thing I can wear is the Burmese silk polonaise. It is very vexing for I have no good clothes besides, except my white alpaca. That nice buff and brown batiste I cant put on. It is crooked, wont meet, and drags from the neck. The violet up my best dress has 4 or 5 different lengths in the skirt, and is fuller in front than behind so that I couldnt even wear the skirt. Well I have re-made it.

Will you put £150 on a deposit receipt – it will be better than sending it out to me. I am caring for it but this weather is sucking away my soul. It is strange to come in for such exceptional seasons on the Mediterranean Portland and Victoria. Dry heat can be borne but one may call this *unbearable.*

My pen is found! This is such a lovely house.

Nov 28. Hot but cleared. I felt so strange and ill and obscure yesterday that I was frightened. This has been a delightful visit certainly enough to make me remember Victoria with pleasure. But indeed I am overwhelmed with kindness so much so that had it been a different season I would have stayed. I have got on my new travelling dress, the most skin fitting I ever made, my luggage is all together and in 2 hours Mr and Miss Budd come here and take it down in a car the Bishop and his wife taking me in their carriage. They are both charming and so droll. There is a west wind today. It is terrible to think of a voyage of 1300 miles. My clothes have been a great toil and misery to me. I care so for it. Dont tell Emily about the photo. It goes via Bermuda. Love to Mary.*

Its Pet ILB

I hope Dr Guthrie† is not dead.

---

* See Mary Macdiarmid, p. 333.
† See Dr Thomas Guthrie, p. 326.

Hawaii

From Australia, Isabella sailed to New Zealand in a steamer loaded with sheep and horses. A lunatic, stowed in the berth next to hers, made the passage very uncomfortable. Nor did Dunedin seem an improvement over Melbourne. If anything, it was worse. Isabella was horrified by the drunkenness and carousing she witnessed, and overwhelmed by the heat and dirt. Restless after her stay in Australia, Isabella left New Zealand after only two weeks. She departed on New Year's Day, 1873, in the *Nevada*, a small, leaky steamer bound for San Francisco. In her book *The Hawaiian Archipelago*, Isabella wrote that the *Nevada* was barely seaworthy: condemned by a government surveyor, she was in 'dilapidated condition', and nearly capsized after hitting a typhoon. Instead of being dismayed, Isabella found this exciting. She enjoyed taking her meals in a dining room awash with spray, and found it amusing that the ship's provisions were squirming with ants and weevils. At night, she wrote, 'We would scare rats and kill cockroaches with our slippers.' Such conditions inspired Isabella to befriend an American woman named Mrs Brigham,* whose husband appears to have been a sea captain among the Hawaiian Islands. Mrs Brigham was alighting in Honolulu, so Isabella did, too. She decided to postpone her trip to California, and instead caught the inter-island steamer to Hilo. Unfortunately, Isabella's first letter to Henrietta about her experiences in Hawaii seems to have been lost. The following are extended extracts from those that remain.

Hilo. Hawaii. Feb 19th 1873
48 pages

Nothing Annoying in This

My Pet

I must write a letter besides the great journal letter which may be read to or by everybody. You need not read it yourself first but you may assemble all the Kers and Emily and read it straight on to them as it will be like a book. I think Mrs Blackie might have it only perhaps she would think the writing too small. I am wearing so to get back. The 10000 miles is such a fearful vision and it is as difficult to get away from these islands as from Barra [in the Outer Hebrides]. There has been no steamer since I came and the first mail from Honolulu arrived last night by a schooner which was ten days on the way. She brings the news very

---

* See Mrs Brigham, p. 317.

56

great to me that the Nevada good old leaky tub which when 7 days out from Honolulu had put back but had sailed again!!! [. . .]

Hilo is an enchanting place. I now know all its ways. It is the most kindly sociable friendly little place you can imagine. There is no morning visiting. If people want anything they come in at any hour, but after supper 6 oclock people take their lanterns and drop in to each others houses or verandahs and have talking and music. As there are no servants there are no doorbells and no one raps but people come in at the verandah windows and if you are in your drawingroom you are supposed to be ready to receive them. There is no dressmaker in Hilo. The ladies all make their own dresses and give each other patterns. When anyone is ill like Mrs Austin* the ladies form a sewing circle and do her mending and making and when anyone needs nursing the ladies take it in turns to nurse. There are only 3 black sheep among the foreign residents at Hilo, one a Scotch doctor the other an Englishman a foster brother of Mr Forster M.P. the 3rd an American sugar planter who is an infidel. There is a large but much dwindling native population very much occupied with politics just now and with petitioning the new King to dismiss all foreigners and fill all offices with natives.

When I came back from Onomea I found that Miss Park† had been ill for a week of what goes by the ridiculous name of the 'boohoo fever'. She is most miserable not having any indoor occupations. Her voice has ceased to annoy me now that she is ill poor thing. She was so delighted to see me back too because she said I 'brought so much noise and life into the house'. I am always afraid of getting it too as I have the same room with her and influenza is epidemic just now with the south wind. [. . .]

Sat. Feb 22. Since I wrote this there have been great excitements in my rat hole and one day I got over nanged with people and have not been well since so I have not written anything. This afternoon I am going to ride out on a toothbrush expedition to Onomea to come back in time for church tomorrow morning rather to get a little quiet than anything else. There are so many people at table now that I find my head getting confused and then I get discouraged. I like the independent ways of going off on my 2 hour journey alone crossing in my scow swimming and fording my rivers and getting in wet up to my waist! How frightful we should think it at home if we heard of anyone 'having had' to swim

---

* See Samuel and Mary Austin, p. 314.
† See Miss Park, p. 336.

a river. The weather has been most lovely. I suppose the rainy season is over.

On Thursday I solely cooked dinner for 10 people. I made a most delicious curry, a rolled pudding, a huge beef steak turnips breadfruit baked. Mrs Severance's[*] beautiful baby was ill, and I could do many useful things for her. You know how useful an unaccompanied person is in a house. She was very glad for me to sit up with him, he was so very ill. I take great interest in the family and have become for the time being quite one of them. It is a very pleasant way of living. But if I lived in Hawaii I should not settle in Hilo. The society is I think too small if one had not local duties. I would live in Oahu within a few miles of Honolulu and come to Hilo for three summer months and board here.

On Thursday I had accepted an invitation to dine with the Thompsons at 4 and teach Mrs T. how to make a curry previously. Then Miss Coan came in the morning to ask me to lunch and I did not like to refuse. Mr Titus Coan[†] related wonderful things of his adventures in the gulches and canoes. The natives were friendly from the first, having cast away their idols before the missionaries came but I should think in no region had they undergone such physical dangers. I went on to the Thompsons and Mr Austin came in from Onomea and then when I came back here Dr Wetmore[‡] came in with his microscope and I got a nervous headache which I cannot lose.

That day news came that the American government had offered to King Lunalilo[§] the U.S. corvette *Benicia* for a tour round the islands, and that he would arrive at Hilo the next morning. He is adored by the natives and each kanaka[¶] feels himself raised by the respect which their elected sovereign meets with from foreign powers. There was great excitement and when at 8 yesterday the corvette appeared inside the reef there was such a sudden blossoming out of flags (the British ensign on a ground of red white and blue stripes) and such galloping in of natives garlanded and wreathed. Mr Severance[‖] and Mr Lyman[**] the Governor went off to receive the King and at 10 he landed. He is a fine looking man of colour with a gentlemanly courtesy and dignity of manner and wore a dark cloth suit with a single decoration. It was most amusing, this

[*] and [‖] See Lucinda and Luther Severance Jnr, p. 340.
[†] See Reverend Titus Coan, p. 321.
[‡] See Dr Charles Hinckley Wetmore, p. 344.
[§] See King William Charles Lunalilo, p. 333.
[¶] A generic term for 'man' in Hawaiian. In *The Hawaiian Archipelago*, Isabella finds the term 'decidedly objectionable', as would most people today.
[**] See Lieutenant Governor Rufus Lyman, p. 333.

propped up royalty which stands between the islands and their absorption by America.

The first person to receive the King sad to say was an Englishman very drunk who rushed at him with shirt sleeves rolled up and shook hands. The natives all cheered and yelled and waved their hats and formed a procession with the Hilo band in white and a great Hawaiian standard. I tried successfully to see it. A rabble of children ran in front, then walked the King over whom the natives had thrown a wreath of crimson myrtle blossoms with Governor Lyman on his right Mr Severance the sheriff on his left, the chamberlain and adjutant general behind, the standard bearer, the Hilo band and then a disorderly rabble of men women and children. They were going at a trot! When he went into the governors he made a speech like any other king and said he would receive them all on Monday.

In the afternoon I went to the woods about 7 miles from here fern hunting with Dr Wetmore. We were cantering round a sharp corner which leads on to the beach when we had to pull our horses almost on their haunches to avoid running over the King his suite the American admiral the captain of the corvette 9 of their officers and Generals Schofield and Alexander.[*] When I saw these strangers and their well veiled stare I remembered that I was in a Bloomer Suit[†] astride a horse and that probably they had never seen such a thing! I wished I were anywhere else. We galloped for three miles down the sands as fast as the horses could go for we had to walk in the woods. We swam the Wailuku River and got among cocoanut and breadfruit trees and then into a bewildering forest of all sorts of things under this a few miles are seas of lava. It was so lovely. Through the trees we saw the soft faint blue of the sky not a leaf stirred not a bird sang, the stillness was perfect there was a slight freshness in the air it only required the soft rustle of a falling leaf now and then to be an exact reproduction of a perfect October day in Hunts. The smell was like it too, so even in this land of perpetual summer I did so long to be with my being and felt so dreadfully homesick. We got some parasitic ferns but some were out of reach. We got on and off incessantly. In the narrow track where one could hardly pass another we met many natives driving horses laden with cocoanuts the beautiful breadfruit live fowls taro poi[‡] and driving small garlanded hogs

---

[*] See Colonel John McAllister Schofield and Brevet Brigadier General B.G. Alexander, p. 340.
[†] A riding outfit with Turkish trousers and a divided skirt, it enabled women to ride astride with propriety.
[‡] *Taro* is a member of the arum family of plants of the genus *Colocasia*; the roots are pounded into paste to make *poi*, a traditional Hawaiian dish.

all as presents for the King who would they say be able to freight a ship with the offerings which will be brought. We did not get back till dark.

Feb. 23. Of course the presence of the King upsets the whole district. The reception is tomorrow and it is expected that 1500 kanakas will come in on horseback. All the plantation hands have got a holiday 200 are coming from Onomea only. This King has sworn to the constitution which his predecessor over rode and his first act was to dismiss the sorceress who had ruled him and to appoint a new ministry which everybody says contains the best and wisest men on the island. He is also going to abolish the household troops and to reduce the number of secure offices at court. In this petty court which rules 50000 people there are nearly as many offices as in ours. He is said to have had a very fine English education, and to have a very superior intellect, and to be a perfect gentleman – when sober. But he has been a drunkard for 20 years a complete slave to drink. It is most unfortunate for in spite of the law against the sale of drink it is ravaging the natives. They distil it for themselves. The American admiral, all his officers and the two generals are abstainers and it is not placed upon the Admirals table. So the King has been sober on board. He wishes to reform he says and has appointed as Lord Chamberlain a good templar also a boon companion of his the adjutant general who is here with him has just taken the pledge. But people think that it is not possible for him to give up drink that the sight or smell of it would awaken the craving for it irresistibly. The subject of drink is being much discussed by the Hawaiian press and in private.

The American papers have come. They are utterly disgusted at the election of a king. It was expected that the annexation would follow on the late king dying without having appointed his successor. The present scheme among the foreigners here is to get the King to go to Washington to negotiate a reciprocity treaty with the U.S. and to induce him to sign away the islands after his death. The natives are very much opposed to his going to Washington. The flute band of the missionary school serenaded him last night and he addressed them saying he had been taught as they were in his youth but had departed from it but hoped to amend. The papers say that such universal interest was felt in England and France regarding the election of a king under the Hawaiian constitution. I daresay in Edinburgh nobody knew the late king was dead. [. . .]

Yesterday morning I did various things in the house and Mr Thompson came and read aloud to us while we worked. At three I went to Onomea my only luggage being your shawl containing my toothband nail brushes and knitting. Mr Husbands, a manager of a plantation who has been here for the last week, lent me his mare to go out on mine being rather chafed with the saddle. He said she was very frisky and must be held fast while I mounted but before my feet were firmly in the stirrups her heels were in the air and she shook herself from the Chinaman who held her and danced away. I rode 5 miles before she would quiet down. She reared and pranced and jumped and tossed about and went in the most undesirable manner for such a track, dancing and fretting on the very verge of a precipice 600 feet deep. She nearly knocked my breath out of me. She was so furious at going into the scow and finally when I spurred her she jumped upon it so as nearly to upset it and fidgeted so that 2 men held her. She behaved shamefully at the fords and swam the Kaiwiki so savagely and with such plunging strides. I met quantities of kanakas. They all bow and say 'Aloha'. I reached Onomea at 5. They were surprised and delighted to see me. I found Mrs Austin worse. My visit and all the Hilo dilts cheered her. On my way I passed a coffin. A crazy woman had thrown herself over the cliff.

I left at 8.30 this morning. Just as I was going away news came that on the way to Hilo a man on horseback carrying a child had fallen over the track. The child was not hurt but the man and horse were killed. At the place where he went over, the ferns and bushes were all torn away. It was not one of the worst places there are several so [sketch] and on 2 of these *palis** as they are called the track is so narrow that one of your feet hangs over a precipice 500 feet deep. I liked my ride, the horse had sobered down the morning was lovely I crossed in my scow I forded my gulches I swam the deep black still basin under the Paipai Falls I saw my glistening snowy mountains for the last time. I wish that all the rest of the time that I have to be away I could have spent in these islands riding and in the open air. [. . .] But I do so wonder how my pet is getting on. The dark winter must be passing into another spring. I wonder if it has felt very dil in that dingy street and what it has been doing and if Mary has been ill. My heart yearns over my good sweet little thing. I wonder if anyone was kind to it at the new year.

Monday Feb. 24th. This has been a grand day of sightseeing the old kanaka customs revived. The two old missionaries said I was most fortunate to come in for so truly national and interesting a spectacle. The day has been splendid too not too hot. I am so glad of it for the people have come in from distances of 40 miles. I must write now for this event

---

* Hawaiian word meaning cliff.

of the King coming here tomorrow evening involves so many preparations. I shall have to spend this afternoon and all tomorrow in cooking. I have made a pound cake and I am going to make 2 dozen cocoanut cakes such as we used to buy in Birmingham and a trifle a dish which has never been seen in Hilo and macaroons and a blancmange which also has not been seen. Dont you think I am a most pleasant boarder for I nurse the baby!!! cook go errands sew.

Last night at the King's request there was service in the foreign church. Mr Thompson preached an excellent sermon on 'Sleep on now and take your rest. Arise and let us go hence' – the subject being 'the irrevocable past the irredeemable future'. There were tropical torrents during the night and I feared for today but it opened gloriously! From early morning we saw the natives on horseback trooping in and when Mrs Severance and I went down to the beach to try to get some things to eat they were still streaming in, and about 1000 horses were tethered on the grass by the sea. The King was to receive the natives at the courthouse a pretty verandahed wooden building which stands on a large grass lawn opposite this house and long before ten crowds had assembled outside the lawn. Flags on bamboos made each entrance look gay an enormous flag on the government flag staff could be seen for miles the stars and stripes waved from neighbouring plantations and from several houses.

We were still hunting almonds when I saw the King the governor the chamberlain the adjutant general and Mr Severance coming down the road and I rushed back borrowed a hat and white cloak and got to the stairs in the verandah of the courthouse before they arrived. They all wore shocking hats and the King was badly dressed in a short brown jacket ash coloured trousers with a blue stripe and a grey waistcoat. But the dress of himself and suite was almost hidden by garland on garland green garlands 2 yards long and beautiful garlands of the crimson and yellow ohia blossoms.* The King dressed in this style to enable the natives to come in anything rather than to compel them to put on their best clothes. The young men of Missionary Lymans Industrial Training School here ranged to the number of 88 in a hollow square round the great signal staff, and when the King appeared to my surprise they sang our national anthem. Then there was tremendous cheering but there is no P. in Hawaii so the men who led it 'said hi hi hi hi hi urrah'. The excitement was tremendous, for the King was elected unanimously by the people and before that he was the highest chief on the island his

---

* A sweet-nectared blossoming tree from the same family as the guava; also known as the mountain apple.

name Lunalilo meaning 'above all' and they were so delighted with his condescension in receiving them as their old chiefs used to do. The late king was a heathen and little better than a savage and was hated.

He took his place in the lowest verandah bareheaded his suite standing about him and nearly all the foreign residents of Hilo and the neighbourhood were in the verandah balcony above the 2 venerable old missionaries and the Romish priest among them. The missionaries were much delighted. I wanted to see the thing better so I stood for 2 mortal hours on the stairs going up from the lower verandah. The natives were admitted upon the lawn in one continuous stream passing through the verandah and depositing their presents in front then seating themselves on the grass. Over 2000 shook hands with the King and lastly the foreign schoolchildren and Mr Lymans Industrial School. Not the smallest child came empty handed. Then the King went to the open verandah and made a speech in which he reaffirmed the Constitution spoke of the political benefits conferred by Xtianity on the islands justified his choice of a ministry and stated that when natives had fitted themselves for the responsibility of the highest offices he should replace the foreigners with them. The speech was interrupted by the most tremendous cheering and at the end the enthusiasm was tremendous. The missionaries said that probably so large a gathering of natives would never again be seen. It was really a beautiful sight the outburst of loyalty and affection towards the King of their choice no ceremony or humbug all real genuine feeling. The King enjoyed it very much and was most affable in his manner.

It was one of the most picturesque and interesting sights possible 2000 brown men women and children with faces beaming with pride wonder or ineffable satisfaction and every variety of costume. The women all wore the native dress. Many were black many green many the brightest rose colour some bright yellow others yellow and scarlet mixed. Many wore some kind of hat made from sugarcane tops many bright bandanna handkerchiefs numbers wreaths of the lovely fern. Nearly all wore garlands of crimson and yellow myrtle blossoms or sugar cane tassels or the great orange pandanus or 3 one of each. Few if any had shoes. None of the children had anything on their heads. One woman terribly affected with quaking palsy a hideous object dragged herself along one hand was helpless and the other in her agitation grasped a fowl she was carrying so tightly that she could not loosen it to shake hands with the King but he good naturedly lifted up her helpless hand which called forth more cheering. Some half dropped down on their knees others passionately and with tears kissed the Kings hand others seized it in both theirs, while a few were so embarrassed by the presents they were carrying that they had no hands at all to shake and the King clapped them on the shoulder. Then a string of 40 Chinamen plantation hands with their front hair shaven and the rest gathered into pigtails wound round and round their heads dressed in dark loose blue cotton pants and blue cotton shirts fastening at the side then came up and each put a piece of money into the adjutant generals hand.

The dresses of the men were more singular than those of the women. Every kind of dress and undress and garlands one upon another. Poor things they came up so innocently many of them with nothing on but an old shirt and a pair of blue cotton trousers rolled up to their knees and garlands. Some had brilliant shirts and blue trousers many wore their shirts over their trousers! Some had good brilliant shirts blue cotton trousers and ranch riders boots rusty and mudcovered up to the knees. A few were in white shirts and trousers with crimson garlands, some had hardly clothes to cover them. A few old men had crash towels tied over their shoulders. Some had diggers scarves round their waists but the general effect was a blaze of colour. There were ancient men who were middle aged when the idols were cast away tattooed all over who remembered the days of tyranny when any man on whom the Kings shadow fell was put to death and when none had any rights or property. There were those who came trembling up almost falling on their knees and kissing the Kings hand with tears. Numbers of little children were brought and babies in arms and younglings carried on parents backs and the King stooped down and shook hands with all and even pulled out the baby hands from under their mufflings amidst tears, and cheers rent the air. There was one crippled man who had only the use of his arms, his knees were doubled under him and he trailed his body along the ground. He had dragged himself 2 miles 'to lie for a moment at the King's feet'.

The great sight was the presents. Most of the women brought live fowl one man a great black hog which squealed most terribly, some eggs hundreds taro and sweet potato artistically done up. Men staggered along carrying clusters of bananas weighing over a hundred weight on a bamboo between them. Many brought sugar cane, quantities cocoanuts, others pumpkins, one a pine apple, some the great delicious gronadilla the melon like fruit of the true passion flower. All these after the donor had carried them before the King were arranged in heaps in front of the verandah the fowls all with their legs tied. There must have been fully two ton of taro and sweet potato hundreds of fowls, cocoanuts and bananas without end. 2000 presents were brought. A few brought necklaces of yellow feathers valued at £6 apiece and exquisite bouquets of flowers. Then there was the speech and the closing enthusiasm and then the assemblage dispersed delighted. Many as there were there would have been more but that the scow by which I crossed the river the day before had reached that point at which it could no longer swim and sank in the morning with 4 kanakas [and] their horses on it who easily saved themselves by swimming.

The spectacle lasted from 10 till just one then came dinner and after dinner I cooked for 3 hours. I made 4 dishes of cocoanut cakes which are perfectly beautiful white like snow just yellowed at the crystalline edges. I was afraid about the baking in the stove but succeeded well. A Chinese prisoner grated the cocoanuts. I made a sponge cake for the trifle a large cocoanut pudding for todays dinner and cocoanut drops for the trifle instead of raspberry. I was very tired. I like work but cannot combine it with society and I have again got a nervous headache so that I disliked going at 7 p.m. to a party at the Lymans to meet the King. They are excellent old missionaries but they are trying to make the King good and I fear the result will be a reaction into a most outrageous spree when he gets out of their hands. It was just like a party at the Cunninghams stiff and dull the verandah filled with lads playing on flutes and singing at intervals to the melodies. When the King came in the lads played the national anthem and everyone stood up. He devoted himself to me on and off the whole evening and today sent for me to ride with him to Kaiwiki a plantation 3 miles from here. He is a very gentlemanly courteous unpretending man very intelligent and altogether unassuming. When one sees him it is hard to believe the wretched stories current of him as Prince William.* I was as tired as I should have been after a party at Edinburgh. The King told me that the Admiral and the two generals though they have seen so many fights were afraid to go down into the crater of Kilauea! He seemed dreadfully bored last night just as I should be and much happier while out riding today with only the adjutant general and me. I hope the Americans who surround the poor fellow are honest.

I have done more cooking today. I have also sold 'Bessie Twinker'† the sweet animal. She followed me about and licked my face. The surf continues tremendous. My drawings in pen and ink though little more than outlines will always keep the scenes of my ravage fresh. Tomorrow afternoon if the surf allows of a boat getting off I begin to turn my steps homewards. I sold my mare to Mrs Severance so she will have light work

---

* Possibly Kaiser Wilhelm II, p. 344.
† See Bessie Twinker, p. 315.

and a good home. I wish I could find in a mountainous district in America exactly the same kind of house to board in that this is.

Wednesday Feb 26. The 'Kilauea' which ought to have been in 4 hours ago is not in sight and the surf is so heavy that when she does come we shall have to scramble 2 miles round the bay and be carried through a river to get on board. Schooners have come down from Honolulu till 3 have accumulated here but since I came a month ago there has been no opportunity of sending either letters or person *away* from Hilo!

Yesterday I rode to Kaiwiki with the King and his myrmidons a pleasant ride. In the evening the great party came off. A party without servants is toil but it has advantages. The verandah 12 feet broad was decorated with flags and festooned with ferns and Chinese lanterns and the rooms were beautifully decorated with flowers. There were chairs in the verandah which when the 3 folding windows were open made one with the room. There were about 30 people. It was considered a most successful party. I cannot say I enjoy any kind of party and I was so tired I could hardly stand on my feet, but still it was a pleasant party. The great object was to prevent stiffness and give the King some real enjoyment and I think it was successful. There was hardly any singing. Games were tried the chair game a very good one and then a refined blind man's bluff, which I dont like so well but it was very amusing as the blind man is allowed to ask 3 questions. The King looked on at first but soon joined and enjoyed himself very much. I like games, anything better than sitting still and primping talk.

Supper was at nine. Several nests of Japanese tables were borrowed and these little things were put so that one did for each 2 or 3 people in the drawing room and verandah. Miss Coan Miss Holden and I brought in and handed round the things. It was real waiting and very tiring. There were 2 large trifles and I never got a taste of one they were so popular. There were 3 dishes of sandwiches made like ours made of potted meat which were all eaten. After supper there was a little dancing in the verandah and then 2 or 3 quadrilles which no one knew how to dance in the drawing room. No one had anything different from a good morning dress on and the gentlemen had their boots. Natives stood along the garden fence all the evening looking on. Hardly anyone knew how to dance. The King insisted on teaching me to dance a polka in the verandah. Think of that. Everyone seemed very happy and they left about 12. Such a party could only be possible in this climate where in and out of doors are all one. The King is really a most pleasant creature so gentle and unaffected. It sounds funny to hear him spoken of as 'His

Majesty'. We sat and promenaded a long time in the verandah. He wrote some poetry for me and brought it just a simple stanza of good wishes. He said he was willing to cede a harbour in Oahu to America for a Pacific naval station in return for a reciprocity treaty but nothing more.

This morning everyone has called to wish me goodbye and I am done up. I shall never be fit for society and dont enjoy it. I like 2 or 3 people. The howl in this house at my going is frightful. I seem to have suited them as exactly as they have suited me. Mr Thompson wanted me to go and stay with them and go to Kilauea with him a great temptation but if I miss the Nebraska on March 8th I am done for. I seem to have taken root in Hilo. The poor King is so pleased that since he came to Hilo he has had no craving for drink he says he would like to stay at Hilo *because there is none*. This very speech says much for a Maine law.

March 1st. To my horror and misery my writing book with my whole journal some landscapes in Hilo and other irreplaceable things was lost off a pack mule on the hills. All my pleasure at once went. I wished I had never come to Hawaii if *it* never got the giant journal letter. I must register them for it would be such a frightful loss.

Well I dont know where I left off. The rainy season is not over till the end of March. So at rainy Hilo you may frequently expect a days rain. On Wednesday it rained all day. [. . .] I was just finishing dinner when the King and his attendants called to wish me goodbye. The King apologised for his dress a short jacket and blue trousers stuffed into boots covered with mud up to his knees. He played the English national anthem entirely from ear. There is something peculiarly attractive and interesting about him but he has a sadly irresolute look about his mouth and I saw from little things that he could be persuaded into anything. Although 38 he does not seem more than 25. He is so simple in his manner and conversation. It is sad to hear him in the most harmonious voice using odious American forms of speech. The American admiral and generals had come down from the volcano stiff sore bruised jaded done and the King said 'I guess the Admiral's about used up.' The missionaries say that it is wicked foreigners who have ruined all the Hawaiian kings. In Hilo Captain Spencer made a heavy bet that he'd 'get the King tight before he left'. That word tight is used by gentlemen and ladies in Australia N. Z. and Hawaii.

The rain still poured when at 4 p.m. in my Bloomer frock over my silk skirt I got on 'Bessie Twinker' on a sidesaddle on which I felt entirely helpless. The King and Colonel Judd his aide de camp escorted me and my luggage went on a native's horse. There were tears and wavings of handkerchiefs till I was out of sight. Bessie Twinker behaved like all other palfreys that bear my elvish freight and was very tiresome indeed and the saddle being too long for me hurt my knee so much that I could not canter which I was sorry for as the King coming from rainless Oahu dislikes the rain. We had to ride nearly 3 miles and ford a river. Quantities of kanakas were on the beach who cheered the King enthusiastically. The rain had soaked all my clothes and a wet man carried me into a wet whale boat in which the water was up to my ankles. It looked deplorable. I felt sadly dil at leaving lovely Hilo and concluding my ravage. It was a long row to the 'Kilauea' which lay rolling on a vile swell and was wet and dirty.

Before long Miss Park came having made up her mind at last to endure the voyage rather than the dilness of Hilo. Mrs Severance thought that she was eaten up by jealousy because they had all taken to me so much and the King had liked me so. I fear it was so and I am very sorry but it could not be helped. She said the Hilo people had been pointedly rude to her and that the King had never spoken to her. I think she is the most ludicrously disagreeable person I ever saw and so thoroughly selfish. She is a traveller by profession and seemed to me a very expert one but the day we rode the 3 miles to Kaiwiki and crossed the first mild gulch she seemed to get such a terror that she never would go again and gave up the Waipio ride which she had always intended to take. She has ridden through the Holy Land the Lebanon and all through Greece where I suppose the riding must be dreadful. However it was a very good thing that she did not go for she would have gone on her side saddle and would have been drained. [. . .]

We sailed at 9 and at 11.30 the machinery broke down, and we had to lay-to for 5 hours in what they here call a heavy gale and heavy sea. It was a truly miserable night. I wondered if my ravages in Hawaii were worth it all. No privacy so hot so wet my spine and head really tortured an impossibility to sleep, so overcome with nausea without being able to be sick so terrified of cockroaches as large as mice! I had got on my rajah robe over my wet chemise and lay outside my berth a Chinaman with a pigtail wound 3 times round his head in the next, a rough customer a guide to the Yosemite Valley in the next. In the middle of the night water began to come in at the skylight in great dashes over the table and soon the saloon was 8 inches deep in water. Then when she rolled while the splashes came in the water dashed into the berths and soon all the clothes and the mattresses were soaked. Then a sea put out the lamp and a ships lantern was swung in its place. In an English ship there would have been a great fuss and stewards flying about with buckets but the native steward sat with his bare feet in the water watching it with an air of comic hopelessness. It was dismal to be quite wet seeing the water and hearing the swish swish. Breakfast of course could not be served but a plate was put at one end for the captain to eat with his oilskins and southwestern on and the steward in pants rolled up to his knees waded about taking food to people who sat on the edges of their berths.

All that day was fine but very coarse the next night was smooth and before daybreak Kilauea was seen vomiting up glorious fire and the huge mountain of Mauna Loa suddenly blazed up sending up a tree of red smoke which looked a mile high. This side of Hawaii to my thinking is hideous. There are 5 lava flows the longest 40 miles long by a mile wide and they enter the sea in the blackness of desolation. There are few trees only a few orange and coffee plantations and groves of palms and were it not for the wonderful blue of the sea which is like liquid sapphire showing the coral at an immense depth it would be wearisome. At nine we were at Kealakekua Bay where Captain Cook[*] was killed. The place where he fell is marked by the stump of a cocoanut tree. Kona celebrated for orange plantations was the next place. Dora Greenwell has a brother an orange planter there married to a very nice wife. Bishop Willis[†] was anxious that I should see them and I had written asking them if they could come on board the steamer but when we stopped I got a very kind note from Mrs Greenwell saying that her husband was 15 miles off and she was too near her confinement to ride on horseback.

Several people came on board here to ask me to their houses. They said I had been expected during the last fortnight at all the ranches and plantations round the island. The husband of the native woman who went down with us into the crater of Kilauea brought me a wreath of ohia blossoms. We got cocoanuts and sucked their delicious milk. They were saying that we could eat their meat with a spoon. I found that the sailing of the next California steamer had been put off till the 15th so I accepted Judge Daniels invitation [to stay at his son-in-law's, Frank Spencer's] and was truly glad to shake off my 'old man of the sea'.

Kawaihae was blue and blazing with a barren shore on which 3 frame houses stand. We came ashore in a whale boat Judge Daniels Mrs Rodinot a girl about 18 her sister of 10 and I and went up to a room above a store to wait till it was cool enough to ride. The store was kept by an Englishman named Chillingworth who said there was no place

---

[*] See Captain James Cook, p. 321.
[†] See Bishop Alfred Willis, p. 345.

worth living in but Hawaii. He had been there 7 years and had never had an English lady under his roof. He produced champagne in honour of such an event which did my head good. We topped another cocoa-nut out of which came 4 tumblers of the most delicious milk. I changed my dress for my Bloomer Suit and once more found myself equipped for real travelling.

We left at 4 for a ride of 13 miles our luggage going on a mule. Mrs Rodinot rode a huge horse in a gown astride with her sister sitting behind the saddle tied round her waist with a shawl. I rode in a native saddle a mere double pad of wood with a horn in front. The great wooden stirrups had such large cumbrous guards descending from the saddle that they could not be shortened and were 6 inches below my feet. The wood of the saddle was not even covered with leather. I had spurs on with jingling bells the real Mexican getup but when I got on I saw that I had no stockings on. It was much more tiring to ride without stirrups and I feared I might come off but I soon learned to balance myself and galloped a race with 10 natives. It was a dreary ascent of 2500 feet along a very tolerable road to the Waimea a great expanse of table land on one side of which the mountains rise like domes. We reached this place (Spencers Ranch) just at dusk. I was so frightened just before I got up. We were cantering over grass in Indian file when Mrs Rodinots great horse in front of me rolled over and in trying to save himself rolled over again. She threw herself off clear of him and before either of us could ride up had vaulted into the saddle with the child still tied to her!

I had not known at all what to expect. The visit so suddenly arranged was literally a pig in a poke. I knew that Mr Spencer had a ranch with 25 000 sheep and 1000 cattle and Bishop Willis who was here said it was a very rough place but I was not prepared for anything so rough. There were a number of native and Chinamens houses and then among some bushes within a wall just sufficient to keep the cattle off a kraal of frame and grass huts (with a cook house) 10 or 12 of them with bushes among them. There were several men about but only 3 seemed to belong to the house. We dismounted and clambered by steps into this enclosure where among the kraal of dwellings we were taken to one which seemed to consist of several rooms with boarded floors not covered with mats. There was one little room which served as a parlour with a table and 2 benches with backs against each wall. An eating room opening out of the cook house several rooms with nothing in them but a 4 post bed and about 9 women and children native half white and quarter white in sacks without shoes and a frightful Chinese cook. In the house in the parlour bedrooms eating room there were tame Australian magpies and cockatoos hopping over the floors bantam fowls dogs – saddles saddlebags spurs and bridles lying about. I dont know what it looked like. I saw too that a sort of small closet contrived the washing apparatus of the whole family and feared great discomfort when I needed rest after the miseries of the 'Kilauea'.

However in the Nevada I had heard that this man had a daughter who had grown up as a flower out of a stony soil and Mr Spencer saying I was to have his daughters room took me across the enclosure over some very rough stones to a frame room by itself which promised at least privacy. There was no mat on the floor and the roof and the upper part of the walls let in the sky through chinks but there was a bed with mosquito nets a washing apparatus behind the wooden partition a toilet table and glass and 2 rocking chairs. It has a door but no windows on one side and a door and a window on the other and the wind screams and howls through it. Outside there is no fastening and when you come out, you have to leave the door open. I always find a duck on the floor when I go back and fowls sitting on the mosquito bar. There is a good piano some plants and sundry indications of piety and refined tastes, though the room would excite pity even for a pauper inhabitant and at home could now not house even such a horse as Vixen with safety. Yet such a shelter is all one needs in this superb climate, and when I came in and padlocked the door (which would admit a cat underneath) I dont feel any need of greater luxury.

March 2nd. This Waimea being 2600 feet above the sea level is cold at night and bracing during the day. I wear my flannel Bloomer frock over my green silk short skirt and tweed petticoat without being too hot and at night have 2 blankets and a quilt. About 3 miles across the plain rises the great ragged dome of Mauna Kea 13 500 feet high its pure snow rose colour each morning and a mile behind the houses or kraal rises the picturesque well formed abrupt wooded Kohala hills 6000 feet their slopes and all this Waimea table land covered with the finest downlike grass. It is a truly singular place 13 miles from the sea on each side a solitude utterly out of the world. This is the life of which white people who hate conventionalities become enamoured. Everyone who lives in Hawaii lives here from choice and they think life is not life elsewhere and in any other climate. Indeed I admit that this is a superb climate and though I dont agree with Disraeli[*] that 'happiness is atmosphere' I think such a

---

[*] See Benjamin Disraeli, p. 322.

climate if one had those one loved with one would induce cheerfulness.
I have been here 5 weeks and there has been no change and they say
there never is any except that the sun is rather hotter in the summer.
There is truly no 'weather'. I have never wished for air at zero because
I have never been afflicted by heat. Then think what toil and anxiety
Bessie would be saved. You get a dress and wear it till it is worn out. You
need no change. You never have to think what you will put on to go
out for night and day. You are in the open air. Then there are no rep-
tiles but harmless lizards or noxious insects except a few mosquitoes
imported from Australia. 30 years ago there was nothing that either bit
or stung. But when a person becomes too old to ride or as many do finds
riding astride produces intolerable pain from straining the muscles then
Hawaii owing to the absence of roads must be dull. Here there is Mr
Lyons[*] with his wife who I went to see yesterday. He has been a missionary here for 40 years, the population has both dwindled and receded.
They can now neither of them mount a horse and it is very doleful for
them. In Maui and Oahu there are roads. [. . .]

Yesterday I rested, called on the Lyons, and sat in the morning with all
the many coloured women. The native women are most clever and ingenious with their needles. You never saw such a rough way of living. I
cant convey an idea of it. The food is such that I find it difficult to get
enough though there is abundance. There was a whole sheep on the table
today. Yesterday most of a side of beef, smoked and jerked. They cut 4
joints from a bullock and throw the rest to the hogs. They give all the
black lambs to the hogs. I am curious to know by what standard this
rough self outlawed class of persons judge others. They dont value people
for their money or surroundings or position or education or intellect. I
think they think more of jollity courage and lack of conventionality than
anything else, and in women they certainly appreciate goodness and
kindness for Mrs Austin is respected and beloved by everybody. Yet I
doubt whether she had not an immense amount of quiet pluck she would
be as popular. I am very much liked! Yet I am very quiet and very grave
and I think it is because I have British pluck and endurance can swim a
horse and have fallen so completely into Hawaiian ways. No man now
ever says of any difficult thing that I could not do it.

I hope to leave this at 5 tomorrow morning on horseback with Mr
Spencer for the Waipio Valley! There he will get me what is called a
Waimanu horse i.e. a horse tried in the Waimanu Valley which conse-

[*] See Reverend Lorenzo Lyons, p. 333.

quently has been accustomed to go in and out over the palis. Reckless as Mr Spencer is he says no other horse could go. A horse and a native and I then start for the Waimanu Valley. It has not long been known to whites and only 2 travellers have entered it. These 2 said it equalled the Yosemite and Mr Spencer says it is most wonderful. I shall sleep there at a natives house one or two nights return to Waipio get the horse I have left and come from thence by myself! These are ways like ways! This will end my ravage which will have lasted 6 weeks! I know I shall be terrified for I saw the place which one has to go up from Waipio. I shall not even take saddlebags only a bundle strapped behind the saddle. It is such a relief to have got rid of Miss Park.

Monday Evening. March 3rd. Sitting at the door of a hut at the end of the world the wonderful Waimanu Valley natives are round about 30 all staring chattering laughing. Now about 15 of us have eaten all sitting on the floor a bucket of poi* in the middle of the mat and a basin of fowl which has been cooking in the stones outside watched by an interested group. The poi is taken out by a most mysterious twist of two fingers. The fowl we take with our hands, as I have forgotten my knife. The brown tattooed legs of one man are lying across the mat the others are sitting cross legged. All the people of the valley are outside many having swum their horses across the river to see the wonderful 'haole'.[†] This is the height of the last and most glorious ravage a ravage which has had no precursors as it can have no successors for I am really *alone*. 20 miles of mountain and gulch, an 8 hours journey lying between me and the nearest white man!! How Alickie will envy such ways to which here no suspicion of masculinity or impropriety attaches!

I am wet up to my knees and have nothing to change but in this superb climate there is no risk of catching cold. This is the most tremendous marauding ravage for I have succeeded in getting not only where no white person has ever been man or woman but where it seems doubtful that anybody has ever been. This is a truly wonderful place a valley without any visible means of ingress about 3/4 of a mile whose gigantic walls rise as precipices 4000 feet. Cascades to the number of 5 fall from the very top one of them only making 2 leaps! It opens to the Pacific whose awful booming surf is within 100 yards of where I am writing but no canoe can leave or land. A placid river about up to a horses body is the road up the valley which must be about 3 miles long.

---

* Traditional Hawaiian staple, made from *taro* roots baked and pounded into paste.
† Hawaiian word for foreigner, specifically a Caucasian; the literal meaning is 'a person with no breath'.

It glides at the lower part through grass of the brightest green then divides into 5 leaping torrents it disappears into forests trackless which conceal the deep unknown basins of the cascades. It is ground solemn imposing. The sides of the precipices are covered densely with wood of various shades. You can only see any bare rock close to the cascades.

About 40 people inhabit this wonderful place. Some of them have never been out of it. They are the merriest people I have seen in Hawaii, and doubtless their isolated world is very dear to them. I fancy they think clothes an ornament rather than a necessity for there was a great shuffling into garments when I arrived. It is so piteous that with an artists eye I have not an artists gift to sketch the indescribable picturesque which I see. This is a grass house and I am sitting at the door looking across to the stupendous walls of the valley. In the verandah formed of mats there are two youths and 5 women in green red and yellow chemises squatting on the ground all with garlands of ferns round their hair. Beyond there is a pavement of great boulders of lava sunk in the ground to keep it dry and groups in all colours wreathed and garlanded are sitting and lounging there some crouched up in red and yellow blankets. Eight dogs 7 fowls 3 cats are picking about saddles lassoes spurs bundles of ti leaves[*] are lying about. 13 horses are tethered just outside some of them having brought riders who escorted me triumphantly from the other end of the valley. Then the broad placid river across which horses and children are constantly swimming and all are talking and staring and watching me write all as kind and good natured as possible.

My guide from Waipio Halemanu's son is discussing about me I can hear. He knows a very little abrupt disjointed almost unintelligible English and sometimes comes up saying 'Any father? Any mother? Married? How came you? Any watch? Kilauea? Saw Lunalilo?' Then he goes back and talks at a great rate. One man a very fine pleasant looking native who made me get on a very beautiful horse without a saddle at the head of the valley seems to have no English but this 'How old are you?' When I told him he said 'Too old' and laughed very much. I had photographs of the Deacon and the Coans in my writing book and when I showed them they all crowded round shouting and clapping their hands as they did when I showed them the King's writing. I did so wish I had more. They were so delighted. My inkstand reassembled them again and they shrieked with laughter when I pressed some exquisite

---

[*] Plant imported to Hawaii by Polynesian settlers, small in stature and growing in wild abundance. The leaves are used in cooking, thatching, clothing and animal feed as well as in traditional medicine.

ferns. I am so grieved that I have nothing with me to show them.

I am wondering how many are to sleep in this den. While I was up the valley the poor people made a wonderful bed on the mat on one side and have screened it with the most flowing curtains, but on the other side are the pillows in a row! I am now writing by beef fat in a hollow stone with a wick and two youths seem obligated to attend on me for if I look up one or other of them rushes to bring something that they think I want. Now 2 of the men have made such ridiculous English. What a wonderful thing it is the absolute security one white woman among 40 'savages'. I must make up an account another time of my wonderful ride. I wish to go to bed for I have ridden 30 miles and explored on foot in the crater 3 hours besides and it is 7 o'clock nearly I should think by the darkness the time I like to go to bed on these ravages.

Spencers Ranch Waimea. March 5th. It is so hard to write. I believe I have quite lost the power of describing anything so as to give anyone any idea of it. I often see this view from Waimea described as so beautiful. I wonder that I don't admire it more but I have never thought the large views in Hawaii so beautiful, only the details. This is a monstrous view with such sweeping lines. All the mountains of Hawaii snow crested rising up at once. But you cant realise their immense height. I like them at sunrise when the clouds and sky are all red and gold showing the snow to more advantage, but it is not a view which will ever float in unbidden upon my memory like views in Switzerland Italy or New and old England.

Mr Spencer called me at 4.30 on Monday morning. We breakfasted by lamplight along with 2 bullock hunters Mr Spencer and these men going with me as far as Waipio where they were to get some bullocks. My luggage consisted of a nightgown comb toothbrush ink, writing book, cholera medicine, and a black leather wallet containing provisions which was slung over the horn of one of the other saddles. My luggage wrapped in your shawl went behind my saddle. I wore my Bloomer Suit a chemise greys trousers under my full ones my great spurs and a pocket handkerchief around my neck. I rode a most spirited and excellent horse on an Australian stockriders saddle which is an English saddle with ruts for the knees and Mexican wooden stirrups with guards. The bullock hunters and Mr Spencer had all good horses and wore gay coloured shirts and trousers tucked into their boots. A native with 2 mules loaded with lassoes and guns was along with us.

It was a gorgeous morning the dew so blue and glittering on the short grass the air so absolutely pure the blue mist lying in heavy lines along the bases of the mountains, and the mountains themselves so white and sharp cut against the reddening sky. It was very fair to look on and the horses danced and chafed at their chain bridles and disliked being reined in. [. . .] We had left soon after 5 and by eight were at the top of the great pali above Waipio. Our horses used to the mountains and the grass-lands of Waimea positively refused to go down and we even had to get off and walk. You cant walk you can only jump and I was afraid of spraining my ankle all the time. Halemanu was much surprised at seeing me back again. He soon prepared breakfast for 4 during which time we all sat in the verandah looking across the valley to the frightful air hung line which is the path to Waimanu. [. . .]

Soon after ten I got on the Waimanu horse Mr Spencer having left me a Mexican saddle and a guide and I galloped along the beach across the valley till we came to the fearful zigzag which goes up the almost perpendicular pali 1900 feet. They would never tell me about this before I went. They always said it was not really dangerous with a Waimanu horse but since I came back everyone has been loud in descriptions of its horrors. They say the mere sight of it from Waipio has turned back every traveller but two. It is hideous. The pali is as nearly perpendicular as can be | not a bush or fern or tuft of anything and terminates abruptly on the sea and on this goes up in zigzags something like a sheep track from 18 to 24 inches wide sometimes broken rocks at other smooth without any foothold in 3 places quite carried away the most frightful track that imagination can picture. But I did not fully realise all this till I came down yesterday.

The guide went first and it was most unpleasant to see his horse strain-ing and stumbling. I dared not look at anything but his horses feet for everyone had told me to be sure not to look down and there seemed such an irresistible fascination about looking down. My horse went up nobly and wisely but slipping scrambling and jumping and sending stones down. Once hanging by his fore feet and for a moment I execrated my merciful spurs which could not hurt him. The higher we went the nar-rower and worse it grew. Sometimes I had to take my left foot and hold it alongside the horses neck to prevent it being crushed while my right hung over a precipice 1000 feet deep. Then we came to a place where the path had been carried away leaving only a declivity of loose gravel. You can hardly realise how difficult it was to get off where there was nothing to get off on. I somehow got down under the horse and then taking hold of his hind legs screwed myself carefully behind him. Then Hananui drove the animals on. It was hideous to see the legs of these surefooted creatures going quite down in the gravel as though they would slide quite down the pali hideous to cross these places myself which I could only do by the guide getting his foot firmly planted and giving me a hand when for 3 steps I put my foot against his both feet sliding. You have to get across as fast as you can. I was glad when I reached the top. Between that and Waimanu in about 10 miles there are 9 gulches 2 of them 900 feet deep none of them very difficult and all very beautiful from the broken ground and varied and luxuriant vegetation. They succeed each other with great rapidity. I am sure that between the two deepest the ridge at the top could not be more than 50 yards wide.

Soon after 12 we came suddenly to the top of the great pali of Waimanu 3700 feet in height and as nearly perpendicular as can be with a track as steep and broken as the Waipio one but without its elements of terror for out of every rift ferns kukuis[*] ti and ohias grow all damp and luxuriant so that it screens from your view the altitude at which you are. It was into this extraordinary valley then densely peopled that the missionaries used to go letting themselves down by ropes from tree to tree. From the dizzy height you look down into the narrow valley and see green grass with a quiet river like a ribbon running through it and a few houses and a church as if under a microscope and sides densely wooded and cascades but it looks as if you could never reach it in a days travel so very far it is below. Yet so steep is the road and so surefooted are the accustomed horses that less than an hour brought us down to the house at which I have written. There were 4 houses huddled on this side of the river and about 6 on the other and between them and the sea a narrow steep beach of round stones upon which the surf roared all day and all night with a fearful deafening sound. Up the other side of the valley there is no track it is absolutely inaccessible.

As we came down several great boys and girls were coming away from school but as soon as they saw a stranger they ran back and all with several adults assembled round the house where we stopped. To get to this house you had to get up a rude ha ha of rough large stones which I could hardly get up, but though the natives are kind hearted unlike the Highlanders they never dream of giving you any help which I suppose arises from the fact that the native women are as strong bold fearless and active as the men. An old man without any clothes was pounding the baked taro for poi in front of the house. A woman with flowers in her hair but without clothes was wading up to her waist in the river with a trumpet shaped

---

[*] Also known as the candlenut tree, with distinctive silvery foliage and oily nuts, the *kukui* is a symbol of enlightenment in Hawaii.

basket catching fresh water shrimp, the other women were clad in the usual picturesque chemises green rose yellow. I only stayed long enough to eat a biscuit, as I wanted to make the most of the 5-hours of daylight left and mounting the horses again we entered the river which for about 1/4 of a mile is the road up the valley. It is still and clear with a smooth bottom but comes about 1/2 way up the horses sides and you take your feet out of the stirrups and bringing them to a level with your body lean a little back and hold them against the horses neck. All the children undressed and swam alongside holding their clothes above their heads with one arm and two log canoes with paddles and outriggers on one side were close to us! It looked very nice and some dogs belonging to the children swam behind. It is quite a new thing to see children swim to and from school as these do every day. Then we reached some very pretty houses under magnificent giant breadfruit trees loaded with fruit. These are the oldest and largest in the island. All the people came out and from the way in which Hananui asked me almost quite intelligible questions I judged that they were asking him about me.

There were lovely coffee trees with blossoms white like snow amidst their dark green leaves and fragrant as orange blossoms and 2 immense orange trees covered with buds and blossoms of which I send one. Beyond the houses the valley became a jungle of Indian shot 7 and 8 feet high guava and ohia trees and soon the guide said 'Horses go no more.' I said 'We'll try' and went on first and he sat on his horse laughing and then followed. That is the way in which strangers are so often deceived. He wanted to go back and gossip with the natives. We fought our way a mile further I should think and then he went out of sight altogether below the jungle his horse having floundered up to its girths in a bog. We then got off and tethered the horses [. . . and] got on on foot until till a beautiful torrent appeared. Then we got on alongside this among exquisite trees moss and ferns in the thickest part of which we came on 3 horses and some clothes the beautiful torrent then divided into two and seeing footsteps and trodden ferns along one we took the other. This was perfectly beautiful and though there were difficulties there were no dangers. It was difficult for a non surefooted person with one weak ankle but it was so very lovely quite peculiar. I did so wish I were an artist. I have seen scenes something of this kind painted though not with the depth and tropical vegetation of this.

There was the stream not so broad as the river in the 'pass of awe[*] all broken by rocks covered with mosses and fragile ferns leaping along

---

[*] Possibly the Waipio Valley, which is bisected by a river.

clear as glass with deep bright holes where fish were sporting a laughing sparkling rushing terrorless stream without mysteries or agonies
which could be crossed and recrossed on rocks and by wading in its
unchilled waters not higher than ones knees. Where it rushed fiercely
I made the guide stand to steady my feet against his. One glorious mass
of vegetation came down to its borders and every green thing went
lovingly towards it or stooped to touch it and over it the whole magic
length arched and interlaced the exquisite pea green ohia gigantic
whose millions of spikes of bright rose coloured bloom lit up the
whole arcade and the light of the afternoon sun slanted or trickled
through dancing in the mirthful water and lighting its dear depths and
brightening into a yet more glittering green the many shades of kukui
and glossy camellia and ferns of all kinds from the majestic tree fern
to the fragile tamarind fern which clung tremblingly to the stem of
the ohia – it shone on huge leafed things without a name on clumps
of the tall and graceful bamboo on mosses of every kind from those
which wrapped the stones in feathery green to those 10 inches long
hardly distinguishable from ferns. Here and there a tree had fallen
across forming an arch from which grew upwards and trailed downwards fairylike some transparent ferns and mosses all glittering with
moisture and sunshine. It was most loveable looking, just the details
which I like.

One could not walk on the land at all we got the whole way up, more
than a mile I should think, by getting from rock to rock and wading
through the water. At last we emerged into full daylight, the home of
the 5 cascades of the Waimanu Valley where they fall from one circular
basin. It was a very sublime sight, this tremendous gulf, the dark deep
basin and the water descending so calmly and so slowly into it, quite
unhurried from an altitude of 3000 feet.

(*Steamer* Kilauea *Thursday Evening March 6th. Off Maui*. I have hardly
any heart to finish my journal so frantic am I at realising that my glorious culminating never flagging 6 weeks ravage is over and that the like
can never be again. It died like a tropic sun for Waimea and its ways were
the wildest of all and so many prospects were proposed for prolonging
and even increasing the ravage, and now off Maui Judge Daniels and
Mrs Rodinot are haranguing me to land and go up Halakala and
through Maui. Hateful hot horrid disgusting America. If it were not for
it and getting through it without injury I would even now stay till the
next steamer. I do so hate leaving my thoroughly congenial life in these
islands, just the life made for me in which I have 'rioted most

luxuriantly' without any annoyances, and have been liked for myself being judged without people being prejudiced for or against me.)

The sides of this gulf were draped throughout with ferns growing in spray and dampness and above the water all the rock was deeply caverned out and filled with maidenhair and other fragile ferns. The water was deep and clear. I got a hollow stalk and leaned over a shallowish place to suck up water and overbalancing myself fell in. My Bloomer dress makes such an excellent bathing dress and once in I enjoyed splashing about. It was as lovely going back wading and jumping rock to rock and the sunshine twinkled through the dense kukui and shining ohia on growths fragile and exquisite.

When we reached the junction with another river still arched over with great trees a beautiful sight appeared of two water nymphs and a dryad 2 women and a man beautifully formed, the water up to their waists with ferns and myrtle blossoms hanging from their necks, their brown skins such a colour in the slant sunlight, their masses of shining black hair dishevelled and bound round with garlands of feathery green moss. They were carrying trumpet shaped baskets for shrimp catching and formed a beautiful picture in a beautiful setting. They joined us and we waded down together till we came to the place where they had left their horses – they slipped into their holukus[*] and the man made me get on his horse without a saddle till we reached ours and then we all galloped over the soft grass and waded down the river till I came to the house regarding which I wrote at the time. The schoolmaster had got all the white visitors names in a book 8 men and Miss Spencer.

When darkness was complete the house filled up with people who all sat round the stone lamp, but I crept within the curtain and went to bed. I had hardly laid down when a monstrous cockroach fully as large as a mouse with projecting eyes and antennae like a lobster mounted guard on the corner of my pillow and another equally terrible looking at my feet. I got up and spent some time in driving them under the curtain but I heard them cracking about like mice and for hours they scared sleep away. About 10 I think the people went to bed, I looked out and beheld ten heads lying in a row. They and I got up at dawn on Tuesday, and when I was dressed about 5 the horses were inexorably at the door and the man whose saddleless horse I had ridden the day before was there to act as guide. My soaked boots would not come on so I went forth a shoeless rider on a shoeless horse.

[*] A colourful shift worn by Hawaiian women.

We first rode up the river up to our horses' bodies in that slow and solemn fashion in which horses walk in water lifting their feet so high trying always to take them out of the water, our feet round our horses' necks, then galloped over the soft grass forded a sparkling river 4 times and then entered a tremendous jungle of guava banana Indian Shot tree ferns with great breadfruit kukui and ohia rising out of it. There were thousands of bananas. Here guavas as large as oranges and as yellow as lemons ripened and fell. Here there was no track except that made by mustangs. One could not see it for the jungle dew laden was higher than the shoulders of a man on horseback the guide often had to get off and look under the jungle for anything like a trail and then the horses shutting their eyes pushed boldly at it, ones feet often being lifted up and carried behind one so that one was in an attitude of swimming. A great crashing as of hippopotami would be heard sometimes but nothing could be seen but the tips of ears as herds of happy mustangs resenting our approach crossed away from us through the jungle. Sometimes deep down we heard the rush of water, but saw nothing and Hananui had to get off and grope to find where the rivulet was. [. . .] The huge palis 3000 feet high narrowed towards the head of the valley walling it in completely inaccessible solemn and grand the valley all in deep dewy shadow till the sun rose above the palis and flooded one side with pink light. About 3/4 of a mile from the head of the valley we were fairly baffled and had to turn back but I had seen all that it was possible to see and for me it was impossible to sketch it. I shall always remember that ride in the cool freshness of morning in dew so heavy that my flannel suit was wet up to my waist. I turned back reluctantly. Every step now seemed not a step homewards but a step out of my healthful life back among wretched dragging feelings and aches and nervousness. How pleasant that 1/4 of a mile down the river was when instead of tucking my feet under the horse's neck I rolled up my trousers and let my feet hang in the clear cool water.

On getting back to the house heaps of people seemed assembled. I had said the night before I would have no breakfast before I went to the head of the valley which in the hopeless ignorance of English they understood to mean none at all and as I had to ride 13 miles alone over a dubious track I could not wait while any was being prepared for fear of being caught in the darkness but I was not very hungry for I had gorged so much of the rose coloured pulp of the guava as I rode along, and had drank so much sparkling water out of cups made of the great green taro leaf. I put up my few things shook hands with all the people, forced 1 1/2 dollar upon my host and departed, knowing that never again should I look upon that most extraordinary scene. [. . .]

All this time I was not thinking at all of the terrible pali by which I must descend into Waipio. I had come up it without more than a few moments of positively breathless terror and I hoped to go down it more easily when suddenly we came to its very edge 2000 feet perpendicular and not only to its edge but where the track was only 2 feet wide turned L thus the point of the turn being also at the edge of the precipice above the sea. Nor was the path rocky or level but a shelving 2 feet of loose soil sun burned and all down the precipice nothing but a little sunburned grass. It was the most appalling prospect on which my eyes ever looked. It seemed as if there were no possibility of ever getting away as if I must return and live and die in Waimanu. In an evil moment I flung myself from the horse thinking I would walk down that I never could risk crossing on him the places where the path was broken away. If my senses had not been taken away I should have seen how much safer it was to trust to his 4 legs than to my 2, and to him who had no nerves or dizziness or fear of death and was above all used to it. I got off just where the track turned. It did not look wide enough for a horse much less for feet on each side of him. The guide and horses went on but as soon as I put out one foot it slipped and the use of my limbs entirely went from me and I clung on there in the most abject terror. Had I known before what they had concealed from me that the nerves and heads of the strongest men had always given way there and that none yet would cross it a second time I would never have gone but they said they thought it such a pity that I should not see it that they did not tell me.

It seemed an hour before the guide having managed to get off his horse came back. I could not make him understand my terror but he got on his horse and gave me the end of a long tethering rope to hold. I went two or three steps but terror took away all my strength. I could not shut my eyes and when I opened them they turned by reason of a horrible fascination to that fearful precipice. I then got hold of my horses tail but he took jumps that I dared not follow and I let it go in despair. My tongue cleaving to the roof of my mouth and screwing my feet round I turned my back to the precipice and my face to the cliff and clung there in dismay. Then Hananui finding he could ride no further got off and came back and I got hold of his hand and we proceeded he leading his horse by a long tethering rope. It was terrible for it was like that | and when from being smooth and shelving it became broken and rocky a new fear arose for the horses following brought down stones with them which bruised the back of my feet and twice struck my ankles so hard as almost to knock my feet from under me and Hananui's horse which was anything but surefooted 2 or 3 times slipped, and so nearly came down upon us that he making strong ejaculations crept aside and sent the animals on first who when they got to the bottom broke their bridles and galloped home. It was a hideous descent hideous getting over those places of which I told you before where the path was broken away and Hananui did not understand helping me and was not surefooted himself. I wished so for a stout helpful Highlander, or for one of the bold bullock hunters who had ridden with me yesterday. Once both my feet went from under me and I fell on my back but did not hurt myself. Sometimes the broken ledges of rock were I suppose as high as the steps of the great pyramid and I had to sit on the ledges and let myself drop down.

I was so annoyed all the time at my cowardice making such a fearful fuss about what a native woman would think nothing of and whose peril consisted in the imagination solely for when we got near the bottom though the path was just as narrow and rocky I felt no fear. It was pleasant when I began to see a wide river instead of a silver streak when houses began to seem bigger than dots and when I not only began to see people but the colour of their clothes. When I got down all my terror was forgotten and I was ravenously hungry for breakfast and reasonably so for by the altitude of the sun I judged that it was midday. A woman had caught the horses and came galloping back with them, and as our bridles were broken and we had only rope halters they both ran away flying over the grass and sea sand till they reached the river where they stopped and we rode up it alongside of two men in a canoe, who with all the people of the Waipio Valley had been watching our descent for an hour − probably laughing at the cowardice of the wahine* of whose courage such singular stories have been invented.

My face was now hotter and redder than any face that was ever seen, and the backs of my hands were swollen over the knuckles. I was riding carelessly up the river with my feet tucked round the horses neck thinking only natives were looking on when to my dismay I saw two white men standing under Halemanu's verandah and presently Mr Spencer and Mr Wilson came down to the riverbank to receive me jovially. I was really glad to see them for I wanted someone to speak to and I had been toiling over the prospective difficulty of making Halemanu understand that at that late hour I wanted breakfast and also that I wanted to get on to Waimea that night. [. . .] So I was delighted to see these people and they seemed so jovial and eager to hear my adventures, and they had breakfast on the table having been watching me from the time I got off

---

* Hawaiian term for woman.

the horse and well knowing the terrors I had been experiencing. Mr Spencer bathed my hands with some pain killer but it did no good.

I did Mr Wilson injustice. He has truly hunted and shot bullocks on the mountains but he bears a character exceptionally good in Hawaii. He is a Canadian and was a backwoodsman, then made £9000 at the Fraser River diggings invested it in a sugar plantation on Hawaii and lost it all when instead of going to the bad he got a situation as manager for Mr Spencer and has a large flock of sheep. His frank jovial manners and handsome fresh looking face are such a pleasant contrast to the icy bloodless Americans. Mr Spencer is by no means a man to be admired but is jovial and any manners are pleasanter than that utterly phlegmatic American manner. We sat in the verandah while I recounted my adventures. I liked the free and easy style. [. . .]

After breakfast, we rode up the pali all holding onto our horses manes to prevent the saddles from slipping back, but this of which people think so much and which I thought so much of the first time seemed nothing now. At the top we got off to rest our horses and did this 3 other times and once I got off to change my huge horse for the stringy spirited one I had ridden before. The Kona or south wind had set in and on the east of the island it was rather sultry, but when we came to the uplands of the Waimea a most invigorating air refreshed us and the horses who had seemed quite tired became frisky and eager to gallop. We walked them for the first 8 miles and Mr Wilson and I talked a great deal about Canada. Each time I got off I found my limbs stiffer till at last I had to be helped on! Mr Spencer was quite good in helping me but I noticed both in him and Mr Wilson what I notice in all the white men from living so much among natives that though very kind they dont render those little attentions to which one is accustomed. Also it comes from ladies riding astride and needing so little attention. But they will say 'Now jump up please' or 'Go ahead please' or 'Just catch ahold of this horse' –

When we got to the uplands plain grass over broken ground with trees here and there and stumps and prostrate trees Mr Spencer proffered a gallop and away the horses went tearing over everything leaping over the rugged ground barrelling over trunks of trees snorting and pulling. I always expected to come off being then on an English saddle and when we got to that part where the grass was very short and the ground dry and hard it hurt the back of my head so much that I was obliged to stop. The air felt delicious. At 4 we reached the ranch where the whole bevy of native women were ready to receive us. I had ridden 30 miles since 5 a.m. yet except that I was stiff from walking down the pali I was not very tired and could easily have ridden 10 miles further! Mr Spencer had to lift me off the horse and when he lifted me off I fell down. This was a most triumphant ravage. I liked it thoroughly. I went to my den and found magpies a duck and some bantams in it the floor covered with shavings and a carpenter's bench in it! A mere shelter. I got a tub of hot water from the Chinaman and changed my dress the only change I had being my Suez silk with the open front which looked grotesque in that kraal, and with my scarlet freckled face which made everyone laugh who saw it and my hands so swollen that they would hardly go through my sleeves. I went to bed rather early and slept till sunrise.

Wednesday was a day principally given to writing to you and working patching my tattered trousers in the delicious air at my open door. After breakfast I went over to Mr Lyons the old missionary. They are such old world people and spoke so strangely of their life. Mr Lyons said when he was a young man he had gone four times to preach in the Waimanu Valley having let himself over the pali from tree to tree by ropes. They gave me custard apples which grow all the year round on a tree in their garden and contain a white very rich vanilla tasting substance like solid-ified cream, so rich that I should not wish to eat another. Also the melon like grenadilla the exquisite fruit of the true passion flower. In the evening Judge Daniels and Mrs Rodinot played at keeka[*] and Mr Wilson and I talked beginning about skating till 11.30. He is a fine pleasant backwoodsman but nobody had any watch and all thought it was only about nine and I thought he never would go. In that style of life and country there is a seemliness about a nice Garibaldi shirt[†] especially when worn by handsome men. [. . .]

Thursday was an exquisite sunrise all bathed in dew. I was up at 5.30 knitting on the wall looking over to the snowy tops of the great moun-tains and howling that my last Hawaiian day had arrived. I felt better that week in Waimea than I had done since I was on Lake Superior. I seemed quite different, no head ache no wretchedness in the morning. I got up refreshed ready for a days riding or a days writing and working as the case might be and my mind seemed clear and bright. We breakfasted very early and then the horses were saddled and loaded. Mr Spencer sent Mr Wilson to ride with me and we started Mr Daniels and Mrs Rodinot with her sister tied behind her in front and Mr Wilson and I behind. After we got out my horse was so very wild that I nearly came off not having my feet in the stirrups which came too long. It was a beautiful

---

[*] *Keeka* is the Scottish word for peep or spy, so this could be a game like 'I Spy'.
[†] Loose red shirt popularised by followers of the Italian patriot.

ride of 3 hours, not that the immediate country is anything but barren, but there were the glorious mountains, and down the hill the gleam of the ever blue Pacific. I found Mr Wilson very pleasant and supposed he was not disliking it though he had said and Mr S. had said too that he was only going a bit of the way. He tried every persuasion to make me give up going by the Kilauea till the next week. I should go up Mauna Kea and get silver swords, I should go through 40 miles of forest, I should go to the Kohala hills and he added laughing if I would stay another week perhaps I could be persuaded to stay altogether. He quite tormented me to stay and was really so jovial that I should have liked to stay. Then taking a note from his pocket he gave it to me in a sheepish kind of way and it was this

Puuloa March 6

Dear Miss Bird
My friend Mr Wilson is most anxious to propose to you but dare not after so short an acquaintance. I can only say that his character is excellent and that he is about the best hearted fellow on the island.

Yours very truly
Frank Spencer

Think how ludicrously taken aback I was! I showed him the note and asked him if he were serious? Of course he said he was and pleaded his cause in a way so unusual as to be almost grotesque everything ending with 'Now dont go, stay and I try if you cant like me.' I asked him why he liked me and he said the first time I spoke he felt strange all over and since I had begun to talk to him he had liked everything I said and every opinion I expressed and that he had never felt so good and happy as the night before when he was talking with me and that the sight of my knitting needles had affected him so by reminding him of his mother in Canada. You would have laughed he was so perfectly respectful yet so perfectly assured. I told him that it would not do that there were 50 reasons against it and he said if I would stay and tell them to him he would dispose of them one by one. He said he would return to Canada by the next steamer if I liked. My heart was in 'the desert land' in which I felt and was so different and for a moment it did not seem that the manly good hearted splendid looking fellow who rode by my side was an insuperable objection! What I might have said if it had not been for *you* I dont know. I dont think I said anything very definite. I felt inclined to laugh for I knew his feelings were not deeply engaged. I wondered what B. and E. would think I ought to say whether I should lecture to him on difference in social position or say any stereotyped thing, but I did not for I have suspected that he was encouraged to propose by my saying the evening before when they were persuading me to stay that I must go home and work for my living.

During this colloquy we came down on the beach within a mile of the landing and the Kilauea blew her whistle 3 times making the pair in front gallop on. I tried to gallop but it hurt my head on the hard sand, consequently there was more opportunity for persuasion. We got there only just in time. Mr Chillingworth had detained the mail boat and would not even let me have time to change my riding suit. The Kilauea was moored by a very long cable to a buoy and instead of sending a boat as is usual to cast it off a kanaka jumped from the deck and swam to the buoy. Mr Daniels had left a dog on shore and a kanaka jumped out of the boat and swam back for him. They do this though the water swarms with sharks. There were 5 minutes in the steamer before the boat left. At last I told Mr Wilson I would write to him from Honolulu more explicitly than I had spoken, he wished me goodbye, the screw revolved in the clear turquoise water and my glorious dream of the desert land was over!

Honolulu March 11th. Well the dream is o'er and the 'Paradise of the Pacific' has no charms for me now. I did not dislike that voyage in the Kilauea except for the want of sleep. It is a very friendly steamer and I seemed on jovial terms with everybody. From the time I left Kawaihae Mr Daniels and Mrs Rodinot were trying to persuade me to land with them on Maui and go up Haleakala, a great temptation but one which had to be resisted. At night the kindly native steward came to me in the saloon saying 'your bed is ready' and carrying a blanket preceded me on deck where a mattress and pillow were laid on top of the skylight. I hardly slept at all and at five he brought me coffee. We were at anchor in a bay in Maui all the night but the kanakas talk as ceaselessly as the Highlanders and that night all the passengers were driven on deck by the cockroaches.

By 11 we were at anchor off Lahaina [on Maui] the most beautiful and tropical looking place in the islands. It is truly beautiful with shapely mountains 6000 feet high and deep ravines behind the little town whose beautiful latticed and verandahed houses peep out cheerfully from amidst a profusion of cocoanut trees breadfruit tamarind kukui mangoes bananas limes while the brilliant green of sugar cane forms the background. I hired a whale boat and landed at 11 and prowled through canefields by a track shadowed by palms breadfruit and mangoes then along the dazzling beach onto which the sea rippled like transparent turquoise rendered bluer by the drifting snow of the surf breaking over the environing coral reef. Such glittering blue such a blazing vault of blue overhead such dazzling various greens such quiet under the blazing noonday sun truly the tropics have a charm. It was all fanned by a most delicious breeze. Some miles away like a great blue morning glory lay the mountainous island of Molokai, a hideous object for on it 400 lepers are doomed to endless banishment and isolation and 300 more are shortly to be sent thither. A sad notice appeared in todays paper 'All lepers are required to report themselves to the government health officer within 14 days from this date for inspection and final banishment to Molokai.' The people hide lepers under mats in the daytime and let them go out at night to keep them from this fate. It is a part of the infinite curse with which white men have desolated these fair and happy islands. [. . .]

We sailed at 3. I lay on the skylight all night and by the crimson sunrise we were abreast of the grand mountains of Oahu and soon afterwards were moored at dew bathed lovely beautiful Honolulu. Of this splendid ravage extending over 6 weeks no record remains but these 2 letters which must be along with all the others most carefully kept. I wonder how you will like such narratives if what was so interesting to me will appear tedious and monotonous to read. At any rate the Kers will enjoy them. I think they may hear them throughout. I hope you will think that I devised a good scheme for myself at last. Alas that it is over, that it could not last the rest of the exile! I even thought that to stay till June or July I would endure a sailing vessel from here round the Horn and dispose of my railroad ticket but there are only two ships for England during the year and these carry no passengers. [. . .]

I should like to have gone to the Leeward islands, people say the climate is even finer than the Windward. The lee side of Oahu would be too hot for me. I dislike a thermometer standing perpetually at 80° even though the nights are cool, and the mosquitoes are dreadful at Honolulu. But they are propitious islands, blossoms of a summer sea upon whose leafy glories cool breezes and sunshine are ever playing. They realise dreams of 'islands blest', 'in the bright Pacific Sea'. But the dream is over and soon the hard prosaic north at the unloveliest time of year will greet my disgusted eyes. But having left the life I like I wish the 'Rolling Moses', now 6 days overdue, would come.

Its Pet

ILBird

*Dr Smiths** Koloa. Kauai. March 23. 1873*

Leeward Islands
Nothing very annoying in this

My darling

This is like the toil of Sisyphus. No sooner is one letter finished than another has to be begun. In Honolulu the toil of finishing the journal letter was frightful amidst interruptions and nangarenes like Edinburgh. I was feeling quite ill and forgetting and losing everything before I came away. The clatter of a hotel dining room is so distracting. Here in the quiet of this cool and bracing altitude I shall do better. I like this plan in a place where there is no fear from man or reptile of detached houses. These are old mission premises and the place allotted to me is an adobe house i.e. one built of clay and grass baked in great bricks in the sun. The walls are two feet thick, the roof is grass coming down on every side 6 feet to shade the 3 windows. It is a large room the floor matted and furnished as bedroom and parlour. It is under the shadow of date palms and algaroba trees and surrounded by great oleanders and daturas. It is about a minutes walk from the house. The cool breeze walks through it through the never closed windows and the trees rustle loudly. Other sounds there are none. The quiet seems like taking a heavy weight off an overtaxed spring. I revive under it.

This seems a superb climate. I had a blanket and quilt on and my flannel frock and thick tweed petticoat are most comfortable. The trades which will blow persistently for 9 months only set in 4 days ago. I had no idea that they would be *strong breezes* and that they would blow for every day and night. I certainly should not like it colder in a land without fires. They fleck with foam the blue Pacific but dont make it rough. I am sorry that I must leave on April 16th. There will not be a steamer again for 3 months and though you can come here in a schooner in 18 hours as I did it takes a week to go back beating to Windward, and everybody says I should be almost killed by the heat and misery. So if all be well I must then go to the uplands of Maui and Hawaii. When one looks at the tropical houses buried under trees especially in Honolulu one thinks 'how lovely now but how dreadful it will be in the winter', forgetting that it was the depth of winter when I so spoke and that the sun always shines.

On Friday at 5 Mrs Brigham drove with me to the wharf. The 'Jenny' did not look a conveyance by which one could travel. She looked smaller

---

* See Dr James Smith, p. 342.

and worse than any of those sloops which be at Oban pier and her little deck was covered with lumber and sitting or sprawling kanakas with their invariable calabashes of poi. Mrs Brigham got into it with me and looking down the hatch into the little cabin was quite sick. The only arrangement for a w.c. was a box by the wheel into which if you went your head and shoulders were above the top. If the passage had been more than 18 hours I dont know what I should have done. On the deck there was just room for me to sit on a box and the captain sat on the taffrail. She spread her white duck sails and glided away like those white winged things which I used to admire so in Portland Harbour. The stars came out the breeze was strong the Honolulu lights sank and in 1 1/2 hours in that little craft we were out of sight of land.

I had soon to go below for fear of being chilled and the captain came down to help me to get to bed. Mr Brigham has been very kind to his wife so he was very kind to me. The cabin is a mere den with two large berths one on each side and a table. The finer cargo was down there. The Attorney General and his wife and a missionary and his wife were to have been my fellow passengers but at the last moment they changed their minds so fortunately I was the only cabin passenger. When there are more boards are laid across the cabin with mattresses on them and sometimes 11 sleep heaped together! I could only take off my hat and boots. In this climate, the necessity in these coastling craft of sharing your room with men is a great evil for it is so hot having on all your clothes. The heat was nearly insupportable and the cockroaches mosquitoes and flies. The other berth was occupied in watches by the captain and his son, who also had their breakfast there at 7 when we sighted land. I was very sick though the schooner was very steady and the anchor was down and the boat was thrown over the side and filled with kanakas before I energised myself to get up and then I thought I should be sick in the boat. The miseries of getting from island to island are great. The island looked green rocky and precipitous with pointed hills like Oahu, and cactuses growing down to the sea.

The thing I disliked in coming here is this. There is no inn or house where you can board, and the residents receive strangers so I came with a letter of introduction to the Smiths, who were to have forwarded me on to the Sinclairs* 20 miles off to whom I had 3 letters of introduction. Though the custom it is so very awkward. Young Smith was at the rocks with a buggy to meet the Attorney General and his wife and drove me up here where I was received very courteously by a very agreeable lady and

* See Elizabeth McHutchison Sinclair, p. 341.

at once shown to this room. The first thing I did was to take off my linen and wash it hang my outer garments in a draught and lie down in my dressing gown till my clothes were dry for I had left my carpet bag in the schooner to go round to the Sinclairs. It is a very elegant tropical house with music photos books about. Dr and Mrs Smith came out as secular members of the mission but he has remained as a doctor on their land. [. . .] With the extraordinary hospitality of these islands they would not hear of my going on. They said I must stay for a few days till I was thoroughly recruited as it was a hard ride. But I am longing to be on horseback again. Later Mr Müller* an enthusiastic young German tutor at the Sinclairs came in. He was going to ride back, and took the note of introduction. So it will not be so awkward there as they will expect me. I slept all night in the rustling coolness unvexed by mosquitoes which really are a most fearful pest at Honolulu. They poison my whole blood with swelling and fever.

Monday. Yesterday was a day of great activity in this house. I two sons and two girls taught a native school twice and went in the morning to the native church, and in the afternoon we all went to the English service. In the evening I told them about the Hebrides. When I went to my house to bed I found a lizard darting over the floor. [. . .]

The last week I have found it very difficult and have not been able to eat but I think I am just suffering from general nervous exhaustion brought on by my unsuitable life at Honolulu. I am feeling very quank.†
Dr Guthrie's death the break up of the Kers the break up of our home the uncertain future and the disappointment which it always is to me to break down when I am among people and ordinary ways make me feel depressed. I like nice genial informal cultivated people, yet I feel that however much I may recover I never shall be able to enjoy more than the very quietest society one or two people at a time.

You see I am now trying to continue the life under which I improved so much and in two days I shall be located at a height of between 3 and 4000 feet above the sea level. I have made no plans. If nothing unforeseen occurs I shall stay on the islands as long as I seem benefited and then try to get to Colorado. I feel very dil when I look at the foam flecked stretch of the Pacific and think that 2 oceans and one continent must be crossed before I can see you and that then there is 'no place to be'. It seems so very far away here and I dont know where this island is on the map. I quite agree with all you say about giving this experiment a fair

---

* See Waldemar Müller, p. 335.
† A term used by Isabella to mean out of sorts.

trial when so much has been sacrificed in order to make it and I also feel that up to the time I left N. Z. all was a loss. So if I have money enough I would be willing to be separated from you even till Xmas to get some degree of improvement. [. . .] How very strange it all seems to have drifted like a waif into such a life. How surprised you will be when you hear of it. It was a plan devised and propelled by no one. If Mrs. Brigham had not been compelled to land I should have gone on to St Frisco.

Mr Sinclairs Makaueli Friday March 28th. On Wednesday I did not write because I was dil and yesterday because I made the journey here and now I don't see much possibility of writing. This is the most delightful of plans, filled with the most delightful of people and this ravage, though less easy to give an idea of and less full of wonder and adventure is just as successful as the Hawaiian one. I wonder if in any part of the world there are such people and such unbounded hospitality. The great thing is that I am better. I have been so poorly since the voyage that I feared I was going to have bilious fever and I could eat nothing from nausea, but starvation and this splendid climate have made me feel much better and I have no doubt that by tomorrow I shall be quite mended.

[. . . Yesterday] we left at nine Mrs Johnson her little native guide and I for our 15 mile ride. There is what people here call a road the whole way i.e. the turf pared off and the stones removed. It was mainly tedious except that I like so well the mere being on a horse for the old lady was timid about going faster than a walk and the country, like the leeward side of Hawaii, is long slopes to the sea without features or trees. It was broken by one deep rich valley with steep palis on both sides and a broad river flowing quietly down the middle the Hanapeipei. All the valley was green with rice surrounding native houses. We rode through rice fields before crossing the river. I was frightened I daresay without cause in that river. It was as broad as the Ouse at Huntingdon and the sea was rolling heavily in on the left and the boy of ten was an incompetent guide and my horse disliked it so and it was up to my knees the whole way. On that side rain seldom falls and in the bright hot sunshine we saw showers chasing each other down the well shaped picturesque mountains. We met quantities of natives both men and women all well mounted who saluted us with the kindly 'aloha' which the foreigners all borrow from them. It means 'my love and good will to you' and is the one form of how do you do and goodbye. People also say thus 'My aloha to you' – or he sends his aloha to you and it soon comes to have a very rich and unique meaning. So also all the foreigners use the word 'Pilikia'. It seems to mean in trouble difficulty or 'a mess'.

At noon which we judged of by the sun ceasing to cast any shadow we sat on the ground and eat some sandwiches after which we turned up towards the mountains. They looked so very beautiful as we began the ascent so cool so green so varied their grey rocky pinnacles so splintered their ravines so dark and abrupt their even slopes covered with the finest grass thin Ohia trees at a distance like pines rising singly then in twos and threes then mingling with the light bright green Kukui in dense forest masses. It did not seem possible that the house for which we were bound could occupy a situation so ideal and when at length ideally placed I saw in the distance in sublime loveliness a roof as of a Swiss chalet I could not hope it was our destination. More beautiful it became as the track wound through deep wooded ravines or strayed along the top of narrow ridges, cooler and damper elixir became the air till at a height of 15000 feet emerging from a wood we came upon this lovely spot a beautiful large thatched wooden house with steps leading to a verandah festooned with roses water lemons and passion flowers a house of patriarchal size with a guest house of 8 rooms joined onto it and all as trim and as beautifully kept as could be standing on a most abrupt natural lawn its slopes dotted with orange trees burdened with ripe fruit ohias etc. Behind rise the forest covered mountains and in front a beautiful wooded ravine very precipitous widens to the rolling grassy hills and the blue sea 5 miles off on which at a distance of about 18 miles floats the island of Niihau which the sun turns every night to a living amethyst. There is no house native or foreign within 6 miles. It is the most beautiful scenery I have seen on the island in fact the place is perfection. The great novelty of the house is that it has a chimney. The crater house at 'Kilauea' also has one.

I must now give as 'legibly' as possible an idea of this family to which I have been consigned. Their story which was told me by Mr Damon I thought too odd to be true till they confirmed it in every particular. Mrs Sinclair the mother about whom I have been hearing ever since I came to the islands was a Miss Semple daughter of a rich Glasgow merchant and her husband was of the Caithness family. When N. Z. was first started they bought land at Wanganui in the North Island where I was and with a young family emigrated thither but on arriving found that the Maories were hostile and would not allow them an inch of the land they had bought and they underwent great hardships till a vessel came to take them away. Going to the middle island they bought the beautiful bay and mountains of Akaroa and later when the Canterbury association was formed Banks Peninsula near Christchurch making them the largest landowners in the province. At that time they had to get all their supplies by boat and this lady's husband and son going to Wellington for them were never heard of again. She then undertook the whole management of the property and sheep stations and everything prospered with her. Her two daughters married and one of her sons and had children but her ruling passion was to keep all her family under one roof or rather to recollect them under one and so she sold her property for some enormous sum and 11 years ago with all her kith and kin left N.Z. in search of an isolated home.

Mr Damon was their seamans chaplain and one day going down to the wharf he found a handsome clipper barque newly arrived with the whole of this immense family and their possessions on board and on deck pens containing sheep and cattle of the finest breeds. He made their acquaintance and found this most fascinating family with a beautiful and brilliant old lady at its head. They had bought the ship and had been for several months cruising in the Pacific in search of an island on which to settle. They had visited the Marquesas Friendly and Society groups and had been tempted by Tahiti but found it too immoral to bring up their children in and were then on their way to British Columbia to look at an island which they heard of in the Puget Sound. They had on board music drawing work books and he said carried about an atmosphere of refinement and Xtianity which made him sorry when they sailed away. In 3 months however the ship returned. They had been disappointed in the climate and were quite at sea. He told them he thought they could get the island of Niihau and in a few days they had bought it from the government and taking 3 wooden houses with them they established themselves there for 7 years. They bought also 1/2 this island all this grand mountainous district and are likely to possess the whole. Two years ago they built this delightful house and the family migrated here from Niihau on which the eldest son his wife and 3 children live the only white people among 300 natives. It is an island of 70 000 acres very difficult of access owing to a tremendous surf which I now see surrounding it like a drift of snow. They have 20 000 sheep there. Mr Sinclair is said to reign there like a prince. He and his wife devote themselves to the natives who are said to be the most religious, moral and prosperous on the islands. Mrs Sinclairs great object has been to keep her family all together and she disliked leaving Niihau but as her grandsons grew up they could not have enough to do on so small an island.

The family living here consists of Mrs Sinclair a bright beautiful lady of 72 with a refined Scotch accent and charming manners. They all admire and adore her and say she is the youngest of them all. She usually wears a bonnet and is in and out all day and up at 5. She is very talented and sparkling like Dean Ramsays ladies. She was away when I came but rode up on Sat. 15 miles, and this morning the 2 ladies of 68 and 70 have ridden away mounting their horses like young girls. Then there is a bachelor son very quiet and an immense reader. Mrs Robinson a widowed daughter highly cultivated and very intellectual and a most splendid rider. She has one son 6 feet high only 19 but with a mature mind and much culture. He has the most singular grace of manner and though not at all handsome he has a face you like to look upon. He is a delightful creature. Then another widowed daughter Mrs Gay and her 5 children. She has 2 sons 19 and 21 over 6 feet very dark and handsome with great beards and mustachios a most attractive girl of 15 as graceful as she can be and very intellectual and a boy and girl of 10 and 8 like the very nicest English children. The mothers say that not one of their children has ever cost them 5 minutes thought of an anxious kind.

These 3 young men are beginning to have cattle here and are settled on the island but they desire to be very highly educated so they have a tutor who teaches the whole 6. Such enthusiasm about study I never saw. They all learn Greek German mathematics music English and they begin at 6.30. The boys retire at 8.30 and unless their mothers hunt after them, they study till 12.

Certainly their tutor is calculated to awaken enthusiasm in the most stolid. He is a singular part of the household. He is Prussian (Mr Müller) he was a lieutenant in the Ülans and there went with those who volunteered to go to Mexico with poor Maximilian.* He was on his staff and after being wounded several times was almost killed at Queretaro, and was liberated by Juarez because he has two bullets in his arm and side. He then went to the States and learned English which he speaks most beautifully, his refined instincts having made him avoid all Americanisms. He was educated at Leipzig University and is a great linguist. Falling into wretched health he came to these islands nearly 2 years ago and on the voyage met with a Bible into which he had never looked and was converted. From that time he threw all his talents and energies into religion. He is a most gifted musician and artist a poet a linguist brilliant sparkling exquisitely refined so radiant a creature I never saw. He looks too *spiritual* to live. They say they think he never knows a moment in which he has not the presence of Jesus. His face sparkles and he has the most exquisite grace of manner, something I never saw in anyone before. But like so many people who have been similarly converted and who have drawn their ideas from the Bible solely he thinks

---

* See Archduke Ferdinand Maximilian of Austria, p. 333.

all literature wrong has given up poetry and the reading of all books and all the things he used to do and thinks that one may not admire the beauties of nature because it is an alien land and under the curse. He plays exquisitely and improvises with soul yet is now thinking about giving up music. [. . .] His prayers are wonderful and everything he says is so beautiful but I dislike those ideas. They were not those of the loveliest and holiest I ever saw or have known and *they* could not have been left in error. It oppresses me.

It is a most singular thing about this family. Down to the youngest child they are all devoted Xtians. They ride 8 miles on Sunday & hold a Sunday school for neglected natives and have 100 old and young and they minister alike to the bodies and souls of all about them. The natives say that they would all have been saved had all foreigners been like this family. All the natives on Niihau and this side of Kauai call Mrs Sinclair 'Mama' and they have an immense number of native servants among whom they live so happily. I think I never was in a family which to an equal extent combined religion love and culture. They all speak Hawaiian as easily as English. They all dress nicely but not fashionably but when the young men go out on horseback they look so picturesque in scarlet shirts grey trousers leather belts and great boots and spurs riding brass bossed Mexican saddles with lassoes coiled up behind. They are the best riders on the islands. [. . .]

I must now go on with my journal. On riding up here we were most elegantly received by young and old and conducted to the guest house where soon a tray came to me with tea and cold beef. I always undress and lie down after these long rides. At 6 we had tea roasted a time by the fire and then spent the evening in the drawing room till 8 when there was reading and prayer. Soon after we went to bed. [. . . The next morning] I breakfasted in bed for the first time since leaving N.Z. and did not get up till 10. As we were sitting in the parlour we saw a strange gentleman ride up whom I recognised as Mr Meyer. He brought a letter to them, and had he brought none the reception would have been equally hospitable. After dinner Mr Meyer Mr Müller Mrs Robinson her son and I went on a fern hunt in the woods. I had on my Bloomer Suit which seemed to confuse Mr Meyer. I got some very rare ferns. [. . .]

On Sat. we went on one of the best expeditions I ever made through exquisite scenery, varying the whole time. It was to the Hanapeipei Falls. I had been told that ladies could not go and I was amused to see that Mr Meyer looked as if he thought we should be a great nuisance when Mrs Robinson and I said we were going. Also it was amusing afterwards to see his unveiled amazement at our riding. We outrode him, I galloped down the hills where he only walked and Mrs Robinson coming up out of the river took a leap where he did not follow her. He is a very good rider but being used only to the easiness of N.Z. he could not do without dismay even the things that I do who have been over two months in the country. He kept ejaculating 'I never saw such riding – I never saw ladies with such nerve' when it didnt require any. Then he never knew how I got into my saddle. It seemed an unceasing wonderment to him. He never saw me get on! He said he had not the remotest notion how to help a lady who rode astride!

It was a perfect excursion but I cant convey any idea of it because I cant describe the style of country. It is all ridges very narrow and abrupt beautifully grassed and sprinkled with trees singly and in clumps like a park. These run up to the highest mountains and down to the sea and the deep ravines between them are filled with trees and streams. We crossed many of these till we reached a height of 2000 feet from which there was a most splendid view of near mountains deep gorges dense wood and waterfalls. We left at nine. Mrs Robinson and I Mr Müller in a green shirt and corduroy trousers and boots Mr Meyer in a green shirt and George Gay in a scarlet shirt. A native went with us to carry the food. All the horses leaped and danced and it looked most picturesque. Mr Müller Mrs Robinson and I galloped up and down these steep hillsides leaving Mr Meyer far behind. I liked the mere fact of wild reckless furious riding, for the horse was nearly running away the whole time. We galloped down hills as steep as Arthurs Seat and along tracks only a foot wide and along knifelike ridges till we descended that steep 2000 feet which led to a broad swift clear river emerging from between walls of rock to encircle a bright green lawn on which a cottage belonging to the Sinclairs stands. The young men had been driving horses down from the mountains and 20 saddled with gay saddles were tied to a fence and there were many natives, and these with the young men in their scarlet shirts looked very picturesque.

We had a most difficult ride of 1 1/2 hours from thence to the falls. It was worthy of Hawaii. How often I recalled the lines 'and linger shivering on the brink and fear to launch away'. In going and returning we crossed that broad deep cold stream 26 times always up to the horses girths and higher and the bottom was so rocky and uneven and the horses trembled and floundered so that one could not tuck ones feet up about their necks and so I was wet up to my knees. It had once been possible to ride along the margin but a flood had carried that away so only here and there was a little foothold and we had to cross and recross to get to that. I cant think how the poor horses managed. Sometimes we rode over smooth round boulders like the top of Ben Cruachan at others like the landing at Iona and most of the rocks under water were covered with a smooth green weed making them slippery in addition to the deception of the rush of the clear bright foaming water over them. I hate crossing water and I think each time I disliked it more as I saw the horses of my companions stumble and flounder in holes and tremble as they were urged in. But it was most truly beautiful, a richly wooded broken glen with great faces of bare rock and terraces of basaltic pillars rudely formed sometimes peaks and pinnacles rising 3000 feet sometimes the glen quite walled in apparently and turning so abruptly as to bewilder and when we came to the end where the river comes in one snowy sheet 250 feet it was very grand. Indeed I suppose one would seldom see river scenery of the kind but people elsewhere would regard scenery as inaccessible which could only be approached in such a way. We had wine and biscuits at the falls. [. . .]

My Pet, if we lived here, we should be 'rich residents'. We could help the natives and others exercise unbounded hospitality keep 6 or 8 horses have abundance of books and periodicals and as people need never ride faster than a walk you could get about and pay visits quite easily and learn this most easy language in 6 months. The artificiality of life at home and the fearful price of necessaries rendering free hearted hospitality impossible for most wear people out. Here if the furniture is shabby the table inelegant the steel and silver dim and strangers come in no apology is felt still less offered. No change is or can be made for visitors and as there are no table servants you are never made miserable by their gaucherie. People have made themselves miserable and their lives a purposeless slavery in England and America and the price of things which is a curse really oppresses everyone. [. . .] You would be surprised too to find how competent I have grown in cooking mending washing managing generally. I never visit at any house without doing things for people or teaching them various kinds of work. There is a knitting pattern which I learned which every person has asked me to teach them! And now I can saddle bridle and pack a horse quite independently of anyone. I can learn all manual labour so easily it is so different from my inaptitude for intellectual acquirements and music and languages. I have learned a great deal since I came to Hawaii nei. I am quite fitted to live on these islands now or in any similar circumstances. I should never bother any more with a woman servant. I would have a man cook who would wash up clean knives and boots trim the lamps, and if I could not get anyone to wash for me I would do it with one of the little steam machines which do it so well.

How you will wonder when you get all my well pleased letters. How glad you will be. But it will seem so strange, a world opened which you have known nothing of. I can imagine how fierce my Bessie will be when eventually she reads or hears my letters, how she will toss her head and say 'She'd better stay where she is for she'll only come back to grumble at everything and hate us all!'

Isabella's happy mood did not last. From April 4 to 6 she camped at the 'Birds House' in the Kauai mountains with Mr Müller, the Gays and the Robinsons to explore the environs around the Waipoo Falls in the Waimea Canyon. She did not find it a pleasant expedition: the group had neglected to bring enough food for themselves (and none for their horses). She wrote that her nerves were in 'a very bad state' and she lay awake each night 'with restlessness and terrible nervous achings'. On April 7, the group returned to Makaueli, to Isabella's relief, which enabled her to depart for Dr Smith's at Koloa. There she mended her clothes, read Robert Browning's poetry, and visited the natural wonder 'the Spouting Horn'. Rather than improving with the Smiths, however, Isabella became worse. The following extract was written after she left the doctor's house, as she prepared for her last excursion on Kauai, a ride to Hanalei.

*Mr Rices** Lihue Monday April 14.* My luggage and I got parted for 2 days, and I have had literally nothing so I could not go on with this. I have had too little rest lately and was very glad of yesterday while these good people went to the native church and of this morning when they have gone to the other side of the island to be quite alone. I shall have to go and bury myself in a grave in Kona. I have never got over the fortnight in Honolulu and on this island in visiting these kind people I have felt that it would be ungrateful to shut myself up in my room. Indeed it would have been impossible. Then I have never been allowed to ride alone and I find talking and riding too fatiguing. I get so dreadfully depressed when I get over done and yet *apparently* no life could be quieter, living simply in remote country places with genial quiet families going to bed at nine. I fear I need drink. If I could only get draught ale. I suffer from debility and exhaustion. I am going to drink a bottle of porter today. Wine disagrees with me. I am disappointed at not having improved in the perfect climate of this island and in such an open air life. I have felt *dil* all the time and so terrified lest you are dead. I am wearying so to see you. You are my first thought in the morning and my last

---

* See Mary Waterhouse Rice and William Hyde Rice, p. 339.

thought at night and because you are the one thing belonging to me in the world I fyke[*] ceaselessly about you in terror lest you are dead.

It is really more and more dreadful about the kindness in these islands. One staggers under the weight of it. Mr and Mrs Rice are young married people. Mr Damon and Mr Morant had written to them that I was in the island and she wrote to ask me here. She is a charming young creature and she and her husband and Mrs Rice her husbands mother are as good as they can be. I came here on my own horse but Mr Rice insists on supplying me with a fresh one for the 60 mile ride to and from the Hanalei Valley, and with one of his natives on another horse as guide enjoining me not to give the native any present. I am only going to ride 15 miles a day so you see I am very prudent and I am going 3 miles out of my way to avoid swimming a river. I hope the long solitary ride will be a rest and when I ride alone I can ride as slowly as I please without wearying anyone.

Well on Friday after luncheon the two Smith girls and I went off 5 miles to the woods to return by moonlight and tethering the horses fern hunted for more than an hour. When they said they would go to the woods I had expected nothing – they said they had been afraid of saying anything because they thought I had seen such wonderful forests in Australia and New Zealand. So it was a surprise. I never saw such woods and the whole scenery though not tropical so beautiful. Deep ravines along which bright fern hung streams brawled among bananas overhung by ohias glowing crimson with their extraordinary blossoms walls of peaked ridged broken precipitous wooded mountains rising behind the trees deep in shadow with mists floating round their spiky summits gleams of a distant silver sea the ground broken into ridges with ravines all round filled with the most beautiful and fantastic forest many tinted not matted together but festooned and adorned with beautiful creepers and tree stems the ground the rotting prostrate trunks of trees all covered were hidden with the most beautiful ferns. I cannot remember ever seeing a forest at once so beautiful and so picturesque with its long cathedral aisles and hoary columns stretching far away making one feel as if soon one would hear anthems and the majestic roll of organs. My eye was satisfied with seeing more so than since I saw the sun set in many tinted Malaga. We got back in good time. [. . .]

On Sat. at one Miss Smith a native child and I went to the glorious woods again and got some fine ferns and at 4 one of the young Smiths joined us and escorted me here which I reached at 6 wet to the skin with

---

[*] Scottish word meaning to fret, worry or fidget.

a very heavy shower. The country we rode through was like an English park fair swells of bright green grass clumps of trees green valleys watered by swift streams but unlike England no houses or sign of men and over each stream bent the ohia with its shining pea green leaves and its flaming glory of rose crimson which you see far off. I was not only wet from the rain but wet up to my knees from crossing a river and the man who was to have brought my things from Koloa never came or all yesterday and they had to be sent for this morning. I had not even pen knitting or toothbrush! Mrs Rice who is nearly as tall as Bessie had to lend me things. [. . .] When she came here as a bride 6 months ago the natives were so delighted Mr Rice had married an island girl who spoke Hawaiian that they gave her a 'luau' or native feast at which there were 2 bullocks 19 hogs and 100 fowls besides poi and innumerable native dishes. There were 500 natives all in leis and garlands and each brought them a present and chanted native songs in praise of her husband and then she had a piano brought, a thing which they had never seen before, and she sang songs to them in Hawaiian.

Mrs Johnsons Valley of Hanalei Tuesday April 15. Yesterday I had an expedition which I thoroughly liked. I had quiet all the morning at one lunch with a tumbler and a half of porter which did me a great deal of good and at 2 set off with a very nice native as guide intending to ride only 17 miles but I rode the whole 30 and was not more tired than when I ride 7 or 8 with people. A journey alone on horseback with only saddle bags and a native as guide is the thing I like. [. . .] I rode galloping over miles of turf crossing 3 rivers and seeing grand mountain scenery till I reached the ranch at which I had been advised to stop for the night Mr Burtelmanns.[*] I will never again ask for hospitality except in an emergency. I disliked it so. I got off and looked about till a rough kind hearted man appeared of whom I asked a nights lodging. He said I could have one but he was sorry his wife was away and he took me down to a room where a very rough man was nursing a baby with a burnt leg (a year old). They had the charge of this between them. I took it while they went to see if they could get some tea and it roared and fought and kicked till they came back. They could not find any tea and said they were sorry they had nothing but poi which I cant eat. I suggested that my remaining was inconvenient and that I really was not tired enough to render it necessary when Mr B. said that if that was really so he would be very glad if I would ride on to Mr Litcombs his father in laws where his wife was staying and I should be very comfortable.

[*] See Christian Bertelmann, p. 315.

So I rode on again the scenery becoming more and more beautiful and past Mr Litcombs as the dark frowning mountains of Hanalei looked quite near in the gathering twilight. But they were some miles off and a pali and two deep rivers though I did not know it lay between. The twilight deepened as we came to a broad beautiful ravine through which a smooth deep river glided into the pure white breakers of the ocean. Here I anxiously looked for the scow which was reported to exist but saw only its broken timbers. My guide and the people at the ferrymans house talked long without result. I saw a punt 1/2 full of water and made signs to them to take me across and the 2 horses swam. When we reached the top of the ravine the last glow of twilight was dying out over the melancholy ocean and the black forms of mountains looked huge in the gathering darkness and the wind sighed through the creaking rustling trees and it seemed nice and eerie. Soon the darkness settled and after riding for some time I saw what appeared to be a valley with twinkling lights lying at the foot of a precipice walled in on all other sides by great mountains. It was queer going down that wooded pali rough and rocky not able to see the ground with nothing in view but the white jacket of the native. Somehow I was not frightened. I was only hoping that Mrs Johnson's was not on the far side of a river which I had seen gleaming in the distance.

When we had nearly reached the bottom the native signified that he did not know the way any further, but just then a man on a powerful horse came brushing through the wood who I hailed in Hawaiian when to my pleasure he answered in English and said it was two miles to cross to Mrs Johnsons over a deep river in a scow that he would ask me not to go further but that he had only rough bachelors lodging to offer and that he would see me across to the scow. He added that he was Captain Ross[*] – manager of the Princeville Plantation and asked my name. I was so afraid that I had fallen in with a low bad foreigner but I afterwards found that he had a very high character as a good and moral man. It was so very dark that when we got to the river I could not see the railless scow which lay there. Then the horses would not jump on or off and had to be dragged floundering in the water. The gentleman then said he would ride to Mrs J.'s with me that he thought he owed a call if I didnt think it was too late and we cantered on 2 miles in utter darkness across the Hanalei Valley speaking in French voices.

Mrs J. was delighted to see me and asked my companion to stay to tea and he staid alas till nearly 10, while I was wishing to go to bed. The cold was great in bed. I had to sleep in your shawl, and this within the

[*] See Captain John Ross, p. 339.

fiery tropic, but one feels cold with the mercury at 68°. The next day Tuesday I did not get up till 10 and played the agreeable nearly all day! Mrs J. and her daughter seemed to enjoy my visit very much. Captain Ross wrote her a note which he did not intend me to know about asking her if she could do so without intrusion to find out if I was engaged for if not he wished to pay me such attention as might enable him in due time to propose to me. It is such a pity that Harriet could not have these lovers! She would marry them. I left at 10 on the Wednesday with my own native and a native who was riding to Lihue to be company for him. I met Captain Ross outside the gate and he rode with me the two miles to the river where Mrs Johnson met me and took me up the pali to an old altar hill from whence a magnificent view of the whole valley of Hanalei was obtained. Captain R. expressed unbounded regret at my going away but had the good grace not to say anything more. [. . .]

At 2 I went a mile off the track and got a cup of tea at a beautiful ranch belonging to a German Mr Krull of whom everyone says 'Oh Mr Krull's a perfect gentleman.' So I found him. He dissuaded me from taking the mountain road back saying I could not get down it by daylight and that there were three bad gulches and rivers. So I gave it up but by a mistake the natives took me that way and I liked it. Oh I liked it though it made the days ride 40 miles and I got in some time before sunset. It was wildly beautiful and indescribable mountains woods waterfalls grassy valleys and grassy narrow ridges on which one could gallop ceaselessly and feel the breezes blowing. Then the beautiful Wailua Falls and the park like scenery round them and the space and freedom and solitude! How I did wild things which I cant do with white people such as galloping wildly up and down hills hallooing to a horse to make it go twisting my knee for a few minutes round the horn of my saddle riding without stirrups and other free and easy ways. I thought of nothing all that day! There were two very bad rivers to cross in which I got very wet. I shuddered to cross them and felt cowardly. It seemed quite 'the desert land'. I galloped down one hill and the strange native said 'Spaniola'* and laughed and when the other came up he said 'Spaniola' to which the other said 'ei' by which I understood them to say that I was a Spaniard, and also when we were joined for a time by two women they said to the women pointing at me 'Spaniola'. When we got to Lihue I asked Mrs Rice what this meant and she said 'Oh lassoing cattle and all that sort of thing,' and laughed very much when I told her about it and said she would have toned down the meaning of the word had she known why I asked. [. . .]

---

* A Portuguese word for cowgirl, adopted in Hawaii. The more common form is *paniolo*, or cowboy.

On the Friday being the 3 monthly steamer day there was a great hunt from early morning. The steamer lies there from 8 till 5 and the passengers land and the Rices keep open house for them all day. At 12 Mrs Robinson Aubrey and Eliza Gay and the invalid Mr Sinclair came. There were 14 at dinner and Mrs Rice being away I had to carve a turkey for the whole.

At 4 we all went down on horses and in caryalls to Nawiliwili a little bay from which the steamer starts. Driving hurts my back sadly. It was a strange sight when we got to the little mountain backed bay. There must have been more than 120 horses and natives women in their brightest holukus dashing about and gay groups on foot and on horseback and a general buzz and bustle and a heavy surf rolling in through which moved stanch whale boats with stirring oars and embarking passengers. The young Smiths were there from Koloa and they brought me a piece of tapa a material made from the immense bark of the hibiscus tree of which formerly all garments were made. The farewells were most affectionate. All the people had begged me to return and spend some time with them before leaving in case a monthly steamer is put on. I delighted in Kauai. It is 'the desert land' and then it is so beautiful and the people are all so good and kind. It is attractive to the eye.

We were all carried into boats our feet much higher than our heads and then natives dashed up to the boat on horses and threw in carpet bags plaids valises and sometimes their horses plunged and threw them into the water! The Kilauea was rolling most abominably. It was more difficult to get in than I ever knew it. I thought everybody would get into the water. The deck was cumbered with natives all in leis and garlands. Mr Krull was most gallant and helpful as a well person can be at sea. It was very breezy and so cold that I had 4 blankets on, on the deck where I slept everybody except Mr Krull and I was dreadfully sick and I lay down at once and could not even go downstairs to look for a berth for a girl who the Smiths had placed under my charge. But I slept better than I had ever done on board the Kilaueu under the cloudless sky and we had a splendid passage aided by the blustering trade getting in to Honolulu at sunrise. The 'K' is a truly beastly propeller but she is as friendly as the Pioneer or Clydesdale and she was sweeter and better this trip having been thoroughly painted and cleansed since carrying lepers. Oahu and Honolulu looked lovely in the dewy rosy morning. I always return to it with fresh admiration which lasts until the nangings begin. But it is beautiful buried in a greenery of tropical trees with shapely mountains just behind it. And lovely it looked and lovely the hotel looked amidst its mist of algaroba trees. I went in great triumph with my friends and Mrs Brigham was delighted to see me and we secured one table. This is the end of the great Kauaian letter.

Mr Alexanders Heiku Plantation Island of Maui. April 24. This letter goes by the *last* steamer. No mail is in and no one knows how mail will be arranged for the future. That one letter of yours is the only one since Xmas Eve! It is still very cool and showery. I am caring so for it, but the lack of letters is dreadful. I never can realise Dr Guthries death. I always think I shall see him at Edinburgh and it makes such a blank. I suppose he died at St Leonards from an attack in his heart.

There will not be any more great journal letters for henceforth I shall only be on the old hunting grounds. The Kauaian ravage was delightful. I liked the scenery. Maui seems ugly after it. Tell E. and B. that I have found it impossible to write by this mail also that when people are 'abroad' it is not well to risk a letter to them written with difficulty.

Its Pet
ILBIRD

Sweetest little thing.

Isabella certainly wrote another letter to Henrietta between April 24 and May 28, but it appears to be missing. From *The Hawaiian Archipelago*, we know that Isabella spent this month exploring Ulupalakua and the Wailuku Valley on Maui; she then returned to Waimea for a longer stay at Spencer's Ranch. There she met the volcanologist Mr Green* and ascended Mauna Kea. She also spent more time with her suitor, Mr Wilson – which is probably the reason behind Isabella's suppression of this letter.

Hilo Hawaii May 28th finished June 15

Nothing Annoying in This.

My own darling

Think of my delight when an hour ago that old 'Kilaueu' brought a letter from you dated March 27. It came by a brig bound for the grassy isles. It is a most delightful letter, nothing annoying in it. It is so good that at last you got letters from the Sandwich Islands. By this time you will have got the letter saying that I am remaining here *6 months*! There is doubtless the heat that people describe on a low level on the leeward side of the islands, but I avoid it and have not suffered from it at all. I have

---

* See William Lowthian Green, p. 325.

never felt so much oppression from heat as often at home. But Honolulu is too hot for pleasure, though the mosquitoes are worse than the heat.

I fear my descriptions convey the idea of greater beauty than exists. There are often beautiful details and Kauai is very picturesque. The Wailuku Valley in Maui is glorious and there are bits of forest scenery and slopes and gulches in Hawaii of livid green which delight the eye from the luxuriance of the tropical vegetation. It is the climate, the eternal summer, the shimmer of an endless sunshine, the equability, the absence of all chill rawness depressing influences from the atmosphere. As I sit now in Hilo in the afternoon zephyrs play all round. Unless you go up to great altitudes you are never cold and are very seldom hot. I have never seen a day yet even in blazing Honolulu in which one could not walk or ride without inconvenience in the middle of the day. One would require to be thoroughly occupied to reconcile one to dull grey sour easterly days. It is a glorious climate.

I am so glad that you are no longer fyking. I fear perhaps you will fyke now about my not coming back as you did then about my coming back! This is such a strange life without incidents. I fear you will be tired of hearing of equestrian feats wild rides mountain ascents. Yet this is the life you have always wished I should have so perhaps that will reconcile you to the repetition. I do hope that nothing happened to the 2 registered letters containing the great Hawaiian ravage sent by the mail of March 10th. Now you will be surprised to find that a second Hawaiian ravage has almost exceeded the first, indeed quite for wilder ways have been inaugurated! And next week I hope once more to see the living fires of Kilauea. How excellent it is in it to be so pleased that I have 'something I can like'.

Puna May 30. [. . .] I must now continue the journal and make comments afterwards, as after all it appears that there will be another opportunity of sending letters by the same steamer that the two former ones are going by as its sailing has been put off for a week. When I reached Onomea on Sat the 24th I found Mrs Austin out of bed and better. I stayed till Tuesday. Stanley[*] was read aloud for 2 or 3 hours each day but it did not seem to me an interesting book and he seemed just a 'smart' Yankee newspaper correspondent. The rains peculiar to the Hilo district fell copiously. I had a pleasant visit and felt very much at home.

On Tuesday at 3.30 feeling sure that I should never get my horse 'Johnny Smoker' into the scow and into Hilo, I rode 'Bessie Twinker'

---

[*] See Sir Henry Morton Stanley, p. 342.

which Mrs Severance found too skittish for her and sold to Mrs Austin. It seemed nice to ride that familiar road with its hideous gulches and tropical beauties again all alone. Hilo is by far the prettiest place where people live on the islands. Such lovely grass houses nestling among bananas and the houses of the foreigners as pretty as those in a New England village. In Hilo I met little Helen Severance walking on stilts and she told me her mother was at Dr Wetmores where I proceeded and found her and leaving her there rode to the Severances and was dressed by the time she came back. In about an hour all the Hilo people had assembled and greeted me most warmly. [. . .]

Yesterday Mr and Mrs Severance and I with Helen on a pillow behind her father set out for Puna 26 miles distant. I only carried a night dress and comb in your shawl and a bag of oats on the horn of the saddle. Mrs S. wore a Bloomer dress on a side saddle. We rode in single file Mr Severance first and a native mounted constable carrying our food last. You see a great deal of the island in coming to Puna and there is a great deal of novelty. For 2 miles we rode over the hard sea sands then for 7 through woods a complete tropical jungle through which you would have to cut your way with axe and jungle billhook if you left the narrow track. It is all lava – lava for 26 miles. After riding for 2 hours we stopped at a native house and had some very rich milk in addition to our lunch. Then again we rode through brilliant green grass and woods of ohia and lauhala trees the ohias with their great crimson apples white and juicy inside with which we quenched our thirst. And all the way we were close to the sea and the snowy surf kept bursting up behind the trees and every opening gave a glimpse of dark blue water. Then suddenly the green ceased and we came upon an awful sight the lava flow of 1840, 11 miles long. You never saw anything more suggestive of fearful work on the part of nature than this black and tumbled sea tossed jagged spiked twirled thrown heap on heap broken rifted upheaved in masses half falling back now in ravines of its own making falling into the sea in perfect blackness, in great masses on which the surf and blue water was breaking. Here and there ferns were springing up. We stopped in one place and found some crystals of a much prized green substance called olivine which might be set in a ring.

The green was a welcome sight again and the country became broken with pretty craters filled with trees and clothed with green and we rode entirely under the shade of most lovely cocoanut trees and breadfruit a most tropic region. The heat would have been fearful but for the sea breeze for there was not a cloud and we were almost at sea level 18° 20′ from the equator in summer! The cocoanut groves were most lovely, the palms all sizes and their long leaves the brightest green. They were loaded with fruit in all stages, and it is in such profusion in this region that nuts lay on the ground in numbers unheeded. For 30 miles beyond this you pass under the shade of palm trees. Then amidst the feathery palms and the great glossy leaves of the glorious breadfruit gleamed the deep rose clusters of the ohia to my mind the most beautiful of flowering trees. And golden guavas as large as oranges were in the guava undergrowth. It was without doubt the tropics.

At 4 we came upon short green grass and going up a hill came to our resting place, a nice frame house standing on one of those green natural lands in which Hawaii abounds. This belongs to an old German sailor named Eldort who from being a bullock hunter has come to have a goat and cattle ranch of his own. He is a good man but has married a native woman who does not even sit at meals with him and sat on the ground staring at us. We had a room to sit in and two little dens to sleep in but one would never sit anywhere but in the verandah in such a climate and with such a sweet green view in all directions. There is a heavy shower every morning in this district and it keeps it perennially green. All sorts of animals specially cows were about. It was a place one could spend a week in very well if one had plenty of occupation though rather hot in the afternoon. The Severances and I went about 1/2 mile to a crater now filled with grass and trees and ferns with a deep green lake almost the only water in the district in it on an adjacent crater which tradition says is the first Hawaiian land upheaved from the ocean. There is an altar for human sacrifices. We bathed in our night dresses by which means I had to sleep in my chemise. On the way back Mrs Severance fainted away and Mr S. had to go and get a horse while she lay on the ground looking dead. I think it must have been swimming after the long ride. We went to bed about dark when all the stars were blazing, the full glory of a tropical night. Helen the child slept with me. I had brought nothing but my bloomer suit and Mrs S. revelled in a holuku with her hair down.

After breakfast we seemed *(Friday May 30)* most indolent. I was tired and it was warmer than I like. I worked and wrote to you. At 12 we had bread and milk. I afterwards went to sleep and awoke miserable. But at 4 we got horses and towels and went a mile to something I really liked. We rode among ohias and guavas into a grove of most lovely cocoanut trees and there tied up our horses. Close to these is a high wooded cliff of lava or basaltic rock with ferns growing out of every crevice on its jagged but perpendicular sides. The side nearest us you could easily scramble down to the famous warm spring a piece of water about 16 feet wide and 60 long 18 feet deep as clear as glass. Everything put into it is transformed, the bottom is rocks stones old cocoanuts old pieces of trees and all have that wonderful blue gleam like the blue grotto at Capri. It looks like heaven in the water a jewelled floor of marvels. Mrs S. and I put on holukus and Mr S. went in a white suit. They swam about. It looked very nice like a merman and maid their garments under the water feet and hands as white as snow but with the blue tinge of a glacier. I had a lasso tied to a tree to hold for I am so terrified in water. But this is so buoyant that you can lie down in it with your head above. It was most lovely to look upwards at the feathery palms rising into the crystalline blue but lovelier yet was the mirrored image of things so very fair. We felt much refreshed and very hungry. I thought there was perfect security in these craters which have not burned for ages and are so green and full of trees but a few years ago just such a one suddenly vomited forth fire destroying the lovely growths of centuries and desolating the neighbourhood with a flood of fire. We hung and sat about till after dark. [. . .]

On Sat. early there was some talk of staying till Monday, but I was glad it came to nothing for I wanted to go to church at Hilo and also had not sufficient occupation. It was showery but we got away at 9 expecting it to clear but it rained nearly the whole way to Hilo which we did not reach till 6. Mrs S. heeded the rain as little as if she were a Skye lady. We went on till we came to that awful lava flow of 1840 where we all got off and hunted for olivines of which I have now got about 40. We looked like something Scotch riding on in that rain Mr S. first with his little girl then the slight well sitting form of Mrs S. on her handsome horse in her well fitting bloomers – then me in my well-worn red dress with your shawl and a bag of oats on my saddle lumbering along on my great coarse horse which by his heavy gait and queer way he holds his head says to everybody he is a bullock horse. Then the mounted constable one of the fattest men ever seen whose back looked monstrous in a heavy poncho he wore. So we jogged on at that trot suited for Hawaiian travel but which after some hours becomes dreadful on a lava track. I had awoke with violent pain in my side (it has been very bad for 3 weeks) & it was so bad that I held one thumb in it all the ride to make it possible to go on. I was so glad when after riding 18 miles we stopped at the large native house. Mrs S. and I at once threw ourselves on fine mats on the floor where we lay an hour and drank some beer. There was a gorgeously coloured fish cooked for us among hot stones and ti leaves, also some roots and we had our own store of cocoanuts, giving food and drink at once, bread butter crimson ohias, and they gave us milk. We were most refreshed by the food and most of the 8 remaining miles was through wood till we got to Hilo Bay where we had a nice long canter such a relief after jogging on the lava. [. . .]

When we came back we found that two gentlemen had made the terrible ascent of Mauna Loa. They had nearly perished with cold and thirst, the water in their canteens being frozen. They say it is the most sublime sight ever seen. A crater 800 feet deep one surging ocean of lava sending up jets 300 feet high and so rapidly filling up they think there must soon be a lava flow in the direction of Hilo. It is most strange that this fearful volcano of which Kilauea is but the safety valve should have resumed activity. I daresay it will grow to be the highest mountain on Hawaii. It is sad that to me it should be inaccessible. One of the gentlemen was sick the whole time as if at sea. There were several earthquakes during the night. I could not sleep. So those red mysterious fires which can be seen for 80 miles are solved.

I am in the house alone tonight the others having gone to a prayer meeting. I have come to bed for the earthquakes and over excitement kept me awake last night. I am pining for it, and thinking wearily of 'ocean waste and desert track'. It pleases me to think that now a constant stream of non-annoying letters will be giving it pleasure and that it will not be fyking about me. Isnt it wonderful that a second Hawaiian ravage should succeed so well? Mrs Austin who is a great doctress thinks I am leading the healthiest life any person could lead. I think so too. I am doing what a woman can hardly ever do, leading a life fit to recruit a man. Now with my horse and gear packed upon it, I need make no plans. I can fall into anything which seems feasible. It is like a snail carrying its house upon its back. It shows some originality and energy to have devised such a life! And some of my old spirit. Bessie may think at my age learning to ride in a new fashion to succeed so completely [is absurd] for without any vanity now that Miss Spencer is unable to ride I know I am the best and boldest female rider on these islands! How disgusted she and Emily will be that instead of writing books I should become a '*paniola*'. I feel energy for anything except conventions and civilisation! And the endurance of heat and hurry. I am always caring for it. Does anyone but it get such delightful letters? I am wishing so for the time when it will read them to the Kers. It is such a pet.

Monday June 2nd. Hilo. How often that phrase occurs to me 'Is thy servant a dog that he should do this thing?' When I left Waimea Mr Spencer said 'I hope nothing will tempt you to go up Mauna Loa' and

I said 'I should never dream of it.' When Mr Wilson wished me goodbye he said 'I shall have no rest unless you promise me not to go up Mauna Loa' and I said 'I shall make no promises but I should never dream of going up. The suffering is too great.' This morning before 8 I saw Mr Austin and Mr Green coming up and (you remember I had arranged to go with Mr Green to Kilauea when he came to Hilo) Mr Green at once said that if I would like to go to Mauna Loa he would be very happy that I should go with him. He is completing a book on volcanoes and came equipped with a tent in order to ascend Mauna Loa 'the matter-horn of the Pacific'.

Crater House Kilauea!!!!! Wednesday night June 5th. I am shaking with excitement for everything is happening that could happen. How will this letter ever be written for I am so tired and 'drunk with sleep'. Well I at once said I would go for since I heard the news brought by the two gentlemen on Sat. my heart was secretly set on going though there seemed no hope or prospect of it. I went to the Severances and then to Mrs Sisson to tell them and they were delighted. The news soon spread through Hilo and offers of warm clothing and help poured in. It is an excitement for Hilo even when people go to the volcano, but you can form no idea of it about Mauna Loa. People seemed talking of nothing else than the 2 gentlemen who had gone up and for a foreign lady to go up is an event only one woman having ever been up. [. . .] Everybody thinks it is such a fortunate thing for me that Mr Green who is very popular and much esteemed on these islands has asked me to go.

Oh what a hunt it was! I went to all the stores and could get so little. Everybody when I went in said 'So you are going to the mountain with Mr Green.' I bought potted tongue chocolate tinned salmon biscuits peppermint sticks oats. Then Mrs Severance Mrs Sisson and I went to Mrs Reid. Her husband owns a large ranch on the mountain which will be the last house at which we shall sleep before taking to the tent. They are old Scotch people and it was thought they might have woollen clothes. Mrs Reid exclaimed 'Oh what some people will do!' but she leant me a woollen shirt of her husbands and a pair of stockings knitted 25 years ago. Then I went to Mr Thompsons. He lent me a cardigan knitted with long sleeves a pocket cup and a heavy blanket. Then Mrs S. called for me. Mrs Sisson lent me 2 chemises, Mrs S. a pair of stockings and large saddle bags, Mr S. a huge blanket poncho. Then to Dr Wetmores to see Mr White who had just come down. The difficulty about a guide seems great as the native who took them up suffered so from mountain sickness that they had to carry him down and he will never go up again. Mr W. thought the spectacle sublime. He suffered dreadfully from cold. The water froze in their canteens and he was sick for 36 hours. I then saw Dr Wetmore to ask if there was any risk of my suffering afterwards, and he said not unless I had any weakness of the lungs or heart. [. . .]

I sorted my things over and over rejecting all the things that did not seem essential and went to bed not early enough however for Mrs S. got into my room to tell me some rat hole news. However I slept till daylight yesterday when I got up unlocked the house unlocked the saddle-room laid a towel filled with oats before 'Johnny Smoker' packed and breakfasted with Mr Green at 5.30. We did not get off till 6.30. The two ladies were up to see us off. We had a very fine looking native from Waimea on a horse who drove a pack mule carrying the tent and blankets. Mr Green was on a fine horse carrying nothing but a waterproof, I on the brute heavily loaded. I had on my usual red suit, my little brown hat, my long white scarf wound several times about my neck a handkerchief tied over my face. A bag with 6 lbs oats tied to the loggerhead of my saddle your shawl with ends hanging down in front of me. Some strips of raw hide and a lasso which I had been obliged to borrow of Mr Wilson for a tethering rope hanging to one of the side rings and the immense saddle bags behind. Several of the Hilo people were at their garden gates as we went by. It was a beautiful day but with less air than usual.

For the whole of that 30 miles you can hardly go out of a walk till you get within two miles of the volcano. Up nearly to Hilo itself it is waves of lava of the kind called pahoehoe* but now thickly covered with forest and vegetation millions of tree ferns and very green. The track is just over the lava where the grass has been worn off by horses feet, such a track though it appears nothing after so much riding. The repetition of the same scene is most singular though when the vegetation is so profuse it does not tire the eye by monotony. We jogged along in single file. I had actually undertaken to act as guide and nearly lost the way, for a guide is so expensive. At one we reached the 1/2 way shed and turned the horses loose to graze. We waited nearly an hour before the native came up with the mule and I lay down on earth with your shawl for a pillow. [. . .] At 2 we started again. My brute was very lazy but never tired and never stumbled. In 30 miles you ascend only 4000 feet, and only by the cold can know that you are ascending at all. The mercury

* Hawaiian term for smooth, unbroken, level lava.

was 78° most of the day but near sunset it began to grow deliciously cool, and was cold so that the gallop with which we finished did not warm us.

As soon as we got off we went to look at steam cracks and then came into a huge woodfire. It was a brilliant evening but with my feet on the dogs I sat shivering even with your shawl on and never got warm till I took some brandy. This grass house is thoroughly comfortable. But wasn't it hideous to find that though we were shivering in this way the mercury was as high as 57°. Such is the result of living in an equable climate that you feel a change of a few degrees so very much. It was very exciting. Here on the craters edge we looked across 3 miles of its black depths to where the lake of fire sent up clouds of red bright light against the star lighted sky and on our right the lofty flat top of Mauna Loa upheaved itself against the moon without a cloud, and far and faint burned that solemn lonely light which ever since I first saw it from the sea at Kawaihae has seemed so mysteriously fascinating. In front the Southern Cross now quite erect seemed out of place. One looked rather for the shivering North Star. I went to bed at 8 and slept all night.

Today *June 5th* has been a day of great fatigue. I see that my travelling companion requires to be looked after. I saw that before I left Hilo. Like many thinking and scientific men who have good wives he is quite in a dream about practical things. I dont know what would have become of us. I have to remind him of everything and suggest plans, and I have now written out a list of things which we must take with us or die. Miss Spencer who lived with them for 4 years was anxious when I went with him to Mauna Kea and said he was headstrong and reckless. That he is the last I have seen today but hitherto I have led him with a thread of silk, and often think how much better it is to travel with a man than almost any woman. I daresay you see that generally I go about with a man or men. This is very customary here.

This evening has been spent in trying to plan with the Indian who keeps this house about our ascent. Our only hope in getting a guide lies in meeting Mr Reid who is to pass this on his way to Hilo but he has two ranches 16 miles apart and we cannot tell which he will take. A good track 18 miles long leads to the lower one and a blind trail 10 miles to the upper. So I and a native with four mules are to take the trail and Mr Green the road. How strange such ways must sound. My fear is that the spasm of activity on Mauna Loa may be over and that all will have been gone through for nothing. I am nearly asleep so I must leave the narrative of this day. I have endured great terrors. Tell Bessie that her knife reflected the awful fires of Kilauea. The things I saw on January 31st were as mere fireworks as compared to today or like a royal salute as compared with the smoke and fire and din of battle.

Oh how horrid how awful how terrible how thrilling! What blackness and darkness and half seen fire suffocating gases scorching heat crashing surging smashing lashing roaring detonating. I saw something too hideous to be thought of. I know I shall be haunted by the terrors of Kilauea all my life. My boots are burnt, I dont know what I shall do. I fell through lava crusts *twice* and have cut my limbs and slightly twisted one ankle but what is anything even burnt eyelashes and brows as compared with such a spectacle. I have not suffered in any other way except one mortal horror that the thing on which we stood was going headlong into the abyss. Mr Green now says that we ran a great risk, that it might have gone any moment, and that only intense excitement would have induced him to go on.

Ainepo Thursday afternoon June 5. [. . .] Well we breakfasted at 7 after which I packed up lunch and with a guide and Mr Greens native we started at 8 carrying alpenstocks. As I before told you the crater house stands on the verge of a crater nine miles round and 3 across with different levels in it. The largest depression of this is occupied by a nearly circular sea of tolerably level lava which has cooled in waves streaked with sulphur and at a distance looks like foamy water. We crossed the very middle of the lake. I had hardly observed before the wonderful surges and convolutions in which the lava lies, sometimes so beautifully formed as to look like coils of wire ropes. Wherever there is a crack there is sulphur and singular growths like mineral lichens of all colours. The new lava flow is in waves streams coils twists tortuosities of every kind, the surface shining and smooth with a bright metallic lustre and a great deal of iridescence everywhere. It was very fine with a nice cool breeze.

Somehow I had expected to find the volcano as I last saw it though the dense white smoke might have prepared me for a change. When we had laboriously climbed that awful looking hill with the crust becoming more brittle and the footing hotter as we reached the top there were no laughing fiery fountains as before tossing themselves above the rim, but the lake had sunk probably to a depth of 100 feet or rather the overflow had raised the precipice above it to that height, and the precipice itself was overhanging the lake a breadth of about 9 feet between which and us was a great crack about 10 inches wide emitting suffocating fumes of sulphurous acid gas. Getting up to the verge of this we tried to look into those dense masses of furious smoke which were rolling themselves round in the abyss and every now and then caught glimpses far below of flames wallowing as if in agony. We tried to get a better standing point but were nearly choked with sulphurous gases. Then coasting this lake we got near to the edge of the other where the whole was incandescent and emitting but little smoke. This fairly conquered us. For a minute or two we kept going to the edge and jumping back again just seeing the agitated lake but a few trials in which throats noses eyes were irritated to torture by the gases convinced us that it would be unsafe to attempt this any longer. The pain and gasping for some minutes following were very severe.

We came back to the other lake. A ledge a few feet wide hung over it and between that and the comparative *terra firma* of the other lava there was a fissure of unknown depths emitting gases and steam. Mr Green crossed this telling me not to come, but presently told me to come for a moment, and I jumped on. Burnt singed stifled blinded only able to stand on one foot at a time, jumping across the fissure every two or three minutes when an unendurable whiff of heat came, or splitting sounds thundered a downfall of the ledge − in that condition we spent three mortal hours! It was fearful. I shall never forget the sight impressed as it was on my mind by every circumstance of terror. Sometimes dense volumes of smoke hid everything and seeing nothing upwards from out that sulphurous canopy rose fearful sounds crashing surging thundering, and we never knew whether the spray of some uplifted wave might not dash up to where we stood. Then the smoke partially lifting but still magnifying all things revealed portions of the lake no more a level surface with fountains playing over it but a literal whirlpool of fire surging and whirling at unknown depths sliding downwards from all parts of the lake into a deep vortex where mingling with indescribable noise and lashing against a sort of bank of solid fire of its own creation this fierce gory fire broke dashing itself in clots and gushes 20 or 30 feet in height while hell itself seemed to yawn. Always changing, always sug- gesting force which nothing could repel agony indescribable mystery inscrutable terror unutterable. What a fearful scene only caught in glimpses, the whole lake never revealed at any one time, leaving so much to the imagination. The sounds were most terrific. Sometimes we saw bits skim over with skim of a most wonderful silvery satiny sheen then it was drawn down into the vortex and presently as the fiery surges broke they seemed mingled with misplaced patches of bright moonlight. I thought at the time of how some of the old Scotch divines would have revelled in the sight. But surely though this may be used as the fittest emblem of the quenchless fire the place of torment cannot be like this terrible with material fires. Who can dwell with the everlasting burnings? It is such an awful glimpse into the fiery interior of an earth whose doom is to be perdition by fire. Never was so horrible a sight seen as those fires wallowing in torment.

Beyond the fiery abyss we saw dense volumes of smoke proceeding from the upper ground and took our perilous way in that direction. The lava often broke and let our feet into great heat. A large crust broke and let me into a place of steam and trying to save myself with my hands my thick gauntlet gloves were in one moment eaten away the thumb of one entirely eaten away by sulphuric acid. My knee was cut and my right ankle a little sprained by the fall. We found a fearful scene. I never wish to look upon its like again. It made me feel quite sick. Mr Green said that these were the most terrible phenomena he had ever seen in connexion with volcanoes and he has seen nearly all the eruptions and lava flows. We came first upon one 'blowing cone' then a group of 3 or 4 but it was not from these that the smoke proceeded. I only went to the solitary one for the footing was so bad the sights so fearful and the eblutions of gas so dangerous that I did not dare to go near the others. Mr Green however got a glimpse into the others and came back quite scared. The one I saw was of beehive shape about 11 feet high hollow inside and with a great rent in one side through which it had been spitting out lava which cooling rapidly looked like lumps of black glass. The inside of the dome was molten at a white heat, a perpetual blast or roaring proceeded from it and below it opened out a great width and seemed to go down about 50 feet to a sea of fire from which a lashing and surging sound proceeded upwards. Intense heat and stinging sulphurous gases only allowed me to take hasty glimpses down this terrific abyss. The group of 3 or 4 blowing cones together looked awful. You see their steady unflickering light all night from the crater house. I think they have been in existence 6 weeks. Possibly the fire is nearly 8000 miles deep.

After this Mr Green took one native and went to another part of the crater while I with the other returned to the crater house. My feet were so bad that every step was painful and the nearly perpendicular ascent of 1000 feet to the top of the crater was a tremendous effort. I at once went to the sulphur steam crack and took a vapour bath which is esteemed a panacea for sore and aching limbs but it made my head so bad that I went to bed for three hours afterwards. They boil kalo* etc in these steam cracks and all the water you drink is condensed steam. There is some-

---

* Another word for *taro*, the root used in the making of *poi*.

thing very awe inspiring about the vicinity of the volcano house smoke & steam coming out of every pore of the ground and that huge crater in front. It is a fearful thing.

My second visit has produced a far stronger impression than my first, and one of awe and terror altogether. These are so different from the volcanoes at the top of mountains which send high into the air fire and stones in spasms and then subside into harmlessness. Ever changing never resting the force which stirs them never weakening raging forever with tossing and strength like the ocean their work unfinished and possibly never to be finished. [. . .] How miserably poor seems this account of this magnificent spectacle. But no one could describe it. Only those phrases which in the Bible figure forth the place of torment give any idea of it. The lake which burneth with fire & brimstone. Poor little Mary must now be in a lunatic asylum if the first Hawaiian letter nearly 'drove her mad'.

> The next morning, Isabella and Mr Green split up to search for Mr Reid. The kraal Isabella found, up a blind trail from the Volcano House, was but a circle of rude huts. The small community of men living there had nothing to give her but some milk in a broken bowl. She worried about provisions for the next day's ascent, as this was 'the place where we were told we could fit out with flour tea sugar beef fowls spoons. If Mr Green has not sense to bring food from the lower ranch I cant go up the mountain.' She could do nothing but wait, however, so she settled down to write beside a stinging fire and fell asleep. Her rest was plagued by nightmares and fleas, and she awoke to realise that Mr Green, who had just arrived, had brought nothing but a young, untrained goatherd for a guide and some powerful green tea. All was not lost: Isabella convinced the ranch hands to sell her sugar, doughnuts, coffee and corn, enabling her and Mr Green to set off at dawn the next morning (June 6) for Mauna Loa.

Now the serious work of the ascent began. We soon entered upon the huge fields of pahoehoe which ground away the animals feet, a horrid waste, fearful to look at and think of extending upwards for 7000 feet. This region exceeds in wildness and confusion the most extravagant nightmare ever inflicted on man. For miles and miles above and on either hand great billowy masses tossed and twisted into a thousand grotesque shapes arrest and weary the eye. Struggling slipping tumbling jumping hopping ledge after ledge is surmounted and still upheaved against the glittering sky rise new rugged outlines to be overcome. Immense bubbles have risen from the confused masses burst and yawned apart. Swift running streams of molten lava have cleft straight furrows through the congealed surface. Massive flows have fallen in exposing caverned depths of jagged outlines. At times we skirted horrid streams of a-a* that have rushed remorselessly down everything and heaped high ragged mounds of brown scoria† into impassable walls. Winding round the base of tossed up fissures hummocks of pahoehoe leaping from piece to piece clambering up places where it looked as if the pack horse must roll over backwards moving cautiously over crusts which rang hollow to the tread stepping over deep cracks travelling hilly lakes that in cooling have been rent into a thousand fissures painfully toiling up the sides of mounds of scoria mixed with pumice stone and again for miles surmounting surfaces of rounded billowy ropy lava on forever on. My mule fell 5 times but hurt neither himself nor me.

So passed hour after hour over that trackless and inanimate region of horror under the tropic sun and the deep blue sky. Colder and colder it grew, the guide became dubious. Our only guide was the faintest mist of smoke far far off against the glittering sky keeping our hopes alive that the lonely fire was still burning. We called a halt to put on warmer clothing and eat food, while the guide reconnoitred. I put your shawl now alas sadly cut with lava over my knees, a handkerchief covered with a woollen square over my face and a French soldiers overcoat belonging to Mr Green. Then upwards still in the cold bright air till reaching what appeared to be the highest ledge we were on the summit but apparently no nearer that thin white smoke than we had been long before. [. . .]

At 4.30 we arrived at the edge of an a-a stream about as wide as the Thames at Westminster Bridge and it seemed that somehow we must cross it. I should have liked to have left the animals there but it was represented that it was not possible to cross on foot and we plunged in. It was so sickening the terror and suffering of the animals the plunging trembling struggling and snorting, the blood and torture. I could never go again with horses in company for they were splashed with blood up to their knees and their poor eyes looked piteous. I thought they would all break their legs. Then over 500 yards of rugged lava then a deep fissure with an overhanging precipice jutting 18 or 20 feet beyond the goal was reached then down a fearful precipice yawned the blackness and horror of the great crater of Mokuaweoweo.

Ha! Ha! Ha! In a deep recess nearly opposite shoots up a thing of beauty from out a black lake a perfect fountain of yellow fire not the bloody gleam of Kilauea but pure fire vigorously rising and falling in several united yet independent jets to a height as we ascertained after-

---

* Hawaiian term for chunky, craggy lava, in contrast to the smoother *pahoehoe*. Walking or riding on it is perilous.
† Lava with steam-holes.

wards of from *150 to 300 feet*. Such a beautiful thing you cannot imagine, the distance at which we saw it divesting it of all horror which may surround it.

(Just now after dinner Ellis the sort of bailiff at this ranch Charley Hall a very nice old bullock shooter and I were sitting on the verandah talking volcanic talk when loud detonations were heard and the whole place was shaken by an earthquake. I seem to have no more fear of an earthquake than of a hail storm. Yet how strange that the severe quake which occurred when I was riding alone through the solitude between Kilauea and Ainepo should not have frightened me. I am very glad to have felt such good earthquakes. Mr Green who was riding on a track 10 miles seaward from me saw the earth upheave and reel and thought he was seized with vertigo and was going to be very ill.)

We sat on the edge for some time and Mr Green actually proposed to pitch the tent there on that side of the great crack but I dissuaded him on the ground that an earthquake might send the whole thing down into the abyss. During the night there were 2 falls and after breakfast we saw another quite near us. For about two miles we had heard a distant vibrating roar – now at the craters edge it was a glorious sound the roar of an ocean at dispeace mingled with the deep hollow thunder of surf wailing in sea caves booming on, rising and falling ceaselessly like the sound of windward Hawaii.

The pack horses were unloaded the tent was pitched with the poles stuck between rocks one of them in a fissure of the great crack so that you could not get out of the tent without getting down into the crack. The tent was 6 feet broad 12 feet long 5 1/2 high at the highest part. The horse blankets were laid over the rude stones, then I went in to put on my last reserve of warm clothing and I got all the blankets and arranged them on the floor. I was to have one end of the tent and I got my saddle and turned it upside down for a pillow. Then I was exhausted and went and sat out again. In the meantime the natives made a fire and boiled the kettle when Mr Green discovered that he had forgotten to bring the tea of which I had reminded him over and over again! I made a great tin of brandy toddy and we all had it, tinned salmon and doughnuts. The sun was now setting, the peaks of Mauna Kea blushed red and the next minute turned ghostly against a chilly sky and with the disappearance of the sun it became severely cold. I got your shawl over my head and shoulders and wrapped my feet and knees in a blanket and we actually sat there till 20 minutes to nine, the first people who have been able to do such a thing. So fortunate were we in having so little wind.

The moon and stars were very bright. Coldly gleamed the pole star above that sublime altitude and strangely shone the beautiful Southern Cross exactly opposite. But as the sun set what wonders made their appearance. It is absolutely indescribable. Everywhere through that vast crater appeared glints of fire, fires bright and steady burning in rows like blast furnaces, fires lone and isolated burning like planets or twinkling like stars, little rows of sparks marking the margin of the lower level of the crater fire in wavy lines, all showing that the vast expanse of blackness was a mere crust all liquid underneath. Indeed the whole interior of this vast mountain must be fluid for the lava flows have not been eruptions but cracks anywhere in the side high or low from which the fluid contents have gushed out. But broad in the glare giving light enough to read by at a distance of 3/4 of a mile, making the moon look *blue* as blue as an ordinary English sky, lighting up the whole of the sides of that part of the crater with a bright rose coloured light bringing out every detail here, throwing cliffs and heights into huge black masses there, rising falling, now in lofty jets, now in glorious shapes like wheat sheaves cascading leaping reddening, a glory and a beauty was the lonely fire fountain of Mokuaweoweo. Every minute some new wonder developed itself.

The lake by daylight had appeared black with the fire fountain rising from the centre of it. By night it showed itself all incandescent with black spots of cooled scum upon it, from one side there was a flow down into the lower part of the crater a river of fire glowing with the brightness of metal flaming out of a furnace. In the bank of crusted lava which seems to support the present lake there were several holes showering the molten fluid within. Heavy white vapour in one place blew off in a jet from the edge of the lake and below there were various jets and ebulitions of steam or vapour. A dark projecting cliff concealed part of the lake. To us it appeared circular but doubtless there was more of it behind this. The whole gorge was lighted up with an intensely bright light. The middle of the lake seemed to be at a white heat – probably waves were surging there and from this the fountain rose solid at its base but churning and frittering as it rose high in the air to fall in fierce sprays. When one jet was about half high then rose up another so that while one fell another rose often two at a time going different ways. Mr Green says they are exactly like those gigantic flames in the Sem so perennial self-born springing up in glorious sparkling light played the mighty fire fountains. Think of this 300 feet in height falling in fiery masses and fiery form with the solemn diapason of the mighty jet and fall, the booming of a fiery sea. How far from all the world companioned only by the solemn stars! So perhaps the grandest display in the world has scarcely a spectator going on by day and night ceaselessly splashing and thundering the only token of all that goes on being the faintest glow visible from Waimea which is merely the reflection of the fires on mist or smoke. There is something strange in seeing what so few ever can see. I was glad to find how well I had borne it so far.

It seemed impossible to stay up all night. I was afraid of getting too much chilled so I climbed into my tent. My bedding was truly on the cold ground. Think of a wooden saddle covered with hide without stuffing above or below for a pillow but I put your shawl under my head. I had a blanket of Mr Thompsons a pair from the ranch and all my warm clothing. I wrapped my head up in the blankets and lay down. The lava was not worse than a very bad bed except one piece which was just under my shoulder. The 2 natives and Mr Green soon buried themselves in blankets in the other part of the tent and tied up the door. There is a saying about 'sleeping on the brink of a volcano' and this was literally done for I was soon asleep and might have slept all night but for fleas which I had brought up in a blanket borrowed at Ainepo.

When I awoke the heads of the others were all hidden in blankets and they were sound asleep so different from the sufferings which others have endured from incessant vomiting vertigo and cold. I lay awake a long time but was thinking about *them** and you and failed fully to realise the extraordinary circumstances. Lava at the height of nearly 14000 feet for a bed 20 miles from the nearest dwelling and the swell roar crash and thunder of one of the most fearful volcanoes in the world for lullaby. How had I come there? It seemed all a wild dream as that majestic sound moved on. There were two loud reports followed by a prolonged crashing parts of the crater walls giving way. I lay listening I should think till past midnight and then a louder surging of the fiery ocean and a *series* of most imposing detonations could no longer be endured and I got up and crept over the sleeping forms, which never awoke even though I had to kneel on one of the natives while I untied the latch and cautiously climbed into the crack and out upon the projecting shelf where putting a blanket under me and your shawl over my head I sat I should think for 1/2 an hour. It may have been much more, for the 4 hours we had previously spent in watching had passed like one.

I shall never forget that time. It seemed the most marvellous circumstance ever self chosen by me. All Hawaii slumbering people having looked out at the mysterious light having wondered what was going on up there I only seeing it. The blue moon shed her pallid light as feeble as compared with that of the volcano as with sunlight but red and

* Her parents.

glorious burned and glowed the splendour of the fire fountain on rock and tent and shivering mules. Oh light that never was on sea or shore! Light at once of beauty and terror unwatched by any mortal eyes but my own. It was freezing cold but what was that in the radiance of earths uplifted central fires! Words can convey no idea of the glory of that mysterious spectacle. Things had changed as they seem to be hourly changing in craters. Those loud detonations were probably the evolution of some fire cones which appeared at the far end of the black depth of the crater, 2 miles off I should think. Fires appeared all round the edge, marking the outline, and here and there all over the expanse lone stars of fire kept bursting out showing that underneath that black crust was a liquid sea of living fire. The fiery river flowing from the fiery lake had advanced and broadened and looked grand. The lake was now all fire and the increased noise was owing to the increased height of the jets which even now were playing regularly and perpetually at a height of 300 feet with the cross fountains playing at their lower part.

I dont know how long I should have watched their inconceivable glory, their beauty of form their radiant reflection on the cliffs 700 feet in height which walled them or how long I should have listened to their thunder music but for this which occurred. The jets which had played to this immense height suddenly became lowered and for a few seconds they seemed only cones of fire coalescing in a sea of light, then suddenly with a sound like the sound of many waters, the boom of the ocean on wave girdled Hawaii, nearly the whole surface of the lake seemed lifted up as if by the impulse of some powerful internal force and rose 3 times with its whole mass afire in glorious jets or one glorious upward cascade of fire to a height (estimated by the height of the cliff) of 600 feet! That was a sight of glory, as the earth trembled, and the pale cold stars seemed to withdraw themselves abashed into the infinite space. After that it returned to the height at which it had been playing before and as it was now very cold I crept into the tent, those words occurring to me with fearful force, 'Dwelling in the light which no man can approach unto'. It was *his* birthday* on which I saw this wonderful sight.

Two volcanoes in one week is too much excitement. I kept myself from being very cold but hardly slept at all more and was glad when the rays of the sun made it prudent to get up. The natives had slept all night but the Waimea one complained of very severe headache and was soon entirely prostrated by mountain sickness, so that he could not help with anything and lay moaning. It seemed worse than sea sickness from the

---

* Apparently the birthday of Edward Bird, Isabella and Henrietta's father.

agony in the head which accompanied it. The guide made a fire and we made chocolate and toddy. I tried to make hasty pudding but could not owing to the low temperature at which water boils or rather milk. I did not care to eat for I felt a sort of nausea and lassitude coming on. I sat out and took an outline of the crater, but soon returned to the tent. Our preparations though small took very long owing to the difficulty of making any exertion in that rarefied air and having only one man left to saddle the mules and load the horses. The tent was a perfect picture of rough life. I thought how little Eastern travellers with their dragomen and their iron beds and their cooking tents and their comforts and their tents pitched when they reach their camping ground know of the exigencies of travelling. Blankets all heaped in confusion my great old saddle upside down spurs strips of raw hide a brandy bottle 2 sets of saddle bags and gear of all kinds.

We did not start till nine. I then felt quite sick and miserable, but owing to the use of snow and the water which had *frozen in our canteens* I had no headache but the usual one at the back of my head. The fire fountain looked as it did when we first saw it. The poor native could hardly get on his mule. The morning was cloudless and brilliant, but the air very keen. The descent took 4 1/2 hours to the camping ground and we never stopped during the whole of that time except once to tighten the girths. Not a rope, strap, buckle or any of our gearing slipped or gave way once such a different experience from that of other people. But it is truly awful that 10 miles journey over that Plutonic region. The a-a streams were most fearful to cross, the two generous horses were terribly cut. It made me sick to follow them for at first they left patches of hide and hair on the rocks then flesh and when there was no more hide or flesh to come off their poor heels and fetlock joints, literally *every step* was tracked in blood, blood dripping on every rock and if they stood for a few minutes each foot left a little puddle of gore. They had all the suffering and we all the interest, and they can't be rewarded. The mules were terrified in the a-a but they are so catlike that they were very little cut. I was so glad that I had left my brute Johnny eating at the ranch, for these wretches were 27 hours without food or water. [. . .] We went in single file over a rough and unknown road in the dark and reached Mr Reids ranch at Kapalapala at 8.30, a collection of nine wooden buildings among mulberry and sugarcane at a height of 2400 feet all surrounded by a cattle wall.

Utterly strange to say I was only reasonably tired and resting the Sabbath Day was such a blessing. We had three excellent meals on Sunday. I read a great deal of *Paradise Lost* with new admiration though

I dislike the helpless, idiotic jellyfish style of Eves speeches to Adam. The rest and quiet of that Sunday were delicious. How much more ease and freedom there is with men than with women! I never miss women! Mr Green would not let me pay any share of the expenses of the guide or pack animals! I think the cost of the weeks expedition will amount to four guineas. We parted this morning on the best of terms. He had never been cross complaining or selfish. He behaved as a quiet courteous English gentleman the whole time. He is considered the best traveller on the islands. I heard him say to Ellis[*] that he had never seen a gentleman on the islands such a perfect rider and traveller as me!

> That morning, with difficulty, Isabella found her way down a blind trail that looped over 'hideous a-a streams'. She had to blindfold Johnny Smoker to get him over the lava and she worried that she would lose the track. She had heard that 'one native who was lost opened a vein and drank his own blood'. Despite her fears, she soon reached that region 'where the whole ground steams and smokes and fumes with sulphur and at two I was comfortably in the Volcano House'. She wrote an account in the register, spent the night admiring the far-off flames from her window, and returned the following day to Hilo. 'They were delighted to see me and I had to give my narrative to a number of people.' Sadly, her return coincided with the removal of several lepers to Molokai, where the Belgian priest Father Damien[†] had just been landed. After writing an account of the lepers' removal, she spent the night with the Severances then returned to Waimea. A gap in her correspondence exists between June 15 and 28, 1873.

Waimea June 29th 1873

My ownest,

Yesterday I never wrote a line to it and I felt so dil but there is not much to write about, and I always feel dil when I am stationary for it is very lonely to have no communion of soul and to see no one to whom the subjects which have great interest for me are interesting. It seemed very dil to have no one to clang to[‡] about the school board in which I take such interest, or to tell about the rat hole. The loneliness is dreadful often. When I am travelling I dont feel it, but that is why I can never stay anywhere. When the wind howls as in November as it is doing now with keen cold I feel so very dil, for it makes me realise the desert track over which I have yet to go. Waimea is like a Hebride in its climate, so blustering and so coarse, so cold and so wild. One certainly would think

[*] The bailiff on Mr Reid's ranch.
[†] See Father Damien de Veuster, p. 343.
[‡] Meaning, no one to talk to.

oneself in latitude 56° instead of 19°. I long for my warmest wool stock-ings and wear my Turkish trousers under my crinoline. Four blankets at night make it possible to sleep. It is really very cold. [. . .Also] Mr Wilson has been away for a week. I think he will not be back before I go to Kona. He is a strange creature. He told me that he would not deceive me that he had been what women call very wild. What this means in Waimea it is fearful to think of.

This afternoon I have read all of its letters from Dec 2. I delighted in them. I hope it is now satisfied that I left Australia and N.Z. Much as I should have liked to have returned to Mortlake the climate was destroy-ing me and N.Z. was worse. They are delightful letters and are perfect when read consecutively. But each letter that I get gives me such a wild despairing wish to 'get back' and see its well rounded face for it is my own and my only pet who never seems absent from my thoughts.

Monday. All last night I could not sleep. I talked till 10 and got very nervous and Mauna Loa the finest view of which is from Waimea was playing such singular antics blazing up to a height of 1100 feet. My bed is close up to the window and I have only to lift my head and see at a distance of 50 miles the glorious reflection of the great fire fountain of Mokuaweoweo! Think of seeing one of the mightiest of earths volca-noes from ones bed! I send the Pacific Commercial Advertiser with an account of the ascent of Mauna Loa and my being the second woman who has been up there. Also the piteous account of leprosy and the peti-tion to the government to appoint a day of fasting and humiliation. Kona the district to which I go tomorrow is the great place for lava flows and volcanic phenomena. I hope something will happen. I dont see how that tremendous sea of lava can be surging and wallowing at a height of 14000 feet without breaking through.

Tuesday. A glorious day. The volcano was tremendous last night. Yesterday afternoon I went for a ride with Mr Wilson and we sat in a tree for some time. As we were riding from Hamakua before he went away for a week he said something about leaving the islands if I would marry him and making a home in any part of the world I would choose. I told him he was mistaking liking for another feeling and that in the four months since he had proposed to me he had never succeeded in making me feel that he loved me, to which he made only the answer that he thought he did. Well yesterday he told me that while away he had been thinking the matter over and he believed that his feeling for me was the greatest liking and respect but not love. I told him I liked him all the better for speaking so frankly, that it relieved me from the annoyance of thinking that my refusing him would cause him pain but that in future I hoped he would never propose to anyone till he was quite sure of the state of his own heart. I could not help laughing, for he is queerer and more blunt than anyone I ever saw and then he laughed and we took a tremendous gallop back again and I asked him to ride with me to Kawaihae today. He amuses me indescribably by his brusquerie. It shows what a good thing it might be for people to 'keep company' instead of being obliged to be engaged.

Also it is a very good thing that I have remained so long on Hawaii nei. Had I left at the end of the first ravage I might have sighed after the islands and thought often that I should like to live on them. Now nothing would induce me to live on them or even to spend the coming winter on them, though 3 things remain delightful, and I shall always regret them. Pre-eminently the riding 2nd the perfect climate either at 4000 feet above the sea on the windward side or 1500 on the leeward, 3rd the life. The riding for 5 months has been life to me, just giving me the air and gentle exercise I need without the pain and dragging either of driving or walking. I believe that now I could (with a change of horses) ride 100 miles in a day without overfatigue. It does not drag shake or hurt me in any way. As soon as I get on a horse I feel thoroughly comfortable and the more I ride the more I can ride. The climate is perfect from its equability. In nearly 6 months there has been no change. You never have anything to guard against and as long as people live here they have no neuralgia or toothache. You live in the open air. Whether the heat of Honolulu the soft airs of Hilo the delicious breezes of Onomea the cool bluster of Waimea it is always the same. That grim gloom which we have so much of and harsh sour malign winds are altogether unknown in regions which bask in an endless summer. The life in its ease and simplicity has great advantages. It is truer better more Arcadian.

It would take too long to write the faults which I find with the islands. The chiefest arise from their heterogeneous and ill-assorted nationalities. There are no fusing great interests such as those which knit vigorous Victoria to distant England or unite the merest log village in the far west with the mighty Empire whose heart beats at Washington. Consequently petty strifes, intrigues and jealousies and an amount of gossip and such knowledge of each others affairs as exists on a ship pervade the islands to an extent grotesque to a stranger, but which as a resident I should find unendurable. Then there is undoubtedly a *low* American influence predominant. Then though it sounds a strange thing to say I find almost no intellectual equals. Then the missionaries with the exception of Mr Lyons are the coldest driest hardest shrewdest type of American piety and have not the manner or tone of American gentlemen with the single exception of Mr Coan. Then there is a class of foreigners on all the islands save Kauai scratching for their living and hating each other, escaped convicts from New South Wales, old whalers, beachcombers, adventurers from the Spanish main, the very dregs and scum of creation who have produced an atmosphere of corruption which is hideous. Then there is the loneliness produced by the absolute paucity of population which is dying out at the rate of 5 deaths to 3 births besides decaying with leprosy. Then there is the general bankruptcy, which everyone says will swamp the islands in another year. Then there is the knowledge that the government is 'run' by Americans, for their own and Americas interests and heaps of other things impossible to explain to anyone who has not lived on the islands for some months. You can hardly imagine what an unpleasant feeling the lack of large public interests gives. You hardly feel the beat of the great pulses of the world. But the travelling about is delightful glorious. Alas that there are no more worlds to conquer or rather that my money in which consists my ability to conquer them is done.

Ridge House S. Kona. Hawaii July 6. I came here on Tuesday night the first and have been too busy and heartless to write more. Mr Spencer has 50 horses yet they were all lost or lamed with bullock hunting so that they had to borrow a horse from Mr Wilson for me to ride the 10 miles to the steamer and if he had not ridden down with me I should have had to go alone! There was immense fyking about this as a little girl had also to come up, and Mrs Spencer got very nervous which made me so. Mr and Mrs Spencer and I rode for 4 hours in the morning hunting a vine fern up such lovely gulches with grottos and waterfalls and at 3.30 I came the three hours ride to Kawaihae and I should never have known that I had ridden at all.

Just at sunset we went up a high eminence to see a heiau or native temple. It is the rudest construction, a wall of lava stones about 10 feet high and the same thickness on three sides and the 3rd open but 3 platforms sloping to the sea for 3 orders of spectators. The paved centre had houses or oratories now fallen in which the high chiefs used to pray and the rest was the altar on which the blood of human sacrifices has flowed in the memory of living men. The short twilight darkened while we came down and I was terrified at crossing a horrible place where a broad stream falls into the sea and with only a gleam on the water left we had to cross in the sea on a narrow sand bar with waves rolling over it and deep water on each side. I hate those watery exploits. [Mr Spencer] was obliged to leave me here and I had to carry my luggage and ride over that unknown beach for a mile in the dark unsaddle the horse and carry my saddle and my luggage to the rocks in the silver moonlight without seeing a soul. Mr Chillingworth the agent and deputy sheriff soon appeared and took me into his house and soon the engineer of the Kilauea came ashore for me and I went off over the heated silver water to that familiar craft. I dont think it has rained at Kawaihae for 3 years. Nothing grows out of its burning rocks but the graceful cocoanut trees. Always clear and the air trembling over its molten soil here they will watch the transit of Venus. Truly it is the fiery tropic whose burning breath is never softened but by the faintest breezes yet only 10 miles from the cold blustering plains of Waimea!

[. . . I am sorry that one of my letters upset you.] You see when anything seems less wild than a Hawaiian ravage it doubtless seems dispiriting. And yet new glories unprecedented ravages are on their way which will make this and every other letter seem flat. You dont say which letter had a gloomy effect. I am always so afraid of your thinking me better than I am. So long as I am riding about on journeys doing literally nothing but riding eating and sleeping then I am much better. I sleep well digest well have no need ever of medicine my back is not specially painful and I dont feel nervous indeed I then feel equal to any horseback travelling where the heat is not oppressive. But when I am stationary I often feel miserable indescribable feelings of nervousness and lassitude as if everything were a drag, but even then if I get on a horse they go away. I think perhaps now a change may be beneficial to a cold climate. I may then feel a greater benefit from having tried this for 6 months, though I dread heat and changes after this perfect equability. The difficulty will be about exercise. Driving is none and certainly I *never* walk without dragging, and even if I had a horse a sidesaddle would hurt me. Disease of the nervous system I am sure I have even had no doctors said so and I suppose nothing but quiet and regular occupation will mitigate it. I have looked old ever since I was so poorly at Ulupalakua. I am wearying so to get back. [. . .] I hope you do not send my letters wandering after the Kers for they will be lost and I would so much rather that you read them to them. Then I should hear their comments and screams.

Sunday July 13th. I have been away for three days on the mountain of Hualalai during which time I have not touched a pen. On the way back

I called at Mr Greenwells (Dora Greenwells brother) and got your letters of May 20th and 29th. They came to Honolulu in 5 weeks. I can never sleep the night after I get the letters. I cant tell what letters of mine you have got for not a *single comment* has been made except on the Hawaiian ravage. Yet you must have got my letter from Kauai or you could not have known about the horse having been given me. Now I am fyking because you must at this time be going about in England incurring the perils of trains. And what is to become of my poor Pincher while you are in England? [. . . I want to know too if] you think Edmunston and Douglas would like to publish my travels 'Ten Months in the Pacific'? My island tour would do for 'Good Words' not the Sunday Magazine. It would be much better for me to publish it there and *afterwards* as a book. [. . .Also] since getting your letter I have decided to sail on August 7th and try Colorado. People insist on it that unless I go much further east I shall suffer from the heat and that the nights in Colorado are cool. I cant get to Kauai owing to the steamers not suiting and though the Alexanders want me to return to Maui the riding there does not suit me. I cant stay in Waimea because I cant accept the hospitality of a man whose manners and morals are offensive to me. Although there is no difficulty in seeing Mr Wilson, remarks would continue to be made and altogether it is not a fit place for me. I feel out of my element. This place though the quiet is absolute, I find too warm. I seem to feel the heat more than ever.

You would think it perfectly beautiful standing 1500 feet high on an eminence not shut in, a very pretty house looking down on bananas mangoes custard apples pawpaws oranges citrons chinese oranges cocoanut trees figs grenadillas water lemons while amidst greenery indescribable are hidden watermelons squashes sweet potatoes pineapples and on the skirts of the burning mountains is a dense forest belt 5 or 6 miles in breadth and interminable length of kukui ohia koa* sandalwood lobelia mamane† festooned with vines and parasitic ferns and carpeted with moss and ferns of every description. No wind ever blows in Kona. The stillness is solemn especially after the windward side of the island. A soft sea breeze blows faintly in the morning and a soft mountain breeze at night hardly rustling the trees. 'Nor ever wind blows loudly' may I believe truly be said of this region. The whole range of the mercury during a year is from 60° to 84°. The greenness now is something wonderful and the luxuriance of everything. The lovely bamboo grows 5

---

* A timber tree used for furniture, with crescent-shaped leaves and white flowers.
† An endemic species of the family *Fabaceae*. Its durable wood was used by Hawaiian priests as a symbol of authority.

feet in a month and things *stride* in the night. Below is Kealakekua Bay, where you land on the very spot of lava where the first circumnavigator fell, and an expanse of unruffled misty blue gleams through the Pride of India trees which are clumped round the house. The dining room is one end of the verandah enclosed with lattice work only shaded on one side by passion flowers. Pretty little houses mostly belonging to men who have married native wives are scattered through the district. Many of these men came here in consumption and having got well remain here. The gardens are very beautiful hothouse flowers growing in the rankest profusion tea roses geraniums 15 feet high Nile lilies Chinese lantern plants begonias lantanas hibiscus passion flowers fuschias cape jasmine the wax plant tube rose the beautiful and overpoweringly fragrant ginger plant while the whole district is filled with shrubs from 8 to 16 feet high of a white pendent, trumpet shaped flower 6 inches long which we had a plant of in the green house and which I think is called the Datura floribunda. It has 70 or more blossoms often on one tree looking beautiful and at night filling the air with a delicious delicate odour vying with that of the night blooming cereus! But the air though suited for consumptives is too mild for me much softer and warmer than Hilo on the sea level.

It is a great piece of news that the fiend has gone to St Kilda. I hope it will suit his wife and that he will not have to go home, but he must dislike going there very much. I thought it the least attractive of the Melbourne suburbs. I think his spirit is broken like Mr Walkers by going to Australia. Of course the fiend would never have gone or have been urged to go to a small suburban church like St Kilda. Doubtless he is a better man for the trial and disappointment. Another summer will show if his wife can remain in that climate. [. . .]

I came here on July 2. As usual I slept on the deck of the Kilauea. It was a glorious tropical morning as we sailed along the palm fringed coast where deep beneath the clear green water the white tree coral formed a fairy forest. At 8 we were anchored in Kealakekua Bay, a small bay with perpendicular cliffs 5 or 600 feet in height and perpendicular below the water which was very deep and clear. Palms fringed the water and waves of lava formed the shore. There were two or 3 grass houses. The whole looked blazing and tropical. Canoes full of splendid pineapples and cocoanuts selling at a penny each came off. Mr Paris formerly a missionary here and his family and I landed on the very block of lava where Capt Cook fell. Then the King had a stone house on the shrine and the district was densely populated now there are very few natives and leprosy is very common. We had a long time to wait in a shed where we eat pineapples all juice and concentrated sunshine quite different in texture and taste from those raised in hot houses. Then I rode up the two miles here on a fiery little horse.

This house is advertised and Bishop Willis recommended it to me. It is kept by an Englishman and his wife. They have a dairy and ranch. He is not so bad. She is a clean active striving vulgar souled sordid avaricious woman doing all the work herself, always spotlessly clean and able to ride about and amuse herself. The terms are £1.1–0 per week. It sounds moderate but the table is very poor and you see that she would rather you did not eat. I have a beautiful room however in which I sit exclusively except at meals. There is a young New Yorker boarding here for his health and a very gentlemanly cultivated accomplished man lately a surgeon in the U.S. Navy. He is the most agreeable and intellectual man I have met on the islands but has gone to wreck with drink and has been divorced from his wife because of cruelty to her.

There is an English church here with a congregation of three adults. Mr and Mrs Davies its clergy were missionaries teachers in Zanzibar and are rather pleasant. Dora Greenwells brother has a store orange and coffee plantations here. He is a very gentlemanly and very intellectual man. He has lent me 3 weeks of the Evening Mail the Quarterly the British Quarterly the Westminster and Blackwoods. He has a disagreeable embittered sarcastic tone and a bad temper. Some time ago he tied a Chinaman to a post and beat him so that he died but on being tried was acquitted. He has a very sweet wife ill-circumstanced. The former missionary Mr Paris has accumulated a good deal of property here both in land and cattle. I rode in the forest fern hunting with Miss Paris one day and dined with them afterwards but was not prepossessed. There are 3 men here married to 3 1/2 white daughters of Charley Hall the old bullock hunter [on the volcano]. They are all steady sober industrious men with nice homes and have all been very kind in sending figs peaches flowers etc. I have ridden alone every day except once with Miss Paris and once with Mr Davies.

I occupy my time thus. Breakfast is at 7.30. After breakfast I write sew and read till one unless I ride. If I ride before dinner I write sew and read till 5.30 after which I sit in the verandah then come up to my room and go to bed at 8. The luxuriant vegetation everywhere is very beautiful but it is too hot. I have almost made a loose robe of this stuff, have done a few trifling things in fern printing as presents, mended frightful holes in my stockings, collected a great many ferns, written a great many letters. When I have written a few more I hope to make some notes of some books on the islands which are now out of print. I dont exactly dislike being here because of the quiet but I sigh to think that there are no more romping ravages. Yet on Wednesday I shall make one more for I intend to go for a week and live 5000 feet high on the mountain Hualalai at a little shanty owned by a man named Wall of thoroughly good character married to a pious native woman who speaks no English. Mr Severance wrote to him asking him to take me as a boarder but he would not do this but came down last Wednesday saying he would take me up Hualalai if I could start the next day for after Sunday he would be busy shearing.

So on Thursday morning at 8 with my clothes strapped up in your shawl I rode two miles to the house of a respectable 1/2 white where I was to meet Mr and Mrs Wall. A party of 12 with two pack mules went all natives or half whites save Mr Wall and myself. It was very picturesque straggling in single file mile after mile through the dark forest every person with one or more leis of flowers and mailé* on. They rode madly at full gallop along the narrow trail up and down hill leaping over trunks of trees stooping under branches with loud laughter and harrouches, and as I was near the middle I had to go just as they went but the ground was soft and I liked it. When at last we stopped having gained a height of 4700 feet, Mr Wall said that the women wanted to see how the 'foreign woman' could ride for the haoles were such bad riders and as they patted me murmuring 'Paniola' and threw mailé garlands over me I suppose they thought I did well. They were all very nice women with nice faces. Mr Wall cut me a piece of sandal wood deliciously sweet. There are huge grand koa trees in that forest and wild boars and bulls. Two of the party carried rifles in the hope of getting some fresh beef.

At midday we came out upon an immense valley covered with mamane scrub and coarse grass, lying between the great mountains of Mauna Kea, Hualalai and Mauna Loa. Deep indigo stains on the last showed where the lava flow of 1858 had come down. Here at a height of nearly 5000 feet the air was cool and bracing. In the midst of this desolate wilderness Mr Wall has built a circular wooden shed to which the sheep are driven down to be sheared with 3 little grass lean-tos as shelter for the shearers. Here we got off and stayed an hour and soon on the floor of the shearing house a wonderful dinner was made round which the whole party crosslegged sat on mats. I wish it could have been photographed. There were so many physiognomies, and all shades of colour from a jet black negro goat herd to my red face. All had garlands round their heads and necks. The shed was full of all kinds of gear guns

---

* Pacific island vine whose fragrant leaves and bark are used for *leis* (garlands).

raw meat fowls dogs dirty wool and our meal was 2 great calabashes of poi into which all present dipped their fingers, a tin pan of broiled mutton, dumplings, some sweet potatoes, a taro root and some tin pannikins of coffee served out of a kettle. The food was cooked in a hole lined with stones outside. I was very hungry. After dinner the bullock hunters left and leaving the others there the Walls and a woman going to act as shepherd and I set out for the higher sheep station a ride of 3 hours. It was trackless over waves of pahoehoe with sand between and scrub over all which we leapt and galloped recklessly. I delighted in that ride for though we went in this way it did not shake or hurt me and the air was so fine.

The afternoon mist came on and it looked not possible that on that bleak mountainside there could be a dwelling. Yet we came on a little frame house with cattle walls all about and sheep pens 15 miles from the nearest human being. It seemed further off than Kalaihae or any place and there are no tents or grass lean-tos as there. There were two native women, one Mrs Walls mother considerably over 100 years old *for she saw Capt Cook killed* and was far from young at the last eruption of Hualalai in 1800. I suppose the old people have never reconciled themselves to clothes they shuffle about in blankets or any old thing huddled and held on about them leaving their tattooed legs bare. The house consisted of a bare room with a large fire place and 2 bedrooms. There is no water save what is caught and sometimes it only rains 3 times in a year. A fire was soon lighted and a comfortable tea produced on a table. Mrs Wall is the first native woman I have seen who sits at table and eats with her husband. We went to bed about 7.30. I had only two blankets and slept with my window wide open, the first person Mr Wall said who had ever done so. There are night frosts there during a good part of the year. Before going to bed I saw a splendid sight, Mauna Loa just across the wide valley burning and glowing far up into the clear heavens like a huge conflagration and beside the fire the largest full moon I ever saw rose over the mountains brow. I know what is going on in the mysterious crater of Mokuaweoweo.

On Friday July 11th I got up feeling refreshed and at 9 the Walls and I on good mules went up the last of the Hawaiian triplet of mountains Hualalai 8000 feet high. The ascent only took about 3 hours and was not steep in any place. It has vegetation of some kind up to the summit and though the last eruption is only 73 years ago the lava is greatly disintegrated into sand and I saw no uncovered masses of pahoehoe or hideous a-a streams. It looks quite a smooth round dome from Waimea and Maui but on this side, it is altogether shapely ragged and picturesque made so by craters all the way up with ragged pinnacled splintered edges and abrupt caverned rocky abysses. The summit has some splintered rocks. It is quite different from the other two volcanoes and has no steam cracks such as exist on the skirts of Mauna Kea to show that heat and some kind of action exist in any part of it. At the very top there was an ohia in blossom. In the earthquake of 1868 the mountain was cracked across. We rode alongside this crack. The ground is treacherous all about it. There was no view because of drifting mists and just when we got to the edge of the deepest of the craters by riding along a narrow ridge between two, a torrent of rain came on such as I have not seen on the islands. It came in sheets and being at that altitude was cold like Highland rain. I had no protection and was drowned in 5 minutes. I thought how I should dislike to see anyone like you without a waterproof. I never was so wet except in the Hilo gulches. When we got back I wrung out my chemise in the basin. My boots were full. We soon had a fire and I put on my nightgown with a holuku of Mrs Walls over it, had some whisky, and soon got quite warm by a good fire. We went to bed at 7.

A boy nearly cut off his toe with an axe. It was just almost severed. I sewed it up and though the blood ran over my hands did not feel the least sick because there was something to be done. I liked the air and the quiet which nothing could interrupt and Mr W. is a really upright worthy man though the only religion he professes is to do to everyone as he would be done by. I should have liked to have stayed only they were coming down to the wool house on the skirts of the forest to shear sheep of which Mr W. has 5000 besides quantities of goats.

On Sat. 12th he a female shearer and I left at nine. We rode the 8 miles to the wool house all down the mountain side at full gallop only pulling up at some bad lava places. I like those breezy regions and huge smooth spaces. The hunters were just bringing in the hides and the best part of 3 wild bullocks, so we had some steak broiled on the wood fire. I admired the forest very much as I rode back so dark and dense and silent. There is a great deal of sandalwood. When we got to the first house in Kona rain began to fall in torrents and I went in and had a dish of figs and a cup of tea. [. . .]

On Monday the 14th I pursued my usual avocations and after dinner walked to the store. While I was at the shop Mr Todd came to say that 4 natives were going to hunt and lasso a wild bullock and there was a horse saddled for me. This is one of the specialities of Hawaii but I had hitherto failed to see it. I liked this *it was wild* and as I was riding about I thought that such a life was the only life fit for giving me health. I cannot think how people out of health can think of packing themselves away into watering places where they lead the same conventional life they are oppressed by at home. One man spoke English the others were lads. Each had a shod horse and a saddle like mine but with a long lasso made of hide hanging from the horn. We rode over shocking ground ran down hills and came upon one herd but none were fat enough. Then they told me to stay on a rocky hill where they would drive a herd down from the wood and they went into the wood to hunt. I think I sat there an hour, apprehending every moment a burst of cattle till I heard deep notes of bulls and saw a herd with hunters in pursuit emerge upon the open some distance above me. Then I rode towards the hunters who called to me to stop till they came and the herd disappeared. I asked the man where I should stand to be out of danger and he said 'Oh just keep behind me.' I had thought of some safe point not of galloping with a ruck of half mad cattle but it was the safest place as cattle till brought to bay or cut off from their haunts flee from a horseman. The only danger is of the horse falling among the rocks.

We rode on slowly till we came in sight of the herd at the foot of a slope. There our horses were urged into a full gallop jumping over rocks till we got to the cattle. Then there was one brief wild rush the ground shaking under the tread of cattle and horses there was whirling of tails and tearing up of the earth with horns a lasso spun 2 or 3 times round the head of the man in front of me and almost simultaneously a beautiful young bull was prostrate on the ground with his foreleg noosed to his throat nearly strangled. Then the lads got off and put another lasso round his horns slipping the first one into the same place so that he was held with 2 lassoes one man riding before and the other behind. As soon as his leg was set free he jumped up and made a mad rush but the captors were too dextrous for him and every rush he made he found himself fast. The lassoers are wonderfully skilled. As the bull rushes from side to side they dodge under the lasso slipping it over their heads and as the horse leans over to give himself purchase when the bullock pulls, the man throws himself off the saddle and hangs in the outside in one stirrup to help the horse by his weight. The animal had to be led a mile to the tree where he was to die and every wild rush he made you would have thought would have upset horse and rider. I avoided seeing him killed but I know a steak of him was on the table the next morning. [. . .]

Wool-shed Hualalai. July 17th. I have been away a whole year today. I dont know how I lived through the misery of that wretched murky evening on the Clyde when I walked on the poop thinking I would give all I had to get back. Then the three miserable months and my bad illness then the violet light on abundant Victoria and the pleasant time there then N.Z. unsatisfactory except Lake Wakatipu and now 6 months here. After the Ben Nevis the year has gone by very quickly and I dont feel as I thought I should that it has been all together lost out of life. I know that I was killed by the Wakatipu journey. It would have been too much anyhow and specially after that very severe illness in the Ben Nevis. But the last 6 months have benefited me at least in body and the last 12 weeks since I returned to Hawaii I have considered myself as well as I could ever hope to be.

If there was any way I could have managed to have two months more of *thoroughly wild* horseback life on Hawaii I would have it but on turning it over in every direction I see that it is quite impossible and even if there were steamers after August which there are not I should not like to lead a flat insipid life of visits in Kauai or Maui. But I cannot help howling. Though I have made so very many pleasant acquaintances and have met with so much kindness there are no people I specially care to leave but 'Oh the life on breezy hills on countless horses. This is the life thats meant for me.' All my gear and occupations on the saddle and no thought or care. And how useless my riding will ever after be! No more shall I tire 3 horses in a day. No more shall I tilt at the ring with brown flower garlanded youths and maidens. No more shall I at full gallop pick up lassoes from the ground while kanakas murmur admiringly 'Paniola' and 'maikai'.* No more shall I go out with the hunters or swim rivers or gallop down mountain sides or fight through forests! No more shall I mingle in the tropical life in latticed houses, or hear the music of the Hawaiian tongue, or sleep soundly on the mats of friendly native houses or take solitary journeys in perfect security. No more will Kilauea's awful fires thrill my soul or my bed be rocked by earthquakes or my eyes be feasted by the lonely uplifted fires of Mokuaweoweo. Come when it would it would be a wrench and it is best to leave when no pale gradations quench its ray than have a finger aye wagging in Kauai or Maui in heat or lower regions.

The next day, Isabella returned to Hualalai to stay with Mrs Wall until July 26, sewing, fern-printing and writing to her sister while Mr Wall (the only other person who spoke English) was away shearing. Being alone with her thoughts had the usual result – illness – and Isabella was prostrated with 'violent pain in my head back and limbs fever and almost constant shivering fits and sickness'. Thankfully, this infection was short-lived, and for the most part 'the days presented little change'. Isabella's comments to Henrietta about these days are confined to her diet

---

* In her letter, Isabella defines *maikai* as good, but it actually means to the sea.

– namely, jerked mutton, boiled goat, coconuts, brandy – and a cave she and Mrs Wall visited that was covered with ferns and icicles, nestled in a grotto. On the Saturday she left Hualalai, with 'a folio on volcanoes under my arm and a lamp full of kerosene in my hand', she concluded the last of her Hawaiian 'ravages'. She had only a few days left to devote to visiting friends in Kona, then she put on her bloomer suit 'for the last time' and made her way to the *Kilauea*.

It was a glorious moonlight tropical night, quite still and the air heavy with the fragrance of the trumpet and other flowers. The saddle hurt and strained me so terribly that halfway down I had to change horses with Mr Davies. When I reached Kealakekua Bay I was so tired that I lay down on the ground within a few yards of the place where Captain Cook was killed and slept till wakened about an hour afterwards by the cry of 'Kilauea' but it was another hour nearly 11 before I got off for there were so many pilikias. Meanwhile I got a boy to climb a cocoanut tree and get me some nuts to add to my bag of bananas. It was truly beautiful the perfectly placed and phosphorous crest of the sea whitening into surf on the rocks, the shadows of the high cliffs darkening the bay, the soft murmur of the leeward surf and then against the sky were the slender stems of the cocoa palms with their crowns of tropical foliage so feathery and foreign.

The Kilauea like some dirty ugly dog wins one by its friendliness. The deck was covered with natives but there seemed few foreign passengers. I went and lay down but did not sleep. In the morning I observed a very distinguished looking gentleman dressing, who seemed attended by several native servants. At 8 am Friday we anchored off Kawaihae and lay there till one. People say jokingly that it is on the equator and the heat did look fierce. There in that blazing cloudless atmosphere they will observe the transit of Venus. It looked a fiery coast with nothing green but the fringe of palm trees and above it rose to my eyes for the last time the three giants Mauna Kea Mauna Loa and Hualalai. The blue of the water was dazzling and at a depth of 7 fathoms you saw the tree coral as distinctly as if it were at the top. A hideous shark was cruising near the vessel the whole time. [. . .] We reached Ulupalakua last night and while there a shark was caught which was hauled on deck by all the crew and passengers.

This morning many young dogs appeared, among them Mr Willie Rice and one of the young Smiths from Kauai. It has been a glorious day. All the other passengers have gone ashore, but I remained to write letters. Mr Damiens gave me a jug of iced claret and water which is very agreeable in this great heat. A strange riff raff of passengers are in the saloon owing to a law which compels all white persons to pay cabin fare.

Certainly the arrangements in this steamer are terrible. Think of men and women living for 3 and even 4 days in absolute publicity. You cannot do your hair or wash aught but your face and hands. To night is the 3rd night of it. The food is the best cooked that I have eaten on the islands but the accommodation is degrading. [. . .]

Honolulu August 4. Late *Monday night.* I am having a tremendous ravage here and am far too nanged and excited to sleep. How often today have I thought 'Fair Paradise of the Pacific, bright blossom of a summer sea'. Such were my first such are my last words. I am howling now frantically as I see my fate lying at the wharf in the steamer Costa Rica. Six 1/2 months and no disagreeable memories! Oh dear Oh dear. I am glad that I am so sorry to go. I should have been sorrier to have outlived the fascinations of the islands. The moonlight is trickling through the feathery algarobas, through graceful tamarind trees and palms – shining on the glossy leaves of breadfruit and citrons and huge lilies and a breeze soft and cool impels the perfumed air in at my open doors and brings in the soft whisper of the summer sea. But a week here would kill me yet I dread the fast coming hour when from the deck of the steamer I shall look my last on the vanishing faces of my friends and on the summer isles *forever*.

I landed at 6 yesterday morning. Mr Damiens brought me here. They have given me the best room in the house sitting and bedroom in one looking up the Nuuanu Valley. I found your 3 entirely delightful letters and one from Emily and Bessie which made Honolulu bright at once. I could not go to morning church I was so tired. Bishop and Miss Willis came to take me to their house, Queen Emmas[*] maid of honour to ask me there, Captain Dan Smith to ask me to Waikiki. I sent word to all that I was in bed but in the evening Mrs Morant got in and told me the shocking news of Bishop Wilberforces[†] death. I went to evening church but *hated it*. This morning the hunt which will know no cessation began. I was at breakfast at 8 and had hardly sat down when Mrs Dan Smith came in her buggy to offer to take me about the town and we started at 9. I went to the man from whom I hired my saddle and bridle 5 months since and he declined to receive anything for it! He said that I had travelled so wonderfully that anyone might be proud to help me! Then with Captain Smith to the steamer office to choose a berth. My ticket is all right. I lose nothing. Then to the bank to cash the last of my circular

[*] See Queen Emma, p. 324.
[†] See Bishop Samuel Wilberforce, p. 344.

notes. I have spent £64 on the islands £10 a month. It seems a great deal as often I have been visiting. £12 I have spent in the Kilauea and £9 in horses. Then doing commissions from Hawaii. I got through a great deal in very little time. I was just beginning to pack when in came Mrs Severance who I was delighted to see. After she had gone I was just sitting down to lunch when Mrs Stirling came and I heard of you and a party at the Blackies where you were. I came up again and was beginning packing when Mr Greens card came up. He had no sooner gone than Miss Willis's came up, but I had her to my room and read her [your poem] 'In the Glen' which made her cry. I toiled then to finish some presents got 'a bit of dinner' and was just going to lie down when Mrs Atherton Mrs Alexander's sister came to ask me to go to stay with them till I left. Then 6 cards with bouquets of flowers, then Mrs Stirling who took me on a drive up the Valley in the short red twilight and then to her house. The moon was shining on it and men were catching fish by torchlight. [. . .]

I must make comments on your letters in the steamer for I am nearly run to death. There is but one thing in which I have never failed to my three beings and that is writing. These letters are 'tokens of gigantic toil'. Ah Ah Ah I hate leaving the islands. They are one large rat hole in which I have rioted most luxuriantly. Still I should be sorry to feel it less. I wonder whether in the purple distance my island life will seem less nice. My spurs my riding suit are put at the bottom of my trunk and my huge collection of ferns. Hawaii nei! So soon to be a dream with its endless summer!

Wednesday August 6th. Well I am longing to be away for each hour is rapidly undermining my strength. I never closed my eyes on Monday night and had all the old horrible achings from head to foot and have been miserable these 2 days. Mr Thompson from Hilo came at nine Mrs Severance soon after for an hour and a half then Mr Green for 3/4 of an hour then lunch then writing hasty letters to Kauai then Miss Willis to drive me up to see the Bishop. When I got back at 4.30 I went out to stores in the hotel buggy and to the Costa Rica, then dinner when the Damiens came saying I *must* call on Mrs W. Rice for she was expecting me in Kauai for 2 months and then I had to spend 1/2 an hour in the verandah in consequence of this card from a gentleman whose civilities I have rejected ever since I came. Since then I have worked like a slave and still two of my boxes are bulging heaps and little things are lying about. I have done and Oh how I hate doing it as a task in the midst of this toil a spatterwork packet for Mrs Robinson and finished one for Mrs

Alexander. In a few minutes Mrs Atherton her sister is coming for me to take me to some places and then I must by a great effort finish my packing. I feel as if the 'Costa Rica' would be a heaven of rest. I am certainly not so well apart from the fagging here. I have missed the riding so dreadfully the last 10 days. It was my life and without it I die. All comments on the altogether delightful letters I reserve for a separate letter. Care very much for its pet.

Its being
ILBIRD

Henrietta's only surviving letter concerns Isabella's adventures in Hawaii. It is reprinted in full below, and was written to their close friend Ella Blackie.

Tobermory, Mull Argyllshire
Sept 10th [1873]

My dearest Mrs Blackie

I have no idea where you are, so must enclose this to Mrs Lewis, in the hope it will reach you sooner or later. I greatly appreciated your long & kind letter, but I thought your life too oppressive to be borne, without great spirit & spring, the public weals, the heat, the living in necessarily darkened rooms, the wants of any interest & of any kindred spirit. However you were sacrificing yourself for the benefit of your boy & you have the approval of conscience.

I have had many affectionate messages for you from Isa. She sent in one letter her 'warm love to Mrs Blackie, & tell her that her not writing makes no difference. I understand it, but tell her I want to know' how her soul is. 'Tell her I see her Pro. greatly praised in American papers.' (This was after I told her you could not write.) Again, 'How nobly Mrs Blackie behaved about Robina, that was friendship stronger than death for Robina's fate was worse than death.' Again, 'My love to Mrs Blackie & tell her I liked the Pro.'s speech about me.' (This was the speech he made when he proposed her health at dinner one Saturday.)

I have since I wrote you last had 3 most delightful cheerful letters from her, she was not to leave the islands till this month, & then will have spent 8 months there! She is evidently better, for she views everything cheerfully, delights in my letters, approves of all I do, worries about nothing. She has continued to enjoy herself wonderfully and has ascended (on horseback) all the 3 great volcanic mountains of Hawaii. The last 3 letters have not contained a single word which has left other than a pleasant impression. Is not this delightful? But I am *very unhappy* about her, for such a sad disappointment awaits her. She is looking forward confidently to finding the Kers on her return (about Christmas) & alas! they are again ordered abroad. They are now in Edinburgh but their house is to be let furnished & they leave soon. It is deplorable, for great as the blank was to me, it will be ten-fold greater to *her*, who is so dependent on Bessie for her daily relaxation & *outlet*, & then the carriage, & 1000 things, will be such an indescribable loss. I should have wished her to have everything cheerful & pleasant in her first winter of 'asphyxiating civilisation', to keep up the good she has gained, & I see no prospect but dull lodgings, which might have been tolerated if *they* had been at hand coming in & out. I detest now the want of courage that held me back from taking that house, & running the risk. She would have liked it! & I *might* have had a cheerful home ready for her. There was everything at the time against it, & she says she quite understands my hesitation. The house is gone now, like every golden opportunity one lacks the pluck to grasp. 'Nothing venture, nothing have.'

I have had a most charming holiday, 'lark', 'spree', since I wrote to you! Did I ever tell you that I had proposed to Miss Kate Simson to go with me this summer to Stromness in Orkney? I never thought I should carry out so great an idea! I improved in strength decidedly before the end of my 3 weeks at Braemar, & much more after I came *here*, & Miss K.S. came up here on July 18th by the Clansman & together we went up the west coast, round Cape Wrath, to Scrabster Roads, whence on the 21st we crossed the Pentland Firth, to Stromness! There we stayed a fortnight on & off, visiting Kirkwall with its grand solemn cathedral, taking a cruise round 'the North Isles' in the little steamer 'Arcadia', seeing the stones of Stenness & Maes Howe.

We then extended our trip to Shetland! which I had regarded as beyond my reach. We were at Lerwick thence by steamer to Unst, then to Hillowick on the west side, where we stayed 4 nights, & saw all the glories of Shetland rock scenery. Back to Lerwick, & then back to Orkney for a few days, & then I made my way by Wick, Dingwall, Stroma, & Portree, & so caught the Clydesdale which brought me here once more. The tour occupied 5 weeks, & I enjoyed it *most thoroughly*, all was *new*, I could not arrange to have my letters sent after me, so I had no worries! I let all bothers *stand over*, & had 'no cares beyond to-day'. Shetland fascinated me even if it had no remarkable scenery, its remoteness & novelty give such a charm, it has the interest of a foreign country with the comfort of excellent English being spoken. There we were 150 miles north of the north of Scotland. It was my ambition to get beyond the parallel of 60°. I *never walked* but when not in boats I went about on nice shaggy ponies or in carts. It was the most thorough *change & recreation*. The weather was almost always fine, & in Shetland the north wind came unmistakable from icebergs not so very far off. Miss Kate S. was a capital companion, she had no fears, or fancies, never grumbled, enjoyed everything, made herself at home everywhere, was never tired, yet took the greatest care of me. It was an experiment, for we knew little of each other, but a perfect success. I feel I have laid in a store of new ideas & pleasant memories. We were for once not tied in any way, & just drifted about, without fixed plans, & I had nobody to be anxious about me.

I am now settled here probably for some time. It is not 3 weeks since I returned, & I had an accumulation of letters to answer, & I felt so thoroughly *dissipated*, that for about ten days I had to *drive & goad* myself to work of any kind. Now, I have got into regular habits once more, & hope to study. Mary is at home, her mother is better for the present, & Mary seems happy, but is not strong. She goes to her new Edinburgh home in 3 weeks. I wonder where you are. Tell the Pro. I saw the Old Man of Hoy look over the sea, & that I was always saying to myself in Shetland boats, 'Landlubbers we, & new to boats, &c. &c.' With much love,

Believe me to be, my very dear one,

Your truly affectionate, HENRIETTA AMELIA BIRD

Colorado

By the time Henrietta wrote these words, Isabella had sailed on to San Francisco. Bothered by its 'clang', she realised she preferred to be alone in the wilderness and decided to depart at once for the Rocky Mountains. Travelling first by stagecoach to Tahoe, then by mail train to Cheyenne, then on horseback for Denver, Isabella had several adventures. She wrote in *A Lady's Life* that she saw grizzlies and wolves; and she spent several weeks on the plains with a family of settlers, helping them harvest tomatoes, squash, pumpkin and maize. Unfortunately, Isabella's letters from this period seem not to have survived. Those we have pick up several weeks after she has reached Colorado, and after she has made her famous ascent of Long's Peak. These later letters chronicle the winter wonderland she observed on a series of snowy rides to Palmer Lake, Halls Gulch and Breckenridge Pass. These rides, while beautiful, often feel rather aimless – which, in fact, they were. Isabella had no real base in Colorado – no foothold in the mountains to call her home – with the possible exception of Estes Park:[*] a beautiful hollow in the mountains near the city of Greeley. Indeed, the most notable part of Isabella's surviving letters from Colorado is her snowbound stay in Estes Park, when she discovered that she had awakened the passions of a disfigured, one-eyed desperado named Jim Nugent[†] (a.k.a. 'Rocky Mountain Jim'). A poet-trapper, Jim seems to have inspired in Isabella equal measures of terror and excitement. 'I cannot but think of Mr Wilson on Hawaii', she remarked to her sister, 'and his quiet undemonstrative un-annoying ways, and comparing him with this dark tempestuous, terrible character, wondering how it is that the last is so fascinating.' Isabella, at this point, was forty-two years old, and she had been away from Henrietta for nearly two years.

Great Platte Canyon Thursday Night Oct 23. 1873

My Pet

I dont see how letters can be written. After a long days ride I am so sleepy and wholesomely tired that I really cant write. Here are 4 days unjournalised.

Monday 19. Left Estes Park with Mr Power at 9.30. Lunched at Millers. Met 'Mountain Jim' and was by him guided to cross a deep

---

[*] A park in the Colorado sense is a high-lying enclosed piece of woodland and pasture, usually ringed by mountains on all sides.
[†] See Jim Nugent, p. 336.

and dangerous river on a beaver dam. Reached Longmount[*] at 6. 40 miles.

Tuesday. Left Longmount at 9.30 Col Heath[†] escorting me 8 miles. Cold and eerie journey over the plains. Reached Mrs Evans[‡] just outside of Denver at 4.30 just as snow storm began. Warm welcome. 30 miles.

Wednesday in Denver. Saw Gov Hunt[§] and Mr Byers.[¶] Mr Power escorted me about. Fitted out.

Thursday. Left Mrs Evans at 10. Gov Hunt took me out of Denver. Reached this (Van Warmers) at 3. 20 miles. Another snowstorm coming on.

This will tell me what I did in these days in case I can never fill up the outlines. They have been pleasant days kindness and courtesy everywhere but the toothache today is burdensome. Evans has provided me with an excellent horse and saddle and I have a new Bloomer Suit with a bear jacket over it. On Monday we were to have left at 8, but Mr Powers horse was lost and we hung on till 9.30. The leave takings were very warm. Mrs Dewy[‖] who is not demonstrative cried and kissed me many times and said 'I do hate to have you go.'

It was a glorious ride. The day was solemnly still and warm. We passed through the gates of rock solemnly down deep gorges in which the unsunned snow lay deep caught glimpses of far off snow clad giants rising into a deep sad blue walked down all the hills and at 2 emerged into the ravine behind the foothills and stopped at a cabin where two brothers and a hired man are 'keeping bach'.[**] It was so trim and clean and never missed a woman. They gave us milk and bread and we left at 3. The day before Mr Waller and Mr Kavanagh[††] had come back from Longmount bringing news that a bridge was broken down and they had both gone in over their horses heads! This was terrible and every new person suggested some new way to get across.

In the narrowest part of the St Vrain canyon I saw a fearful object in the distance who Mr Power said was Jim. He looked more terrific than I ever saw him & I wanted to turn back fearing either he was not sober or in an 'ugly fit'. However Mr P. said his chivalry and respect for women never deserted him and when he got up to us he dismounted and my

---

[*] Township on the plains.
[†] See Colonel Heath, p. 327.
[‡] See Jane Evans under Griff Evans, p. 325. Given the inaccessibility of Estes Park, it made sense for the Evans family to winter in Denver – especially since Jane Evans was pregnant with her sixth child in 1879 when Isabella visited.
[§] See Alexander Hunt, p. 327.
[¶] See William Byers, p. 318.
[‖] See Mr and Mrs Dewy, p. 322.
[**] Colorado expression, used for a group of men (usually bachelors) who have set up house together in the mountains.
[††] See Mr Kavanagh, p. 329.

fears diminished. He is a most extraordinary man. His appearance was frightful but as soon as he spoke he was fascinating with his gentle cosy manner low musical voice and slight Irish brogue. He told us it was a fearful place ahead but if we followed the tracks of his horses through the bush we could cross on a beaver dam. He leant on my horse and said 'I'm so happy to have met you so very happy God bless you' and his poor disfigured face literally beamed with nice kindly feeling. Mr Power remarked 'What a thorough gentleman Jim is and how very much he likes you' both which things were true. He likes Mrs Dewy very much and Mr Dewy says he sees a great difference in his manner since he began to like two such good women. I asked him to call on Mrs Dewy.

We had the greatest difficulty in finding the dam a fearful place just room for a horse on it with 8 feet water on each side but the horses being afraid went over daintily. It was a delightful ride then for 12 miles in the purpling evening. I altogether liked Mr Power. It was not very nice riding along fast in the dark along an unknown road but we found our way to the same inn where I was with Dr and Mrs Hutchinson.[*] They are very kind there but they make strong pure green tea which kept me awake nearly all night. When Mr Waller came back from Longmount he said there was 'a dreadful man' who had been a colonel in the rebel army who was determined to be introduced to me an amateur sculptor who talked largely about art and before I had finished tea Mr Sigley[†] the landlord said this Col Heath was there tormenting him to introduce him and he could do nothing but do so but he thought I could easily make an excuse for getting rid of him. He brought him up to the ladies parlour and I said I had only a few minutes for I wanted to finish my English letters, and he stayed 1/2 an hour and was more 'dreadful' than I expected. I saw at once that he thought because I was travelling I was rich and that he was resolved to make up to me. I was rude as I could be with politeness but he never went till Mr Power came and asked for my letters.

Mr P. went 3/4 of a mile to get me bromide of potassium. He had told me on the way a sad story which had wrecked his life and when he wished me goodbye he said my sympathy and kindness had made him happier than he had been for 10 years, that he should never forget the ride he wished there were anything he could do for me. Everyone had delighted in him at Estes Park because he was always doing little considerate things for people and never thought of himself and though a

[*] See Dr Francis Blake Hutchinson and Alice Hutchinson, p. 328.
[†] See Captain William Beach Sigley, p. 341.

very shrewd and humorous observer of character he never said an unkind thing. Mountain Jim who likes me very much said I could not have a nicer escort and it was true. I do like a gentleman who always knows the right thing to say and do. It seemed very dreary without him on Tuesday and the day though fine looked as if a storm were brewing.

As I was getting directions Col. Heath came up and said he had brought his horse to escort me over the intricate part of the way and as Mrs Sigley said that he was not a bad or disreputable man I was obliged to make the best of it. It was very cold then changed to very hot and finally to an east windy cold that was insupportable. If my sense of the ludicrous had not predominated I should have thought of the deadly weapon in my pocket. He was egregious. 'Making love' was the only phrase that could be used, delicate flattery, all arts by which he supposed he could make himself agreeable. I might have said he proposed 10 times. I never spoke but to snub him but a man bent on money is not easily snubbed and I very much fear and have good reason to fear that when I return to Longmount unless there is some jovial spirit down from Estes Park he will ride up with me on pretence of elk hunting there. If I had any means of knowing when I should get back I would get Mountain Jim to come for me for there are things which become unendurable.

It is a dreary ride of 30 miles over the Plains to Denver very little settled and trails going in all directions. The only directions given were 'Steer south and keep the best beaten track.' It seemed like embarking on the ocean without a compass. Those rolling brown waves on which you see a horse a mile and a half off impress you strangely and at noon it began to darken up for another storm. The mountains swept down in blackness to the Plains and the higher peaks assumed a ghastly grimness horrible to behold. I cannot say that I disliked the ride though on horseback I think any company is better than none. It was free and breezy and the horse which bucked on leaving Longmount went well and was quite companionable. Sometimes herds of cattle were browsing on the sun cured grass, sometimes herds of horses – now and then I met a horseman with a rifle slung on his saddle or a rude waggon but oftener a waggon with a white tilt called 'a prairie schooner', sometimes a train of them with cattle mules horses the exodus of whole families lured from the States by colonised accounts of Colorado. I met one large lean drove of Texas cattle herded by 3 wild looking men on horseback who were followed by 2 waggons containing a large family with young children. They had come 1000 miles. That night they must have been nearly frozen to death camping out in the deep snow. Once I rode off on the prairie to get a nearer view of the prairie wolf which illustrated the danger of leaving the beaten track for it was long before I could find my way back again. This beast is like a very large jackal dark gray and runs from you. Everywhere there were the carcasses of those who fell in the wilderness.

At two I came to a bleak ranch where I got oats for Birdie* and bread and milk and an hours rest for myself. It was fully cold and windy when I came out and the next 11 miles were a race with the fast coming storm. At the top of every prairie roll I expected to see Denver but it was not till past 4 that I looked from a considerable height on the great 'City of the Plains' the metropolis of the territories. Then I got off put on my skirt and got on again sideways using the horn as a pummel. To ride sideways now seems to be as if having the use of 2 feet one was compelled always to hop on one. There the great braggart city of 16000 souls lay spread out brown and treeless upon a brown and treeless plain which here seemed to nourish nothing but the Spanish bayonette or soap plant and southernwood. The Platte with a scrubby fringe of cottonwood wound along by Denver and up its course 2 miles I saw a fearful sand storm coming which in a very few minutes buried the city, blotting it out of sight with a brown cloud. I had to trust entirely to Birdies wonderful sagacity to find Evans shanty. Just as I got up with a wind that doubled one up a snow storm began. Had it come an hour sooner I should never have found the trail.

Mrs Evans was quite delighted to see me for the sake of my budget of news. They have only a kitchen with a bed and 2 bed closets with windows in them in one of which I slept with Mrs E.'s niece.† They made me very comfortable as their guest the 2 nights I was there. Mrs E. is such a very nice Welshwoman and brings up her children beautifully. She is expecting her confinement soon and is nervous and sleepless but one dose of bromide of potassium took away all her nervousness and gave her a good night. It is a truly blissful medicine. It has done Mr Dewy a great deal of good. I seemed to have so much news to tell Mrs E. I slept all night. We rose very late the next morning. It was cloudless and an intense frost and everybody thought it too cold to get up and light the fire – 4 inches of snow were on the ground.

After breakfast Mrs E.'s niece and I walked into Denver. We first went to see Jinny, Evans eldest daughter who is living with Mrs Edwards‡ sister. Then I went and saw Mr Byers editor of the leading Denver paper

---

* See Birdie, p. 316.
† See Mary Jane Roberts, under John Buchanan, p. 317.
‡ See Mrs Edwards, under Sam Edwards, p. 324.

and he advised me not to take the cars for Colorado Springs but to ride. Then I went to Mr Powers who walked with me to Gov Hunts office. I found Mr Hunt as pleasant as Miss Kingsley* said he was a jovial genial spirit. He also advised my riding to the Springs not by the road but by the cañons at the base of the mountains. He wrote down the settlers houses where I was to stop and gave me a circular letter of introduction. He said I might ride as safely alone through the mountains of Colorado as down the main street of Denver. This is truly a glory for the territory. He said he had heard that I was an invalid but could not think such a horsewoman could be one. Then Mr Byers went with me to the Bank where the panic being over I got 2 circular notes cashed, which must be the limit of my tourist expenditure. Both prognosticated superb weather & now I fear that I have come in for a terrible exceptional winter.

Barkers Ranch Plum Creek 26 miles south of Denver Friday night Oct 24. I then went to an English hotel where Mr Byers got me 3 English mutton chops! Then he went with me to see after the mare and order it for tomorrow morning, then I bought a bear jacket and went back to the Evans. Denver has composite streets with good stores, but being the outpost town of civilisation they present a singular aspect. Here are 'rig stores' with every article for the Plains and camping out saddle stores, where nothing is sold but huge Mexican saddles, Indian stores and no end of fur stores and fur depots, for Denver is the entrepot of the whole fur trade of the Rocky Mountains. Crowds solely masculine. I only saw 5 women the whole day. Men in every rig, hunters and trappers in buckskin suits, men of the Plains in huge blue cloaks with belts and revolvers, teamsters in leather suits, horsemen in fur coats and caps and buffalo hide boots with the hair outside and camping blankets behind their huge saddles, Broadway dandies in light kid gloves, rich English tourists clean comely and supercilious and heaps of horse Indians on their small ponies and their buckskin dresses sewn all over with beads and red blankets wound round them faces painted vermilion and long straight hair and squaws riding astride with furs over their saddles all picturesque and wild. I had to mend my clothes and make a new bag.

Yesterday morning at 9 the man brought my mare saying she was a little demon she had bucked on the bridge and had thrown him. I found it was that he had put the wrong bridle on it. It is a wild horse lassoed and tamed after their fashion by the Ute Indians,† and when it dislikes

* See Rose Kingsley, p. 330.
† See the Ute people, p. 343.

anything it bucks. Birdie is a nice beast, except difficult to mount, always going away when one gets one foot in the stirrup. I kept riding sideways and thus rode through Denver without attracting any attention. I called and wished Jinny goodbye and then went for Gov Hunt who went outside the town with me to put me on the right track. He gave me a sort of pass, as I may come up on a large Indian camp of the friendly Ute Indians but they scare people sometimes in order to get tobacco. It is sad about these Indians. The Indians of the mountains and those of the Plains are traditional antagonists and the Utes have taken the war path against the Cheyennes who are on the war path against the whites in the neighbourhood of Colorado Springs.

I got off and took off my skirt a mile from Denver being in very bad pain and you cannot imagine the unspeakable relief of getting on astride. It was a lovely Indian summer sky and so warm that snow on the ground seemed strange. The first few miles are over the plains but you gradually come on rolling country along the base of the mountains and a stream well fringed with cottonwood along which there are settlers houses about every half mile making it a very cheerful ride. I passed and met waggons frequently and often came upon the track of the quaint narrow gauge Rio Grande Railway. I picked up a muff with 500 dollars in it and found the owner.

At 3 I left the road for the ranch indicated, Mr Van Warmers, a large frame house the door of which was opened by a most repulsive man. On giving him Gov Hunts note he said their house was full but a very agreeable ladylike looking woman coming out said she could make up a bed on a sofa. The house had more pretensions than any I have yet seen being papered and carpeted and there was a hired girl. There was a lady there a Mrs Hutton from Laramie who kindly gave me 1/2 her bed, a very tall elegant woman the first woman who settled in the Rocky Mountains. She had a waggon with beds tent and tent floor cooking stove and every luxury a man to manage everything a light buggy and a most superior hired girl. She is consumptive and had been camping out for 3 months. I soon saw that there was a screw loose in the house and that the man was a perfect brute and this lady told me at night that he was nearly killing his wife with cruelty. She was very attractive. At meals the 3 hired men and 2 hired girls sat with the family.

It turned black and cold at night and Friday opened fearfully with a hard frost a biting N.E. wind and a sky surcharged with snow. Mrs Hutton an old friend of the lady was leaving because of the domestic troubles and I left just after breakfast, giving up the Platte cañon because of the weather. It seemed awful to face a coming storm. I saw the car of the Rio Grande Railway pass all cushioned and warmed while I was on the bleak hill side among snow and I rather wished to be in it. I only got 4 miles and the storm came on so badly and I got into a kitchen where 11 wretched travellers were sheltering all with the snow melting on them and dripping on the floor. I was so pleasant in the two hours I waited that though they keep an 'accommodation house' they said they would take nothing for I was such 'good company'!

It continued snowing but seemed as if it would not be deep and at one I saddled Bird and set off again and rode 4 more miles, fording a frozen creek which let the horse through the ice to my great terror. I cant describe my feelings on that ride. The utter loneliness and dumbness of all things, the quietly falling snow, the obliterated mountains, the darkness, the intense cold, the appalling look of nature. There was nothing to be afraid of and though I cant say that I enjoyed it yet I felt it was all doing me good. I was well clad except my feet and kept myself warm and had an excellent horse, but still it was eerie. I resolved to stop as soon as the snow hid the track, and put up at Mr Barkers, a ranch which had been recommended to me. It was very tolerable. The cold became awesome. It reminded me of a scene in Whittiers Snowbound.[*] All the stock came round the house with mute appeals for shelter. Sheep dogs got in. Men went out muffled up and came back shivering and shaking the snow from their feet. A most pleasant settler on his way to Denver came in all snow covered unable to get further. The 'gray man' had a stentorian voice, smoked a clay pipe, derided the courtesy of English manners raged at English people but it was a pleasant and diverting evening. I had no sheets, and the cold in the night was so awesome that I pulled the rag carpet from the floor to put over my bed.

Colorado Springs (Mr Lillers[†] Oct 28. [. . .] On Saturday I left the Barkers at 8.30. More snow had fallen the frost was intense the sun brilliant the snow sparkling like diamonds. I lost the track once but footmarks of some beast made it pretty legible. After riding an hour I had to get off for the horse could hardly keep on her feet because of balls 4 inches high in her shoes. I met a boy who told me I could get a chisel at a house nearby and when I went up it was the people whose muff I had found and they received me very warmly and made me hot coffee and gave me two tumblers of cream. they were a most pleasant people, Welsh from Glamorganshire. I started again and rode 12 miles. It was

[*] See John Greenleaf Whittier, p. 344.
[†] See J. Elsom Liller, p. 331.

getting very awful. At one I turned off from the road and went 2 miles into the hills by an untrodden path with many gates to open, forded a steep sided creek and at the entrance to a fantastic gorge came upon an elegant frame house to which I had an introduction belonging to Mr Perry son of a millionaire banker at St Louis.[*] He was away but his sister a very elegantly dressed girl came and asked me in to dinner. There were all the refinements of a table and a black table maid and stewed venison and various luxuries. They have 5 negro servants who were their slaves.

After dinner a man cousin rode with me into the Park.[†] It is very grand and beautiful with singular 'monumental' rocks from 50 to 400 feet high and the gates are formed by these. They are bright vermilion green buff orange and sometimes all combined their gay tinting a contrast to the disastrous looking snow and the sombre pines. A grand cañon comes down on the Park and we crossed the creek at the foot of this on the ice which broke through and let both horses through which was not nice nor was it nice for Birdie afterwards to put her foot into a marmots hole covered with snow and in recovering herself fall 3 times on her nose. When we got back Miss Perry pressed me to remain. She has been travelling with her father and family in Europe for 3 years to Egypt Palestine Asia Minor Turkey Moscow and the other European countries and was most intelligent in her descriptions. It seemed so odd to have a beautiful bedroom (icy cold though) hot water and all luxuries. The snow began at 6 and fell all night with intense frost so that in the morning there were 8 inches of pure bridecake looking snow glittering in the sun.

Miss Perry gave me a pair of her brothers sox to put over my miserable boots and some wine and I set out to break my own way for 2 miles. There a single waggon had gone through making a legible track for 30 miles otherwise the snow was absolutely pathless. The sky was cloudless and I made the long ascent up the Arkansas Divide the mountains came sweeping down in great cañons on my right to the valley and on my left the foothills rose crowned with fantastic rocks like castles. All was buried under a glittering shroud of snow. Silence reigned. The babble of the streams was bound in fetters of ice. No branches creaked. No breath stirred. I rode 4 hours in this solemn solitude till I came to a ranch where I got a basin of bread and milk and feed for Birdie. She is really a good beast considering that she not only has the wild horse blood which makes the bronco so dangerous but is the real wild horse herself. She

---

[*] See John Dietz Perry, p. 337.
[†] Perry Park (as it is known today), not Estes Park.

bucks if she dislikes anything and makes huge shies but her soul is harmless and she is so very wise. She puts out one foot and tries a bridge and smells it and if it is not safe she backs off it. At this house I found that it was Sunday so utterly had I lost count – now I have to give my beast today the Sabbath out of which she was cheated.

On again I rode an awful ride the snow now 13 inches deep always ascending in the loneliness and silence. 'Beware the pass the old man said' but just as the sun set behind a snowy peak I stood on the top of the Divide 7975 feet above both oceans. Here in unutterable loneliness lay a frozen lake. Now I felt eerie. Owls hooted among the pine trees, the trail was obscure, the country was not settled and the cold was something fearful. My feet had lost all feeling and one was frozen in the wooden stirrup. I found I had only gone 15 miles in 8 1/2 hours and must look about for a place to sleep. The eastern sky was something such as I never saw. It had been chrysoprase that turned to aquamarine and that to the bright full green of an emerald! Then suddenly the whole changed and flushed with the pure bright rose colour of the afterglow. Birdie was sliding with every step and I was almost crying with the intense cold when I reached a house Gov Hunt had mentioned but they said 17 snowbound men were lying on the floors and I had better ride 1/4 further which I did and reached the house of a German from Eisenau with a sweet young wife and her mother. Everything about them was attractive and their house so tastefully ornamented. My feet came to themselves with something that could only be called torture. I had excellent food and a room to myself with a basin to wash in!

The morning was gray and sour but brightened and warmed. I rode 12 miles over the snow without any incident till I came to a large ranch where were 8 boarders each one looking nearer the grave than the other. I got bread and milk and feed for my beast. Then a most charming old lady a most intimate friend of the Coans at Hilo kept me for 2 hours and kissed me when I came away. Here I was to leave the main road and diverge through Monument Park a ride of 12 miles among fantastic rocks but I lost my way and came to an end of all tracks in a wild cañon. I went about 6 miles. I came back and took another track and rode 8 miles without seeing a creature. I then came to strange gorges with wonderful upright rocks and turning through a gate of rocks found myself in what I knew must be Glen Eyrie as wild a glen as imagination ever pictured. I could not help riding up it then rode down a valley close under some of the highest and ghastliest peaks of the Rocky Mountains wild cold awe inspiring scenery. I forded a creek several times and then came upon a cluster of decayed houses, Colorado City, and then 2 miles off on a ridge looking towards the mountains I saw the bleak scattered looking houses of Colorado Springs, the goal of my ride of 150 miles.

I got off put on a skirt and rode sideways but it did not look like a place where any deference to foolish prejudices was necessary. Such a queer embryo place just set down there. I found the Lillers a single room at the back of the printing office serving them for kitchen parlour bedroom and 2 prairie dogs a kitten and a deer hound also inhabit it. They made me at home at once. They are very bright pleasant people. I like them much and felt in 1/2 an hour as if we were old friends. Mr Liller cooked a steak while Mrs got the tea. There is an air of English comfort and refinement about this room. It was a very pleasant evening. Mrs L. at 8 walked with me to the boarding house where I sleep. We sat some time in the parlour talking with the landlady and some were reading and others playing backgammon. Opposite me was a door into a bedroom and a young man dressed was sitting on a bed supported by another and a very sick looking young man kept going in and out. A great deal of laughing was going on. The door was half shut then one young man came to the door saying 'Shields quick a candle' and then there were movings about in the room. All this time during these movings I saw two large white feet at the end of the bed sticking up. I watched and watched hoping those feet would move but no and somehow they grew stiffer and whiter to my thinking & then my horrible suspicion deepened that while we were sitting there a human spirit untended and desolate had passed forth into the night. Then a man came out bringing clothes and then the sick young man came in groaning and sobbing and then the man who had supported the other said to me the man who had died was this young mans only brother. And the landlady took no notice but said afterwards to me 'It turns the house upside down when they just come and die we shall be half the night laying him out.'

I could not sleep for cold and all night heard that groaning and sobbing. Yesterday Tuesday I went into the parlour to get a needle and the door of that room was open and children were running in and out and the landlady was sweeping there and called to me to come in for the needle and there with the sun shining through the unblinded window lay that thing of terror the corpse not even covered with a sheet laid on some chairs not even placed straight! It was buried in the afternoon and from the looks of the brother who continues to sob and moan I should think he would be gone in less than a month. The dead man was sitting in the parlour 2 hours before he died and walked alone into his room. The Lillers say that so many come in the very last stages of consumption, thinking that Colorado will cure them, without even money enough to pay for the coarsest board.

Wed. Oct 29. [. . .] You will see that though there are no unearthly glories and fascination as on the Sandwich Islands that I am getting on very well much better than I expected before or at first. I am glad I decided to remain, for 3 months of such a nomadic open air life in which I feel *tolerably* well *should* benefit me. It is a mans life but all people here seem to think it fitting for me! I am caring always for it, but I get letters seldomer than on Hawaii. I cannot get any now till Nov. 15th and that makes it dill. I hope it is enjoying itself. It is such a sweet little thing. I wonder if it will hate that harmless photo which I sent from San Francisco. It is exactly like me.*

You should propel me to people who will get me employment to write, for I seem to have so much to say now and writing travels is not hard brain work. [. . .] Have you read the description of this place in Good Words. The scenery though Pikes Peak is 14 300 feet high is nothing to Estes Park and the more I see of houses in which people board the more delightful I think Evans where I can 'riot most luxuriantly'. It is its last year. A waggon road is to be built this winter and a hotel next spring. Everyone says there is no similar place in Colorado. I cannot yet send the thrilling Longs Peak letter for Mr Liller wants me to write the ascent for 'Out West' the Colorado monthly and I must keep the letter to copy out parts. I should like to find myself riding down the McGinns Gulch in the glory of the sunset into the matchless beauties of Estes Park!

Its thing
ILB

Great Gorge of Manitou Rocky Mountains Oct 29/73

My own Pet,

I dispatched a 12 page letter with nothing annoying in it this morning from Colorado Springs and now begin another. These are wild ways. Having my luggage in a pack and my conveyance a horse I can stay wherever there is feed and shelter for us both. Feed for me has become a most unimportant matter. I am now eating and sleeping like a hunter. This is a fearful place a rushing torrent in a valley and mountains covered with snow rising on 3 sides and overhanging it to a height of nearly 15 000 feet. It is grand and awful and has a strange solemn beauty like the beauty of death and locked in these snowy horrors a mile from here is the Ute Pass

---

* See the photograph of Isabella taken in San Francisco in the plate section.

by which if all be well tomorrow I traverse the heart for the Mountains. But all may be lost for want of a horseshoe nail. One of Birdie's shoes is loose and not a nail can be got. She amuses everyone just as Pincher does with his queer ways. She always pushes after me and today got quite into a house and pushed the parlour door open! She always follows me with her head on my shoulder, licking and nuzzling, all for sugar and sometimes when anyone else takes hold of her she rears and kicks and all the bad bronco soul comes into her eyes. She has such a cunning pretty face and makes such a funny noise when I go up to her. At the stables the men make such a fuss with her and call her pet. She gallops up and down hill and over the roughest ground and never requires a whip.

The weather is again perfect, a cloudless sky and hot sun and the snow is all off the plains and these lower valleys. If it keeps so my tour will be truly magnificent. Everyone has encouraged it. I packed my pack and carried it and went to the Lillers where I had been mending stockings all the morning – they drove in a buggy and I rode by them. We crossed the mesa a high hill from which the air was extraordinary – huge leaves 200 feet high of vermilion rock against a black ground of snowy mountains surmounted by Pikes Peak. Then into cavernous Glen Eyrie with its fantastic needles of coloured rock. Here we 'called' at General Palmers* to say I could not stay there – a perfect eyrie and the beautiful hall full of buffalo elk and deer heads skins of all animals stuffed birds bear robes and all kinds of Indian and other trophies. Then through a gate of huge red rocks we passed into the fantastic valley called the Garden of the Gods from which the views were grand. Then into a gorge down which the Fountain River rushed. The Lillers were afraid of going further, it was getting so cold and I left them with regret, and rode into this chill and solemn gorge seeing only far off the bright sunlight reddening the peaks. I put up Birdie at a stable, and there being no other place to put myself up but this huge hotel I came here for once to be in luxury. They charge 6 dollars a day but it is now 1/2 price and instead of 400 fashionables flirting and dressing there are about 15 people. There are huge fires and 6 blankets on the beds. There are 7 medicinal springs. There are the usual dying people speaking fast like Ella and coughing their hearts out. It will be the 3rd night in Colorado I have slept on anything but hay or straw. It seems strange to have the luxuries of life in my room.

I am indescribably shocked to see a telegram in the paper that Dr Candlish[†] is dead! Oh how melancholy how sad how dreary! Edinburgh losing him and Dr Guthrie in 6 months never more to see that grotesque

---

* See General William Jackson Palmer, p. 336.
† See Robert Smith Candlish, p. 319.

face and those nervous ways never to see him managing the Assembly. It is sickening to think how they are all going. There is no security about anyone past 60. [. . .]

Bergens Park Oct 31. Well this cabin was so dark and I was so sleepy that I could write nothing last night but the frost is so severe this morning that I cannot start till the bright hot sun melts the ice for fear of slipping. I left Manitou at 10 yesterday morning having waited 15 minutes at the breakfast table before the waiter came and 15 more before he brought anything! I went down to the stable and Birdie who was loose came trotting down the middle asking for sugar. I forgot to tell you that one trick that amuses everyone is that she swells herself out 6 inches when she is saddled then collapses leaving the girth hanging loose. It is a very tiresome trick for unless one always remembers it, as soon as one takes hold of the saddle to get on it turns round and she runs back kicking! No nails could be got and her shoe was hanging by 2.

The morning was perfect so was the whole day not a cloud freezing in the shade and summer heat in the sun. Awe inspiring the snowclad pine skirted mountains looked as I entered their dark recesses and on the edge of the Fountain torrent began the ascent of 20 miles. I saw the mineral fountains sparkling in their basins and sending up their full perennial jets. There was all the time the snowborn Fountain, brighter than any stream because it tumbles over rose red granite, rocky or dis-integrated, a truly fair stream cutting or forcing its way through fringes of crystalline ice thumping with a hollow sound in cavernous recesses of darkened cañons or leaping in foam from heights with rush and swish always bright and riotous, dashing through gates of rock, pine hung, pine bridged, pine buried, twinkling and laughing in the sunshine or frowning in dowie* dens in the blue gloom of pines. And here for a time owing to the more Southern latitude [I] met trees of other climes. Here were dwarf oaks willows cotton woods large rustling aspens shivering in undying remorse the hazel and the filbert white cedar trailing juniper and spruce jostled each other for a precarious foothold and the majestic redwood of the Pacific met the exquisite balsam pine of the Atlantic slopes. And above towered the toothy peaks of the glittering mountains rising in purest white against the sunny blue. Grand glorious awesome but Oh not loveable. I would not give for it all one Hilo gulch or one day of those soft dreamy skies whose very tears are balm. (I cant write for with my left hand I am rocking a cradle.)

---

* Scottish word for dismal, low-spirited or sad.

Up ever the road being blasted out of the bright red rock which often overhung it the natural width of the cañon not being more than from 15 to 20 feet. The narrowness made it superb ever winding with the thunder of the Fountain which you cross about 8 times almost deafening. Sometimes the sun in all its glory struck the rock and it was very hot then one entered gorges never sunned where the snow lay deep and the crowded pines made dark twilight and the river roared under ice bright fringed with icicles. There was one gorge so dark and tomblike that I felt quite eerie. But at last the Pass opened out on an upland park sunlit. I stopped and got Birdies shoe fastened and got some shoe nails and 2 miles further I stopped at a house to get feed for us both. They were very pleasant people though like all Western folk they asked legions of questions. A very gentlemanly looking traveller came in who after some talking introduced himself as Colonel Kittridge* from Mount Vernon, VT. [. . .]

I then turned off the road up a long ascent deep in snow. It did not seem the way, and I tied up the pony and walked some distance to a cabin to enquire when I found her just like Pincher trotting after me! We had 8 miles to go part of the way through pine forest which I disliked particularly for it was all snow and ice and we could hardly keep on our feet and we had to cross several creeks on ice which broke through. I saw a beautiful white fox a skunk some chipmunks and squirrels owls crows and crested blue jays. I dislike forest alone because it is so dark and one never knows what may appear from behind the trees. That forest is full of bears and pumas. At last when the sun was slanting I got through the woods to Bergens Park which Mrs Lillers thinks the most beautiful thing she has seen. It is a fair mountain park all buff sun dried hay with a stream fringed with the everlasting cottonwood and from low ranges the pines sweep down in clumps leaving fair glades of grass where one looks for mansions. The south end is completely closed up at a distance by the huge bulk of Pikes Peak very like Mont Blanc snow clothed and pine fringed while beyond the other end are peaks and towers, wonderful in blue and violet colour and beyond these sharply defined against the clear green sky the mere glistening peaks of the snowy range 200 miles away! It was truly fair but not loveable and freezing hard, making one think of the land where 'their summers always last'. I dont like winter. It is true of that glorious climate [of Hawaii] 'Who so drinketh of that water shall thirst again.'

---

* See Colonel Kittridge, p. 330.

Isabella continued to ride back to Denver, encountering miners, teamsters and hunters on the way. The solitary ride was punctuated by the hospitality of the set-tlers' homes, as well as by the howls of wolves and the hooting of owls in the barren winter landscape. 'I fear you will be tired of these monotonous unenthusiastic Rocky Mountain letters,' she wrote her sister. 'I am wearying so to hear from you. In my long lonely rides I think mainly of you and of *them* and how very poor the world now is.' But the scenery too was fantastic. The mountains impressed her even when she was lost, as happened temporarily on November 4, 1873, in the vicinity of Pike's Peak.

That ride concentrated all my faculties on finding the way. The trail for the most part keeps in sight of Tarryall Creek one of the large affluents of the Pratte and is walled in on both sides by high mountains some-times so close together as to leave only the narrowest cañon at others breaking wide apart till after winding and climbing for 25 miles, one arrives in a barren park rock girdled watered by a rapid fordable stream as long as the Ouse snow fed and fantastic rocky hills snow covered brightened only by a small growth of the beautiful silver spruce. It was most wild and unlike other parts. I went up one great ascent where hills were tumbled about and suddenly across the broad ravine rising above the sunny grass and the deep green pines rose in most glowing and shaded red against the glittering blue a magnificent and unearthly range of mountains as shapely as you could see rising into colossal points, cut by deep blue ravines, broken cuts sharks teeth, with gigantic pinnacles and knobs rising from their forever inaccessible sides a sight fair to look upon, a glowing heavenly unforgettable sight and only 4 miles off. They were just the colours which painters give to mountains in the desert and Asia Minor and one could not believe them forever uninhabited for on them rose as in the east the similitude of stately castles not the grey cas-tellated feudal towers of Europe but Moorish architecture the out-growth of the solid rock. They were such an indescribable colour deepest and reddest near their pine draped bases softening into inde-scribable tenderness till their highest summits rose all flushed and as clear so that you might believe they were taking on the flush of sunset. Broken ravines, all fantastic rocks cleft and cañoned by a river and a tender unearthly light over all, the apparent warmth of a glowing clime, while I on the north side was in the pure unsullied snow.

I rode up and down hills laboriously finding out a track getting off and walking in deep snow down ice clad hills, often stopping to enjoy that changeless glory, always seeing some new ravine or miraculous colour or fantasy of form. I did like that. Then down where the trail was locked in a deep cañon a beauty of another kind, barely room for both, and then the stream wound in and out, pyramidal spruce and the beautiful silver spruce fringing its banks and often falling across it in artistic grace while now behind as if in the glory of an eternal sunset lay those flaming and fantastic peaks. One singular effect was produced by the combination of winter and summer. The trail all the time was on the north side of the hills and the snow lay deep and pure while not a trace lay on the south side whose abundant lawns basked in the summer. The pitch pine with its monotonous and somewhat ungainly form had also disappeared, the white pine was becoming scarce both being displaced by the shapely spruce with its picturesque slim spires. Valley and cañon were passed as the sun lay low and slanting. I crossed a lake on the ice then came on a park surrounded by low contoured rocky hills above which huge mountains rose. Here in some brushwood we crossed a deepish stream on the ice and fell through and the water was fearfully cold. All these streams become bigger as you reach the neighbourhood of their source and the trail disappeared in a rapid river as wide and deep as the Ouse which we forded twice. Then ever ascending to the verge of the timberline in eternal frost and unsullied snow timber scattered and dwarfed by cold and wind, solitudes such as one reads of in the High Alps, no sound but a crackle which the snow makes the pitiful howls of wolves, the hoot of owls. The sun to me had long set, the peaks that had blushed were pale and sad the twilight deepened into a green but still excelsior!

No happy homes I saw, the light of household fires beaming warm and bright. Above the spectral mountains lifted their cold summits against the sky. I for some time feared that the cabin to which I had been directed had been confused with the rocks when just as the ground was freezing too hard to be safe I saw a log cabin up a gulch and found it was Mrs Links daughter in law of the pleasant people I was with last night. Her husband had gone to the Plains yet she with 2 infant children was in this forlorn solitude in absolute security. Two peddlers peddling their way down from the mines with a pack horse had got shelter. It was a cabin of 3 rooms and I had to sleep with the mother and children while the peddlers slept in a room through ours. I had taken a few spoonfuls of coffee and could not sleep much also the room was too warm and airless.

Halls gulch. Platte cañon. Thursday Nov 6. Yesterday morning was too glorious, the light too dazzling, the sun too fierce. The cabin was papered with the Phrenological Journal and my eyes opened on the very best picture of Dr Candlish I ever saw. I felt grieved to think I should never see that fantastic face again. Mrs Link was an educated and very intelligent young woman. The peddlers were Irish yanks and the way they 'traded' was as laughable as Sam Slick.* I had admired their pony very much and after they had gone, one came back to know if I were 'willing to trade' and would 'swop the mare for it'. They trade their souls I know.

There was another dispute about the way I should take. Yesterday was the most critical day of my journey. If I once got through the snow and reached the Denver stage road though I may be detained by snow I could not be blocked in, but the peddlers insisted that I could not get through for the road was not broken. Mrs Link thought it was and advised me to try it. [. . .]

I saddled Birdie so well that the saddle remained firm all day [... but] as soon as I got out I felt as if I should drop off. I had bought a large figured handkerchief to keep the sun from my neck, but the fierce unwinking heat caused soul and sense, brain and eye to peel. I never saw the like. At that great height, the snow was perfectly pure dazzling so that I kept my eyes shut as much as possible to avoid snow blindness. The sky seemed a different and terribly fierce colour and the sun was a horrid white scintillating ball. I felt sick and ached from head to foot. I felt as if I must lie down in the snow. I cant do with heat. We passed on this for 4 mortal hours, seeing nothing but an ocean of glistening peaks against that sky of infuriated heat and glare. How I found my way I never shall know, for only one persons foot tracks were visible and I had no means of knowing whether they marked the way I ought to take.

Deeper grew the snow – I think Birdie fell 30 times. She seemed unable to keep up at all so I was obliged to get off. At this time I felt in heart to proceed for I saw a lie of country which I knew must contain South Park and we had got under cover of a hill which kept off the sun. The trail had ceased – it was one of those hunters tracks which so often mislead one. It was awful work the snow was 2 feet 8 inches deep and we went down in one drift (which was rippled like sand) she up to the saddle I up to my shoulders! It was a great fight but I can do quite well when it is not hot. At last we got down and I beheld with some sadness the goal of my journey, the snowy range and this great prairie sea 10 000 feet high, and 75 miles long, rolling, treeless, bounded by mountains and so rich in grass that all the herds of Colorado might one would suppose find pasturage there. So lonely, so indescribably mournful a 'silent sea' significant of 'the muffled oar'. No snow on it I galloped across the

* See Sam Slick, p. 341.

narrow end of it delighted to be out of the snow and when I struck the 'Denver Stage Road' I supposed all difficulties were at an end. Not so. They only began.

The 'Denver Stage Road'. The worst rudest dismallest darkest road I have yet travelled. A winding ravine the Platte cañon pine darkened walled in on both sides for 6 miles by mountains 13 000 feet high! Along this huge abyss for 50 miles there are only about 5 houses, but just now there is a great exodus of miners from the mountains and the freighting trams are going down to get winter stores otherwise the loneliness would be awful. As it was I saw not a creature. It was 4 when I left the park and with those mountain walls it soon became dark. The snow had melted and the road was *one sheet of ice*. Birdie could not keep on her feet and refused to go any further. I had to get off and with great difficulty dragged her along. It was freezing so very hard and we were at the very bottom of the narrowest part of the cañon with a rushing river on our left side. The pines were very thick and sighed & creaked most mournfully. So in the dark we 'got along' 2 miles. I feared we were much further from a house. I saw aloft the blaze of a campfire with 2 hunters sitting by it but no 'household fires', till at last on the other side of the river I saw a camp fire at the mouth of a gulch and something that looked like buildings. It seemed very eerie.

We got across that river partly on the ice and partly wading and there really were buildings and it was the place I had been recommended to. A man came out who I at once saw was in the sapient and polite stage of drunkenness and the door being opened I saw to my disgust 'a bar'. This was the worst place I have put up at as to food and lodging, an old and very dirty log cabin not chinked with one room used for eating in which a miner was lying very ill then a very large shed unroofed and then the bar. They are building and all is in disorder. They asked me was I the Miss Bird written of in the Denver News? A most horrible meal was served greasy, dirty, disgusting. Then a celebrated hunter Bob Craik came in with a young man in a rough miners dress whom I at once perceived was an Englishman. There really is something too ludicrous about the upper class of Englishmen 'High Toners' as they are called here. An American is nationally assumptive, an Englishman personally so. He took no notice of me till something passed which showed him I was English when he at once became gentlemanly and agreeable. I think he is Lord Dunraven.[*] He said he was an officer in the guards on 4 months leave of absence hunting buffalo and elk. I cant think why Englishmen

[*] See Dunraven, 4th Earl, p. 323.

put on that broad mouthing voice. The woman then asked me if I should be afraid to sleep in that large unceilinged canvas sided doorless shed? as they could not move the sick miner. So I actually did sleep there and slept all night! A fearful place with drifting clouds overhead.

Deer Valley Thursday night Nov 6. Tonight I am in a beautiful place like a Dutch farm large warm bright clean with abundance of delicious food, and the cleanest little bedroom all to myself. But it is very hard to write for 2 Irishwomen from Fairplay are telling the most fearful stories of Lynch law and people being 'strung'. It turns ones blood cold only to think that here where one travels in absolute security only a few years ago people were shot like skunks. That place last night at the opening of Halls Gulch up which there are many miners working only 2 months ago saw 2 men strung! It was a horrible place for dirt, obsequiousness, awful food. I hear the worst accounts of the man. He will be getting strung. Those 2 men were strung really for keeping a whisky tavern up Halls Gulch contrary to the will of the miners. At the mining villages in South Park, Alma and Fairplay there are vigilance committees and when people act outrageously they get a letter with a tree, a body hanging from it and a coffin below on which is written 'forewarned'. They 'git' in a few hours.

[. . .] Here more than anywhere perhaps whisky is significant of all evil and violence for I hear people never take it except to excess. The great local question in Colorado is drink or no drink, it is the great electoral issue. Mr Lillers paper is battling against drink. He said he had never thought upon the subject till he came here. It is truly the 'Whisky Fiend'. This territory would be almost without legal crime but for it, and all the great stock raising district through which I have travelled *is* without crime! I dont think there is a lock on any door at all events doors are never locked and on the main road the miners leave their silver bricks in their waggons unprotected all night. There is no danger and no fear. People say after coming from the States it takes long to realise the absolute security in which you live. It is a noble population in many respects moral without religion. Churches exist not. It is often said 'There is no God west of the Missouri' but as to what is called morality, its condition is wonderful and the settlers are very friendly.

Evans. Denver Sunday Nov 9. Friday requires very little to say. I left that beautiful place at 10 on Friday. The day was unutterably glorious with such depths of atmospheric colouring. There was very fine scenery, but certainly Rocky Mountain scenery is monotonous owing to the pines.

I never overtook the freight train owing to having to wait 3 hours when I had ridden 12 miles to get my brute shod with calks. 24 oxen were being shod. I had to sit on a barrel in the forge all that time. The next 8 miles were very beautiful and I enjoyed the ride very much after the heat of the day was over. I went through streams and cañons and cool glades till I came to a grocery store the only stopping place for 9 miles. I had ridden 23 but it seemed a short ride. I slept in the eating room behind a curtain and the wifes brother and 3 freighters slept the other side. I was in bed and asleep by 7 and consequently woke at 4 feeling very miserable thinking of so many things past and future and wondering how I should ever endure bubblings and sleeplessness again.

I wish I had anything arranged about writing my travels so that on returning I might once begin easy literary work for 1 1/2 hours daily, but now that Dr Guthrie is gone there is no one to help me at all in this way. I dislike going back with nothing fixed for me to do. I should think you would go to Edinburgh next month to begin prospecting for a house. I am beginning to be so afraid of breaking down as soon as I give up this life.

Yesterday I left at 9 and enjoyed the 18 miles ride very much. The Turkey Creek Cañon is one of the grandest I have seen, quite magnificent and the road ascends and hangs 600 feet above the edge of a precipice so narrow that meeting a wagon I had to get off because I could not pass with my feet. From this there was a gigantic and wonderful view down over the rolling foothills and over an ocean of grey brown plains to Denver not a tree all rioting in summer heat and dryness, August heat, while behind lay the last cañon of the mountains dark with pines and cold with snow. I followed the creek down to the plains and then devised a way for myself over the prairie. While the head chiefs of the Ute and Arapahos are in Washington and an attempt is being made to reconcile them the 2 tribes have met on the plains with great slaughter. I came by a circuitous route to avoid the sight of the corpses which scalped stripped and hideous had laid there unburied for 2 days. They are a most difficult problem treacherous and savage as enemies and when subdued paupers apparently equally impossible and uncivilisable.

As I left the mountains behind the view became glorious as range above range finally crowned with the purest snow came into view. I knew that 3 glistening peaks 70 miles north must be the peerless shapeliness of Longs Peak the king of the Rocky Mountains. They looked lovelier than the first day I saw them with atmosphere enough to spiritualise them. A mile from Denver I got off put on a skirt and rode sideways. I went to Mrs Edwards one of my hangers on and saw Jinny Evans. She said they have been very anxious about me and were expecting me

163

every day. I put up the pony at a coral and found to my dismay that my luggage left at Halls Gulch had not come so I have had nothing to go about in but my riding dress in which I have even been to church having my old green skirt on underneath it. The day though summer hot was wonderful in its beauty and after sunset the afterglow was as I have never seen it. I suppose that heavy crimson tokened fierce heat. It was redder and deeper than any chrome of the Egyptian afterglow. I met the warmest welcome here and just as I got in Evans drove up in his wagon containing carcasses of 3 huge elk 1 grizzly and one ibex.

Regarding a place one likes one always thinks (in spite of all lessons) 'tomorrow shall be as this day and much more abundant'. All my tour I have been revelling in the thought of returning to Estes Park to explore its glories and stay 3 weeks. Yesterday the weather promised to continue so splendid that I made up my mind to take a mountain tour of a week among the Grays Peak mountains the goal of my ambition being Green Lake just below timber line and stay till Dec. 1 at Estes Park when my projects were annihilated. The whole pleasant fraternity is broken up. Mrs Evans comes down on Tuesday for the winter and for her confinement. Mr and Mrs Dewy and Mr Waller all came down with Evans bound for California, Mr Buchanan[*] and Mr Kavanagh are baching in a cabin, and when Evans (who is really ill) is able to return he and Edwards[†] are going to bach together. I dont know what to do, but must settle tomorrow. I must go up there for my things. Some letters are there for me which I cant get for a week. [. . .]

Monday. Last night Mrs Evans Mrs Edwards and I walked into Denver to get cool. Today is piping and glorious. I start at 2.30 for the mountains which I expect to leave on Dec 1st for New York. I must now go to the depot to meet the Dewys. I care so unspeakably for it. Tell my Bessie and Emily that they are horrid creatures they have not written to me for 6 months and I have written twice to each of them since I heard once from Kona and once from San Rafael.

Its own Pet
ILB

I have lost all my clothes but a nightgown that is I believe they were stolen at Halls Gulch with Bessies knife and my locket with her picture.

9 p.m. Edwards has not come so directly at 8 tomorrow morning I start

[*] See John Buchanan, p. 317.
[†] See Sam Edwards, p. 324.

for my 40 mile ride carrying not only my luggage but the mail bag. A snow storm I fear is brewing. Mr Glazer has been spending the evening with me. I daresay I shall meet Edwards coming down but still cannot make comments as he never travels on Sunday and will be hurrying to get in to Denver. It is 5 weeks and 3 days since I heard, and you hear every week. I generally dream of you, and awake so disappointed because you are not there.

Golden City Monday Evening Nov 13th [1873]

My Ownest

I mailed a 16-pager in Denver today. I fear you will be so weary of the detailed monotony of these letters, yet if you are they will still be of use to me for if I live I shall like to know what I was doing. I never expected to have such extraordinary ravaging as this in Colorado. This will have been an unbroken ravage of 32 days. Doubtless possibly in answer to the prayers of yours a kind providence led me to Estes Park into that nest of generous kindly Welsh people. It is all Evans who by lending me that horse has enabled me to take the tour. I settled with him today and absolutely had to force him to take money for my board. I could not induce him to take anything for all the horses I have had, or for my board in Denver, or the keep of the horse I took from Longmount, and am either to keep Bird for my use or take the pick of the 50 horses, and if I like ride it to Cheyenne. He and his wife delight in me. After all it was settled today that after this mountain trip is complete I am to go back and bach in Estes Park. Edwards will be there and will bring in wood and water and I shall cook and do for myself for the remaining time. Evans will probably be up before I have been there 2 or 3 days.

I was obliged to leave the 'wearying world' today, though seeing so many jovial spirits who like me so was very pleasant. I was so very good, I went to a doctor this morning about that troublesome malady and from what I told him he said as I thought that there was nothing wrong. He gave me a medicine to take and a lotion which I got made up and advised hot water also which I can heat for myself when I get back. I got my luggage, got some knitting yarn, got a very nice russia leather diary for Mr Nugent, sweeties for each child, and then went with Evans to the hotel to see the Dewys who came by the cars but they were out so I went to Gov Hunts, and in coming back I met them on the main when to my immense surprise he as well as she kissed me most demonstratively! I went with them to the hotel dined with them and spent two hours with them very pleasantly. I never see a face like Mr Dewys. He has been very ill but I thought looked less like a dying man than 3 weeks ago. I knew they liked me but I never knew that they delighted in me until today. Then Evans came in so many kindly spirits all together. Then they walked with me to the corral where Birdie was and I got on sidewise with all my parcels and rode to Evans. [. . .]

I galloped over the plains towards the mountains and at dark got to the opening of this gorge and rode an hour in the dark and in utter darkness got into this dark unlighted mining town the second town in the territory. I had forgotten to ask about a stable or hotel but fell on my feet for getting off at a large livery stable I enquired of the gentlemanly proprietor for a hotel and he said he thought I should be more comfortable in a private boarding house and brought me to a ladys house who only takes weekly boarders but he boards here and so she took me for the night. It is the prettiest trimmest house I have seen and very quiet with courtesy and good food. I dont love Colorado but I must ever admire the cordial politeness one everywhere meets with. It is a great thing for a country not to be infested and overrun with women. The 16 miles from Denver seemed like one. On one day at South Park I rode *51 miles* and thought nothing of it. I shall have been 10 months on horseback. I ride so well now and understand all the arts of travelling. Evans said he never saw a horse brought back from a journey in such good condition.

I dont think the last letter was very annoying. I dread the letters which await me, I feel so sure the Kers will leave Edinburgh. It makes me sick to think of it. All the 'tomorrows' which were to have been as this day fail. I cant think what I shall do without Bessie and Emily, without one friend.

Georgetown deeply buried among huge mountains Tuesday night. Nov 11. [. . .] Golden City by daylight showed its meanness ungraded with here and there a piece of wooden side walk supported on posts up to which you ascended by planks, brick frame and log houses huddled together every other house a saloon not a woman to be seen. My landlady apologising for her very nice little bedroom said she had never had a lady sleep in her house before. At breakfast the young lady who waited said 'I've been thinking and I'm sure you're an authoress.'

The day was as usual glorious and very bracing. Winter never 'sets in' here. There is this weather for 4 months with now and then a snow storm but the snow only lies on the mountains and cattle require neither food nor shelter all the winter. People say they never remember a finer fall. Think of Nov nearly 1/2 through without a cloud in the sky except the exquisite cloudlets which are vermilion at sunrise. Mr Clarke thinks the skies more brilliant than those of Italy. I went and found my steed who I found as usual gorging but she licked and nuzzled for sugar when I went into her stall. They never told me that she is in foal till yesterday – I might have ridden her to death.

I was thinking that except last Sunday, since I left the Guthries [in California] I have never heard the Divine Name uttered or alluded to except in blasphemy (except at the Alexanders).* I wonder if such a nation of abominable swearers exists elsewhere. Golden City seemed resounding with oaths and curses specially at the depot. It stands at the mouth of *Toughcuss* cañon otherwise Clear Creek which is considered by many the most wonderful thing in the mountains. There is no road up this, and it winds and turns constantly while its stupendous sides are nearly perpendicular. Up this for the benefit of the mines which are scattered all along it a wonderful narrow gauge railroad, itself one of the wonders of the region, has been built, partly by blasting and partly by actually laying rocks in the bed of the river and laying tracks on them. Never in Europe or America have I seen such churlishness and incivility as in all the officials of that R.R. and stageline or heard of charges so preposterous. Had I known before I embarked I should not have gone for *we* could have travelled for 8 days what this 42 miles costs for 2. There are handsome cars on the line but paying full fare they put the passengers into *a baggage car* where I sat the whole journey on the floor at the door!

Probably no one ever saw the cañon better for that reason. Words cannot describe its singular grandeur. One might heap all epithets on it. One feels terrified too as the engine slowly claws its way up hill on those narrow rims of steel. One keeps thinking 'this must be the last of it' when new wonders open. It is a mere cleft through which the torrent has cut its way probably 3000 feet deep heaped and walled and chasm'd and weather stained with the most brilliant colours, generally dark, sometimes the sunbeams penetrating it, utter devastation, only a few stunted pines and cedars clinging here and there in rifts. Sometimes the walls of the abyss seemed to meet overhead, then just opening they broke into fantastic forms. No beauty, all sublimity and terror and it may be said truly cold. After 2 hours of this the track came to an end and the cañon widened enough for a road all stones and poles with sidings. Here a huge 'Concord coach' intended to carry 20 and a mountain of luggage

* See the Alexanders, p. 313.

awaited us. I sat on the seat above the driver with another lady and one man. There was no luggage, and the high huge thing bounced and bumped on the straps on which it was hung making me realise again all the horrors of New Zealand staging. The driver couldnt speak without an oath and cursed his splendid team the whole time.

The road still pursued the cañon to Idaho Springs a hateful place where we waited 3/4 of an hour and then went on with 6 superb horses. When we got near Georgetown the scenery became wonderfully grand and beyond the town the cañon looks as if it terminated in precipitous and inaccessible mountains sprinkled with pines up to the timber line and covered thinly with snow. We reached a height of 10000 feet and then by a rapid descent of 1000 came upon Georgetown, crowded into the most fearful gorge or cul de sac ever selected as the site of a town. It is so circumscribed and steep and the houses are so perched here and there and water so rushes and snakes through it that it really looks something like a Swiss town. In fact it is the only town I ever saw in America to which the epithet picturesque could with any truthfulness be applied. But truly seated in that cup in the chill and darkness it is a terrible situation. It was only 3.30 and yet to it the sun had set and it lay in deep cold shadow nearly surrounded by Alpine heights. I have not seen anything in Colorado which has impressed me so much except Longs Peak.

Now it seemed getting dark and I have no money to stay over tomorrow and it seemed impossible to see Green Lake the goal of my journey tonight which was a disappointment. We drove through the piled up irregular and really picturesque streets crowded with men and up a declivity to this very good hotel where I at once asked if I could set to, to Green Lake. The landlord said it was impossible, no one had been there for 5 weeks, but to satisfy me he would send to a stable and see. The answer came that no lady could go up, but if it was the English lady who was travelling in the mountains they would send a horse for she was said to be the boldest rider in Colorado. I heard this answer given outside the hotel and presently the landlord asked for my name and then asked if I were the lady who had crossed the continental divide in the snow. In about 5 minutes or 15 from my arrival a large horse with a 2-horned sidesaddle came and I started. This is the only 'mad bad' thing I have done.

The shades of evening buried Georgetown and I had 2500 feet to climb up to the timber line along an unknown road. It was evil excitement highly spiced with terror. I shall forget many things but never the impression of the awfulness and hugeness of this scenery. I went up a steep trail by the Clear Creek now become a series of Falls with a widened and then narrowed valley whose desolate sides looked 5000 feet high. Mining, mining with all its destruction and devastation, its digging burrowing sluicing washing. Up all along the seemingly inaccessible heights were holes log supported in which unsure miners were toiling and selling their lives, down by the rushing stream miners were washing and sluicing all the precipices covered with stumps and charred trees a very picture of fearful desolation and everywhere were hardly passable trails showing where pack jacks bring down the ore. But even from all this I turned.

The last miner I saw told me how to go and I struck upwards into the icy solitudes. It was very awful. Sheets of ice at first then deepening snow pure and powdery a foot deep and a frightful ascent, then through a pine forest where it was almost dark, the horse wallowing in the snow. But the goal was reached. At a height of 12000 feet I halted on a steep declivity and below me in the deep forest with mountains rising all round bright and glorious in the sunset only a few feet below me was Green Lake looking like water but in reality a sheet of ice about 2 feet thick. I had gone up into the pure air and the sunlight. It reminded me of the verse 'The darkness is past and the true light now shineth.' It was a wonderful vision fraught with terror. I doubt if any other woman would have got there up that almost Hawaiian track in the twilight through a foot of untrodden snow. As I stood there, the only human being at that glacial altitude, the glory faded and the peaks passed into ghostliness. Then I thought of the hour of steep downhill riding, the deep snow, the sheeted ice. There was one steep ice sheet which the horse could not go over, and there were only a few inches of bare ground between that and the loose crumbling edge of a tremendous precipice. Think how strong my head has grown with practice that I guided him for about 50 yards along that edge. This was the only ride which involved real riding since I left Hawaii and it was shocking to be taking it on a sidesaddle. The view as long as I could see it was awful so fearfully steep it looked as if you must jump down a precipice to get to Georgetown.

It was long after dark when I returned. I think they hardly believed I had been there. It was an exciting exploit but on a horse I can do anything and it rested me after the terrible jolting of the journey. I like to breathe the cool elastic air at 12000 feet. Here the air is so dry that one thinks several degrees of still frost warm. I hate to be in a house unless it is open to the air and has a great open chimney. They feel so stuffy. You see I have lived in the open air for 10 months. I had no food today from 7.30 till 6.30. Tomorrow directly I leave for Golden City at 8 so I must go to bed.

Boulder Thursday Nov 13. My exploits came to an untimely interruption today. I got here at 2 intending to ride up the Boulder Canyon but was obliged to go at once to bed owing to vertigo faintness and violent headache produced by the fierce heat of the sun in riding across the prairie. I nearly fell out of the saddle for the sun smote me by day and there was no shadow of a great rock in all that weary land. I quite fear tomorrow's ride to Longmount, my last over the Plains till I go away. I left Georgetown at 8 yesterday in glorious cold outside the stage. The sun does not rise there till 11. I doubt it rises there in the winter at all. After 4 hours fearful bouncing the baggage car again received us, and I was again sitting on the floor when the conductor gave me his chair on the platform from which I had a splendid view. I think no language could do justice to the sublimity of Clear Creek Canyon.

Arriving at Golden I dined in a restaurant, and at 3 remounted my steed, from which I never should have separated to ride here. Like Colorado she is not loveable but she is an excellent truly gentle beast, and is an important element in the life which I like. It was a glorious brilliant summer afternoon and not too hot. They could not direct me here at the stable, but told me to go along the Denver road till I could get directions, thus starting me on the wrong track at once. I rode 2 miles and then met a man who told me I was all wrong and directed me across the prairie till I met another man who gave me so many directions that I forgot them and got irretrievably lost. The afterglow seen to perfection on the open plain was wonderful. Just as it grew dark I rode after a teamster who said I was 22 miles from Boulder, and the nearest house to which he directed me was 7 miles off. I suppose he thought I should know, but he told me to cross the prairie when I should come to 3 tracks of which I was to take the best travelled one. He pointed to a star which he said I was to keep right ahead. It did bring me to tracks, but it was so dark I could see nothing and I was lost and benighted. Hour after hour we trudged on, no sound but the wolf. Oh how I longed to meet some one to hear advice. I saw what seemed a house roof and it was a deserted shed. I felt very eerie and made up my mind to trudge on all night steering by the pole star but I feared Birdie would fail for want of water. It was gruesome. Several times I heard the lowing of cattle and hoped there was a settlers house but it was the lone wild prairie. At last I heard the undertoned lowering of a bull and he seemed to be disputing the road snorting and tearing up earth and Birdie was afraid to pass. While she was scuffling about I heard a dog bark, then I saw a light and in another minute I recognised Mr Churchs large house where I stayed to lunch on my way to Denver and knew that I was 4 miles from Denver! There I was most comfortably housed and slept all night.

This morning I left at 8. You can form no conception of what the glory on the plains is just before sunrise. Like the afterglow, the horizon has for a great height above it a shaded band of the most glowing and intense orange imaginable and the mountains reflecting the yet unrisen sun are the colour of amethysts. I left at 8 and was in 2 miles irretrievably lost, but knowing that a gash in the mountains was Bear Canyon 3 miles from Boulder I boldly made tracks right across the prairie for 17 miles till I got there when I struck the Boulder track. I should have enjoyed the ride very much for the mountain view was glorious, but for the blazing heat of the sun. It was awful, and it is quite hot tonight. 7000 feet here is the lowest altitude at which for me it is healthy. When suitably clothed I am now quite impervious to dry cold but heat kills me. It must be hardly bearable in the cars now. People aggravate all the time telling me I shall never bear the damp dark climate of England, but today I would have welcomed anything as a refuge from that solar fury.

Truly the Americans are bone of our bone and flesh of our flesh, hideously, grotesquely, revoltingly our progeny. The Anglo Saxon race will doubtless conquer or replace all the feebler races but it seems to me it is losing nobility as it passes to universal Empire. I do so hate the practice of exclaiming 'Christ' or 'Jesus' at every trifle. I never write any slang in case the Kers should get hold of it and use it.

Longmount Nov. 14. I breakfasted at 6.30 this morning and having hired a horse went up the Boulder Canyon finding it quite cold as soon as I got within the mountains. I was very much disappointed with the horse which would not go for any amount of whipping. I left as soon as I got back intending to arrive here at noon to comment on all your letters, as for a fortnight there will be no opportunity of sending letters. My excellent Birdie came the 15 miles quite lightly. They can hardly believe here that wise thing has taken such a journey. She looks so well. I should have lost my way but a young man joined me 10 miles from here which made it much pleasanter. To my utter dismay there are no letters. They think there are some at Estes Park and that Edwards who with his family is expected tonight will bring them. If so I will make separate comments. If not, there will be no opportunity of making any till I come down myself.

Its poor Pet
ILB

Colorado

My Ownest,

I am always delighted in it and reading over its most delightful letters the nicest letters that ever were. I am today absolutely alone in the Park. All its other denizens have gone away hunting and there is no woman for 23 miles. They put a supply of logs outside the door before they went away and another by the cooking stove. It is a brilliant day of intense frost or else the solitude would seem fearful. I have got the horse in the corral and shall ride soon. I wrote comments but I must now take up my journal letter for four days and I cannot say there is nothing annoying in it for first I came up here under a delusion, secondly there is no proper food for me to eat, thirdly the letters of Bessie and Emily have made me so miserable,* and 4thly and worst, there is a tragedy about Mr Nugent otherwise Mountain Jim which has made me too terribly nervous.

I never can dissever myself from a keen interest in the concerns of people still less would I desire to do so in a life which otherwise would foster selfishness. The nice Evans are suddenly placed in a disastrous plight and it so far affects me that I cannot leave this till he pays me the 55 dollars I left with him in Denver.† The weather became fierce the night I got here and the beavers yesterday came down the river bringing their stores of winter food with them, a thing they have not done for 11 years and which is a sign of a tremendous winter.

I left Longmount at 8.30 on Sat. Edwards had not come down and Mr. Glazer persisted that several letters for me were here. Several people saw me off. They all expected a heavy snowstorm for the sky was overcast except that over the mountains was a deep still sad blue into which snowy points rose sunlighted. It was a mournful looking morning, but when I reached the beautiful valley of the St. Vrain the sad blue became brilliant and displaced all the clouds and the sun was hot and scintillating. The ride up here was far more beautiful than anything I have seen after you have crossed 7 miles of prairie. There is first this beautiful hill girdled valley of fair savannahs through which the bright snow bound

---

* As Henrietta indicated in her letter to Ella Blackie, Bessie Ker and Emily Clayton had both left Edinburgh to travel abroad. Presumably Isabella had only just discovered this, as she previously remarked to Henrietta that neither had written to her for six months. 'I can't think what I shall do without Bessie and Emily, without one friend.'

† Apparently Isabella had given Evans a large promissory note to cash at a Denver bank for her, both to pay him for her board and to save her the trouble of cashing the note herself. Around this time, there was a brief failure of Colorado banks. Because of this, and Evans's failure to return as quickly as Isabella had expected, she was temporarily stranded without money. Evans returned on December 1, 1873, giving her $40 of her $55.

St Vrain curves in and out amidst a tangle of cottonwood and now withered clematis and Virginia creeper which 2 months since made the valley bright with their scarlet and gold. Then the cañon with its rocks of fantastic staining then the long ascent through growing foothills to the gate of rock 9000 feet high then the wildest and most wonderful scenery for 20 miles in which you cross 13 ranges from 9 to 11000 feet high pass through countless cañons and gulches through 13 dark fords and finally descend through McGinns Gulch upon this, incomparably the gem of the Rocky Mountains.

It was a weird ride. I got on very slowly. Bird was either not well or very tired, and 40 miles of such a track is enough to kill a horse. All the time the letters were unopened. When I had ridden 15 miles I stopped at the ranch where people usually get feed but it was empty 2 miles further at another which was also deserted. There remained but the one where I stopped when I rode down with Mr Powers where 2 young men are baching. I was very sorry to impose myself on them, but truly thankful to find one of them in. This house is a model to all women. He cooked me a splendid dinner with good tea. He has the clear eyes and manliness which abstinence gives young men in this country. He confirmed my idea that Evans is simply killing himself by hard drinking. I have told him so over and over again and he admits it but seems drawn to it by his lavish social genial nature. No doctor can do him any good unless he gives it up and I dont think he will live two years anyhow.

I did not mention what a good doctor I have been. When I came here Mr Dewy in addition to lung disease had been suffering from chronic diarrhea which threatens to carry him off and (doctors are such nangs) they only gave him the palliative of laudanum draughts. He also suffered from sleeplessness and nightly fever. I got tannin pills and not only is the diarrhea quite cured but he has gained 7 lbs and after the first dose of bromide he slept like a child and now taking it regularly continues to sleep. I gave Evans nitric acid and bromide. He had not slept for 10 nights and the first bromide made him sleep 10 hours. At Denver he paid 5 dollars to a doctor and when I looked at the prescription it was just bromide and tannin. Mrs Evans was quite nervous and sleepless and she has been quite well ever since she took one dose.

I sat much too long at Millers reading your letters with 20 miles to ride. It was then splendid. I had not realised before the magnificence of that ride but I could not get the pony on and it seemed interminable as after every range I crossed another rose. Then came a region of deep dark densely wooded gulches only a few feet wide and fords and on the tops of precipices high above 4000 feet high I saw the last sunlight glow while I was in gloom and bitter cold. It was most eerie as evening came on and winding in and out often on ice and groping among wood at the bottom of these tremendous chasms. Wolves howled in all directions said to be a sign of storm. I had met 2 companies of hunters coming down & they not only told me that the Edwards had not left but that Mr Edwards had said they should not leave for 2 weeks. So I expected great comfort after my terrible ride. It really did seem endless. At last I got over that last huge range through the last solemn gulch and reached Mr Nugents ranch 5 miles from here hoping he would ride with me but the house was locked. I got on my bear and trudged eerily and tediously down McGinns Gulch which was quite dark though the stars were bright ahead.

Soon I heard the welcome sound of a barking dog. Then one has no fear of meeting human beings, but a great longing for it. As the dog drew near, I supposed it was hunters, but calling 'Ring'* at a venture Mr Nugents noble hound jumped actually up on the saddle with his nose licking my face and I discerned 2 men on 2 horses. It was too dark to see but Mr Nugents musical voice and infinite grace of manner seemed truly welcome and sending the man on he turned and rode with me. To my dismay he said that Edwards had left the day before and that Mr Kavanagh a miner and Mr Buchanan a young man here for his health were keeping house till Mr E. returned. The cold was awful a fierce wind had come on. I was obliged to get off and walk the last mile to keep my feet from freezing.

We found the two men sitting smoking by the parlour fire the carpet gone and everything dismantled and wretched looking. The two men decent creatures showed no annoyance but set themselves at once to get supper and courteously made Jim stay for it. Jim is a strikingly handsome man with a massive brain and is handsome in spite of the loss of his eye, but he had grown old and haggard in a single month and seemed sadly dil. There was a great difficulty about sleeping. There is a spring mattress in the Dewys room opening from the parlour but nothing on it. However they went and filled a bed tick with hay which on the springs makes the most luxurious bed I have had in Colorado. They said there were neither sheets towels nor candles. I got a wash bowl but had only an old chemise for a towel. I slept all night in spite of a gale which lasted until Monday afternoon which seemed to lift up the cabin and which unroofed the room between the parlour and the kitchen where we used to dine.

* See Ring, p. 339.

Sunday was brilliant but a hurricane. I never stirred out of the house. The parlour was *two* inches deep in the mud from the roof. The men cook wash the dishes clean the kitchen bring in wood. I do my room and the parlour which last until today has been a truly dreadful business. Each day I have swept it 5 times taking out 4 shovelfulls of powdered mud each time. I found sheets and towels and an old green shawl which answers for a tablecloth. I swept a path through the ruined dining room to the kitchen where we feed. I dressed in black silk on Sunday. Mr Nugent came in the afternoon but all the life seemed beaten out of him and he seemed not to hear what one said.

Food is the great difficulty. Of 30 cows only one remains and it does not give enough milk for drinking. The only meat is some pickled pork very salty and the hens only lay less than an egg a day. Yesterday morning I made some rolls and made the last bread into a bread and butter pudding. The men are both abstainers. Today I found part of a leg of beef hanging in a shed and we were delighted with the prospect of fresh meat but on cutting into it we found it corrupt. There is nothing. Had it not been for a pound of tea which Mrs Sigley at Longmount gave me I should have had none. But the air is superb and I sleep well and probably the quiet is good before I go to the States. Anyhow I can hardly eat anything because of my teeth and sore mouth.

The gale moderated at noon yesterday but a great snowstorm threatened. Mr Nugent and a trapper he is employing passed in the afternoon on their way to Fall River Cañon which I have never yet seen and he asked me to go up and see it, but he was so dil that it was really depressing, no more singing or talking to his Arab mare or bright repartee. We had not ridden more than 2 miles when a blinding snow squall came on and I had to turn back and he turned back a little way with me to show me the trail. Then came a terrible revelation that as soon as I had gone away he had discovered: he was attached to me and it was killing him. It began on Longs Peak he said. I was terrified. It made me shake all over and even cry. He is a man whom any woman might love but no sane woman would marry. Nor did he ask me to marry him, he knew enough for that. A less ungovernable nature would never have said a word but his dark proud fierce soul all came out then. I believe for the moment he hated me and scorned himself, though he could not even then be otherwise than a gentleman. My heart dissolves with pity for him and his dark, lost, self ruined life. He is so loveable and fascinating yet so terrible. I told him I could not speak to him I was so nervous and he said if I would not speak to him he would not see me again, he would go and camp out on the Snowy Range till I was gone. He said such fearfully bitter things. I could not bear to think of him last night out in the snow neither eating nor sleeping, mad lost wretched hopeless. It is really terrible. For 5 minutes at the camping ground on Longs Peak his manner was such that for a moment I thought this possible, but I put it away as egregious vanity unpardonable in a woman of 40 and afterwards he explained his emotion satisfactorily, and never showed a trace of it again. I miss him very much. He is so charming and can talk on all subjects and has real genius. It takes peace away.

The snow cleared off changing to intense frost. My room is almost the open air being of unchinked logs. I slept with my head under the blankets. Today has been brilliant. I went a most beautiful ride this afternoon to Black Cañon. I thought the Park more beautiful than ever. Nothing compares with it, and now the mountain tops above the black pine wood are pure white. Nothing can be named along with it.

Wed. Nov 19. Like you after you returned to Tobermory I am getting to like my life after the unquiet of my ravage. It is so very healthy, pure air night and day pure water absolute dryness and such glorious beauty. Every day I see something new. I believe there are hundreds of wonderful rides. The whole of the rest of Colorado is nothing to it and the weather is again magnificent not too cold. If only it were not for 'Jim'. It is so sad to think of him and no more to see his Arab mare tied in front of the house as it used to be almost daily. It was very wrong in him to speak as he did he should have let me go without the sorrow of knowing this. Thus again that hideous whisky fiend crosses my path.

You would like him so. He is so quick like a needle a thoroughly cultured Irishman and like most of his nation he has 'the gift of the gab', such an agreeable facility of speech. I cannot but think of Mr Wilson on Hawaii and his quiet undemonstrative un-annoying ways, and comparing him with this dark tempestuous, terrible character, wondering how it is that the last is so fascinating.

This has been a day of manual labour. We did not breakfast till 9.30. Then they went out and I never got done till one. I cleaned the parlour and the kitchen washed up baked and then made 4 lbs of sweet biscuits and baked them after which I had to clean all my tins and pans and do my own room and haul water. Then being tired of riding Bird, I went out on her and lassoed a large horse on which I have since taken a most delightful ride – only I do like a companion on horseback. I wonder if I have told you that I have become tolerably expert with the lasso. I sleep wonderfully well here except the night after getting the letters. I never saw more harmless men than these two. But there is something stupen-

dous in the winter solitude of the Park. I have never experienced anything like it. No possibility of anyone coming or of any communication
with the outer world after Evans and Edwards return. I could not like it
unless I had so much which I must do which is such a different thing
from playing at work. I shall dislike to look my last on this place. Its lakes
and bright streams are such an attraction besides its marvellous beauty.

Thursday. I am liking my life though seriously suffering from inabil-
ity to eat. I am going this afternoon to look after another cow and try a
purely milk diet which I know from experience suits me. This is the
height of 'free leggism'. The work is now better arranged. Mr Buchanan
was doing too much and it was hard. I do the house work make the bread
and any little knick knack and wash up the breakfast and lunch things.
We breakfast at 9.30, take something at 1.30 and sup at 6. Mr Kavanagh
sleeps in a cabin which is better chinked than this, I sleep in the Dewys
room and Mr Buchanan who is delicate in the parlour with a fire. I heat
a great piece of granite every night for my feet which keeps hot all night.
There is only one fire and we dont go to bed till 10. The men smoke
all the evening. They are the most harmless of human beings. Mr
Kavanagh milks the cow and chops the wood. We all do our own
washing.

My clothes are at the lowest ebb. I have only the chemise I have on
for at Longmount I had to tear up the other to patch my riding trousers. I had one nightgown and got it so beautiful bleached on Monday
and hung it to dry and when I went for it, it was torn literally to shreds,
in fact only the lower half was left! I now sleep in my Hawaiian flannel
riding frock. I have only 1 pr woollen stockings made by Rowena
darned all over. I should like her to know that I have worn them for six
weeks, and always think of her when I put them on. When I come in
from riding I put on the gray and white striped gingham dress which
Mrs Brigham gave me and which I am going to give to Mrs Hutchinson.
I have now got the horses Bird and the large thoroughbred mare I lassoed
yesterday. I keep them in the corral and feed them on sheaf oats. I can
saddle both these myself.

The day before yesterday a cow died in the shed by the house. Mr
Buchanan and I had attended to it for two days. It suffered dreadfully
and looked so pleading as it died. There is something to me infinitely
pathetic in the death of a beast, so truly made subject to vanity. We are
now in a great difficulty about it. Meat will keep all winter, but an animal
with an inside swells and bursts and it is horrible – all the wagon horses
were in Denver and as soon as we attach a rope to the carcass and try to

get our saddle horses to pull it to where the wolves can get it they buck and plunge. Edwards and Evans were both to have been back it seems the day I came, but they are most uncertain and they dont know that I am here.

It is delightful to go to bed as I do in the mountains be asleep in 10 minutes and sleep for 10 hours. But it seems to me that I am much more nervous than when I left home the second time, ever since that illness in the Ben Nevis. Such a small thing, one bad night. Anything that befalls anyone a letter from you even one from the Kers upsets me. My appetite is good but I cannot eat from the misery of my teeth and sore mouth. That other malady is much better owing I think to the use of ice cold water. It is a wonderful air here and such a singularly suitable life except for the want of food. We have only a miserable lamp and no candles! You see there is absolutely no possibility of getting anything. Evans wagon with the elk 6 miles from here went over a place and fell 60 feet. The gulches are sheeted with ice, it is difficult to get through on horseback.

I am always thinking of my own darling. I keep its picture always on the table by me and when it says any nice words to me I read them over and over again. I care for it unspeakably.

I dreamt last night that as we were sitting by the fire, Mr Nugent came in with his revolver in his hand and shot me. But there is no such peril. I wonder if he really will stay up on the range? He can't go home without passing through this corral. He was to have ridden over with me a short cut to Dr Hutchinsons – I am beginning to fear I shall not get there and I have some things for them and wanted to make them a grand dinner for Thanksgiving day.

This morning was black with clouds and about 700 head of cattle and all the herds of horses that maraud in the valley and cañons came in long troops towards the cabin but it has again cleared up into inconceivable glory with a warm sun. I am most anxious that there should not be a storm before I get away, for the rivers and gulches are so very bad and 40 miles of mountains and 30 miles of plains must be crossed on a horse before I can reach the railroad, and if only Edwards is here, great difficulties will surround the getting away, he is so negligent and 'do less' and I shall be obliged to have a pack horse as my carpet bag is here. [. . .]

Thursday evening. I was sitting alone eating some milk when Mr Nugent walked in. He asked if I would like to go up Fall River Cañon and ride back alone for he was going back to the Snowy Range and would be glad to show me the trail. He sat by the fire without speaking.

I didnt like to refuse as he asked me before the others and the cañon was glorious but it was a truly dismal and depressing ride. He coughed all the way and hardly spoke at all. No allusion was made to anything that had passed. The dead past has buried its dead. His manner was freezing, courteous of course, but the manner of a corpse hardly touching my hand. He said he would call to bid me goodbye on Sat or Sun night on his way to Denver and he was then going buffalo hunting.

That cañon is superb and as I came back the sunset glories were reddening the mountain tops. Wonderfully magnificent but oh so solemn. There is an immense beaver dam with which they have actually diverted the course of the river. It is well made with a beaver house by it and an immense store of bark for winter use. I rode a very large mare and she fell with me twice – I have let her go again. It was most difficult to get through the Thompson River coming back. It is half frozen and half rushing and it frightens the horses. I came back over two miles of grass at a very large gallop which I liked but that mare though gentle is not safe on her legs. I thought again that if Bishop Wilberforce had been riding a Mexican saddle he would not have been killed.

Friday Nov 21. This is a piteous day freezing hard quite black and with a piercing N.E. wind. The absence of sun has a most depressing effect and all the scenery appears in its fierce grimness of black and grey. My work took me two hours and since then I have been feeling very dil perhaps partly from want of food. I cant even eat bread now. Mr Buchanan has gone to a squatters cabin (the only one for 23 miles except Mr Nugents) three miles off to try if they can let me have a quart of milk daily for the cows we brought in are all dry. I hope he will succeed.

However much I wished to leave I cant for I have only 75 cents and we have lost the horses and have nothing to entice them with. Having lost Bird I cant go and lasso a horse. I put her in the corral last night with a horse that I drove in and Mr Kavanagh put his mare in there too. They had succeeded in hauling the cows body to the back of the shed and last night wolves and catamounts came down and were howling fearfully when I went to sleep. We suppose the horses scared and stampeded and leapt the fence of the corral and as they had no lariats on we dont know how we shall get them unless the prospect of snow drives them down.

I have written this note to 'Jim'. 'Dear Sir, In consequence of the very blameworthy way in which you spoke to me on Monday, there can be nothing but constraint between us therefore it is my wish that our acquaintance shall at once terminate. Yours truly ILB.' I cannot endure it, it makes me so nervous and after that note unless he comes to shoot me he will never speak to me again. There was a revolver at half cock lying on the table yesterday when he came in and I found my hand instinctively verging towards it. He has never come here armed before and yesterday he had 2 revolvers in his belt. Mr Kavanagh had ridden 5 miles out of his way to avoid him saying he saw he was 'awful ugly'. I pity him with an inconceivable pity but for him there is no balm in Gilead and no physician there, no hope for time or eternity. It is a terrible termination of what otherwise as far as local things go would have been a very unharrassed time.

Oh my sweetest how I long to see its sweet unworldly face again. It must care for me, and be demonstrative. I like names, and to be cared for. I seem fearfully walled in beside the ocean waste and the desert track which will take 8 days and nights to New York. I shall write to Mr Guthrie [in California] about investments though I fear we may not succeed in investing our money at a high rate safely. I wish we could help others more, and be free from low corking cares. I often wonder whether we shall 'take up house' again. I dont think I shall be back before the middle of Jan.

Mr Kavanagh says that Jim has just passed on the other side of the creek, so probably he has gone to Denver without seeing me this evening. We have the most enormous log fire. It is not snowing yet but looks sublimely awful in blackness. Mr Kavanagh very kindly hunted a horse and found Mr Wallers, a very large one, which I liked very much better than riding 'a narrow pony'. I wished you could have seen me galloping on that large horse in my ragged Hawaiian dress with 2 huge hounds galloping with one the very picture of outlawed 'free leggism'. In McGinns Gulch I was terrified to encounter 'Mountain Jim' but he was quiet and courteous. I had the note in my pocket and told him I was going to send it to him. He said I was very kind to write and put it into his pocket. He said that he was feeling so very ill that he was going home that he had caught a bad cold on the Range that an old arrow wound in his lung had become very painful. He looked so ill and wretched going to his dark lonely lair, and I felt that I had stabbed him and had not made sufficient allowance for him. He said if he was better he should like to call tomorrow evening. I said nothing for I well knew he would never call after reading my note. I wished him goodbye wishing I could bring him here and make him warm tea and be kind to him rather than kill him as I had done.

I came down the Longmount trail to get the view in the grimness which I had first got in the glory. It is the most wonderful of all views, and in its peerless grandeur dwarfing and marking the whole of the rest

The letters in this volume were written before Isabella Bird became famous. On the left, we see her in San Francisco in 1873, just after her Hawaiian tour (1). At right Isabella is at the height of her fame, *c.*1899, dressed in a Manchu outfit she purchased in China (2). The difference in attitude and dress is just part of Isabella's transformation during these years

(3) Tobermory, on the Isle of Mull, *c.*1885. Isabella and Henrietta's cottage is just visible at the top of the cliff, second from right. Today, a clock Isabella erected in memory of Henrietta stands near the church

(4) Isabella on her wedding day, 1881. She is dressed in mourning for Henrietta (5), who died of typhoid at their cottage in Tobermory in 1880. The groom was John Bishop (6), a distinguished doctor then in practice at the Edinburgh Infirmary. He was ten years younger than Isabella, but died shortly after their marriage. The freshness and vitality of the letters in this volume reflect Isabella's attitude before these tragedies

Melbourne, Australia, was the first stop on the round-the-world tour Isabella took in 1872–3 to regain her health. Here we see a suburban house (7), Collins Street, the centre of the city's religious life (8), and a bottle tree (9). Isabella's doctors thought she might improve in the Antipodes, but Isabella dismissed the colony as 'England in the Pacific' and moved on

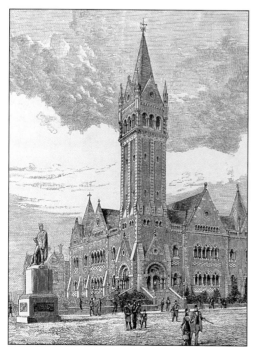

'Hilo is an enchanting place,' Isabella wrote on arriving there in 1873. She danced the polka on a missionary veranda with King Lunalilo (10). She also enjoyed picnicking on Coconut Island (11). Seated from left are: Dr Charles Hinckley Wetmore, Lucinda Severance, Hattie Coan, Luther Severance, Gertrude Severance Sawyer, Mary Austin with Helen Severance on her lap, and other members of the Hilo community Isabella met on her tour. In Hilo, Isabella's health dramatically improved

(12) This letter to Henrietta – written on June 6, 1873, from the crater of Mauna Loa, the world's highest volcano – is reproduced close to its actual size. The original is in the John Murray archives

(13) Hawaiian palms. (14) The crater of Kilauea, Hawaii. This etching was done from a sketch Isabella made of the volcano's 'fountains of fire', which she saw on her second ascent, in June 1873

On her way back to Scotland from Hawaii, Isabella visited Colorado. While there, she spent several weeks snowbound at Estes Park (15), where she fell in love with the one-eyed desperado, Rocky Mountain Jim. Long's Peak is visible behind the ranch

Part of what made Isabella unique on these travels was her willingness to try new inventions. In Hawaii and Colorado, Isabella discovered the Bloomer Suit (16), Turkish trousers with a divided skirt falling mid-calf, which enabled polite women to ride astride. (The horse in this Colorado etching of Isabella is presumably Birdie.) (17) Later, Isabella experimented with photography. This picture, taken in China in 1895, shows Isabella photographing villagers

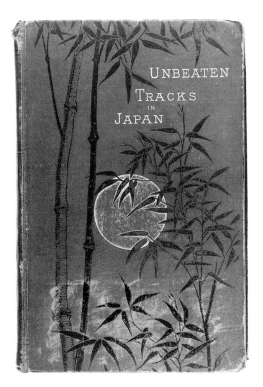

Isabella's second world tour, also undertaken for her health, began in Japan in 1878. Here we see (18) the cover of the book she wrote on that country; (19) a ceremonial entrance at Nikko; (20) the Ainu of Hokkaido; and (21) a Buddhist monk in a Japanese cemetery. This last photograph was taken by Isabella

A devout Christian, Isabella was particularly intrigued by the Eastern religions she encountered; but she did not always regard them with sympathy. These two photographs titled (22) 'Divinity in Wen-Shu-Yuan Temple, Chengtu' and (23) 'Rock Temple, Li-Fan Ting', Isabella took in China, where she travelled in 1878 after Japan

China became, in later years, one of Isabella's favourite places; there, she felt at home among the expatriate community. These photographs, taken by Isabella, depict (24) a group of English missionaries in Chinese dress; and (25) a group of English children in Fujian being taken to school

(26) 'The Street of Tsa-ku-Lao' taken by Isabella

(27) Another of Isabella's photographs – 'The Bridge at Mien-Chuh', published in 1899

From China, Isabella travelled to the Malay Peninsula, where she indulged her passion for the natural sciences. She ate dinner with a party of monkeys, rode elephants, and wrote about alligators and tigers. Here we see a captured tiger (28). Isabella witnessed a similar event in Malacca, noting that the tiger's claws were given to her as a gift. Below (29) is an engraving from *The Golden Chersonese* of Isabella's first elephant ride in Perak

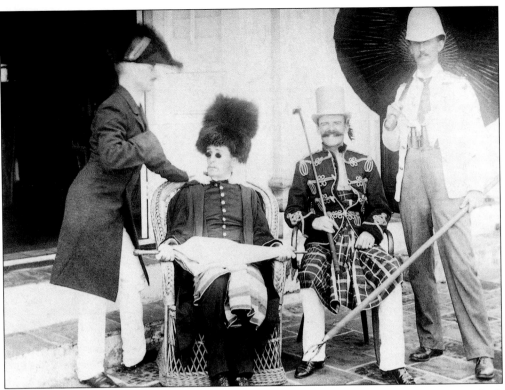

Isabella's letters from this second world tour are particularly notable for their portrayal of the British Empire. Here we see (30) British administrators amusing themselves in Penang in a photograph taken by Hugh Clifford in 1896; (31) Hugh Low, Resident of Perak; and (32) the young daughter of Sir Harry Parkes, with whom Isabella stayed at the British Legation in Tokyo in 1878. This second tour marked the beginning of Isabella's transformation from 'tourist' to 'travel writer', a distinction that affected her later work

of Colorado. So utterly walled in fearful in its loneliness the ghostliest of white peaks lying against the dense black snow clouds the once bright river frozen the pines black the lawns of the park looking so strange the world shut out. I thought if you were here I could spend the winter here and well provided there was no one else. Jim says that I cant get out now till ice bridges form at the fords, and that if another storm comes the gulches will be almost impassable. It is a truly strange life.

Mr Buchanan brought back a tin of rich milk so I have not attempted any meat today. They are grumbling. They say Edwards asked them to keep house for 5 days at the end of which he would return and he has been away nine and they dont see the fun of paying 8 dollars a week for pickled pork and doing their own work. Nor do I but the place suits me and there is a great deal in that. But it really is strange that neither Edwards nor Evans come back. There are two calves dying, and we dont know what to do for them and if a snowstorm comes we cant bring in and feed 800 head of cattle.

Sat. 22. The impending snow began to fall early this morning and there is a white world. Still it does not look like anything serious. We did not breakfast till 10 and then there was a dish of stewed venison tender enough for me to eat. We think Edwards will surely be up tonight unless there has been a heavier storm in the valley but unless he brings supplies the case is becoming serious. There is only flour for one week coffee for one and the only tea is a little I brought with me. The yeast is done and the baking powder nearly so. The venison we had is part of a deer the young men were going to pack down to Longmount to sell and it is hard on them to have to eat it. I have got Bird back and lassoed and brought in 4 other horses. I went out on one but the snow balled so that I had to get off and lead her back and then I went out and walked where I had never been before.

Dear me what wondrous sublimity it is and each day I see something new or under some new aspect. I think there can be no other such place in the world. I fear I shall grieve to look my last on its peerless grandeur and the associated 'free leggism'. I think of my Bessie with infinite yearning, and beloved Emily who has written me such sweet tender soulful letters. I always think my Bessie the pleasantest person in the world. This mornings snow falling without wind has perfectly whitened the mountain down to its timber line.

Sunday Nov. 23. The mercury was at zero this morning. I had to take my basin and the tin of water from my room to the cooking stove and melt them before I could wash. It has been one of the most beautiful days I ever saw a warm sun, and a mercury at zero here is warmer to ones feelings than 40 at home. I wear my gingham dress and old silk petticoat only. [. . .] I have spent 4 hours in reading its most delightful letters over again, also the 3 of Emily and Bessie. I have thoroughly taken in all yours. I think it is such a very nice life at Tobermory. I long to see those sketches. Make heaps of them.

A trapper passed last night and said Mr Nugent was very ill. We did not breakfast till 10, and as soon as I had washed up and swept the house I saddled Bird to ride to his cabin for he is my fellow creature. It is 5 miles off but to my surprise when I had ridden 1/2 way I met him in McGinns Gulch. He said he did not wish to intrude on me but he was coming down to ask a favour for an hours conversation. We rode a little and then got off and sat under a tree I daresay for 2 hours. He was perfectly calm & rational and entered into the fullest explanation of his circumstances. I told him that if all circumstances on both sides had been favourable and I had loved him with my whole heart I would not dare to trust my happiness to him because of whisky. I told him he must not be angry and I told him what I had heard of him from the first and he admitted everything. He said he would never say another word of love he thought on the whole it would be better for him not to see me again. He rode about a mile back with me. He said he felt much happier for having come to a thorough understanding.

I dont know whether I shall see him again or no – I think so but I feel quite at ease about him now. He ought not to have told me that he loved me but it was a mistaken notion of honour and from my first acquaintance with him until now he has acted and spoken as a perfect gentleman. I said a great deal to him about drinking but I think failed to make any impression. Poor fellow he had built such castles in the air of your coming to live in these mountains. I think he has all the faults of an Irishman.

I still have not the remotest idea of how I can get away. There is no-one to go with me and bring the horse back not a soul and I could not leave a pack horse. I should like as I must go to leave on the 27th or Dec 1st. We are living nicely now we are cutting up a deer and Mr Buchanan goes 6 miles to get the milk each day. Things are nearly done, and we are going on the principle 'Let us eat and drink for tomorrow we die.' Mr Buchanan said tonight we were taking 11 hours sleep and getting 3 meals into 8 hours which is true. It is strange how well we get on in such a singular and enforced partnership. Our work goes on like clockwork, sometimes I attending to the horses, sometimes they. We might be 3 men living together, except that they always make the fires and bring in wood. [. . .]

Monday Nov. 24th. It is a most singular thing the non-appearance of Evans and Edwards. You can hardly imagine the majestic loneliness. I fear I am howling at the near prospect of leaving it. I like the place and the life and the people are no annoyance to me. It is such a completely healthful life. I find getting up later suits me much better. I used to drag myself to the 7 a.m. breakfast. Now I get up at nine, and sweep the house before breakfast. Today has been the usual routine of work and riding. I wrote to Dr Blackie a long and 'very nice' letter this morning. I asked him to try and arrange with Good Words for my Hawaiian papers naming terms. If it cant be managed then I shall write a book but I need money, and eventually those who cared to keep them could buy them as a book.

I am now writing a note to thank Dr Hanna* for his, telling him what I have written to Dr Blackie. I had to mend my riding trousers which will hardly hold together another week. The days go very fast – it was 3.30 before I knew it was 1. I then rode with Mr Buchanan for the milk. Bird with rest and feeding has grown quite wild. We had a race, and she beat Mr Wallers immense horse quite easily. I then rode alone another grand ride. I am beginning to wonder if there is so grand and varied a place in the world. But I remember no details. One rides for miles and there is nothing on the ground to look at. I often recall the Wailuku or rather the Iao Valley [in Maui] the most *beautiful* thing I ever saw and wonder at my admiration of this but it is perfectly glorious. Every day I admire it more and the melancholy of its winter loneliness suits me.

Oh how glorious it was tonight when crimson clouds descended just to the mountaintops and were reflected on the pure face of the snow. I think I never saw the procession of the stars so glorious as here. The door of this room and my window look due north and the Plough is quite a dipper now and so luminous and a cold pure crescent hangs over the ghostliness of Longs Peak. This scenery makes a deep impression upon me yet it is not loveable.

I like the serenity of the life. The men are so easy to live with, they never fuss, and they now seem quite at ease. It would amuse anyone to come in before breakfast these two mornings into the wretched little kitchen where we feed and find Mr Kavanagh busy at the stove frying venison, I with sleeves pinned up washing the supper dishes and Mr

---

* See Dr William Hanna, p. 326.

Buchanan drying them or they two busy at the stove while I am sweeping the floor. Our food is a great object to us. I have not had so much to eat for all the months my teeth have been bad as since we began to use the venison – it is so tender. Mr B. says he has not had such an appetite since he came to the Park as since he cooked his own food and rode for my quart of *cream*. I think I am feeling as well now as I did on the Sandwich Islands, better perhaps than I ever did there when stationary. I have so much work and am now really getting enough to eat. It relieves my mind that 'Jim' is not ill and that he was so sensible and quiet yesterday. But 'better a finger off than aye wagging'. It is no use staying here. I feel so convinced that the old miseries would begin at whatever time I gave up this life that I intend to leave the first day I can get anyone to go down with me. But at present, unless Edwards returns this is not possible. It probably will be the beginning of next week. It is so sad that you can never see me as I am now with an unconstrained manner, and an up-to-anything free legged air. I did not expect to have so 'good a time' as this in Colorado because I had no idea I could ride here. [. . .]

Tuesday Eve. 25. Somehow I have had a great deal of work to do today. I never got done from 10.30 till 1.30. After washing up I made a 4 lb spiced gingerbread cake, which is a wonderful success. But oh what a day it was getting a cask of butter open in the milk house getting molasses from a keg so cold as to be torpid assembling everything. I found some buttermilk which had stood a fortnight in the churn and raised the cake with this and soda. Then I baked 3 loaves of bread and during the baking I washed my clothes and ironed them in preparation for going to the States. Then Mr Kavanagh and I lunched together I again washed up and then I wrote to Mr Dunlop. It was so very windy that I did not ride but took a magnificent walk or rather a walk of glorious views. It was nearly dark when I came home but the melancholy glory lingered chiming with my melancholy feelings. It is the grandest place on this continent I suppose, but oh so mournful or else my feelings make me think it so.

Sometime after dark our solitude was broken in upon by the arrival of a young man with Evans team. He had met with an accident, and the wagon lies broken in two 7 miles from here. He says that Evans and Edwards will both be up in a day or two. He is a slangy assured youth. I asked him where he lived and he said 'Ive come to live here.' I am howling frightfully, fearfully about leaving the place and the life. It will be better when it is over now. It is strange that a place and life totally unconnected with people can have such charms, but I am thoroughly attached to it and though I cant say that I have any feeling of wellness because my back always drags, I should be puzzled to say what ails my body and I sleep for ten hours, and have no pain except the gnawing in my spine. Yes Estes Park is loveable after 5 weeks. I should not have had an annoying recollection, had it not been for poor dear Jim. Like Meg I say 'Theres a man I could have married'! But 'Better a finger off than aye wagging.' As soon as these men return and I get my money directly I shall go. I believe I should always be pretty well here, but that whenever I left it would be the same miserable downfall so what good is there in staying, when I weary to see its blessed little mean face again.

Bessie says everyone has grown so old. I fear she means you. I dont feel old here. I do so dread the thought of getting back with literally no place to be the homeless life without its charms. I picture to myself sitting by a fireside with you and not desiring ought else, but that fireside is always Castle Terrace. It is so dreadful about the Kers [moving away from Edinburgh]. I try not to think of it but the thought and the bitterness will come when I once more see those cold grey streets. One reason the chief one for wandering off to Portland by an Allen Steamer is that Mr Dunlop would arrange all about your meeting me and smooth things so well. I always fancied E. & B. coming with you, and our staying a week with them first. I have the highest respect for Mr Dunlop and like him very much. I think he is truth and honour itself, but I am afraid of him, for I think he sees through one. I have not yet borne to write to E. and B. Tell them as *soon as you can* that I received the three last delightful letters from each of them and delight in them more than ever, but that my heart is so broken I have not yet been able to write to them. Tell them I never got their letters from Interlachen, Geneva or London, and knew nothing about this terrible break up till I *gathered* it from their first letters.

The new young man is playing the harmonium *all the time.*

Wednesday Nov 26. [. . .] Last night was fearful. The wind lifted the cabins up and took off much of the roof. We sat with gravel driving in our faces from the chinks and bits of the roof falling all night. I took out 4 shovelfulls of mud from the parlour this morning. As soon as we had breakfasted Mr Kavanagh I and this youth Mr Allan* with two wagon horses went 10 miles to the scene of yesterdays disaster in a fearful gale of wind. I felt so like a servant 'getting out' for a days pleasuring. I hurried 'my dishes' and sweeping and left my bed unmade. It was a beautiful and very pleasant ride in fact the acme of magnificence but such a

---

* See James Allen, p. 314.

wild day. The wagon was overturned and only a large pine prevented it from going over a precipice. I did not like to think that my next ride over that trail would be my last. I left them to fix it and turned back till Mr Kavanagh overtook me and then we raced our horses against each other for 2 miles. I liked that. I now feel like a centaur on a horse one with it. The thing that makes riding not hurt me is that I never move from the saddle. We got in first before the wind fell and the snow began.

Since then Ive swept the parlour did my own room corrected the youths poetry and finished a 12-page letter to Dr Hanna. My 4 lb ginger cake is 3 parts eaten though only made yesterday. While I was waiting for Mr Kavanagh this morning I saw Mr Nugent for some time. 'Better a finger off than aye wagging' applies sadly in his case. He always says he is going and never goes. He seemed perfectly wretched fierce bitter about everything and his voice choked often. I never saw anyone so changed. It makes me wretched to see him. I told him the young men wanted him to come and eat Thanksgiving supper with us and he said he was not fit for society and could not come. He is writing on Spiritualism. It is really miserable to see him. I could not prolong my stay here because of him. I believe he hates himself and me and every-one else. How sad it is that no walls of rock can shut out human woe and evil. I cant do with this at all.

Thursday Thanksgiving Day Nov. 27. The thing dreaded has come at last. Last night the snow began to fall with a N.E. wind. It ceased about midnight but not before it had well covered my bed. Then the mercury tumbled down to zero and everything is frozen. I melted a tin of water by the parlour fire but it froze as I tried to wash in it. One half of the parlour is white with snow. The milk is all frozen and the treacle. Two calves froze to death in the shed. The ink froze. At 8 the snow began again and now at one it is still snowing quietly like fine dust coming in at all the open chinks. Strange to say I dont feel it cold though my hair which I washed was frozen on my head. I have no petticoat under my crinoline and only an unlined silk one and my short wincy riding frock over that. I cannot wear my Shetland next to my skin it caused such a sore eruption. On my shoulders, I have nothing to keep me warm and where I am sitting the room is below the freezing point. Yet I am quite warm.

Ever since I came the lake has been frozen hard enough to bear a wagon and in the hole where we draw water the ice has daily been broken by an axe. This snow *may* melt or snow weather will set in. If I am blocked in I can't help it and shall not therefore distress myself, but

I dont see how Edwards can get up with the winter supplies. And it really is serious about food. There is coffee enough to last tomorrow and the same of tea. There are 1000 lbs of butter in the milk house but the sugar is just done and the flour may last out a week. It is really bad to have 'another mouth to feed', though he is a very nice boy of 18. He told me this morning he could eat the whole of what was on the table. He is mad after food and I see Mr Kavanagh is starving himself to make it hold out. Mr Buchanan is not so well and he is fearing the result of '1/2 rations'. It sounds laughable but it would not be so if we have to look actual hunger in the face. They think the snow wont lie 2 days except in the gulches. Had I known that Edwards had gone to the Plains I should certainly not have come up but being here I have liked it very much. These are such steady men and so easy to live with and the quiet is delicious!

There must be 2 weeks letters from you at Longmount. I wonder if Edwards will have the sense to call at the Post Office. The letters take 8 days to reach N.Y. from Longmount. Mr Allan says there is a pilikia between Spain and America and immense excitement all over the Union. I think this is a very nice letter! Much made out of nothing. I am so glad that Emily looks better. She has less to worry her now. How I wish I could see her bright face and hear the strange things she says so unlike the dull ways of other people. Her letters are so bright and intellectual. I dont see how I shall get about without her everlasting kindness about her carriage such kindness as was never known. Driving hurts me badly in every ordinary conveyance, and walking gives me pain on the back of my head lasting all night even here. She is so wonderfully good. I wish she had a friend who could fully sympathise with her faith and religious feelings as neither Bessie nor I can do with all our love for her! They are such noble women and so are all the Kers. And all my nice letters will be stale to them and when I see them I shall have forgotten so many things which vividly impressed me at the time. Emily describes Dr Candlish in such beautiful language just reading and appreciating his truly noble character, for he was noble a really great and good man.

I like this place to be stationary in, i.e. the house and its ways better than any I ever was in. The snow clouds which have hidden the mountains all day are lifting and disclosing a wonderful winter scene, but the wind is rising. *9 p.m.* About 4 it cleared up and is a brilliant night perfectly still with the mercury 5° minus. It is 3° plus in my unchinked room the cold of which takes away ones breath. I have to keep my tin of water by the parlour fire to keep it fluid. Poor Mr Buchanan can hardly get his breath. I am making him a ginger plaster. They are two such worthy young men. I am glad when I can find anything to do for them. They like ceaselessly to hear of my islands a subject on which I can talk ceaselessly.

I spent the afternoon in cooking the Thanksgiving dinner. I made a wonderful pudding. I had saved eggs and cream for it and dried and stoned cherries took the place of currants. I made a very rich custard sauce for it and having some essence of lemon flavoured it. They all said it was 'splendid'. They have eaten my 4 lb cake in 2 days and hint that they would like another. It is this new boy, he confessed that he had eaten it twice as he came through the kitchen. He helped himself 3 times to my pudding. Tonight we had tea made of tea leaves we used last night.

There is something sublime in winter in the heart of the mountains. I daresay there will be a bright hot sunset to morrow. Unhappily the stumps of the two teeth I lately broke off are aching violently at times. I have not been out, the snow is so deep but in crossing the unroofed room between the parlour and the kitchen the cold sets up jumping toothache and it has to be borne. The snow lies all along one side of our parlour. It is so cold that we gave up sweeping it out because of opening the door. Mr Kavanagh has made the most delicious bread I ever tasted. He sets flour and water to turn sour by the fire and uses that for yeast. It is the lightest sweetest most cakelike bread I ever saw.

Sat. Nov. 29. I did not write yesterday, the day was thoroughly sunless with impending snow mist and after the intense frost was comparatively mild and damp. It looked triste, I had stounds* of toothache in a stump and all day long felt that the spectre of depression which is never far off was brushing me with his wings. Thoughts of 'What had been and might have been,

And who were changed, and who were dead'

crowded in upon me, so I did not write and today the sky has resumed its delicious blue and the Park its unrivalled beauty.

Yesterday was a vile day. A hurricane began about 5 in the morning and the whole Park and mountains were one swirl of drifting snow like wood smoke. My bed and room were white with snow. Later than this the frost was so intense that in my room warm water froze as it was poured into the basin. Then the wind fell after blowing most of the snow out of the Park and it became fine but mildish and damp then a snow mist obscured all the mountains but at night it cleared. I worked in the kitchen ceaselessly till nearly one and made a 4 lb. cake. I then wrote

* Pangs.

'Long's Peak' for 'Out West', but I felt very dil, and actually set to work and cleaned all the windows, a filthy business. I only wish I had done it before. Then Mr Buchanan and I took the organ to pieces and cleaned it. Then I went out but felt truly mean, and could not walk more than a quarter of a mile, then attended to the horses, then wrote again till supper. I usually write after supper and we talk for about an hour before bedtime. Today has been beautiful though too windy and with the bright sun and the dry air I have felt quite better again. It is such a serene life, 'uplifted above war, and hate, and storms of passion'. I howl about leaving it, yet if Edwards comes, and we fully expect him tonight, I have only 2 more days.

It is in some respects like being on board ship, there are no mails, and one knows nothing and has no vision beyond ones little world, which is a very small one in this case. We talk a great deal on subjects. The 2 men though they have no culture are very observant, well informed and intelligent and Mr Kavanagh, the miner, though as quiet as Uncle John,[*] when he can be got to speak imparts much. Of course having known these men for 2 months and having tried each other under these circumstances, and found each other true we esteem each other and consequently get on very well. I should for instance go out of the room leaving this book open, certain that they would never read my letter. They are thoroughly honourable true discreet men, but of a type which has no antetype at home. If we lived a year together I suppose we should get on as we do now.

All women work in this country, so there is no fuss or bother about my working, or saying 'Oh let me do that' or 'Oh you mustn't do that'. They know I cant lift any weights, and there is a tacit understanding as to the work. The last 2 or 3 days they have brought me a brass pan of hot water to wash in! They dont like my 'working with horses' but when I told them that all sorts of light work were good for me they said nothing more. They are thoroughly sensible. I cant do hard work that is obvious so I never could take a servants place but I should make an excellent emigrant when I could take my own time. I now even understand management of an American cooking stove. It seems dreadful to think how helpless I was when I first went to the [Hawaiian] islands, yet even then I could do more than most English people. It is all hollow and sickly that idea at home of degradation in manual labour. I am quite sure all women except weaklings like you would be better for stirring about their own houses. But it is such a vile damp dirty climate – everything

[*] See John Bird Sumner, p. 342.

you touch makes you dirty. Here I 'riot most luxuriously' in doing work. [. . .]

Sunday Nov 30th. The last day of Nov! We sat up till 11. last night, so confident were we that Edwards would leave Denver the day after Thanksgiving and be here last night. Our anger boiled over and we have I think determined to break up this fraternity. Tea coffee and sugar are done, and the venison is turning sour. The men have only one month left to hunt in and on their hunting their winters living depends. Now as the new boy is nominally working for his board, I dont think they are in the least bound to injure themselves for a man who has been so thoroughly faithless and I wont have them stay for my comfort. I cant leave the territory till I get my money! but as I have my horse I think as I cant get a guide I shall take my foot in my hand and ride over the mountains to Big Thompson to Dr Hutchinsons, thence to Longmount for the mail and to see if by any marvel Evans has paid that money into the bank for me, back here and finally away on Monday 8th. This is a very long delay but for one thing I cant help it and for another I cling to a day or two more of a place and life which give me better feelings.

Yesterday was a beautiful day. I worked (in the original sense the sweat of the brow), wrote, and in the afternoon took a beautiful ride with Mr Kavanagh to look for our milch cow which had been missing for two days. This morning the two men from up the river came and we had quite a concert. I have practised the organ a good deal and I played the accompaniments for one hour. They all play. I played our national anthem and they asked me to play it again and all began

'My country tis of thee
Sweet land of liberty etc'

In their books it is called 'America'. Ours is an effete and faded patriotism as compared with the American pride and love of country. They have all gone out for the afternoon, since which I have washed up the lunch things and made two roly poly puddings with molasses for supper which require their boiling attended to. How easy cooking must be when you have all the appliances. We have only a kettle, a frying pan and a 6 gallon brass pan and use a cup for a rolling pin. I cooked some trout which looked and were perfectly delicious, rolling them in coarse cornmeal and frying them.

The new boy is partly amusing and partly a plague. I thought he was 23 at first but he is only 19 and very pretentious, but in some things singularly childish for his years, and so fond of eating, a most unfortunate predilection here. After getting strong he is going to a theological semi-nary and thence into the ministry, but he is quite unfit for it for he is not honourable. He writes in the St Louis Republican and in a maga-zine called the Western and he showed us long pieces of his poetry. In the printed one there are 12 lines Mr K. says copied verbatim from Paradise Lost and a few very long M.S. one which is to be published then there are 2 stanzas from Resignation with only the alteration of *stray* for dead lamb, and all the 'Meeting Place' only slightly altered. Again he lent me an essay called 'The function of the Novelist' entirely made up of quotations which I recognised. Again the men tell me that he has been 'bragging' that he took shelter in Mr Nugents cabin in his absence and opened his box and read his letters and manuscripts! He is amusing but a plague from ignorance and lack of self-sufficiency.

The first morning when I was washing up he said he intended to do all the dirty work. I finished and leaving the knives and forks in the water asked him to wipe them, and 2 hours after I went back and found them not done. He doesnt know how to catch a horse and talks grandly of las-soing not even knowing that a lasso is made of cow hide and he cant tell one cow from another. Two days ago he spent the whole morning looking for the cow and brought one and milked it, bringing into the parlour the pail with a wineglass full of shine in it and when Mr K. went out he found it was a cow dry since last summer! Today I told him to fill up the 4 gallon kettle and just now found it empty and red hot on the stove. Nothing can be kept from him. He has eaten 2 lbs of dried cherries from the shelf, half my 2nd 4 lb spiced loaf, licked up my custard sauce in the night, and pri-vately finished my bread and butter pudding! He confesses to it all and says 'I suppose you think I'm a case.' He sleeps in a lean-to from the kitchen so he can get at everything. Mr K. says that the first thing this morning he said 'Will Miss Bird make a nice pudding today.' All this is harmless, but the plagiarism and dishonourable conduct regarding private papers is wrong. They told me not to leave my writing book on the table.

It is freezing yet I am wearing today being Sunday my grenadine pol-onaise with unlined sleeves and feel too warm. I suppose the rarefied air at this height quickens ones circulation. We have decided on breaking up 'The fair order of this table round'. The men very kindly will stay till Tuesday to get me off early. Tomorrow we are going to advance the breakfast hour from ten to 8 as they will be out hunting all day, and I want to write. I wonder how you will like the Longs Peak letter. I like it almost better than any for it represents what I thoroughly liked. I never saw such a foolish mismanaged random dog as Pincher. It is so miser-able that B. & E. can never see my letters and that before I see them if

I ever do see them my Hawaiian ravages and life here will be almost forgotten, and I shall be the old dil person again. I cant trust my letters to the foreign post, unless they are registered.

I dont think I ever liked a room so well as this. The huge log fire gives it such a cheerful air and I like the bare warm tinted walls of hewn logs and the huge hewn pine which is the roof tree and the round young pines, which closely laid together form the roof. There is certainly no place like it, no life like it for health. The difficulty is the mail. They say that after I leave they probably will not get letters for 4 months! I hope you are liking Tobermory all the time. As Mrs Blackie would say, I am not 'amiable enough' to like a place with so many people. It seems so like a rabbit warren. Yet 'Each one to his taste'. If my health or something were stronger I too should like to be among people. My teeth have been better since the weather settled again. I have thought since times what I should do if I were ill, with no woman or even a competent man within 25 miles! I have almost forgotten that there are such things as women and for woman in the abstract I never wish! It is so strange never to hear dress mentioned — anyone would be surprised to hear men talking about cooking when the 5 were here today they were asking one another minutely how they made their yeast and bread, and one asked me how I made the spiced cake and in return told me how to make molasses candy. My puddings have turned out perfection.

Monday Dec 1. I think I forgot two things, first that on Friday night I was awoke twice by fine snow like pin points beating on my face. Second that the day Mr Kavanagh and I rode we met 'Jim' and that Mr K. usually so reticent said 'Whats wrong with that man! He'll shoot himself or somebody else.' He looked so dreadful that if he had not had as one *supposed* a human soul he should have been destroyed. Today we were up early, but all plans were upset by a snowstorm. So after washing up I washed my clothes and the towels I had used and then made before lunch a pair of drawers out of the relics of my nightgown.

After lunch Mr Allan rode with me to take my paper on Longs Peak to be corrected by 'Jim', but he said he couldnt read it and insisted on our coming in, which the boy was most anxious to do. The dark fit had passed off he was as pleasant as he could be. Amidst those black and hideous surroundings he seemed more a gentleman than ever. The cold was awful. I had got a chill in the morning sitting without nearly all my clothes in my fireless room while I mended them and I was glad to get 'into' the fire. I read aloud my paper which sounded very nice. The geography and altitudes were all correct. He made excellent criticisms on the style and pointed out repetitions of the same idea. I entirely forgot all the time that the disastrous affair began on Longs Peak. I could not help looking at him as he stood talking to Mr Allan. He drinks, swears, has an ungovernable temper, he has led a 'desperate' life, and is at times a ruffian undoubtedly, and I suppose there is hardly a fireside in Colorado where fearful stories of him as an Indian fighter are not told. His faults are glaring. Yet I suppose he is the most popular man in the territory. I think him fascinating as I have before seen him or as he was today. The boy asked me if I should be afraid to ride alone with him because of his terrible reputation, but I should never dream of being afraid of him. Those ninety and nine just persons which need no repentance are different.

We stayed till it began to grow dark and we had a fearful ride back, a snow wind nearly blowing us off our horses, blinding drifts and cruel cold. I got some whisky from Mr Buchanan when I came in, for I had 'claws' from the chill this morning! Though until evening it was not freezing. The men say that if a storm prevents my going tomorrow they will stay. They said they were horrified when I came for they didnt see how they could make me comfortable, and they didnt think I was used to doing anything for myself, but they said 'We've got on all right, I think we could get on for a year.' I told them that was just what I had written to you. Their behaviour has been perfect. I never live more easily with people. I am shrinking from the prospect of riding 100 miles in this wild winter, but unless I go I see no hope of getting the money here out of post and telegraph facilities.

Longmount Dec 3. I am here 'rioting luxuriantly' so as to justify Alickies awful language about 'the roughest Devil'! which made me laugh. I have got all your letters and enclosures with thankfulness and will make comments. The mercury is *17° below zero.*

I left Estes Park alone yesterday morning in fine weather and in 2 hours was caught in a sudden and awful mountain storm succeeded on the prairie by a terrific N.E. snowstorm. I shall never forget it. It was the 'roughest tiggling' I ever had. I was nearly *frozen to death.* I once thought I should never see any human face again but perish there in the wild drift. No mail carrier dared to cross that disastrous prairie yesterday. It was fearful. I had to make across or die for I could not turn back. Today is still the snow dry as dust. I am going to make for Dr Hutchesons 26 miles. Evans is here and I have got 40 dollars of my 55. I hope to get to the Park* on Friday to cut the finger off on Monday my last ride, my

---

* Estes Park.

last ravage, my last free leggism. I have bought a mans cardigan and mittens to go over my lined leather gloves. Yesterday the bridle froze to my hands and my eyelids froze together. Anything more fearful could not be seen. I will write again about lodgings. Nothing can be done yet. The idea seems so hideous of having no fireside [in Scotland].

Its Pet
ILB

Dr Hutchinsons Big Thompson Cañon
Dec 4. 1873

My ownest

This paper which was strapped round some sweeties is all I have and I have to keep my ink on the stove to keep it fluid with a temperature so far below zero. I have on only my riding drawers and frock chemise shetland vest and my short old green silk skirt and require no more. My teeth have not ached at all since this tremendous cold set in because it is so dry. I must reserve comments till I have more time except on the fearful weather which is shocking to think of and your requiring so many clothes. I am glad I am not there, I should be distracted with neuralgia. I cant write well a thong of my stirrup broke as I crossed the prairie yesterday and taking off my glove to mend it I got my hand slightly frozen and my elbow and right knee were frosted from the day before. They are none of them bad but my knee because I knew how to treat them only not useful.

I am 'shrieking, howling, roaring' after my glorious rathole and my congenial life and my altogether out of the world wild windy beast-haunted snow blocked den. But it is again changed for Edwards has gone there and the men said they would not stay an hour after he came, they detest him so. He is as much hated as Evans is liked. I could not spend the winter there with him.

Now I cant write the eldritch* ride of Tuesday. It should if possible have been written at once. On Monday night I drank hot water with a pinch of cayenne in it which removed the chill. We all got up at daylight on Tuesday and breakfasted at 7.30. It was a very fine morning west wind and we all thought promised well. I was well clothed but took no gear except a dress and middlemarch for Mrs Hutchinson and sweeties for the children, and lunch in a pouch on the saddle, and the mail bag also an additional blanket under the saddle. I had not been up out of the

---

* Weird.

Park at sunrise before and it was glorious the purple depths of McGinns Gulch from which from a height of 9000 feet or 1500 higher you look down on the sunlit Park with its pearly acicular formed thus [sketch] by mountainsides dark with pines. The *purple* sun rose in front. Had I known what made it purple I should have gone no further. Then clouds, I supposed the morning mist lifted up themselves in the gulch rose lighted showing the purple sun through as Tyrian purple as a jar in a druggist window. But it grew thicker, grew grey shut out the sun and began to freeze hard so that the horse and my bearskin were snow white.

It was a dense easterly fog! I galloped on. I could see nothing before me thinking to get out of it but my hands and feet were nearly numb with cold. 4 miles further I met 'Jim' nearly rode over him. His tangled ringlets were snow white making him look 100 years old. I suppose he has concluded to let the dead past bury its dead. He stormed and scolded, pulled me off the pony, and dragged it along at an immense rate so that in the darkness I often had to run to keep them in sight. I was off the road in a thicket of scrub all white like coral I knew not where. Then we came suddenly on his cabin where he made me come in and lighted a fire and insisted on my getting warm raging just like E. or B. He wanted me to go back. He said all sorts of things but never that it was dangerous. All he said turned out true. I still said I would go and he said 'Ive seen many foolish women but never one so foolish as you. You've not a grain of sense.' He seemed quite merry and laughed at the stories I told him of young Allan. I dont know now how much of his dark ways and dark language were assumed, he is such a consummate actor and so strange altogether.

As soon as I got warm I started again. I was not frightened but it was an eerie ride and the fir tree tufts of foliage looked like white chrysanthemums. The snow lay a foot deep in the gulches with an unbroken surface so solemn only footmarks of bears here and there so awe inspiring. These gulches looked fathomless abysses with clouds boiling up out of them. Everything looked vast and undefined. A huge thing apparently like Doré's[*] notion of Satan in his illustrations of Paradise Lost with breathing of wings came sailing towards me. As with a strange rustle it passed only about 3 feet over my head I saw for the first time the *gigantic mountain eagle* carrying a good sized beast in his talons!!!

10 miles of metamorphosed gulches silent awful 6 ice bridges. One gave way and let us through. Wind N.E. came on and a frozen drizzle. We were unrecognisable. Birdie was clad in exquisite crystals and the long mane and

---

[*] See Gustave Doré, p. 322.

the beard which covers all her throat were pure white. I knew then I must give up coming here by an unknown trail and I struck the old trail to the St Vrain which I had never travelled before but which I knew was more legible than the new one. The day grew colder and windier but Bird who in all difficulties proves her value never flinched or made a false step. It was a shocking day but still I was not sorry that I came on. I got down somehow to the St Vrain Cañon and stopped at a house 15 miles from Longmount to get oats. I was white from head to foot and my clothes frozen stiff. The woman gave me the usual invitation 'put your feet in the oven'. I got my things thawed and dried and a delicious basin of cream and bread. They said it would be worse on the Plains for it was an easterly storm but they thought as I was such a good rider I could get on. So we started at 2.30.

Not far off I met Edwards who said I ought to have passed Evans. I began to wonder very much about my money.* If it had not been for these men being so unreliable I might have been saved this ride. Soon after I passed Edwards the snowstorm began in earnest or rather I entered what had been going on all day. I had then reached the prairie only 8 miles from Longmount and pushed on. It was simply fearful. It was deep twilight from the snow and I faced a furious east wind laden with fine hard frozen snow. I could only see a very short distance anywhere, the drift was nearly 2 feet high and only now and then through its blinding whirl I caught a glimpse of snow through which withered sunflowers did not protrude so that I knew I was on the track. But reaching a wild place I lost the track and yet galloping on trusted to Birdie whose instinct failed for she took me on a lake which I did not know till we both fell through the ice and then had to fight through ice and water for 100 yards to get to land. It grew worse. The sharp frozen snow beat on my eyes the only exposed part of my face bringing tears into them which froze and closed up my eyelids. You cannot imagine what that was. I had to take off one glove to pick one eye open for as to the left eye the storm beat so furiously against that, that I left it frozen and drew over it a double piece of flannel which covered my face. I could hardly keep the other eye open by picking it open with my numb fingers. It was truly awful. I often thought suppose I was going south instead of east, suppose Bird fails, suppose I am frozen! I thought of people who had perished on the prairie in similar storms. I calculated that if I did not reach Longmount in another hour it would be dark and that I should be frozen or so paralysed with cold that I should fall off. My elbow and right knee were already frozen.

* See footnote, p. 172.

It was not many minutes after I had thought how long I could hold out that to my surprise I saw close to me 1/2 smothered in snow the scattered houses of Longmount! How welcome that wide dreary lifeless soundless road looked. At the hotel I could not get off, and when off Mr Sigley had to carry me in. They had not expected any travellers and had no fire except in the bar so they took me into their bedroom with a stove and brought me hot grog and blankets. They said they had said 'If there's anyone on the prairie today God help him.' My teeth chattered so that it was long before I could speak. I had not suffered so from cold as I did yesterday it was the fierce wind and the fog. All my outer clothing was frozen stiff. I did not cease shivering till I had plenty of food and hot tea. Evans was at tea waiting at Longmount because he thought it too bad to go up. I went early to bed and slept all night. The air had cleared and the mercury had gone down to zero (17 below).

I waited in Longmount till nearly 12 to be certain of the weather and it was a glorious day. At first on going out at those temperatures one does not realise the cold – indeed if you only stay out a short time you can go out in your house clothes. I had to get ice shoes put on Birdies hind feet first then to get myself a cardigan and knitted mittens to go over my gloves. I bought some little things also for the Hutchinsons mailed the letters did some commissions for the men at Estes Park saw Evans off and an English gentleman who came with him and then went and spent the rest of the forenoon with the Glazers two very gentlemanly and thoroughly cultivated Englishmen who keep a store in Longmount. They were very pleasant. I have seen almost no people in Colorado of education or refinement still less of culture so that I have always enjoyed talking with these two young men. And they are so amusing in the things they say about Dr Hutchinson. I hung about afterwards waiting for a freight train to break the track but at last went away alone seeing Longmount for the last time. I little thought that miserable broiling day I drove there with the Hutchinsons of the glorious den to which it was the entrance. Everyone speaks to me by name in Longmount and all down the St Vrain Cañon and indeed everywhere now because I have got such a reputation as a mountaineer, and so many newspaper paragraphs have described me that when I meet people on the road they know who I am and I daresay speak to see what kind of monster I am.

It looked icily beautiful quite pure and the sky a dreamy blue. I could find the track from its greater smoothness but I left it soon and starting for Storm Peak struck out upon the trackless prairie for about 13 miles. There is no house between Longmount and here and I did not see man beast or bird. Even in that bright sunshine it seemed very awful. The cold always great became piteous. I did not know what to do with my hands and feet and I got a part of my hand frozen in mending my stirrup. The snow was so dry that it crunched and squeaked under Birds feet. When the sun went behind the mountains, the colour was lovely but the cold was hardly endurable and I got off and walked the last mile, holding a snow poultice on my frost bitten hand. I think the foothills and the Thompson Cañon are rather improved by snow.

I arrived here without anyone seeing me and was most warmly welcomed. They have got a boarder a very rich Englishman who has come out for the winter to hunt. A new room has been added and there are signs for the present of easier circumstances. But Oh it is a life painful to contemplate and this inclement weather further brings out its woes, when 4 little children have to live all day in one small room with 3 adults. They are delightful children but it is hard for them to be subdued all day. Mrs H. is a charming person, highly intellectual and accomplished and bears up nobly and unselfishly. They are quite set on going to the Sandwich Islands, should the replies to their letters turn out favourable and the notion of moving makes him more neglectful of his place than ever, milking the cows only every two or three days so that they run dry, not re-chinking the house. The cold of it is fearful. In this parlour where they now have the cooking stove the boards of the floor are 1/2 an inch apart letting up all the cold. In the boarders room which he has kindly given up to me, it is the same and those walls being only made of planks you might as well be in the open air. While lying in bed I could see the stars through the roof. I had a dreadful night of cold. There were no bed clothes except my horse blankets and some coats of Mr Haig's.[*] I got 2 sheep skins which were on the floor but nothing was any use. The mercury above my pallet was 8° minus. Mr Haig a luxurious Englishman who had never slept on the floor before and thought it would be 'fun', never slept.

One great trouble is that before each meal the food has to be unfrozen the bread butter eggs cold meat preserve pickles are all hard frozen and the water freezes even in a bucket by the stove. I can only keep the ink from freezing by keeping it on the stove. Yet I only feel the cold in bed. The bed clothes are of the length and breadth of those des

[*rest of letter missing*]

The next day Isabella returned to Estes Park. From there, Jim accompanied her to the nearby town of Namaqua, where she caught a stage wagon east to begin the

---

[*] See William Haigh, p. 326.

long journey home. In *A Lady's Life in the Rocky Mountains*, Isabella gives what must be an edited account of their parting; yet even in this slimmed-down version, Jim cries out, 'Too late! Too late!' and sheds tears over her departure. Even worse, her final act was to introduce him to William Haigh, Lord Dunraven's agent, who proved the agency of Jim's murder at Griff Evans's hands. The experience haunted her. In *Phantasms of the Living*, published more than ten years later by the Society for Psychical Research, Bird claimed Jim appeared to her at the hour of his death. At the same time, she was never fully comfortable with her feelings. As she wrote to Ella Blackie in 1879, 'Don't let anybody think that I was in love with Mountain Jim for I have never been in love but once, but the pity and yearning to save him that I felt have taught me a little of what I think may at an immeasurable distance be the pity and yearning of the Father.'

PART TWO
THE SECOND WORLD TOUR
1878–9

Japan & the Way Thither

For the next five years, Isabella stayed in Scotland. She published her adventures in Hawaii as a book, and those in Australia and Colorado as articles in *The Leisure Hour*, a polite family magazine. She bought a microscope to study at the Edinburgh Botanical Gardens; she corresponded with Charles Darwin[*] about mountaineering in the Andes; and she helped establish a college for medical missionaries in memory of David Livingstone,[†] the African explorer. Most dramatically, Isabella received another proposal of marriage, this time from a respectable doctor from Sheffield named John Bishop.[‡] Such events enabled Isabella to come into her own: she was a famous writer, a respected traveller and a desirable woman at the age of forty-five. But she was far from well. When friends from Hawaii visited Mull, they were amazed to find that the woman who had scaled Mauna Loa couldn't get out of bed. The only thing to do was to journey east, and in the interests of her health Isabella complied. At this point, Henrietta fell ill. Perhaps a long voyage might benefit her too? No one seemed to agree. Instead, Henrietta was left in the care of the kindly Dr Bishop, and Isabella sailed away for her next adventure: by rail through America, and thence to Japan. The following are letters she wrote to her close friend Ella Blackie.

Grand Hotel San Francisco May 1st 1878

My dear one

I am so thankful to hear that you are better. May God bless you and bring you all safely back again, with stores of new interests and memories. A day in Italy is worth more than a year of ordinary American travelling.

Now I will only tell you about myself that I had the best passage to New York I ever made and that it was very pleasant owing to having my friend Mr Robertson on board. Did I tell you that Hennie was very poorly and in bed for a week before I left and that she decided on calling in Dr Bishop who treated her with more judgement and skill than she has ever been treated with before, and was delightful in the capacity of a doctor. She was able to see me off at Greenock. Parting from her is 'the bitterness of death' and is not 'past'. As her sweet calm face faded

[*] See Charles Darwin, p. 321.
[†] See David Livingstone, p. 331.
[‡] See John Bishop, p. 316.

away in the golden sunset I felt, as I feel still, that if she were to die I should never return to Scotland. We slept together for a fortnight before I left. I came on from New York to Chicago at once where I stayed with Sandwich Island friends for one night then on to Salt Lake City for 2 days where some excellent introductions enabled me to see something of 'saintly' life! But I was so poorly and have been so ever since, completely shaken by the railroad journey, so much so that I had to leave the cars at Colfax for a day and night when within 12 hours of San Francisco. To my joy Alick met me at Oakland 7 miles from here. He has been so delightfully kind and has given up so much time to helping me. He seems already au fait of all the ways here and has managed all my business matters so competently. I dined at his *splendid* boarding house last night. It is on the top of a high hill in pure air with a fine view and is very airy and altogether for the kind of place desirable. I sat for a few minutes in their little sitting room which is both pretty and cosy with a fine view towards the Golden Gate. All the pretty mementoes of friends and home were about it. The photo of Altnacraig[*] looked beautiful. I think A. is hardly acclimatised yet, but I cannot see any reason why the climate should not suit him. He seems in very good spirits. He is so very *gentlemanly*. I wish I could write more about him but I sail for Japan tomorrow, and have a great deal yet to do. With much love, I remain

Your loving friend
ISABELLA L BIRD

Hakodate Island of Yezo August 12/78

Dearest One

Your letter and the Pro's delightful addition, with his splendidly truthful criticism of Ruskin[†] were forwarded to these northern wilds this afternoon and I must put in a line to thank you both for remembering your lonely far off friend. I feel much for the Pro's detention among mosquitoes and am very sorry for his disappointment in Egypt. Tell him I agree with him as to the charm of the heather and the Highlands. Nothing in Japan pleases me *one half* so well as the strolls around Altnacraig in the long twilights of our beautiful June. If I am spared to return I shall never again cross any sea wider than the channel. My spine is so much worse that I cannot ride and without that I should prefer

---

[*] See Altnacraig, p. 314.
[†] See John Ruskin, p. 340.

Mull. My journey hitherto has been a great disappointment as far as health goes – I am much worse than when I left home. Otherwise all has been most propitious. I have a congenial and a delightful home at the British Legation with Sir Harry and Lady Parkes,* all difficulties suggested as to my getting into the interior turned out myths, the government has afforded me every facility and I have just successfully accomplished a tour of 700 miles through the heart of the interior without molestation, although on much of my route no European has ever been seen. After being for two months exclusively among Asiatics I find the society of English people fatiguing and *clattering*. My soul hankers for solitude and freedom so in two days I go off into the interior of Yezo to live among its aborigines, the 'hairy Ainos'† till the summer heat be over. I do not enjoy my tour mainly owing to pain and debility but I am accumulating much interest for the future. Japan involves severe brain work. I give myself entirely up to studying it. In the middle of September I purpose to return to the Legation for a month, and then to go to Kioto and Southern Japan. British Legation, Tokio is my address.

Do not forget your loving friend
ILBIRD

Unfortunately, there appear to be no letters to Henrietta from the six months Isabella spent in Japan. All that remains are a few torn pages from her diary, covering a two-week journey from Kyoto to Ise in late November of 1878 – a journey, incidentally, that does not appear in *Unbeaten Tracks in Japan*. These notations are brief, perfunctory and lack interest: a tedious chronicle of inns, temples and mud, unlit by the enthusiasm that had shone so brilliantly in her earlier travels. As Isabella wrote to her publisher, 'I am not fascinated with Japan. It is deeply *interesting* and tempts one to make it a serious study but the scenery is monotonous, the modes of travelling slow and painful, and there is a want of colour which is flat.' A scholarly book might do for such a country, but as to printing her letters, that would be impossible. 'I have made careful notes only,' Isabella explained. 'There is nothing fascinating or ecstatic in the style.' Does this mean she sent no other, more personal communications to her sister at this time? Or were they too morose, too self-absorbed to preserve, as seems to have happened with those from the Antipodes? Maybe Isabella was unable to enjoy Japan, thinking of the sister she had left behind. Whatever the case, once she arrived in China her mood improved, allowing her to resume her journal letters.

---

* See Sir Harry Parkes, p. 336.
† Popular (if derogatory) Victorian term for the aborigines of Hokkaido, the northernmost island of Japan. Isabella's writing about them is generally considered to be the most original and valuable part of *Unbeaten Tracks in Japan*, later inspiring Henry Savage Landor's 1891 travelogue, *Alone with the Hairy Ainu: or, 3,800 Miles on a Pack Saddle in Yezo and the Kurile Islands*.

China

St Pauls College Hong Kong Dec 29th [1878]

Circular

My Darling

Unless I write a journal letter everything is lost. I like Hongkong, though so civilised a life does not of course suit me and I dont like travelling in palanquins, but it is so pleasant to have come in from the dark, misty, coarse, loud tongue'd Pacific and from the winter colourlessness of Japan to bright blue water crisped by a perpetual north wind – to the red flaming hills of the Asian mainland which are red in the early morning, redder in the glow of noon to pass away in the glorious sunsets through ruby and vermilion into an amethyst haze, passing into the glories of a tropic night when the heavens are one blaze of stars. I see the beloved Southern Cross quite low in the sky. On this island there are (though by no means in their glory) the things I love. The spurious banyan, the banana, the papaya, the tree fern, the dendrobium, the date, sago and travellers' palms, the dazzling scarlet passion flower and 50 other things, children of the bounteous tropics and of the burning sun, nothing grey or pale.

My voyage here was about the worst I ever made. Mr Johnson & Mr Keswick* took me on board in a luxurious house-boat and as I went immediately to bed in the salon des dames a good cabin with a nice bathroom attached I thought it was very comfortable but when I got up the next morning I found a miserable steamer not near so good as the St David but arranged like her with no place to sit in, and nothing to sit on but the benches by the dinner table. The captain, a lieutenant in the French navy, was a perfect boer goth Vandal Hun Visigoth all in one. The ship was cold, dark, damp and dirty, no steam pipes and the fire could not be lighted because of a smoky chimney, no lamps and the candles grudged, the stewards dirty and disobliging, the serving disgusting, the cooking dirty and greasy, a coarse imitation of French cookery, the food scanty. I got up the two first days but I could not bear the sitting

---

* See William Keswick and Francis Bulkeley Johnson, p. 330.

206

up on the benches, and the damp cold was so unbearable that each day I went to bed in the afternoon about 4. There were about 4 French and 2 Japanese passengers and they sat at meals in top coats, comforters and hats! *No one on board* knew any more English than yes and no. The third day heavy weather came on with a high violent sea and this continued till we got into Hongkong harbour 5 days afterwards. I never got up the whole of that time and was never able to do anything owing to the darkness of my cabin. The berths were athwart ships and the whole of every day and night I had to hold on with my hands to avoid being much hurt in the rolling. I was very seasick and suffered very much in my spine, and it was truly aggravating to have so much writing and sewing to do and not to be able to do any of it!

About 1 on the 26th when I was fearing that we should have 2 days more, we came up with the land 2 hours from Hongkong – the mainland of eastern Asia bare, lofty, rocky, basaltic – perpendicular cliffs and islands of naked rock separated by narrow channels, a desolate uninhabited region with a heavy lashing sea, driving mists, screaming sea birds, and Chinese fishing boats very high at the stern with double reefed 3 corned sails scudding before the stiff breeze. Soon we were among mountainous islands and then by a narrow and picturesque channel entered the outer harbour with this scorched arid island with its high peaks on one side and on the other the yet redder and rockier mainland without a tree or trace of civilisation and only a few stone huts clustering round inlets in which boats were lying and still the coarse bluster went on so that it was only possible to stand on deck in shelter of the deckhouse. Then turning westwards through another channel we entered the inner harbour, and sailed into the summer! Blue sky blue water a summer sun a cool breeze mountains veiled by blue haze. Hongkong looked magnificent like but far finer than Gibraltar with its Peak 1800 feet high rising above the town which clusters along its lower slopes. A forest of masts lay above the town, P.&O. steamers,[*] Messageries Maritimes[†] Steamers, ships of war of all nations, store and hospital ships were at anchor in the harbour itself. Evergreen woods surround the town and the line of streets can sometimes be traced by dense foliage. Huge sugar factories, immense barracks one above another, batteries, the English and Romish Cathedrals, this Palace and College with a high tower, great high blocks of buildings, stone wharves, all came one after another into view, and over all its rich silk folds spreading out fully

---

[*] See Peninsula & Oriental Steam Navigation Company, p. 337.
[†] See Messageries Maritimes, p. 334.

on the breeze floated 'the flag thats braved 1000 years the battle and the breeze' the flag to which Disraeli in the opinion of everyone out here has given a new *prestige* in the East 'worth more than 50 victories'.

But 'what can it be'? I thought those dense volumes of smoke wrapping the lower part of the town and even as we anchored came off the ringing of bells the roll of drums and the murmur of a city at unrest. No one came to meet me. A few Chinese boats came off and then a steam launch with the M.M. agent. 'How can I get ashore' I asked. 'Its no use to go ashore the towns half burned and there's not a bed at any hotel.' However I did go ashore with the mail agent in the launch, but we had to climb over at least 5 house boats and steam launches which were piled high up with all sorts of household goods which were promiscuously tossed into them to save them. 'The Palace of the English Bishop'[*] they said was untouched so I got into a palanquin with two bearers and went there.

What a sight! The streets choked up with household goods and the contents of shops treasured knicknacks on the dusty road way with beds pictures goods of all sorts, Chinese dragging their possessions to the hills, Chinese women with hoofs not feet tottering along with their children, officers black with smoke working at the hose like firemen, portions of troops moving vaguely, Mr Pope Henessey[†] the civil governor ubiquitous in a chair with 4 scarlet bearers, men belonging to the insurance companies running about with drawn swords, everybody running hither and thither and one vast loud confused hubbub of human voices such as I never heard before, with frequent explosions and the rapid tolling of the bell of the Catholic cathedral in imminent peril. Utterly unmoved in grand Oriental calm with the waves of tumult breaking around them stood sentries of the Sikh contingent, majestic men with swarthy faces and great crimson turbans. I was carried up the encumbered streets and up grand flights of stairs to these grounds which were covered over with furniture and goods brought hither for safety and Chinese families camping out among them. In the great covered corridor which runs round the Palace everything the Burdons value most was lying, ready for removal.

She was out but the Bishop and I went down to the fire which was got under and saw the wreck of the city, and the houseless people camping out among the things they had saved. Fire was burning everywhere walls falling whole streets blocked with masses of bricks telegraph

---

[*]   See Bishop John Shaw Burdon, p. 318.
[†]   See Sir John Pope-Hennessy, p. 337.

poles and fused wire lying about 1/2 burned ledgers half burned everything. The noise was fearful. We went to the prison where nearly 500
desperate ruffians of all countries are shut up and the governor said that
it was held by 100 soldiers each with 10 rounds of ammunition, prepared to convey the criminals to a place of safety or to shoot them if
they tried to escape. When we got back, I was just beginning to unpack
when I saw the flames burst out again and called Mrs Burdon and some
friends. It was a sight of lurid grandeur in the darkness, the tongues of
flame lapping up house after house the crashes producing leaping up
flames the glare. The wind was very strong setting this way and for a
whole hour there was so little prospect of this house being saved that
important papers were sent to the cathedral and several of the refugees
fled to the hills with their things. A lighted fragment at last fell on the
window sill when poor Mrs Burdon who was quite done up from
fatigue and excitement having been up all the night before exclaimed
'Oh God spare my home' and fainted. Just then the wind changed and
the great drift of flame and smoke was carried in a comparatively harmless direction and by 9.30 when we were first easy enough to sit down
to food, the fire was got well in hand. I think that everybody has been
upset as much from personal peril as from sympathy. All parties and
picnics for Friday and Saturday were given up. No newspapers came out
on Friday, the types of one were in this garden. I cannot get the China
Mail which had a very good account, but send one. The mismanagement appears to have been something fearful and the drunken state of
the troops on Xmas night rendered them nearly useless. The city is now
patrolled night and day by strong parties of marines and Sikhs, for the
disposition to loot and the facilities for it are so great.

On Friday we walked about in the town. It is a beautiful town or
looks so after the Japanese towns – so like Genoa, semitropical coloured
deep colonnades, green balconies with covers, high houses, very narrow
streets too steep for anything with wheels, some of flights of stairs only,
shade trees arching over the road ways, processions of Portuguese priests
and nuns, people and costumes of many nations, and the blue sky and
bright sun above. It is cold enough for fires and winter clothes and 5
blankets at night, a hot sun and in the shade a temperature of about 65°
falling to 40° at night and a very dry air. There has not been any rain for
4 months. In spring & summer it is damper than Japan and very hot.
Everything is arranged for heat. In this fine building the rooms are very
large and 15 feet high. They open on each side into covered corridors
20 feet wide which are scantily furnished for sitting in hot weather. They
and the bedrooms have highly polished floors and no mats. The family

only consists of Bishop and Mrs Burdon and Mr Henderson, chaplain to the forces, who lives here but a very nice person Captain Edwards of the gun boat Kestrel is staying here to recruit from injuries received in the fire.

The Burdons are very nice people. He is a remarkably able man. He is only 52 but has hair of silver white and a very full beard nearly white with rather a florid complexion and very dark eyes and eyebrows. He is very tall and gentlemanly looking and in his lawn sleeves looks very Episcopal. He talks very well. It is a very pleasant house. Half the house is the Palace and the other half St Pauls College of which Bishop Burdon is Warden. The *mountainous* grounds are beautiful and the entrance blazes with poinsettias. There are no female servants and the Chinese men look severe.

The 'Pidgun English' is revolting. Everyone demeans himself to speak it. If you order a fire you say something like this – 'Fire makee chop, chop here makee fire No 1.' Chop being quick and No 1, good. If a servant tells one that someone has called, he says 'One piecey manee here, speak missy.' Then if one asks who he is the servant says 'no sabe' very likely or 'No 1 think.'

S.S. Kin Kiang Dec 30. I do not like the Chinese. They are rude, rough, disagreeable, threatening, so different from the courteous kindly Japanese. They speak of foreigners always as 'Barbarian Devils'. I have often heard the word in the street already and Bishop Burdon says that before his servants found that he knew Chinese they were always speaking of him and Mrs Burdon by that name. Their rude stare and the way they push you about and shout at you are unpleasant. You remember about 2 years ago, the Chinese rising on the officers & passengers of one of these Hongkong & Canton boats massacring all and going off with the ship. On board this boat there are 1500 steerage passengers, all Chinese men, and 450 second class with about 10 white people. Such an awful Babel it is for the Chinese are such a noisy people. In the salon there is a stand of rifles, 6 rifles and 4 revolvers, and as we started a man carefully loaded every one of these with ball cartridges and took the sheaths off the bayonets. Then gratings were padlocked over the 2 exits from the steerage and a European heavily armed patrols in front of each ready to shoot the first who attempts to force the grating. It is an immense deck above deck American steamer so white and comfortable but there is only one other European passenger. They look and seem such a powerful independent race as if in force 1 were equal to 4 Japanese. They are so big and tall but nearly always their faces are so disagreeable. They are so cruel. Last week near Canton, they cut off the legs and arms of 4 native Xtian catchecists tied a cross to the trunks wrapped them up in oiled paper then burned them alive. There was a placard last week on the walls of Canton calling for a massacre of the native Xtians in the Canton Province on Xmas day & a good many of them took refuge in the mission compound. There has not been any news since. In todays paper there is a translation of the placard. It attributes every vice to the 'barbarian devils' and says that 'to preserve the peace and purity of Chinese society those who they have corrupted must be cut off'. One phrase is, 'The wickedness of these barbarian devils is so great, that even pigs and dogs would refuse to eat their flesh.'

[That said,] foreigners have misused and do misuse the Chinese. The great corridors of this steamer are full of them in dreamy vision smoking the opium which we forced upon them. You cannot be 2 minutes in a Hongkong steamer without seeing Europeans striking coolies with their canes or umbrellas. No one would dare to misuse a Japanese. [. . .]

This morning I left Hongkong for Canton at 8. The number of picturesque craft the hundreds of them in the harbour was quite interesting. I saw many women standing working the heavy oars with babies strapped on their backs. In the lowest class there is very little difference between the clothing of the sexes each wearing *very* wide trousers with a loose garment over them, that of the women reaching halfway below the knee. It is a most healthy and sensible dress. The dress of the men above the coolie class is rich and beautiful trousers of brocade becoming tight at the ankle, good black satin shoes on soles about 1 1/2 inch thick turned up at the toes, a loose longish garment of silk fastening at the sides, and over that a long sleeveless jacket of wadded and quilted brocade. They put on one wadded garment over another till their size is prodigious. They wear silk caps, but the women have uncovered heads and very large earrings. They wear silks and brocades of beautiful colours, and the general effect is beautiful. But nothing pleases me so well as the Sikh policemen with their swarthy faces and crimson turbans of monstrous size. The yellow skins of the Chinese and Japanese are very unpleasing.

I was shocked to hear of the death of Princess Alice.[*] How bitterly the Queen will feel the first death among her children and of the one who nursed Prince Albert and the Prince of Wales. 'The brutal baldness' of the telegram was even greater than usual. 'The Princess Louise of Hesse is dead.' Another telegram is that Yakoob Khan has succeeded

---

[*] See Princess Alice, p. 314.

Sher Ali* which will I hope prevent the war. If it be true it will be another proof of the influence which England has gained in the East. But there is great need of *rest* at home and freedom from warlike rumours. The 'spirited foreign policy' has gone far enough I think. It is the fashion to speak of it at home as the cause of the dullness of trade, but out here people speak of the dullness of trade in the East as arising from completely glutting the market with goods, reckless and unprincipled speculation, and the sending out of shoddy goods. In Japan they now import immense quantities of cotton yarn from Manchester and dye and weave it themselves because they have found that English cottons are so weighted with clay and so rotted with chemicals that they wont wear. The 'Barbarian Devils' have a bad reputation for many reasons.

Chinese China is hardly to be tolerated after the grace and beauty of the Japanese and their lacquer is hideous, but their carvings in ivory ebony and sandalwood and their gold and silver filigree are most lovely. But their shops are very tastelessly arranged and their manners are curt and impolite. Bishop Burdon has applied for 2 medical missionaries one for the island of Heinan south of this with a million people and the other for Pakhoi a newly opened treaty port. I fear that the Edinburgh Society† cannot pay their salaries. The tenacity with which the Chinese Xtians undergo persecution and even torture and death is something wonderful. So many have been 'faithful unto death'.

Canton Jan 1st 1879. The river for 90 miles up here has nothing interesting the country grows very flat and there are large rice swamps, varied by enclosures of bananas much tattered with the constant strong winds. A very high pagoda marks Whampoa now a deserted looking place and about an hour later we arrived at the beginning of Canton but after that it took 1/2 an hour of cautious threading of our way among junks, sampans, houseboats and slipper boats before we moored to the crowded and shabby wharf. Canton is on a perfectly level site and a broad rapid tidal river flows through it. Not far off are some low rocky hills. One cannot see much of the city because of the boats and masts. It is said to have 1500000 inhabitants. Few objects rise above it − one or two pagodas like shot towers, a double tiered Romish cathedral of great size not yet finished and some singular looking high square brick buildings something like square towers which are the godowns‡ of pawnbrokers.

---

* See Sher Ali, p. 314.
† See the Edinburgh Medical Missionary Society, p. 324.
‡ A neologism, derived from the Malay word *gudang*, coined by British merchants to mean a warehouse or storeroom in the East.

There are some large foreign buildings along the water but everything is hidden by a crowd of boats. These house boats about 15 feet long with two roofs of bamboo circular lie along the shore in thousands or ply for hire to ferry passengers, being sculled at both ends by the tidy vigorous looking housewife often with her baby strapped onto her back. Then there are very large two storied boats much crowded with glass sides, floating hotels in which the Chinese give entertainments. Then the great galley shaped junks are anchored in the middle of the river. You see the shrine or joss house* one in each. These junks carry from 4 to 12 six pounders according to their size and their big black muzzles are always prominent. Besides all these there are the market boats moving shops which supply this floating population and the slipper boats just like large shoes propelled by 3 men at the stern. These go with inconceivable speed but look quite absurd.

Mr Smith[†] of Jardine Matheson and Co.[‡] met me and I was carried in a palanquin to the beautiful house which belongs to the firm here and received with unbounded hospitality and kindness by himself and his young wife. The palanquin could hardly get through the crowds of people in the covered street about 6 feet wide which I thought was a bazaar. We crossed a stone bridge with an iron gate which leads to the island of Shameen which was given to England after the war. It is wedge shaped and is surrounded by a bund a very high sea wall with a broad walk laid with concrete the whole way round 1 1/4 miles, the walk with banyan trees along it. One side is the Canton River with its shifting life and the other is a canal on which an enormous population live in house boats moored stem and stern without any space between them. On the island there is fine grass along with long avenues of banyan and walks laid with concrete connecting the immense tropical houses and gardens of the rich merchants. The community consists of only 45 people and has a nice English church of which Mr Smiths brother is rector, a club bungalow, a lawn tennis and croquet ground, a book club and a hall used for dancing, lectures and amateur theatricals. In Canton not far off there is a large hospital erected and supported by the foreign residents as a medical missionary hospital, but on the island there are only these handsome foreign houses no poor and no Chinese except the servants of foreigners. No vehicle with wheels is ever seen for none can pass through Canton.

---

* Altar. Joss is English slang meaning both a Chinese idol and the incense sticks burned before it.
† See Mr Smith of Canton, p. 341.
‡ See Jardine, Matheson & Co., p. 329.

The houses on both stories have verandahs 20 feet deep in which people live in summer for here there is no cooler place to which they resort.

In the evening we went to the little hall where 6 gentlemen acted a little play called 'Cook or Secretary?' to an audience of 14 people. It was clever, refined, witty and though the room was very cold I thoroughly enjoyed it. On Tuesday we crossed the bridge and went to some of the stores to which foreigners are taken. A china store where everything looked coarse in design and execution after the exquisite grace and finish of Japan – to a store for carved ivory where the things are *perfectly* beautiful, to one for Canton embroideries on silk and embroidered crêpe shawls and one or two others all solid buildings of slate coloured brick, with stone floors, lofty ceilings, and great shrines with joss sticks burning. The big tall richly clothed, rich looking independent looking Chinamen who dont make a bow even and indulge in as few words as possible are a contrast to the bowing smiling pleasant chattering Japanese. In the evening I had to dine out. It was cordial and pleasant, and the New Year was ushered in by the singing of Auld Lang Syne. It was to me very pathetic but I would rather have seen the New Year as I have seen so many before it, alone by my bedroom fire, for then I should have felt less alone.

Yesterday morning I went to church at 11 where there were barely more than the literal 2 or 3. Then before tiffin I went into Canton for an hour with Mr Smith. Canton is worth all Japan. It is intoxicating from its picturesque colour and novelty. I have been out six hours today carried 18 miles through it – revelling. I have now drunk for the first time of that water of which it may truly be said whoso drinks 'shall thirst again' – true Orientalism. Ah I like it! As the glories came and went, I wished the sun would stand still and let me dream my Eastern dream of gorgeous sunlight and narrow lanes blazing with colour with the sun glinting down here and there on eastern fabrics resplendent even in the darkness of blue sky in narrow strips high above of gorgeous marriage processions and 'the voice of the bridegroom and the voice of the bride', of the glittering trains of mandarins of the Tartar city with its pagodas of the city walls and outside the hills of graves extending for miles, a fiery red under the tropic blue, of the Aceldema the potters field with its pools of blood and sacks of heads and the cross for crucifixion now as on Calvary a symbol of the lowest degradation – and all the busy crowded costumed life of this exclusive eastern city and the blue banners hanging from houses here and there showing that the death angel had stilled some busy brain for evermore. This is something to see.

Tomorrow I go to stay 4 days with Mr & Mrs Henry* who both speak Chinese and with them I hope to see the prison etc and more street life. There has not been a cloud on the sky since I reached China. I have put off leaving from the 4th till the 11th. Tell Harriet that I am shocked to see the death of Mr Asford in the paper and sympathise truly with her in the loss. I must finish abruptly.

Your most loving
ILB

Jan 3. 1879

Yesterday I went with Mr Henry who speaks Chinese to the great prison of the Naamhoi magistrate, turning aside from the street called Sze-P'aai-Lau into a small dirty square on one side of which is a brick wall with a large composite quadrupled in black paint upon it, and on the other the open entrance gate of the Yamun.† The road continues through this square and either side of it, and on the other the open space by the prison gates is crowded with unshaven, ragged, forlorn dirty wretches, heavily chained round the legs and with long heavy chains locked round their necks attached to large stones with holes in the centre or to short heavy bars of iron. Two or three were lying in a heap on the ragged mat in the corner, some were sitting on stones, but most were standing or painfully dragging the heavy stones about and the clank of the heavy fetters made a jarring and dismal sound. These unfortunates are daily exposed to passers by as objects of scorn and contempt. For petty larcenies, criminals are also exposed at this gate of woe wearing large heavy squares of wood round their necks, heavy enough to weigh down their heads, and big enough to prevent them from reaching their mouths with their hands to feed themselves. This wooden collar is called the cangue.

The bearers set me down at the gate amidst the fettered wretches dragging the heavy weights, the filthy beggars, the fortune tellers and the hangers on of what is said to be the worst prison in China, and passing through the gate we went down a short narrow passage enclosed by a door of rough wooden upright bars above which a tigers head with wide open jaws and staring prominent eyes is represented, a fit emblem of cruelty and greed, but regarded by the Chinese as possessing virtue. Further on, by the inner entrance, there is a small blackened altar with

---

* See Reverend A. Henry, p. 327.
† *Yamun* or more correctly *yamen* is the office and residence of a Chinese government official or mandarin.

a blackened, worn, granite figure of a tigers head above it and the ashes of unnumbered joss sticks below, for the gaolers, who are responsible for the safe keeping of the prisoners, invoke the tiger's assistance morning and night by burning incense before it. At this place there were 2 or 3 small rooms for the gaolers, dark and forlorn, most inconceivably untidy. Here we met the head gaoler – of all Chinamen that I have seen the most repulsive in appearance, manner, and dress, for his long dress of frayed and patched brown silk looked as if it had not been changed for a year, the lean brown hands which held the prison keys with an instinctive grip were dirty, and the nails long like claws, and the face worse I thought than that of any of the criminal horde, with its merciless look of grip and greed, looked saturated with opium smoke. For this wretch pays for his place, and his gains arise from bribes wrung by torture and cruelty, and from defrauding the prisoners of their allowance of rice. With this guide we saw every part of the prison.

Going down another passage he unlocked a grated door or rather wooden grating through which we passed into a small roughly paved courtyard about 40×20 feet one of 3 similar ones, this wretched man standing in the gateway. From the dark doorways which led into their dens 50 or 60 men swarmed out all heavily chained with long dishevelled or matted hair, filthy clothing, skin caked with dirt, sores, skin diseases, swelled lips, sore eyes and surrounded us closely. Not without some tremor I passed through them and entered one of the wards (!), they following me in and blocking out the light, their voices all clamouring *kumsha* – i.e. backsheesh. These wards are walled on 3 sides, but on the side next to the court are enclosed by cribs, a double row of very strong palisades, black both from dirt and age as are the interiors. Through these such light and air as enter the interior proceed. Each is roughly paved with granite slabs, slimy with accumulations of dirt, in the middle and along the sides are platforms on which the prisoners sit and sleep a sort of coarse black gridiron. The blackness, the filth, the vermin, the rubbish of potsherds etc cannot be described or the awful stench even in this cold weather as only tubs inside the door close to those containing the wretched allowance of foul water are provided for the relief of the needs of nature. No washing water, no bedding, no fuel, no light at night, no current of air, no food except 2 lbs daily of rice, reduced to one by the jailer – no hope of justice with nameless cruelties practised without restraint, the tried, the untried, the condemned, the guilty and innocent, the murderer and pirate, the debtor and petty thief all huddled together without hope of exit except to the neighbouring judgement seat with its horrors of 'the question by torture' or to the 'field of blood' where I saw five heads in a mat only the day before. 'For all prisoners and captives, we beseech thee to hear us good Lord'!

Among men, could one see any more abject than these with chains round their necks and ankles, their coarse standing out black hair contrasted with the shaven heads of the free, the fleshless skeletons covered with vermin and running sores to which their forms have been reduced, the long claws on their lean fingers and toes, the hungry look in their emaciated faces, and their clamorous cry *Kumsha, Kumsha*? In each 'ward' there is also one unchained man, a felon, who acts as deputy demon. One of these told us he had been there 14 years. In each ward there is a rough shrine to a god who is supposed to possess the power of melting the hearts of the wicked into contrition, and to this mockery on his birthday a sort of feast is made, the money for which is raised by 'squeezes' from the rice of these wretched beings. They thronged round us, the cries of *kumsha* increasing, clattering their chains. One man said they had so little rice that they had to drink the foul water 'to fill themselves' – another said 'I wish I were in your prison at Hongkong'! Others said in the prison at Hongkong they had fish and vegetables, and more rice than they could eat, and baths and beds to sleep on! We could not give alms among 200, and as we eluded them with difficulty and squeezed through the narrow gate, they called after us *fan-quai* 'Barbarian devils'.

We went into 3 other yards, foul with horror, and into a smaller one just as bad where there were 15 women some of them with infants devoured by cutaneous diseases. Some of these said they were there for kidnapping, others were probably female hostages for criminal relations who have not been brought to justice and who may spend many years or even their whole lives in this place. There are likewise some single hovels in which criminals who can afford to bribe the jailer can enjoy the luxury of solitude. The whole prison so far as I can make it out consists of four of these yards with 4 wards in each, their walls abutting on each other, while round the parallelogram so formed there is a narrow paved passage, bounded by a very high outside wall. In this outer wall there is a porthole just large enough to allow of a body being pushed through it for no malefactors corpse must be carried through the great entrance lest it should defile the 'Gate of Righteousness'! Within is a hovel called a dead house into which they throw the bodies of those who die in prison till the grave has been dug in some 'accursed' place. Besides the numbers who die of starvation, disease and the exhaustion of repeated tortures, in the hot weather epidemics break out in the dark and fetid dens and sometimes clear out the jail. At night the hands of the prisoners are chained to their necks and it appears that during the day even, only one hand is liberated.

There is a turnkey for each ward and these men, with the unchained felons of whom I spoke before, torture new arrivals in order to force money from them under which process many die. Some of the faces looked imbecile. The gaoler, as we went out, kept holding out a lean brown hand and muttering about his promised *kumsha*, very fearful lest we should give it to any of the turnkeys, two of whom were lying on their beds smoking opium. Has conscience no hell for them on earth I wonder?

Shortly afterwards, passing once more through the 'Gate of Righteousness', we crossed a dirty court infested with fortune tellers and gamblers to the porch with the red insignia of Mandarinism, and two huge figures on the doors which is the entrance to the residence of the Naamhoi magistrate one of the greatest dignitaries of Canton. In the great porch were many official palanquins and many official servants and attendants of the mandarin with hats turned up from their faces and red silk crowns and some of the city guards dirty and shabby persons. One of these took us not through the closed door but along some passages to the left, from which through a circular opening in the brick wall we passed into the front of the judgement seat, at which all the inmates of the Naamhoi prison may expect to be tried. Somehow my nerves were rather shaken with what I had seen and I trembled as a criminal might on entering this chamber of horrors. [. . .]

In a high backed armchair of dark wood such as one might see in any English hall sat the man who has the power of life and death in his hands a young looking man in the usual black satin cap with a blue brocade robe and a sleeved cloak of dark blue satin lined with white fur over it. He spoke loudly and with much rapidity and emphasis and often beat his foot impatiently on the floor. He spoke in the Mandarin tongue, and put all his questions through an interpreter who stood at his left a handsomely dressed old man who wore a chain with a dependent ivory comb, with which he frequently combed a small and scanty grey moustache. Notaries attendants with scarlet crowned hats, city guards, and a small rabble of men and boys stood behind and down the sides. The open hall, though high, was shabby and extremely dirty with unswept broken pavement, strewn at one side with potsherds and disfigured by a number of more or less broken black pots and other rubbish making it look rather like a shed in an untidy nursery garden than a judgement hall. There are certain inscriptions on the pillars one of which is said to be an exhortation to mercy. Different pieces of bamboo used for the bastinado were ranged against the wall and there were other things at which I looked once and no more for a shuddering dread came over me that they were for use in the 'Question by Torture'.

The civil case took a long time and the claimant an old man was so exhausted with kneeling before the judge that he had to be assisted away. Then another man knelt and presented a petition which was taken to 'avizandum'. Then a guard led in by a chain a prisoner heavily manacled and with a heavy stone attached to his neck who knelt with his forehead nearly touching the ground. After some speaking a boy who had been standing during the trial dangling a number of keys came forward and after much ado opened the rusty padlock round the criminals neck and he left dragging the stone after him with his hands. He had made a formal petition for this favour, and the granting of it looked like a solitary touch of mercy, but it all came about through bribery for without that the petition would never reach even the first official through whose hands it must pass. All this time 1 1/2 hours and I know not how much more the 4 chained men were undergoing the torture of kneeling in an immovable position. I was standing so close as to touch the dress of one with my feet, and heard their breathing become a series of gasps, and cool and fresh though the afternoon was the sweat of pain fell from their brows upon the dusty floor – so emaciated were they that even through their clothing I saw the outlines of their bones. The judge asked but one question. The 4 were accused of an aggravated robbery and they were told to confess but they said that only 2 of them were guilty, and they were then sent back to the tender mercies of the opium smoking jailer, probably to come back again and again for other forms of torture, and when no money could be squeezed out of themselves or their friends to be beheaded.

Here there is no regular legal process, no jury, no one admitted to plead for the accused but I could not bar from my heart the trembling hope as I stood so long beside the kneeling wretches that for them, and such as them, a higher than an earthly intercession was pleading before the Judge of all the earth. The legal instruments of torture consist of three boards with proper grooves for squeezing the fingers and the bastinado with bamboos of different weights but the illegal modes of putting the question as commonly practised are – prolonged kneeling in a bent position such as I saw – twisting the ears with roughened fingers and keeping them twisted while the prisoner kneels on chains – beating the lips with a stick – putting the hands in stocks behind the back – suspending the body by the thumbs and fingers – tying the hands to a bar under the knees so as to bend the body double – and kneeling upon pounded glass sand and salt mixed together till the knees are excoriated – severe flogging, successively, with the bamboo, rattan, cudgel, and whip is used more than any other means of extorting confession and when death results the magistrate reports that the criminal has died of sickness, or if he has reason to dread being complained of he bribes the man's friends. The *cangue* or wooden collar is rather a disgrace than a torture if the wearer be fed and screened from the sun but it weighs nearly 30 lbs and the wearer cannot feed himself.

It is doubtful for what crimes the death punishment is inflicted, but for robbery with murder, arson, highway robbery and piracy prisoners may be at once beheaded without a trial. For aggravated robbery death is inflicted and probably the 4 men would lose their lives. It is supposed that about 500 are annually executed in Canton, and that in the Naamhoi prison half that number die annually from starvation and torture. Sometimes 100 are beheaded in an hour as it is feared will be the case soon when the governor goes out of office when it is usual to make a 'jail delivery' in this fashion. These prisons are called 'hells' by the Chinese. In hundreds of cases when a press of business occurs, the criminals, accusers and witnesses are all imprisoned together, sometimes for months and as the government takes no measures to provide for them in the interval, many of the poorer ones die. Anything more awful than the administration of justice here and the state of the prisons cannot be imagined.

We left the judgement seat and passed out of the gate of the Yamun, where the prisoners with the heavy stones were dragging and clanking their chains, or lying in the road full of sores and though the red sunset light was bathing all things, the glory seemed to have died off from Canton and the air to be heavy with a curse. The original provisions of the Chinese code are just on the whole and even merciful. I have just been reading them, observing how all their good intentions have been frustrated through centuries of mandarinism and human cupidity.

Steamer 'Kin Kiang'. Although I went to the execution ground the day before going to the prison, the account of it seems to belong to this place. Passing (after traversing the Tartar city) through the crowded and bad smelling salt fish market and thence along a street where raincoats made of the leaves of palm trees seemed the speciality we arrived at the Ma-T'au, a cul-de-sac with its broad end opening on the street. This Field of Blood which counts its slain by tens of thousands is also a Potters Field occupied during its whole length by large clay pots drying in the sun or being made such as the Chinese use instead of tubs. This place Ma-T'au the 'Horses Head' is simply a pottery yard and when men are executed more or fewer pots are removed to make room for them. The spectacle is open to the street and to all passers by.

We had not gone far before we came to a great pool of blood and dust mingled blackening in the sun, then another and another till there were five almost close together, with great blood splashes on the pots and blood trodden into the thirsty ground against the wall. Just opposite a cross rudely constructed, about 8 feet high, was leaning dark with blood in patches. Among the rubbish at the base of the wall were some human fragments under a piece of matting, a little further on some jaw bones with the teeth in them then some crosses and near the pools of blood some heads tied up in a piece of matting. A blood-splashed wooden ticket with a human name on one side and the name of the Naamhoi prison on the other such as is tied to the criminals neck when he is beheaded was lying there and I picked it up as a relic as the same blow which had severed the neck had severed the string which attached it. The place was ghastly and smelt of blood.

The strangest sight to me was the cross in such a place not an emblem of victory and hope, but of the lowest infamy and degradation, the lowest death which the vilest man can die. Nor was it the solid, lofty structure 15 or 20 feet high which painters represent, but a rude thing of unplaned wood barely eight feet and not too heavy for a man to carry on his shoulders. To it criminals whose crimes merit a lingering death are tightly bound with ropes and are then gradually cut to pieces by sharp knives unless they or their friends can bribe the executioner to give a death blow at once. The cross standing by itself had just been used. Perhaps Paul had such a cross in view when he wrote 'but made himself obedient unto death, *even the death of the cross*'. It is to this death by crucifixion, hacking with knives, and fire that the one rich and 3 poor Romish converts were put who ten days ago for their faithfulness unto death joined 'the noble army of martyrs'. These facts do not need to be dressed out with words. They are most effective when most baldly stated.

In some cases criminals are brought at once from the judgement seat to the execution ground on receiving sentence but usually they are taken back to prison and are not acquainted with the date of their death till an official carrying a small board with the names of those who are that day to be executed enters the prison yard and reads the names aloud. Each man on answering to his name is made to sit in a dust basket and after being carried for the last time before a judge for the purpose of answering some formal questions he is borne through the gate into the outer court of the Yamun where it is customary for his friends (or in their absence at official expense) to give him food such as soup betel nut fat pork and cups of wine. Betel nut is invariably given for its stimulating properties. The prisoners still wearing their chains are then pinioned and a superscription, with the name crime and sentence of each is attached to a piece of bamboo and tied to their heads. A small wooden tally (such as I picked up) with the name of the criminal and that of the prison to which he was confined upon it is attached to each neck. In case of crucifixion the superscription is put over the criminals head. On arriving at the ground, they are tumbled out of the dust baskets as if they were rubbish. A space has been cleared of pots and there the criminals kneel down in one or more rows with their heads bent forward in the attitude of the men who knelt before the judge. A district official who sits at a table covered with red cloth, having been informed that everything is ready, gives the signal, and at one blow of the executioners scimitar a head falls on the ground. Mr Johnson of Yokohama saw 100 heads fall there one morning – 14 is a common number. 5 were taken off the day before I saw it. It is said that the criminals are usually so worn by torture that they meet death with indifference, but in the case of malefactors of a higher rank they are stupefied with wine – i.e. sake. It is possible in some cases to buy a substitute. A coolie sells himself for 100 dollars and for the week before his execution indulges in every kind of expensive debauchery, finally stupefying himself so completely with wine and opium that he knows nothing of the terror of death.

Such is a literal account of the Naamhoi prison and of the execution ground. The part about the executions I learned from Mr Johnson and Archdeacon Gray* who saw many of them. It was from a far worse prison than this in which he had been chained by his head to the roof and by his feet to a ring in the floor that Sir Harry Parkes was led out to be beheaded in the common execution ground at Pekin!

Rev. A. Henrys Canton Jan 5/79

My own Pet

I cannot write about Canton because there is so much to say and I am always either out or too tired to write or 'making myself agreeable' which is the least return that a stranger can make for unbounded kindness and hospitality. Oh I wish I were stronger! I can do so little and at such a cost of exhaustion and 4 or 5 people in a room tire me so much that I cannot see all the people I should like to see. I must only pick out some of the sights to tell you about, as I have written on the prison at

---

* See Archdeacon John Henry Gray, p. 325.

such length. I should be quite content to see nothing but the strange ever moving river life quite distinct from the land life, and the wonderful street life with its crowds processions and din.

I have got pictures of most of the boats you see in Canton but the thousands of them and the rate at which they are propelled cannot be described. There are junks with open bows with 2 six-pounders grinning at the opening and a great eye at either side without which the junk could not see its way. Along the sides there are ten guns and at the lofty stern which is square and of great breadth there are 2 more. The projecting guiding part of the rudder projects 6 feet and more. The masts are single poles and the sails are of fine matting. There are 'passage boats' from all parts of the interior for it is a network of rivers and canals. These sail when they can and when they cant are propelled by large groups each worked by 6 men who stand on a platform outside. These passage boats are always crowded and are heavily armed as a protection from river pirates. There are tiers of large two storied house boats with entrance doors 7 feet high always open, and doorways of rich wood carving. The interiors of these boats are very handsome richly decorated altars great numbers of lamps chairs of carved ebony with white marble let into the backs and sides and embroidered silk hangings. These often have gardens on their roofs. They are called 'Flower boats' and have a very bad reputation. Then there are very large 3-roomed houseboats most comfortable in which people go up the network of rivers and canals – marriage boats green and gold with much wood carving and flags and emblems of all kinds – restaurant boats etc, and almost every kind of cargo has its own fashion of boat.

But the marvellous feature is the moving city of houseboats in which 200000 people are born live and die. The 'slipper boat' and the large one are both houseboats, but the largest is only 15 feet long. The bamboo roofs slide and the whole can be enclosed and divided. The bow of the boat always is the family joss house and the river is starred at night with the dull mournful glimmer of thousands of joss sticks with their faint scent and smaller than a glow-worm's light. Unlike the shore houses the houseboats are models of cleanliness and neatness and space is economised by ingenious adaptations as in a tiny yacht. The house which has neat matted seats by day turns into a bed at night and the children have a separate 'room'. In these boats not only one whole family lives but the eldest son and his wife and children. The men get work as coolies on shore in the daytime, but the women go on shore very little and do all the rowing. These boats by day and night are flying over the river carrying and ferrying passengers one woman at the stern and another at the bow. They are splendid boatwomen, and as strong as men. They are a pariah and alien caste. The women dont bandage their feet. It looks so odd to see numbers of them propelling their boats standing in their wide trousers and loose upper garments, hair stiffly dressed, jadestone earrings and with big bare feet with babies on their backs supported in wrappers with red square embroidered centres. You see a woman sitting sewing or cooking but if you call the boat in one moment she is plying the heavy oar with strength and dexterity.

Not one of the boat people has ever received Xtianity – very little is known about them, but it is said that the river is the speedy grave of a great many of the female children who are born in the boats. I three times went up and down the river in a boat alone to see all I could of this interesting and highly picturesque boat life. On Wednesday afternoon I spent most of the time alone in a boat, and went down and called here.

On Thursday I had a great day of very interesting sightseeing. I was carried 18 miles in a bamboo chair the two Mr Smiths walking and we lunched in the open air on a stone table under a banyan at the 5 storied pagoda which forms the N.E. of the great wall of Canton which there has an inner wall enclosing the city of the Tartar Conquerors and the Tartar garrison the Yamun of the Tartar general and the unmixed Tartar population through whose narrow dirty streets we prowled with their mean low houses with tiled roofs nearly flat, small courtyards and strangely Oriental look. They do not differ much in physiognomy from the Chinese but their stature is shorter, and the women always wear 3 rings in their ears. It was most interesting to come upon this sign of the almost forgotten Tartar conquest. The view was so beautiful (to my thinking) from that corner of the wall – the flaming red pagoda, the singularly picturesque up and down grey wall with its many watch towers and strongholds – the tartar city below with the 'Flowery Pagoda', the mosques, the bright foliage of the banyan trees and the grace of the bamboo outside the wall, the White Cloud mountains and ranges of hills burrowed everywhere for the dead, and all their flaring reds and pinks and oranges harmonised by a thin blue veil which softened without obscuring all revelling in the glory of the tropic noon under a cloudless sky, light without heat, colour without glare. Vanish all memories of greys and pale greens and cloudy passionless skies before this wealth of light and colour! Colour is at once music and vitality and after long starvation, I revel in it. The sights of the day were many and each one is sufficient for a letter.

Isabella then explained the process of literary examinations: 'The Chinese classics are the foundation of all upward progress and the Literary Chancellor is the 2nd

person in the Empire.' As the examinations were not then in progress, she was able
to tour the candidates' cells and reading rooms.

After this we went through some crowded and most picturesque parts
of Canton and reached the wall which is a fine old structure about 20
feet wide and as many high with a broad pavement on which you walk,
and a high platform on the outside with a battlement pierced for marks-
men. The wall is seldom even for 20 yards but follows the inequalities
of the ground up and down and has most picturesque towers occurring
frequently. The wall is everywhere draped with beautiful forms. The five
storied pagoda which flames in red at one angle is an oblong building
very striking as a part of the whole view. Close to it are two stone tables
with stone seats where we lunched under the cloudless heaven with the
pure Orientalism of the Tartar city spread out at our feet, that unimaginable Orientalism which takes one captive at once and like a palm or
banana satisfies a longing of which one has hardly previously been con-
scious. But it was two oclock and our dismay was great not only to find
that the cook had put up lunch for only 2 when there were 3, but that
the chicken was so underdone that even hungry as we were we could
not eat it. I soon got some bananas (food of gods) but the others were
starved, their lunch consisting of porter and dry bread. [. . .]

Crossing the Tartar city we went to the execution ground which I
described and then by the malefactors gate we passed through the outer
wall which surrounds the oldest part of Canton and through some streets
of the better class of dwelling-houses. [. . .] It was pleasant to get out of
these aristocratic and silent streets into the mercantile quarter which is
one vast market or bazaar – one throng of masculine humanity from
morning till night every human being bent on one object the getting of
money. Eight feet is the width of the widest street but one and between
the passers by the shoppers the loungers the people stopping at stalls to
eat or drink tea and the itinerant vendors of goods it is one long push.
Then as you are elbowing your feeble self among the big men who are
made truly monstrous by their many garments of wadded silk and
brocade, you are terrified by a yell and driving out of its way a procession at a rapid trot hustles all foot passengers to one side. Several men in
red and then a handsome closed palanquin borne on the shoulders of 4,
6 or 8 bearers in which reclines a stout magnificently dressed mandarin
either reading or absorbed never taking any note of the crowds and the
glitter which I find so fascinating. Some more men in scarlet and then
the crowd closes up again to be again divided in a moment by a plebe-
ian chair or pariahs running with a circular coffin shaped like the trunk

of a tree with the roots represented 15 feet long – or coolies carrying burdens between them on bamboos with deafening cries or a marriage procession with songs and music all succeeding each other incessantly. All the people in the street are shouting at the top of their voices – all the bearers and the coolies are yelling, and to complete the terrifying uproar the beggars at every corner are demanding charity by striking two gongs together.

Colour riots. Imagine these narrow streets paved with broad granite slabs the high houses with projecting upper stories much carved and gilded the deeply projecting roofs tiled with shells cut into pairs, which let the light softly through, and through the narrow slits between the roofs a sky of deep bright blue. Then in the shadow below but lighted constantly by sunbeams, which at this season are allowed to find their way into the streets, hanging from all the second stories at every possible entrance of height each house having at least 2 are richly painted boards from 6 to 10 feet long some red some black some heavily gilded a few orange the majority red – perfectly plain the red and black having a single row of characters down the middle in gold, several inches long, and the gold and orange having the same characters on them in black – these with banners window draperies and the bright blue draperies which for 100 days indicate a death form together a spectacle of street picturesqueness such as my eyes have never seen and which everybody now tells me is unequalled in any city of Europe or Asia.

Then all the crowd is in costume and such costume! One would think there were no poor. The prevailing colour for the robe is bright blue, even the coolies put on such a garment when not working, and all above the coolies wear it in rich ribbed silk lined with silk of a darker shade. Over this is a sleeveless jacket of rich dark blue or pure brocade, plain or quilted, the trousers of which little is seen are brocade or satin the stockings are white and the shoes which are on thick canoe shaped soles are black satin. The cap which is always worn is black satin quite on the back of the head and the pigtail of pleated purse silk hangs down nearly to the bottom of the robe. Then the most splendid furs are worn and any number of quilted silk and brocade garments one above another and these who are so richly dressed and look so rich are only the shopkeepers and lower classes of merchants – the mandarins and rich merchants never put their feet to the ground.

Then all these thronged streets are composed of shops open in front, usually square, and with handsome paved floors, very lofty and indeed the second story usually being taken into its height. Always opposite the door the whole centre of the back of the shop is taken up with a niche in which there is either a painting of a divinity or the characters in gold which form his name with incense burning, the whole surrounded by heavily gilded fretwork and in the street outside every shop and house there is a projecting niche in which joss sticks are burned night and morning. As darkness comes on and the streets become deserted you see their sides indicated by the dull red glow of hundreds of these fragrant sticks. There is usually a counter at the end of each shop and the goods are arranged in shelves at the sides, and in glass showcases on a bunch at one side 2 or 3 handsomely dressed men sit smoking and sipping tea and there is always a niche near the door in which offerings to the ancestors are placed.

The shops are very handsome and just now are filled with all sorts of brilliant things in preparation for the New Year the great Chinese festival which is to be on the 21st. Streets are given up to shops of one kind. Thus there is the jade stone street entirely given up to shops of jade stone jewellery which is very costly a single bracelet costing $3000 dollars. These are among the richest merchants in Canton. Most of them wore brocades and furs of the costliest kind. At the new year the shops are all closed and the rich merchants vie with each other in the length of time they can keep their shops closed he who can keep one closed the longest gaining a great reputation for wealth – sometimes closing for two months. There is one whole street of coffin makers several in which nothing is sold but furniture from ordinary folding tables up to the costliest settees and chairs of massive carved ebony, chinaware streets, book streets, streets of silk shops only, streets of workers in brass or gold who perform their delicate manipulations under your eyes, streets of secondhand clothes most gorgeous in their gold and silk embroideries and so on every street blazing with colour splendid with costume and abounding with wealth and variety.

We came on a yamun or official residence with the vestibule hung with scarlet the marriage colour. Inside the door were the wedding garments for the wedding guests in embroidered scarlet. Some time later the bridal procession swept through the street, adding more glory to the colour and movement. First marched a troop of men in scarlet carrying scarlet banners each one emblazoned in gold with the literary degrees of the brides father and his ancestors. Then came two heavily gilded, carved and decorated pavilions carried like palanquins under which were borne the bridal presents and last of all the bride being carried in a locked palanquin to the bridegrooms house, completely shrouded, the palanquin one mass of carvings in gold and blue enamel the carving fully six inches deep, a gorgeous thing and behind a long procession of men with banners and instruments of music. It is the China of 1000 years ago, unaltered by foreign contact.

There are many beggars too and a 'Beggars Square' but they form a regular guild with their King and pay an admission fee of $5. The shop-keepers are obliged by law to give them so much and when there is a marriage or any other festivity the giver sends a fee to the King who then keeps all beggars from importuning the guests. They make a fearful noise with two gongs. There is one on the bridge near Shameen who has a callosity like a horn on his forehead, and he strikes the stone pavement with this with an audible thump.

We went into an opium den, a long narrow high room with matted platforms along each side on which men of the poorest class were lying indulging the rapturous dreams so expensively bought, and I thought with shame of the greed for gain of certain men among ourselves of which this is the fruit and of the shameful use made of force to compel an unwilling people to submit to this traffic.

Then we went to a 'dog and cat' restaurant where a number of men were eating of savoury dishes made of these animals. There are thousands of meat shops in Canton and fishmongers. At the former there are always hundreds of split and salted ducks hanging on lines and pigs of various sizes roasted whole or sold raw in joints and kids and buffalo and thousands of chickens and numbers of dogs and cats which though skinned have the tails on to show what they are. The fish shops and fish stalls are legion but the fish looks sickening as it is cut into slices and is always covered with blood. The boiled chrysalis of a silkworm is a great delicacy and so are certain kinds of hairless fleshy caterpillars. I had some 'bird's nest' soup at Mr Duvals without knowing what it was but these nests are brought from Sumatra and are a luxury of the wealthy. A great deal of eating and tea drinking goes on in the streets. [. . .] We saw many other things and after a peregrination of 18 miles reached home at 5. This is a wretched letter describing nothing.

The Colonial Secretary's Singapore Jan 15. This must go unfinished.

ILB

St. Pauls College Hongkong Jan 8th 1879

I see that George Henry Lewes[*] is dead!

My Own Pet

The year seems getting old already. It is only by the date that I know where we are, for under these blue skies and with all windows and doors

---

[*] See George Henry Lewes, p. 331.

open it might be midsummer. Oh how I like sunny skies instead of grey and grim ones, and blazing colour, instead of dismal greys and greens! It is so hard to write letters when one is visiting and especially when one has little strength. I like this visit as a visit very much. It is such a reposeful house so beautifully situated and so large. That would be nothing if they were not such nice people. We have so very much in the way of common acquaintances and interests, and I got to know them so well in the week which I spent with them in Yokohama in May that it was very pleasant to come to them here. She is very pleasant but perhaps is a little like 'Mrs Proudie'.* Bishop Burdon is a scholarly Xtian gentleman, a reposeful delightful talker and the quiet evenings of talk are just the society that I am able to enjoy.

The governor is the Mr Pope Henessey who got into or *made* such trouble in Barbados. He has made so much here that the leading residents have just memorialised the Home Government for his removal on the ground that 'life and property are not so unsafe in any town of the British dominions as in Victoria'. I have heard so much of him and of the insecurity of Victoria that I was curious to see him. Now for some occult reason though I delayed leaving my card at Government House till yesterday, Mr Henessey has shown me as much attention as if I were a Princess. He wrote to the Bishop to say that he wished to serve me in every possible way, so I said I wished to see the prison. Well he spent 3 hours in showing it to me and then making me ascend his palanquin with 6 scarlet bearers he walked beside it here. I had also said I wished to see the Chinese Hospital (solely managed and treated by Chinese) and he said he wished it to be a 'state visit' and he should accompany me and he was arranging that I should be received by the committee and the leading Chinese residents! He wrote asking me to dinner tonight and when I declined because we have people here he wrote again and asked me to dine alone with them tomorrow night, and when I accepted he wrote and asked the Burdons whom he has not asked before and furthermore he has sent me an introduction to the governor of the Straits Settlements asking him to put the colonial government steamer at my disposal, a thing I should not desire within 60 miles of the Equator! I believe he must be thinking that I am writing a book and that in his low estate he thinks a eulogy might be pleasant! Sir Harry Parkes has sent me introductions to all British Governors and Consuls as far as Cairo, so that you need have no fear of my being a waif in any of these strange Eastern parts.

* See Mrs Proudie, p. 338.

But to begin. Mr Smith sent the houseboat down to Mr Henrys at 8 on Monday and Mr H. took me to the steamer 'Kin Kiang' to which several people from Shameen the foreign settlement came to wish me goodbye. There were 2000 Chinese passengers, 1500 of whom were below the gratings in front of which a man with a cutlass and revolver kept guard. On the 'Tchang' they have a much better plan. A large hose connected with the boiler is laid on to each grating through which in case of need boiling water could be sent under strong pressure. These sound dreadful things but such precautions are necessary. They are quite different from the brutal treatment of innocent coolies such as kicking them and striking them on the head.

We came down the Macao passage which was much prettier than the Whampoa one, but the Pearl River is not pretty. Just as we landed about 500 large fishes were passed through a net from a well in the steamer into a fishing boat with a large well to which all the Hongkong fishmongers at once came down. Mrs Burdons chair met me but I walked up. I found poor Dr Golt of Hangchow and 3 small children here. His wife had died on the passage down, and had been buried at Amoy. I found letters from Emily Bessie A Wyld Mrs Blackie, etc etc, a week of the Scotsman addressed in an unknown hand but *no letter from you*! The accounts of the Bank failure are dreadful. I had no idea that the Coans and Chalmers would suffer so severely. I don't like to write to Miss Chalmers till I know more. Mrs William Nelson wrote also – she said it was the finest summer which people could remember in Scotland. In the China papers there are some very severe articles on the failure of the bank. They are said to have been insolvent for years and I also saw some very severe things said of them at a meeting of their creditors. B. & E. have been such excellent creatures in writing. I also had a very kind note from Sir Harry Parkes with introductions.

It was the 2nd day of the 'week of prayer' and there was service in the private chapel here a mixture of liturgical and extempore prayer with Jacksons* 'Te Deum' and 'Praise to the Holiest in the Height' which some people would not like so well if they knew that it was from the Dream of Gerontius. We had a very pleasant evening alone. I stayed in bed all Tuesday morning, and in the afternoon prowled alone in Hongkong, and bought a few things which I needed. It is a very picturesque place, but the whole centre is in ruins. The great fire turns out to have been the work of incendiaries. The city was set on fire by an Englishman at one point and by 4 Chinese at others and several

---

* See William Jackson, p. 329.

Chinamen cut the hose off the engines. There have been fires *every day* since and now one hardly notices the clang of the fire alarm bell. It is not a good place. The river is infested by pirates and the city by the scum of the East. It has 140000 inhabitants of whom only 1000 are Europeans. The Chinese are as 100 to one.

Jan 9th. Yesterday after lunch the Bishop & I went to the prison which is one of the largest in the Empire and I stayed for 3 hours. The governor of the prison took us round. It is simply splendid, and to the Chinamen must seem a palace. There were about 800 human beings there in cleanliness and comfort, each one individualised as a human being, a record kept of his good and bad deeds and every one *sure* of both justice and mercy. I felt the wonderful change in which Xtianity has made in the treatment of prisoners yet punishment without reformatory influences is a sore thing to see. The warders are Englishmen, mostly retired sergeants, but to ensure that the wants of all shall be attended to there are interpreters of different nations who act as deputy warders. There is a strong Sikh guard and one Sikh sentry with a loaded rifle occupies a raised and strongly barred platform in each yard in spite of which several have been murdered.

While we were in one of the yards the governor *chassied* in – 'My dear lord, I'm overjoyed to see you' – a little man much overdressed in white kid gloves and patent leather boots with a mouth which smiles perpetually and sinister eyes which never smile. He was very voluble. In every ward and yard some of the prisoners desired to speak to him, and these were all sent down to the office, to which he wished us to accompany him, and I did so and remained till the end. There were nearly 60 with petitions. The governor of the prison was there to be referred to in each case, and Chinese and English secretaries with the books of records and Sikh Chinese and Italian interpreters and the two senior wardens. Each man prayed for pardon or remission of the rest of his sentence the governor being able to exercise the Queens prerogative. When each man was asked his crime it was horrid to hear murder stabbing piracy in such numbers of cases. There was one Englishman mate of a ship who had beaten and tortured a boy to death on a long voyage, and the governor was going to remit his hard labour and a part of the sentence when he asked me what I thought, which was that for such a crime on the lonely high seas no punishment could be too severe, *as a warning to other men,* and consequently the sentence was not remitted. The man scowled frightfully at me but it is one of the worst of crimes. Of all the petitioners all but 3 had more or less of their sentences remitted. The prison governor, the secretaries and the wardens were all on the side of mercy – all pleaded for those who had been well behaved. I dont wonder that the captives in the Naamhoi prison exclaimed 'I wish I were in your prison in Hongkong!'

The prison pleased me, but Governor Henessey obviously has a diseased sympathy with Orientals. The accommodation, food, etc are as much superior to the houses and manner of living of the poorer Chinese as our rooms and way of living in Atholl Crescent are superior to that of the dwellers in Cowgate. On the way back the Governor began to defend his policy both here and in Barbados! It strikes me that he *is posing* as a humanitarian. I was *awfully* tired, but the Chief Justice a *most* agreeable man, Captain Edwards and Mr Ede dined here and they did not go till 11.30. I was so tired that I did not wake when they came 3 times into my room this morning with my breakfast.

Friday night Jan 10th. I feel as if I could never be rested again a fine climate is nothing if the exactions and fatigues of civilised life surround one. Yesterday morning I tried to write up my Canton letter but I had to cut out some cool clothes for the tropics also. In the afternoon Mrs Burdon & I went to some shops and I bought some rice paper pictures. Those I send you are bad ones less than a cent each. It is fine shavings of the pith of a tree, not rice paper. I have had such nice presents in Hongkong and Canton that I have had to send them home in a box. Mrs Smith gave me two boxes of large rice paper pictures and Mrs Burden has given me a number of things. Captain Edwards gave me some Amoy cut stone ornaments and 2 carved cocoanut bowls from Heinan lined with silver. There was service of a chilling kind each evening in the chapel at 5.30.

On Thursday evening we dined at the Governors, being carried there in closed chairs. There were only the Henesseys, Major Palmer the a.d.c. and Mr Pitman consulting engineer to the Japanese government, a very agreeable man but most severe in unqualified condemnation of the motives and policy of Sir Harry Parkes. Mrs Henessey sat in a dream, spoke to no-one, and only roused herself to fire up fiercely at her husband who retorted with cold sarcasm. After dinner, the Governor talked to me, and though I dislike and distrust him more each time I see him, I was much interested in the things he said, among others that the number of Romish converts in China exceeds 700000 and that many of these are the descendants of several generations of Xtians. As not one of these will worship the Confucian tablet they are shut out from all office and honour. He criticised the plans of some of the Protestant missionaries as was natural.

The weather is indescribably lovely. The pink sunrises are like those of the Sandwich Islands and there is a morning freshness such as I never felt in Japan. I think Hongkong truly beautiful with the city crowded round the majestic peak which is all day long changing and rises perpendicularly out of the town. It has 140000 people of whom 120000 are Chinese and about 15000 more parsies and other Orientals so that shady narrow coloured streets are enlivened by all sorts of costumes. I went to lunch at Chief Justice Snowdens and as they were alone found it very pleasant. The Hawaiian book and the Rocky Mountain papers which everybody reads at Hongkong seem to make all people receive me like an old acquaintance. People are all rich here and have large houses and many excellent servants and here one encounters the hospitality of which one has heard as existing among foreigners in the East.

After lunch I called for Bishop Burdon and we went to Govt House and there the Governor joined us in a chair with 8 bearers in scarlet and some Sikh orderlies in scarlet turbans for the 'state visit' to the Tung-Wah Hospital* a purely Chinese institution built a few years ago by a number of Chinese merchants and supported by them at a cost of $16000 annually. In it nothing European in the way of either drugs or treatment is tried. There is a dispensary connected with it where advice is given daily to about 120 people and they are building a lunatic asylum at the back. Lunacy, however, is very rare in China. We must avoid the mistake of thinking that charitable institutions are solely an outgrowth of Xtianity, though doubtless their management differs widely from that of the charities of Xtian countries. The blind asylum, the asylum for old men and women, the leper asylums and the foundling hospitals of Canton were founded centuries ago and their charters contain humane and admirable rules. This one is only a few years old.

> Isabella found the Tung-Wah hospital to be impeccably clean and humanely managed, and she collected some samples of Chinese medicine to be analysed at home. She was most impressed by her guide, Ng Choy,† a well-spoken barrister educated in London at Lincoln's Inn. The visit concluded with ceremonial tea drinking. The Chinese doctors and Mr Choy raised their cups to her, saying, 'May your happiness be as the eastern sea' and 'May you have many sons.'

I came home then and met a procession of Portuguese nuns on the way. Hongkong or rather Victoria is picturesque in all ways and so crowded with costume and colour. The streets are so steep that to gain standing

* See Tung-Wah Hospital, p. 343.
† See Ng Choy, p. 320.

room for the houses they are built one above another on terraces or steps of stone and some streets are nothing but flights of stone stairs.

I hope the Governor will be recalled. Pleasant as Hongkong is to a stranger I believe that half the people dont speak to the other half – none of the missionaries except 2 are on speaking terms – those of the Xtian Missionary Society[*] & Bishop Burdon are on just speaking terms and no more. Dr Eitel[†] of the London Missionary Society[‡] has just left the mission to become the Governors secretary and is helping to advance Roman Catholicism, the governor is only on *official* speaking terms with the members of the Executive Council and not with the Chief Justice at all and is believed to be as much as a personally restless and ambitious man can be anybodys tool, the tool of the Portuguese Bishop Raimondi.[§] I now think that the reason of his attention to me is that he wishes to appear on friendly terms with the English Bishop for the gaol visit was put in 'HE the Governor accompanied by the Right Revd the Lord Bishop of Victoria etc.' Life is a queer inscrutable thing everywhere and the 'wheels within wheels' are curious. I dont think that the government will supersede Mr Henessey because when he was in Parliament he made himself so obnoxious.

I have now been 17 days in China instead of the one week I intended to be and should like to stay longer but that I want to pass through the tropics while the sun is south of the Equator. I am very glad to find that Mr Dickens[¶] to whom Sir J. Hooker[||] gave me an introduction and his wife are to be my fellow passengers to Singapore. I only saw him twice as he had a severe illness but he is considered about the ablest man in Japan and has studied the country and people for some years. I daresay that you will like these better than the Japan letters.

Your 'Thing'
ILB

---

[*] See the Church Missionary Society, p. 320.
[†] See Reverend Ernest John Eitel, p. 324.
[‡] See the London Missionary Society, p. 332.
[§] See Father Giovanni Timoleone Raimondi, p. 339.
[¶] See Frederick Victor Dickins, p. 322.
[||] See Sir Joseph Dalton Hooker, p. 327.

The Malay Peninsula

Hotel de L'Europe Singapore
Jan 13/79

Lat. 1°22

My Own One

I wonder if you know that Singapore is in the Straits of Malacca only 1/2 a mile from the Malay Peninsula and only 70 miles from the Equator? Mr Cope a very rich banker and old resident has just called to take me to his house, in that unboundedly hospitable way which seems to prevail in the East, saying that some one at Dunfermline had written to him that I was coming. This must be through Mrs P. Fraser will you thank her for me. The gentleman's name was Beveridge. I mean the one who wrote. I have had a very fine passage from Hongkong here in the French Mail Steamer, a beautiful well ordered refined ship made very pleasant by the Dickens from Yokohama being on board. We were 24 hours at Saigon in Cochinchina in lat. 11°, 40 miles up the Mekong River! The heat, 86°, & the mosquitoes will not easily be forgotten!

This is absolutely tropical. Here are mangrove swamps and fringes of coco palms and banana groves and date and sago and travellers palms and tree ferns and india rubber and mango and mangostein and orchids and lianas, all kinds of parrots, blossoms and strangling trailers and monkeys and birds of gorgeous colours and greens of all vivid shades from the freshness of spring to the dark deep green of the magnolia and the yellow plumage of the palm, all rioting in a heavy shower every night and the heat of a perennial sunblaze every day and every costume from Arabia to China floats through the streets. Truly Darwin says that a visit to the tropics is equal in novelty to a visit to another planet. It is hot – so hot but not stifling and all the rich flavoured, juicy, coloured fruits of the tropics are here, fruits whose generous juices are drawn from the moist and heated earth and which have imprisoned the rays of the sun of the fiery tropic – such pineapples! Here too are glories of the heated crystal seas. Big canoes manned by dark skinned men in Turkey red turbans surrounded the ship these canoes loaded with forests of coloured coral white as snow, red, pink, violet in massive branches and fern like sprays, fresh from their warm homes beneath the clear warm waves where fish of hues as bright dart among them like 'flashes of living light', shells of wonderment there were too, of pale rose pink and others of rainbow tints which like rainbows came and went, nothing scanty, feeble, or pale! It is two miles from the ship here and it seems like a new world. This is all *splendid* – if only I were stronger then I could fight the heat. This is Asia – the Far East. I only took my passage here, and if I find any facilities for getting to the mainland of the Malay Peninsula I think I shall not leave the Straits of Malacca for a fortnight. I daresay you will be surprised by this – it is a new idea but these are the enchanted sun lands and I shall never see them again and they are said to be healthy though hot. What singular people all seem to me now to be who live in our dim pale islands and wear our hideous clothes! I am spending this whole day in writing to you among your pale snow leaved trees. Yet I should like to see the *Kientalis Europa* on a strath Affric hill slope. But I forget it is only January. I wonder what you will think of this and my ravage in Canton. I could write deliriously once more here in the bounteous tropics. No! My pen I know has not lost its cunning when there are things to inspire it!!

Your Pet
ILB

S.S. Rainbow. Singapore Roads
Jan 19/79 4 p.m.

My Darling

  With the beginning of what if I carry it out may be regarded as a new tour I will try to begin the good old system of journal letters at any cost even though in this small and entirely miserable looking cabin the mercury is 82°. But so far I am agreeably surprised with this equatorial heat. It is quite bearable and the evenings and mornings are cool i.e. 79° in consequence of the alternation of land and sea breezes. It is not an exhausted or depressing heat though one does long 'to take off one's flesh and sit in one's bones'. I dont know how this strange and quickly planned excursion into the Malay States will turn out. It is so unlikely that the arrangements can fit in. Yesterday afternoon Mr Cope sent a chit to say that he heard that a steamer was to sail for Malacca in a day or two would I like to go. I had only five minutes to think but I wrote back 'If I can get the letters needed, and if I can get the money I will go.' At 7 I went up to dinner at Mr Cecil Smiths* the Colonial Secretary

---

* See Sir Cecil Clementi Smith, p. 342.

the 2nd Governor, as the natives call him, Sir William Robinson[*] being absent a truly charming man with a very nice wife at whose house I spent the day before, and on my telling him he at once said that the letters should be ready by 11 to day and further that Captain Douglas[†] the Resident at Selangor was in Singapore with a small govt steamer and that he had arranged with him either to take me up to Selangor from Singapore or to call for me at Malacca at the end of this week on his return. This plan is sure to break down from weather or other circumstances.

Port of Malacca. Jan 20th. I arrived so far after a most pleasant voyage in a steamer one would have thought too bad to voyage in. I had a delightful evening at the Cecil Smiths on Sat. only they two and revelled in the atmosphere of intellectuality, culture and courtesy. So that I did not leave till 10.30 when I drove back and found everyone in bed. The heavens were one blaze of stars amidst a dust of nebula like the gold specks on Japanese lacquer amidst a dust of gold, and a heavy scent like attar of roses filled the air from countless flowers.

Yesterday I went with Mr Cope to St Andrews Cathedral a fine colonial cathedral beautifully situated on large grass lawns with clumps of trees near the sea. Except some stained glass in the apse there is not glass in any window even in the clerestory, but venetian shutters take its place, as in all the houses without exception. There were 32 punkahs worked by Klings[‡] from Southern India outside the Church. These Klings of whom there are several thousand in Singapore are the most superb race of men I have ever seen. Almost every one in face, figure, and colour might have been the model of the bronze of the Tired Mercury in the Naples Museum. The service was simple and the music very good but in the Te Deum just as they were singing 'Thou art the King of Glory O Christ', I caught sight of some of the faces of these punkah wallahs all bigoted Mohammedans to whom there is 'One God and Mohammed is his prophet' and the thought of how little progress Xtianity has made in the world was very sad. An excellent sermon was preached by a Singhalese D. D.[§]

We were going to remain to the communion when word came that the steamer which was to have gone today was just leaving. So we came away and getting a boat manned by 5 splendid Klings were soon on board a

---

[*] See Sir William Cleaver Francis Robinson, p. 339.
[†] See Captain William Bloomfield Douglas, p. 323.
[‡] Muslim settlers from India, particularly the Coromandel coast.
[§] Doctor of Divinity.

steamer which looked about the size & trimness of the 'Scant'. There were none on board but Chinese and Malays but they showed me a minute cabin swarming with mosquitoes into which I put my things. They said the captain was not a white man and presently a coloured lad who turned out to be he came on board and said they could not be ready till 4 so we went back to Mr Copes had some food and were back again by 3.30 when there were several Chinese cabin passengers and one who spoke English to whom Mr Cope introduced me. He found that the engineer was a Welshman and asked him to look after me to which he replied that he was a family man and that nothing gave him greater pleasure than seeing that ladies were comfortable. He has been most kind and considerate.

It was 1/2 an hour before we sailed and I lay on the little poop watching the continued and manifold life of the harbour, the Malay boats of all sizes but one form, sharp pointed at each end, and like the Chinese and Mekong boats with eyes on the bow, and large sails of matting under which they reeled as though they would upset. There was a steamer discharging 600 pilgrims who had returned from Mecca in most picturesque costumes and boats with men in crimson turbans and graceful dresses of pure white muslin, others with bright blue umbrellas and Brahmins with the mark of caste conspicuously on their foreheads, all in the setting not of a fringe but of a deep forest of coconut palms. We did sail at 4 with a strong favourable breeze and the sea was really enjoyable as we passed through many islets with brilliant green vegetation, right out into the open water of the Straits with the sun setting in flame and blood as I think he only sets in the tropics just in front. Then dinner for 3 was spread on the flat top of the cabin skylight and I eat with the captain and engineer.

This steamer was presented to the Rajah of Sarawak[*] by Lady Burdette Coutes,[†] then sold to the Straits Colonial Govt. and now belongs to some Chinese merchants. The tickets are Chinese and everything else. The supercargo, who took my ticket, was a Chinaman in only a pigtail, girdle and drawers! The Chinese owners do not allow anyone to bring any intoxicant on board lest it should be given to the captain and engineer, and they should take too much and lose the vessel. After dinner the engineer took me below to arrange in various ways for my comfort, told me his history and of his 16 children under 17 and of his colonial wife and his pay of £35 per month, was considerate in every way, lent me a box of matches and had a mattress and pillows taken on

---

[*] See Sir James Brooke, Raja of Sarawak, p. 317.
[†] See Lady Angela Burdett Coutts, p. 317.

deck. When he went to his engine he said 'If you want anything in the night just call engineer down the engine skylight.'

Stadthaus Malacca Jan 20th 3 p.m. They tell me here that this engineer is one of the kindest and nicest of men. It does one's heart good to meet with such a countryman. I had a most comfortable night lying on deck in my dressing gown in the brisk breeze, and though I watched 'my stars' hoping to see the Southern Cross set I fell asleep, and woke not till at dawn a most formidable Oriental awoke me by shouting as I thought fiercely to me with a fierce face till it occurred to me that he was trying to make me understand that they wanted to wash the decks, when I lifted my mattress on a bench and fell asleep again, soon waking to find the anchor running down in the Malacca Roads 6 hours before we should have arrived. I was delighted with the look of this one of the oldest places in the East, originally Portuguese then Dutch now English – a long bay with dense forests of coconuts, islets green as green could be lying on the south, mountains at some distance in the interior a town of antiquated appearance low houses much coloured with flattish red tiled roofs, straggling for a long distance, and built out over the water on piles a hill rising in the middle with a ruined cathedral the oldest Xtian church in the Far East crowning the top with slopes of bright green grass and palms and trees in spring green nearly lemon colour and glimpses of red flat roofs behind the hill. To the south of the old world looking town, there were glimpses of villages, of steep reed roofs under the coco palms, a long deserted looking jetty ran far out into the shallow sea, a few Chinese junks lay at anchor and all looked asleep.

Presently a crowd of Malay boats with sails made rudely of reeds came off and by one of these I sent my card and introduction to the Lieut. Governor. An hour afterwards the Captain told me that the Lieut. Governor usually went up the country on Monday for 2 days. This seemed unfortunate as there is no hotel of any kind in Malacca and as the Captain and engineer went ashore shortly afterwards I sent another introductory to Captain and the police magistrate. The result did not appear till 2 hours afterwards, during which time I sat on deck the only white person with a mingled crew of Malays and Chinamen, the steamer lying 1 1/2 miles from shore. At last I saw the welcome sight of a European well manned boat, manned by 6 native policemen and with 2 peons in white with scarlet and gold sashes which swept up to the ladder and a beautiful gentleman in white who introduced himself as Mr Biggs[*]

---

[*] See Louis Courtier Biggs, p. 315.

the Colonial Chaplain said that the Governor was just leaving when my card arrived and had deputed him to welcome me and that quarters were ready in the Stadthaus. So it turned out all right.

We were soon on a lovely shore under the cathedral crowned hill where the lawns sloped down to the sea in vivid green under palms, and trees whose trunks were one mass of ferns. Very hot sleepy and tropical Malacca looked utterly antiquated a place left out of the race – 'a land where it is always afternoon', to which Portuguese and Dutch have given their impress but which seems so far as I have seen unique. It is called Sleepy Hollow and looks like one. Going over lawns up a steep-ish hill (*Jan 21*) I was taken to my quarters. Such quarters! in the old Dutch Stadthaus, the prominent building in Malacca in the grand old days the residence of the Dutch governor and now used as treasury post office and govt office generally, the state receptions being in it the Lieut. Governor's office, and a number of rooms set apart for the use of the Governor of the Straits Settlement, the Chief Justice and other high officials on their visits to Malacca. Governor Robinson only left the day before so I had his suite of rooms. Dont imagine anything grand. The floors are red Dutch tiles partially covered with some reed matting – the walls as in all these tropical houses are very thick and are coloured blue and the ceilings are whitewashed rafters. There are 2 doors mainly composed of German shutters, and 2 immense windows on each side with the same. The furniture is old and scanty. A staircase leads from my room to a tiled lower room containing a large Shanghai pottery bath, into which as everywhere you must not bathe, but you stand on the tiles and with a dipper pour water over yourself.

The Stadthaus is only one story high at this end but in going down the hill it becomes 3 and even four. This upper part is built round 3 sides of a Dutch garden and a gallery under the tiled verandah runs all round. A set of handsome staircases on the fourth side leads to the lawn like hill with the old cathedral, the Lieut. Governors bungalow and the Colonial Chaplains bungalow. Stephanotis, passiflora, tuberose and climbers of gorgeous colour trail over everything. There must be more than 40 rooms in this old place besides great arched corridors and queer corners. The worst of it is that after 4 o'clock there is not a human being in it but myself but 2 Malay guards walk along the verandahs one on each side of my room all night and 2 English soldiers patrol the corridor by the Treasury. Last night I went about and barred myself in so far as was possible. The view of the green lawns the sea the forest of coconuts along the shore the small stream and bridge just below the Stadthaus and the quaint tiled roof of the foreign town below is most interesting.

I just saw my rooms and then went to tiffin at Mr Biggs. He and his wife are very pleasant. He is a devoted hymnologist and has written a good deal on the subject. I was pleased to find that one of the best books on it that I know is by him. We were soon in the full swing of talk on this congenial subject. I pass their open door as I go to the Governors bungalow and it usually proves a trap. I am quite at home here. There are so few people and the few are nice and the place is wonderfully attractive to me from being as much out of the world as Tiree [in Scotland] and the Lieut. Governor and his family and Mr & Mrs Biggs are not only so very kind but so pleasant and do everything they can to make my stay agreeable. Indeed I am enjoying myself very much and neither the heat nor the mosquitoes are trying. I can hardly believe that I feel the heat so little so very near the Equator. It is quite different from the heat in Japan.

After I changed my dress Mr Biggs walked with me to the Lieut Governors the Hon Captain Shaw,[*] a fine hearty merry Irish naval officer. Mrs Shaw is a daughter of Sir Richard Hill[†] Governor of Newfoundland. They have 2 girls of 16 and 18. I found Mrs Shaw a petite attractive looking very attractive person about 36 and the girls most nice. It has been long since I have seen such thoroughly nice girls. I have not made it clear that I am on a visit to them, but as they have no spare room in their bungalow I am put up in the Stadthaus. It is a nice old bungalow up by the cathedral. Nobody would live in it for some time because close by are some old Portuguese graves. It has deep verandahs above and below festooned with flowering trailers. You would like to see the snowy orchids and the wonderful flower del Espiritu Sanctu on which a snowy dove hovers in blessing.

In the verandah were 2 Malay policemen and 2 scornful looking Bengalis in white trousers, white short robes with sashes of crimson silk striped with gold and crimson and gold hats nearly flat above their handsome but repulsive faces. One of these is a Hadji. He has been twice to Mecca at an expense of £40 each time, and comes out every Friday in a gorgeous Hadji suit. These Hadjis here are bowed down to by those who meet them in the street.

Before lunch was over Captain Shaw returned and it was easy to see that he was the light of a loving home, for he was welcomed as if he had been long away. I soon found that I had made very nice acquaintances but I did not think that any encouragement was given to my project of going into the native states. Mrs S. said that she had never been allowed

[*] See Captain E. W. Shaw, p. 341.
[†] See Sir Stephen Hill, p. 327.

to go. So I came back here and wrote to you, during which time a policeman came with my tea. Then I went to the Biggs and we went over the Stadthaus and then Mrs B. took me a drive through the town and for three miles along the coast. (My pen has lost its cunning I believe or I always write under the pressure of hurry!) We crossed the bridge over the little stream which is in fact the roadway of a picturesque street and drove down that street of Malacca which is nearest the sea. On its left each house consists of 3 or 4 roofed divisions the rearmost one being built on piles over the sea. In the middle there is a court yard. The entrance room always has the door open, and you see houses showing a high civilisation, handsome altars opposite the door massive centre tables, ebony and marble chairs ranged against the wall kakemonos* on the walls and bronzes and fine pieces of porcelain on brackets and stands. At night when these rooms were lighted up with 8 or 10 hanging lamps the appearance was splendid. These are the houses of the middle class of Chinese merchants. The town of Malacca has 30000 people of whom I think 20000 are Chinese, and still their junks are rolling down on the N.E. monsoon bringing more. Nearly all the wealth of Malacca is in their hands, either in plantations or mercantile houses. The upper classes live in immense houses outside of the streets and besides these have handsome bungalows in the coconut groves. The women are secluded in the back parts. Captain Shaw says that these houses are an exact counterpart of the interiors of the Canton houses but that here under British rule they are not ashamed to show their wealth. They rejoice in our rule at Hongkong Singapore and here and show it by [Jubilee] spirit and splendid benefactions. The lofty clock tower of the Stadthaus and the handsome bridge over the creek below it are the gifts of a rich Chinaman. When I remember the judgement seat of the Naamhoi magistrate and the total hopelessness of justice in China and the oppression of the mandarins, I feel so thankful that in the main the rule of England is justice and mercy, just laws righteously administered. I am so delighted to hear that throughout the native states the rule of England is called 'the rule of the just people'.

We gradually got out of the town, the houses became fewer, the wonderful trees denser and then we were in the great dark forest of coco betel and sago palms so awfully solemn almost oppressive in the perfect stillness of the evening. Ha! This is all to my liking, every sight is new for though I have seen the palm before, the palm fringes of the coral islands in their feathery plumage are quite unlike the dark crowded coco

---

* Japanese name for a wall hanging, usually painting or calligraphy on a narrow, oblong scroll.

forests of Malacca, with their endless vistas. There were small muddy streams up which you can go in a boat if you lie down, each thickly shaded by the *attap* a species of stemless palm whose magnificent fronds are often 20 and 22 feet in length and from which the poorer Malays make their houses. The road was often bordered on each side by trees of immense size and spreading foliage, bearing golden yellow blossoms of delicate sweetness and great glory. Jungles of sugarcane often formed a foreground for masses of palms, then a jungle of pineapples surprised one, then overhead fell the long tresses of the orchid – the flower of the Holy Ghost which is only not grown in our hothouses because its dove like blossoms last but a day – then a dead tree appeared transformed into a thing of beauty by orchids and ferns, the shining fronds of the asplenium nidus, often measuring 3 1/2 feet in length – huge tamarinds and mimosa added the grace of their feathery foliage, clumps of the betel or arica nut palm with their slender & absolutely straight shafts made the coco palms look like giants, the gutta percha india rubber and other variations of ficus were there with their shining dark green leafage, the great cashew nut tree whose fruit is an apple with a nut below the breadfruit with its cantaloupe melon looking fruits and 50 others all with their fruits and flowers and very frequently a crowded cluster of Mohammedan graves each with a stone like a pawn at its head and the beautiful frangipani blossoms with its ethereal fragrance called 'the flower of the dead' planted among the tombs. But these great coco groves are by no means solitary. I seemed among things of long ago, such things as are the pictures of Williams' missionary enterprises.[*]

After leaving the town of Malacca with its wonderful fruit gardens one comes upon Malay hamlets thick and fragrant under the coco groves, almost in twilight even at noon, so dense is the shade. Thickly together they are, each house of wood or palm leaves, with deep steep roof and raised from 5 to 8 feet above the ground on posts, thoroughly tropical looking dwellings. The entrance is by a broad ladder. In coming back there was a fire underneath every house for the purpose of smoking out the mosquitoes. Men women and children were lounging about the houses, some cleaning fish others pounding rice but they dont care to work. They need not work as they only need money to buy clothes and they can get that by selling jungle fruits. The women are thoroughly clothed in a garment usually red reaching from the waist to the ankles, the *sarong*, and a long loose garment coming halfway down to the ankles called the kabaya clasped in front with ornaments. The hair is done in a

---

[*] See *Missionary Enterprises in the South Sea Islands* by John Williams, p. 334.

twist at the back and gold or silver pins are put through it. The *sarong* is girt and held up with a clasp of *enormous* size, in silver in the poorer classes, called the pinding. The children at least the boys had not much clothing. The women are very little and bright looking and the children very pretty. The men wear the sarong but only just below the knee, and short sleeved jackets *bajus*, also a turban or a red handkerchief tied round the head. In these little hamlets the people are said to live very happily and to have great domestic affection.

Everyone likes the Malays here. The verdict here is that they are chaste gentle hospitable honest honourable but their honour is sensitive and blood alone can wipe out some insults. The men all wore the *kris* a long knife. They say they are happy and have no more wants so why should they toil. There is one large mosque with a minaret outside the town and in 4 miles we must have passed 10 small ones all very clean and nice looking. They are really ruled by the law of the Koran and except where the Imam who interprets the law is absolutely wrong Captain Shaw confirms his decisions. The Malays highly appreciate English law. We passed 3 women in pure white veiled from head to foot with only holes for their eyes. These are Arab women who have been on pilgrimage to Mecca. The Shaws head servant Babu has been twice to Mecca. It is so strange to come up on a Mohammedan people in the Far East. It was a most interesting drive, though nothing can ever come up to ones first impression of the tropics. We had a most pleasant evening. A chair with 3 bearers came for me at 7.25 and brought me back at 10 to my lonely Palace. It was so pitch dark that I had to feel for the chair in the verandah.

Thursday Jan 24th. Malacca is a place to become quickly 'imbruted' in. Its repose is deep yet I have seen so much that is new, besides coming in for the Chinese New Year. On Tuesday something seemed to be going on all day. Captain Shaw said that 'pluck should have its reward' and that I should be sent to Sungei Ujong in the steam launch and that the superintendent of the police of the Province should go to make all right. Since then the 2 delightful girls have clamoured to go, and we start at 7.30 to morrow morning with the superintendent and Babu the Hadji who said 'Young ladies go then I go' and several Malay peons. It is a wild expedition and could only be undertaken under Govt auspices.

Then a royal tiger was brought in a bullock cart for the reward of $15 and its claws were given to me. The same sum is offered for a rhinoceros, $3 for a crocodile, $5 for a boa constrictor or python. This tiger was got within 6 miles of the settlement. Lately at 5 in the morning a black tiger came down the principal street of Malacca tore a Chinaman in pieces, and then the police being in pursuit jumped through a window into a house. Every door in Malacca was at once barred. The police entered the house but the tiger pinned the Malay corporal to the wall when the 2nd policeman, a white man alas ran away, the 3rd at peril of his life going up close to the tiger shot him and beat him over the head till he let go the corporal & turned on this man but in the act of doing so fell dead. The corporal is just coming out of hospital completely paralysed and the other man has got promotion and a pension for life. A short time ago a fine young tiger was brought to Captain Shaw and he ordered a cage to be made to send it to England telling Babu to put it in its bamboo cage into the godown, but he put it into the kitchen and in the morning the tiger was gone, the cage broken, the shutters torn down. There was a complete panic. People did not dare to go out even on business and not only was the whole police force turned out but all the English troops. It was some days before people believed that the beast had escaped to the jungle. I like wild beast stories but I most sincerely hope that I shall nowhere see in the jungle the glaring eyeballs of a tiger nor the loathsome folds of a boa constrictor.

You will not know the least, nor will anyone else know where I am, when I tell you that I am going to Sungei Ujong the capital of the Datu Klana[*] or referee Rajah of 7 native states and that after that I go to Selangor on a short visit to the British Resident at that Rajahs capital and that then the Shaws are arranging for me to go to the Island of Pulo Penang, and then to recross to the Mainland and go to Perak where we had the war 2 years ago to avenge the murder of Mr Birch.[†] Perak is said to have some of the most magnificent tropical vegetation in the world with wild beasts innumerable. There the travelling is on elephants. All this was planned at Singapore by the Colonial Secretary and the Shaws who are delightful people are arranging all the details. These are 'ways like ways'. How surprised you will be. The last thing I ever thought of doing was travelling in the Native States of the Malay Peninsula. I shall be able to 'swagger' about there without anybody having the power to contradict me! Neither the Governor nor the Lieut. Governor have ever been to Sungei Ujong. I do like to get into the quiet of the wilds, and beyond the hurry and worry of shoals of tourists.

(This is truly terrible. I am alone in the Stadthaus in the midst of a tropical thunderstorm, and the rain is falling in such deluges that even

[*] See Syed Abdul Rahman, p. 339.
[†] See James Woodford Wheeler Birch, p. 315.

if I could find my way through the darkness through which the lightening is flashing perfectly blue, I could not get to the bungalow.)

Ah it is beautiful here. I shall be sorry to leave the grand picturesque old Stadthaus with its tale of two centuries. It has a subterranean passage to the cathedral 100 feet above. Smooth lawns slope steeply down to the sea and these are studded with the 'Flame of the forest' the *poinciana regia* trees which look as if a number of gaudy parrots had alighted on their foliage. Then the little narrow Malacca river just below into which the launch Moosmee has been brought for an early start, and its picturesque irregular row of blue and yellow houses with steep red tiled roofs and balconies and projections over the river and all the dreamy coloured slow-moving Malay life which I see – I like it all. This still endless afternoon is a rest. There is not a single European merchant, no foreign shops, a mail only once a week and no hurry.

On Tuesday afternoon Mrs Shaw took me on a wonderful drive, round three hills used by the Chinese as cemeteries. Each grave on the hill side has a stone horseshoe and an entrance to the grave in the hill side by a door inscribed with characters in a stone archway. These cemeteries are beautifully kept. We saw quantities of grey buffaloes with enormous curved horns, mostly lying or standing on the leeward side of large fires which the Malays make to protect their bare thin skins from mosquitoes. These large animals like the Malays and are so gentle to them that a young child can lead them, but the sight of a white skin infuriates them and they are apt to charge with great ferocity.

The fires under the houses and on the ground in the forest as it grew dark had a wonderful effect. It was the Chinese New Years Eve and Captain Shaw allowed fireworks from 7 till 12. The noise was something awful. I imagined it like the final assault on a city in old days. I saw the streets traced by smoke and fire with crackers squibs rockets going off in hundreds, cannon petards and gingalls being fired, gongs drums and tom-toms being beaten, a din ceaseless, tremendous, universal. At one o'clock every house being decorated and illuminated the Chinese began to make their calls and at 6 a.m. the din began again. After breakfast the Lieut. Governor drove out in state to call on the leading Chinese and was offered 2 dishes of cakes, 12 dishes of candied and preserved fruits, and champagne and mandarin tea at each house.

About eleven all the Chinese children came forth in carriages shaped like boats turned up at each end painted red and yellow and with fringed canopies over them. These were drawn by servants and in the case of the richer Chinese a train of servants accompanied each carriage. This was a fabulous sight. The wealth of the East in its gorgeousness seemed poured out upon these infants who wore crowns of gold and diamonds stuffs of cloth of gold brocade and satin sewn with pearls and whose cloth of gold shoes glistened with diamonds. During the morning four children of a rich merchant with a train of Chinese and Malay servants came to see the Shaws a boy and girl of 5 and 6 and 2 small children. Such a sight it was I cannot give you any idea of. The girl wore a petticoat of treble satin mandarin colour with a broad pleat in front and behind exquisitely embroidered in flowers in shades of blue silk and narrow kilted pleats between each with a trail of blue silk flowers up it. Over this there was a short, sleeved robe of crimson brocade silk with the most exquisite embroidery of blue flowers on white satin all round it above this a tippet of 3 rows of tabs of coloured satin each one embroidered and shaped so. [sketch] On the head was a crown the basis of which was black velvet. At the top there was an aigrette of diamonds the centre one of which was as large as a 4d piece. Solitaires flashing forth blue flames blazed all over the cap and in front was a large dragon in filigree work in the red burned gold of Malacca set with diamonds.

Round the childs neck were seven necklaces of gorgeous beauty, the beauty of the stones (unlike those in India) being enhanced by the beauty of the setting. The first was one of diamonds, in roses and crescents some very large and all of the purest water, the second of emeralds some of them as large as a wrens egg but spoilt by being pierced, the third of pearls set whole. Yellow pearls of large size, the fourth of hollow balls of filigree gold the red burned gold, the fifth of pearls and diamonds, the 6th of a number of fine chains of gold supporting a filigree gold fish set with diamonds, the 7th what they all wear a heavy chain of gold supporting a shield with the characters of the childs name raised in the middle and fishes, flowers all round it and at the back a god similarly surrounded. Magnificent diamond earrings and gorgeous manacles of gold completed the display. And all this weight of splendour and riches was carried by a frail mite with a powdered face and sadly gentle expression who came forward and gently shook hands as did all the others who were all loaded with gold and diamonds but some sugar plums dropped on the floor and one of the gentle grave children crawled on the mat to pick them up and diamond solitaires fell out of her hair! Mrs Shaw thought that the two eldest children wore £20000 worth of precious stones.

Then came the children of the richest Chinaman in Malacca but these dear, gentle little creatures were motherless and mourning for a mother lasts three years so they were dressed only in plain blue and white and their ornaments were pearls and sapphires of great beauty set in silver. Chinese children are quiet gentle, docile, not selfish rude exacting as most of ours are. Just as this brilliant display was leaving the verandah a figure in richer colouring of skin appeared. Babu the head servant in his Hadjis dress. Now this was beautiful. (How abominably ugly our clothing is!) He wore white full trousers drawn in tightly at the ankles over black shoes, but very little of the trousers showed beneath a long linen tunic of spotless white with a girdle of orange silk. Over this was a baju of rich green silk or satin embroidered in front with green of the same colour and over all an open robe of pure white. The turban was a Mecca turban of immense size of soft white silk many yards of it, flowered in white silk.

After this the Datu Klana, Syed Abdulrahman, the reigning prince of Sungei Ujong came with his principal wife and his favourite daughter a girl of 12. Babu interpreted but the girls said that instead of interpreting he was making enormous demands on our behalf. The Datu Klana is an enlightened ruler. He apologised for their dress by saying that they had only just come from a journey. He wore a Malay handkerchief round his head tied in a peak, rich brocade *baju*, dark *manila* sarong, trousers of mandarin satin striped with red and sandals with cloth of gold straps. He was very pleasant and said as he should be absent from Sungei Ujong he would give me the key of his house there. The wife was very pleasing looking. She wore a black veil over her head and her kabaya fastened with 3 diamond clasps. The bright little daughter wore a green gauze veil with gold stars over her head and ornaments of the rich burnished gold. When they departed the 2 ladies drew sarongs over their heads. Captain Shaw & Mr Hayward* the Superintendent of Police are the only men privileged to see the Chinese women and this afternoon the latter and his wife took me to a Chinese merchants house – but this letter must be brought to an abrupt end.

ILB

Sempang Police Station at Junction of Lobah-Chena and Linghie rivers.
Territory of the Datoh Klana. Malay Peninsula
Jan 22nd [1879] 1 p.m. Mercury 87°

'Great' Sungei Ujong letter

My Pet

Probably no one in England has ever received a letter from Sempang but you! We landed here an hour ago to wait for water to proceed on our journey. This is a promontory covered with coconuts and bananas. On either side are small rivers densely bordered by mangrove swamps

---

* See Mr Hayward, p. 326.

uniting below to form the Qualla Linghie. Behind the jungle stretches out with all its terrible inhabitants no one knows how far for no one has ever penetrated the interior, but out of it rise the forest-covered Rumbow Hills. In its tangled twilight depths roam the rhinoceros the royal tiger the black panther the leopard the elephant and many other beasts in any number. Now in this burning sun they must be all asleep in their lairs. The python the boa constrictor and 15 other loathly forms besides the cobra are also lurking and monkeys large and small and flying foxes and peacocks and I forgot the elephant. No roads no tracks. One cannot go 150 yards from this house. I suppose it is very like some parts of the interior of Western Africa. We are beyond the British territory of Malacca but this bit of land was ceded to England after the Malay disturbances of 1875 to have a station with 4 policemen and a corporal in order to put down the pirates who then infested the rivers. Our little launch moored to the shore under a coco palm flies the blue ensign, and the Malay policemen here have an imperial crown on their caps both representing the might of the island lying among the grey mists of the Northern Sea but not her might alone but safety and justice.

Two or 3 canoes hollowed out of trees have gone up and down, those going up paddled by 4 men sitting facing the bow, which always has an aboriginal look, and those going down have a single square sail of very coarse matting. Before we had this post, such boats could not go up and down without having to pay blackmail to the piratical rajahs. The sounds are only the rustle of the palm fronds waving in the air, and the sharp din of the cicada. This 'Police Station' is a four roomed shelter supported on high posts and we are sitting outside on the verandah. The notices are written in Tamil and Arabic and the reports are written in Arabic characters. Soon after we sat down a Malay ran up the ladder and passed through us with the most feline movements I ever saw in a man. His eyes were large and fixed tiger like on a rifle at which he darted snatched it up and with a feline leap passed through us again. For a moment I had feared he was running *amok*, of which I have heard so much lately, but he ran down towards Mr Hayward the Superintendent of the Malacca police who is our escort, who was standing by the river and I ran after him just in time to see one alligator jump from a sand bank into the water. Mr Hayward took a steady aim at the remaining one and hit it when it sprang partly up and then plunged into the river where he supposed it would die.

Permatang Pasir. Sungei Ujong 5 pm. Police Station of the Datoh Klana. This is a far wilder and more adventurous expedition than ever we expected. Things are not going altogether so straight as might be wished and it is an absolute necessity to be out all night which I am sorry for especially as one of the girls has suffered from the sun today. We left Sempang at 2. I cannot imagine what the mercury was in the sun the copper sheathing of the launch gunwale was too hot to touch the river narrowed rapidly and we had to crawl along heaving the lead every two minutes. We were not more than an oars length from shore. We saw a large alligator asleep on the mud which did not wake when we passed him and a gun was loaded and we backed close up to him, but Babu who had the gun was too frightened to fire and the creature awoke and with his hideous form and knotted hide plunged beneath the water. It *must* be like Africa the narrow turbid water, the mangroves, and the attap palms dense along the river side, the heavy plunge of alligators, the gleam of beautiful kingfishers, the intense heat, the muddy creeks only a few feet wide arched over to within a few feet of their surface by trees and lianas, the infinite variety of trees and palms the great fruits the flowers on the trees the *hoya carnosa* and other trailers matting the trees together and hanging down in great festoons, the sunblaze of the fiery tropic vivifying the very mud itself and stimulating all this over-production.

It was very silent, occasionally we saw a little proa[*] with a savage sitting in it fishing, but no houses till at 4 p.m. we came upon large coco groves, and a considerable space where the jungle had been cleared away and 2 very large Malay villages on either side of the river with houses built on posts sampans large and small some of them with attap thatch lying along the shore, and projections on stilts thatched answering the purpose of piers. These villages or campongs were quite unlike anything I ever saw before, more like pictures in books of African travel. Now up to this time we had expected to get chairs from the police station, then (*British Residency Sungei Ujong Jan 26*) be carried 6 miles through the jungle to a point where a gharry could meet us and get here at the latest by 9 pm. (You *must* appreciate this letter for the mercury is 91°.) We had sent off a canoe from Sempang to this place ordering chairs and a runner was to be sent from thence to Captain Murray[†] but 'The best laid schemes of men & mice gang aft agee.' These piers were crowded with Malays in their red *sarongs* or pleatless kilts and white trousers and with small boys dressed in silver fig leaves and silver bangles only looking at us silently. Then two policemen of the Datoh Klana with a crescent with

[*] A Malay boat.
[†] See Commander Patrick James Murray, p. 335.

a star between its horns on their caps came down and threw cold water on our getting on at all till Captain Murray sent for us. We had to be dragged up these piers and then to walk a long way with the policemen to the police station of the campong.

The village was very neat each house under its own palms and its compound sanded the paths were also sanded. There was a street of shops exclusively Chinese, much decorated, then a lane of detached Malay houses and then on an open neatly sanded a police station, a regular Malay house on high posts with 11 policemen and four small guns on carriages underneath it and a gong outside on which the policemen beat the hours. We had to climb into it by a ladder of 3 round rungs where there should have been 8 steps. There was a deep verandah with a roof of steep slope and at either end a low bed for 2 police corporals with the ends bolsters of red silk with gold and silk embroidery. There was also a table with 4 chairs, a Sam Slick clock,* an engraving from the Graphic and some curious Turkish pictures of Stamboul. Rifles *krises* handcuffs hung on the wall inside.

At the river we had been told that the boatmen would not go up the roped narrow stream at night and now the corporal said that no one would carry us through the jungle, that trees were lying across the track, that the men would fall with us or put us down and run away and he added very gallantly for a Mohammedan that he should not care about Mr Hayward but it would not do for the ladies. The tigers who are in numbers in the jungle were no obstacle because they never attack a party. So we had to give this up and with it any prospect of reaching this place before daylight. Babu the Hadji had recovered from a sulk into which he had fallen in consequence of Mr Hayward having taunted him with cowardice about the alligator and had made everything quite comfortable and asked us just as in Govt House when we would have dinner, one policeman brought us coconut milk in tumblers another sat outside and pulled a small punkah and 2 more mounted guard over us.

Mr Haywards knowledge of the Malay character was most useful. He sent for one Malay apart from his fellows and induced him to make a bargain for taking us up the Linghie, but this man soon returned in a state of great excitement complaining to the police that the others had set on him for taking us up, on which the policemen went back & interfered. The youngest Miss Shaw was completely prostrated by a bad sick-headache produced by the sun which I feared might be the beginning of bilious fever and lay all the time on one of the beds, but her sister and

---

* See Sam Slick, p. 160.

I strolled out and visited the grave of a Hadji 'a great prophet' they said who was slain in coming down the river. There was a grave with a post at each end, and a jar of oil on it, a reed lattice round it on which curtains were hanging, and the whole was covered by a thatched roof sustained on posts. There are village officers in all villages and each village above 40 houses has its own mosque and religious officers.

The Malays are certainly not savages, though they commit very savage actions. They have quite a high code of civilisation. They are not pleasing, they have a haughty indifferent manner, but after the Japanese who I think must be the most indelicate people on earth it is very pleasing to see people so well clothed especially as their clothing is most becoming both in form and colour and no amount of severe work in the heat causes them to take off anything more than the *baju* or jacket. Instead of the promiscuous bathing of the Japanese there are little bathing sheds by the rivers used by one person at a time who throws a sarong on the thatch to show that it is occupied.

Babu had heated some excellent soup and made a curry which with fresh coconut milk made a good dinner and he waited as grandly as in Govt House though only in simple Malay costume. Miss E. Shaw was feeling so wretched that she wanted to stay in the police station all night but I was most anxious to get her on because I thought if she were ill I could nurse her at Captain Murrays but certainly not in the verandah of a Malay police-station, and Mr Hayward was of the same opinion. The worthy man who is a brave man and used to facing danger, who was the first European to come up here and acted as guide to the troops in the war and who afterwards disarmed the population, quailed at having the charge of these two lovely girls. 'Oh' he said 'if anything were to happen to the Miss Shaws, I should never get over it – and they dont know what roughing it is – they never should have been allowed to come.' His idea was to give the sick one two tablespoonfuls of whisky and to make each take it for it was a risk to sleep out in the jungle especially in the rainy season. I was really afraid about this for the miasma rises heavily for about 20 feet and the heat of the day had been tremendous.

We started at 7 Mr Hayward in front with a torch composed of strips of palm dipped in dammar a most inflammable resin and bound tightly together, a policeman then the sick Miss Shaw leaning on the arm of her sister and me then Babu and then a train of policemen carrying our things and more torch bearers the torches dripping flame all along the path. We walked fully 3/4 of a mile to cut off some considerable windings of the river, 'dragging' till we could hardly stand on our feet, crossed a river by a plank bridge and found our boat lying at one of these high wooden piers with a thatched roof. There were many torches there lighting irregularly the lofty trees of the jungle the skeletal pier the sampan the dark swift flowing river and the dark lithe forms of the Malays. This sampan was a broad flattish bottomed boat about 22 feet by 6, its whole length covered by a gridiron of split bamboo. About 7 feet of the middle was covered with a circular roof of attap. It was steered by a broad paddle lashed loosely and poled by 3 men who standing at the bow planted their poles firmly in the mud and then walked down as far as the centre. All boats must go up by this laborious process as the current of the river is so strong that the Japanese would call it one long rapid. Coming down the river carries them down and they only use their poles to keep off the banks. The boat was essentially 'native'.

(*Monday Jan 27/79*. The 'Golden Chersonese' is very hot, and much infested by things which bite and sting. How a night can be cool at 80° I cannot imagine yet so it is. I have not suffered from the heat at night since I reached Singapore. These climates are said to be very healthy but the heat has to be fought all day and the mosquitoes from sunset till bedtime.)

A fire was burning in the middle of the boat which smoked the mosquitoes from under the roof. Babu & Mr Hayward arranged blankets and pillows under the roof and we lay there 3 abreast and Mr Hayward who had never been up the river and who felt very responsible for the girls sat on the floor at our feet only occasionally sleeping. Babu who wrapped himself in true Oriental impassiveness and a police servant of Mr Haywards sat or lay in front and so we started for our jungle voyage which though we knew it not was to last for 18 hours in which time I suppose we travelled about 20 miles. This does not exaggerate the torturousness of the river nor the sharpness of the turns. [sketch] The boatmen measure the distance by turns. When we asked them when we should reach the end, they never knew in how many hours but always said there were so many turns. Captain Murray the Resident here spent £5000 and 2 years in a solitary exploration of Africa between Cape Colony and Lake Nzami, then going westward, and he says that our journey by the Linghie is an average specimen of African travelling.

Silently we glided away from the torches into what appeared impenetrable darkness, but the sky was ablaze with stars and ere long forms of trees over and round us became quite distinct. Ten hours of darkness in the jungle. Loudly clattered the restless cicada – a steam whistle constantly blown in the distance was the cry of some monkey, yells hoarse or shrill were any of the wild beasts with which the jungle swarms –

253

splashings and plungings that I thought were alligators, Captain Murray says were more probably wild elephants disturbed in drinking at the river – sheet lightening every now and then revealed the strong stream eddying past, and a canopy of trees falling and unfallen – trees with straight stems 150 feet high surmounted by a crown of drooping branches palms with their plumage, lianas, hanging and looping and twisting great black snags, and the lithe forms of our Malay boatmen, and the motionless white turban of the Hadji all for a second against the flashing blue flame to be again lost in darkness. The river with its sharp turns and muddy hurry was I think from 20 to 35 feet wide but a mere path through the jungle.

Now do not think of a jungle as I have as an entanglement, or thicket of profuse and matted scrub but think of it as the noblest of forests of majestic trees so heavily buttressed at their roots that 50 men could find shelter behind them. On the top branches of these, other trees have taken root from the seeds being deposited by birds and these send down the most extraordinary single cylindrical strands perhaps 150 feet long and 8 inches in diameter smooth and perfectly straight which root themselves in the ground and look like the guys of a mast. Under these giants stand the lesser trees in glorious confusion, coco, sago, betel and nibong palms, the wild nutmeg, the artocarpus, the angsenna – I have counted 76 species of trees nearly all of them bearing striking flowers – and under these again are flowering shrubs with flowers of heavy delicious odours and the attap palm the bamboo the rattan, which often extends itself for 200 feet, tree ferns 20 and 30 feet high with ferns, selaginellas and lycopodiums in their shade and all the giants and all the lesser trees are twined or loaded with lianas trailers ferns epiphytes, all twining together the huge masses of the antler fern and the 5 feet fronds of the asplenium nidus being everywhere. Not only do orchids crowd the branches but one sees as in a hothouse a tendril dangling from a branch, sustaining at its base some bright hued epiphyte of quaint mocking form, or a branch hangs across the river supporting a festooned trailer from whose stalks hang almost invisibly suspended conical fruits almost vermilion coloured as large as a small melon. There the beautiful vanilla and hoya wreathing the same tree here and everywhere a trailer with great clusters of orange blossoms festoons four trees at once then again an audacious trailer with richly veined and highly coloured leaves has leapt across the river at a height of 200 feet from tree to tree and sends down a profusion of festoons but it is useless to describe to understand anything of a tropical jungle one must see it in all its wonderment with its colossal flowering trees and inextricable involvement, its butterflies and moths, its bright birds its bats and flying foxes, and its infinite variety of monkeys sitting hanging leaping grimacing chattering pelting each other with fruits and its loathly alligators lying in wait on the slimy banks under the riotous vegetation.

All this and far more the dawn revealed, but in the darkness there was the black river under the foliage with scarce 10 yards of its course free from obstruction, great snags all along it, trees lying half across or quite across sometimes under water where the sampan 'drove heavily' over them, sometimes above ripping the thatch from its roof in hundreds and as one obstacle was safely passed the rapid stream always canted us close on another but the great skill of the boatmen averted all accidents. 'Jaga Jaga' Caution! Caution! was the constant cry. The most unpleasant part was the constant ripping and tearing sound made by branches catching the thatch and the perpetual bumping against timber. The girls were terrified. The whisky had cured the younger ones sick-headache and she was alive to terrors. They thought the boat would be ripped up, that the roof would be taken off, that a tree would fall and crush us, that the boatmen when they fell into the river as they several times did would be eaten by alligators, that they should see the glaring eyeballs of a tiger and they were always awaking me with some new thing that was either happening or going to happen and they were so angry because they could not sleep while I, an old campaigner, slept whenever they let me.

Dawn revealed all the glories of the forest seen through a veil of mist before the sun rose in great power. Then we had soda water and bananas, the Hadji worshipped with his face towards Mecca and one man prepared the morning meal of curry and rice for himself and the rest a most elaborate curry of salt fish for its solid and for its condiment *blachang* a Malay preparation which such Europeans as those who relish decomposed cheese also eat. It is made of shrimps and prawns which lie in heaps on the seashore till putrefaction has well advanced and are then trodden by bare feet into a paste – the smell is penetrating and lingering. The men rinsed their mouths in the river made the boat fast and eat as the Malays always do without chopsticks. This was about 7. Then one prepared the betel nut for the rest. All Malay men and women chew this nut for its stimulating properties. Everywhere humanity weary in body or spirit craves something to chew or pull. The betel nut is a small nut of the arica palm, a very beautiful palm. They first take a fresh green leaf of the *sirih* a creeping plant grown on poles like hops for this purpose. Then from a small tin box they take a little moistened lime and smear a little over the leaf – then a little paste made of gambier or a mixture of other spices is added with a piece of the nut and the whole is wrapped up in the leaf and chewed. If you speak to a person while chewing this and he answers you his mouth appears to be full of blood. The day was fiercely hot, the mercury 87° and magnificent as the forest was, there was some suffering from the heat.

At 9 having been 14 hours on the river we came on a small cleared space where a bearded man in linen clothes and a pith helmet hallooed jovially to us and we were soon hilariously greeted by Captain Murray, English Resident in the Native State of Sungei Ujong in which we then were. On seeing him we hoped to find a gharry and to get some breakfast and he helped us on shore and dragged us in the boiling sun to a long shed the quarters of 100 coolies who are engaged in making a road through the jungle. Here we sat down on the long platforms which served as beds but instead of getting breakfast we only got some cups of bad tea given us by a half naked Chinaman! We then learned that the runner who should have given Captain M. the note at 1 am. had not delivered it till 8 a.m. so he had not been able to arrange anything by that hour and to our dismay we had to go back to the *sampan* and toil up the shallowing and narrowing river for 4 hours more, the boatmen sometimes jumping into the river to heave the boat off the mud.

When we landed at last Captain Murray met us on horseback and we found a road and two buggies of extreme antiquity much lashed together with rope in one of which I drove Miss Shaw, with reins so short that only by sitting on the edge of the seat could I hold them and a whip so short that I could not reach the pony with it. At the Chinese village of Nioto the police brought us coconut milk. After that the pony could not or would not go and the Malay syce with difficulty got it along by leading it, and we had to walk up every hill. At the large Chinese village of Rassah a fresh pony met us and we arrived here at 4 an open valley, with a good deal of cleared land and the large Chinese village of Serambang upon it and beautiful hills some of them over 3000 feet high surrounding it and stretching away to the northern state of Selangor. In the midst of the valley a steepish hill on which the arica palms were waving their deep green fronds was crowned by the British Residency two unpretending bungalows united by their upper verandahs in front of which the blue folds of the British ensign were slightly bulging in the afternoon airs. Food was the first necessity, then a bath, then dinner at 7.30, then more sleep. We had been 33 hours in coming 60 miles!

Residency. Sungei Ujong Jan 29th. We have been here 4 days. We were to have gone back yesterday and by not doing so I have lost the opportunity of getting to Selangor and fear that I shall have to go on direct to

Prince of Wales Island to join the Ceylon Steamer, but I felt that I needed a longer rest, and the girls were longing to stay. I have never travelled in such great heat before and it hinders one from getting the exercise which makes travelling so much easier. It is wonderful that one gets on at all, but the nights are cool and this is a very dry soil and a dry air though 100 inches of rain fall in a year.

These bungalows are hot but airy. One has only an attap roof without a lining. No one sleeps at night in the one in which my room is but since we have been here a sentry has been on duty at night and a bulldog is chained at the foot of the step ladder which leads to both bungalows. It is most strange to see the things belonging to civilisation in the heart of the Malay Peninsula. The drawing room has a good piano and is as liveable looking as a bachelor would be likely to make it, there is a billiard table in the corridor and the dining room to which we have to go out with its floor of large red tiles and its walls of a dark unpolished wood is very pretty, with a plateau or lake for flowers in the middle of the table with a flower vase rising out of it, exquisite crystal – menu cards with holders of Dresden china 4 classical statuettes in Parian* and a beautiful pineapple, a grenadilla, bananas and a durian blanda† always upon it.

The food except the fruit is too elaborate for me but plain meat is hardly to be got. Curry is at every meal but not made with curry powder. Its basis is coconut grated and made into a paste with coconut milk. The spices are added fresh. Turtles are kept in a pond and we have had turtle soup and stewed turtle. Fowls dressed in different ways are at each meal but never plain roasted or plain boiled. If we had been here a little sooner we should have had elephant trunk which is said to be like beefsteak. The dressing bell is a bugle. In houses in these regions you always have a tiled bathroom of large size under your bedroom to which you descend by a ladder. It is often concealed by a trapdoor which is often concealed by a couch. You lift the cushion and find it. Here it is an open trap in the middle of my room. Each night one has to look under the pillows for snakes and centipedes. We have all found the latter.

Babu has taken command of everything, puts on his grand clothes, carves at the sideboard, scolds the servants, pushes them aside when they attempt to offer 'his young ladies' anything at table, and saves Captain Murray all trouble.

The native prince the Datu Klana applied for a Resident 4 years ago, and Captain Murray has been here since. He is a little sunbrowned,

---

* A type of porcelain.
† The Malaysian name for the graviola, or *Annona muricata*.

restless, eccentric misanthrope, never still for five minutes and very *disconnected*, very kindhearted, very blunt, very undignified and hasty, never happy out of the wilds, very well meaning. Practically he rules Sungei Ujong which is a small state supposed only to have 12000 people, 10000 of whom are Chinese. The villages are exclusively Chinese – the Malays never join house to house. The Chinese are just as Chinese here in dress, houses and customs as in China. They have been here for nearly 40 years, and are principally engaged in tin mining. Captain Murray is judge tax gatherer Board of Works – everything. He sits 'in equity' for there are no laws and the Malays are judged by the Koran. He is doctor also, and has been so successful that people come from the neighbouring states for his advice. There is no other European except one from Australia who is making roads. He is an honourable man and means well. If I were made 'Judge in Israel' I should act differently in some respects but the state enjoys security for life and property and several of the neighbouring states also desire Residents, and one or two had been promised them when Russia accused England of designs on this Peninsula, when the giving of such officers ceased and only Perak, Selangor, Sungei Ujong have them, and in these 3 states, piracy, insecurity and plundering by petty Rajahs are at an end. It is well that England can always command the services of able, brave and honourable men, and that those who appoint them are conscientious in their appointments, for practically these Residents have no check upon them. [. . .]

Monday was a day of fierce heat 91° in the shade. I went with Mr Hayward to the police court to see some Chinese cases tried by Captain Murray. What a contrast to the judgement seat of the Naamhoi magistrate at Canton! A large whitewashed room with a clean floor of red tiles, 3 long benches at the end for witnesses and friends, a punkah constantly going – a tiled dais with a desk for the judge a table with a charge and other books and a clerk a Chinese interpreter who speaks six dialects and a Malay interpreter who puts the Chinese interpreters words into English. The benches were quite filled principally with Chinamen and a number of policemen stood about. I do not see how truth can be arrived at in an Oriental court yet the judge took great pains to find it out and the prisoner had every advantage, and when found guilty was put into a good jail from which he would daily be taken out to work on the roads. The question to be arrived at is the simple one, 'Did the prisoner commit the crime or not?' If he did he is punished, if not he is sent away free. The police there as with us like to sustain a case. 114 persons were convicted last year, theft being the usual crime. It does not seem many out of a population of 12000, considering that most of it is an unsettled, foreign mining population. The resident is a most eccentric little man just over 40, never still for two minutes and even in the court he was hammering with a knife, whittling on the desk, humming snatches of airs, making desultory remarks to me, exclaiming 'Bother these fellows' or 'Do get on and dont keep everyone broiling here' or 'Get along young man' knowing that no one understood except the Malay interpreter. Mr Hayward, through whose hands the crime of Singapore and Malacca had been filtering for 20 years, was very critical of the rough and ready method here, and constantly interjected suggestions such as 'You dont ask them questions before you swear them' etc. I doubt not that justice is done for Captain Murray though eccentric and hasty is a most worthy honourable man. [. . .]

At 4 we had a very pleasant expedition to a hill 1300 feet high 3 miles off where Captain Murray has built a cabin on the very top for the bracing air. We left in buggies at 4 and where the road ended, a chair with 4 bearers carried Miss Shaw, her sister rode part of the way up and I rode to the very top on an Australian stockmans saddle and enjoyed that. It was a steep path cut through the jungle, the last of it being 200 steep steps up which the sagacious pony went cunningly. The growths were wonderful. One charm of these tropical forests is the endless variety – every few yards there is something new. How glorious the forest giants looked with their trunks straight and smooth as the mast of a ship to an average height of 150 feet and their branches supporting all sorts of orchids and trailers. One cannot see 'what like' the foliage is which is borne so far aloft into the summer sunshine but on the ground I found great red trumpet flowers, and flowers like red dragonflies and flowers like large single roses in yellow wax, and looking up I saw that these came from the immense trees, and that thousands of such flowers were wasting their beauty and their rich fragrance on the desert air.

I should like to be there alone to have time to study the habits and ways of ants. On the top there was a large tree containing an ant town at its base with a double entrance at the top. To this an army of millions of ants in a column 3 inches wide converged the whole time marching in rows as regular as a British regiment, over all sorts of inequalities, rough ground and imbedded trunks of trees, never breaking their ranks, larger ants who looked like officers, marching outside the column and sometimes turning back as if to give orders or look after stragglers. I followed this sinuous column for about 15 paces till I came upon a scene of singular hurry but of orderly activity – a stump of a tree quite dead and about 3 feet high was completely black with ants who appeared to be removing the bark in infinitesimal portions. Another column was always returning from the lower entrance to the nest but as this was only half the width of the other I suppose that many of the carriers stay inside to work. I never saw a more busy scene. They were working from the top downwards, and about 7 inches had been peeled. Captain M. destroyed both entrances to the ant hill but before dark a new one had been made much lower down, and the next morning a second. Towards night the smaller column of ants ceased to emerge from the hill I suppose because it became too dark for work but at 5.30 the next morning both columns were in full activity.

I should have liked also to watch the ways of the white ant,* the great timber destroying pest of this country a large ant of a pale buff colour. He builds a tunnel of sand held together by a viscid secretion up the trunk of the tree at which he works, and under this tunnel he cuts a groove extending the tunnel upwards as he works. I broke away 2 inches of a tunnel but by morning it was restored. There were a number of ants two inches long whose works must be on a great scale, but I had no time to follow these, and their bite is to be feared.

The great tree crickets kept up for a time the most ludicrous noise I ever heard one sitting in a tree and calling to another. From the deafening sound one would suppose the creature making it to be as large as an eagle. It is on two notes. Early in the morning the apes began to call to each other with a plaintive Hoo-hooey and I saw an iguana fully 5 feet long silently glide down the trunk of a tree. Captain Shaw asked the imam of one of the Malacca mosques about alligators eggs one day since I came and he said that when hatched the young which went down to the sea became alligators and those which remained in the rivers became iguanas!!!

When we got up to the top of this very steep hill I was well pleased to find that only the undergrowth had been cleared away and that there was nothing but a house of a single room partitioned into two, elevated a good height like a Malay house with a deep verandah up a step ladder. A smaller house could not well be or a more picturesque one from the steepness and irregularity of its roofs. A small attap shed cut into the hill outside was the miniature cookhouse, and a barrel in a little place under the house with attap screens served as a bathroom. The edge of the hill from which a few trees had been cleared was so steep that but for a bamboo rail one might easily go over. Some coffee shrubs some tea and ipecacuanha were growing under the trees. The view in all directions was beautiful to the north a sea of wooded mountains with blue indigo

---

* The termite.

shadows to the south the country we had threaded in the Linghie river, forest and small clearings and little valleys where rice was growing and scars where tin mining was going on and the 'capital' the little town of Serambang with its larger clearings, and to the west the glitter of the shining sea. We got chairs and I actually 'got out' till after dark and oh the relief of the absence of mosquitoes! It was a gorgeous sunset of the gory, furnace kind one only sees in the tropics, waves of violet light rolling over the land, and the low Sumatran coast lying like a purple cloud amidst the fiery haze. Our host said 'Now if you are smart you can have baths' and he sent our 11 servants to the knoll above where he and Mr Hayward mounted guard over them till we were ready.

The indoor accommodation was very limited. The girls slept on two camp beds in the inner cabin and I in a cot-hammock in the outer cabin, the table being removed. The two gentlemen with their arms and the bulldog slept in the verandah and the 11 men stowed themselves away under the house. Dinner was well cooked and served with coffee after it just as at home. The Chinamen made a huge bonfire such as I never saw with great trunks of trees, and pieces of dammar gum several pounds in weight obtained by rotting in the ground, and this was kept up till daylight throwing its splendid glare over the whole hill top, lighting up the forest and bringing the cabin out in all its picturesqueness. The cot was most comfortable but I did not sleep so well as usual owing to some absurd fears. 'Parochial' as the Scotch papers are, as Mrs Cosmo Jones was one of the persons implicated, perhaps they have given an account of a tragedy which occurred at the Dindings on this coast a few weeks ago and I was just thinking of this and the ease with which the Resident could be overpowered and murdered in this lonely place by any ones having a grudge against him when (as I thought) the door behind my head from the back ladder was burst open and my cot and I fell down at the floor at the head! It really was that the rope not having been properly fastened gave way with a run! An hour afterwards the foot ropes gave way in the same manner and I was deposited altogether on the floor. When it grew dark tiny lamps began to move in all directions some came from on high like falling stars but most moved among the trees a few feet from the ground with slow undulating motion the fire having a pale blue tinge as one might imagine an incandescent sapphire to have. It is 21 years since I saw fireflies and unlike some other things they were so much more beautiful than I remembered them to be.

We got up at daylight and after coffee and bananas walked down the mountain. The forest was glorious but I wished for time to take in each beautiful detail. Unlike the coarse weeds which form so much of the undergrowth in Japan, everything which grows in these forests rejoices the eye by its form or colour but unlike the Sandwich Islands, things which hurt and kill lurk amidst all the beauties. I found the steep descent most painful to me – I could hardly get to the bottom. There buggies waited for us but in going down one hill the crupper broke and the breeching consequently giving way the buggy came down on the horse and we had to stop and take him out and mend the harness. I should think that there is not an emergency for which Mr Hayward is not fully prepared. I like a man of his quiet strength. He has a great spear wound in his brow which Captain Murray says was received in holding 60 armed men at bay while he secured the retreat of some helpless persons. The only thing which seems to disturb him is his responsibility for the Lieut. Governors fragile looking girls. He says they should never have been allowed to come but they are enjoying themselves very much and will be none the worse.

Almost as soon as we got back a large number of Chinese carrying banners and joss sticks came up to give a representation called a mein mein, the first part of which is a representation of a huge dragon, and the other parts representations of fights with spears, shields and battle-axes. The whole was accompanied with the most *infernal* music of tom toms etc. Tomtoms always seem to me an accompaniment of devil worship.

In the cool of the afternoon we drove and rode 4 miles to a Malay campong called Mambu to visit the Datu Bandar,* the 2nd prince who in the Datu Klanas present absence takes his place. His dwelling with three others, a godown on very high stilts, and a mound of graves with a great many coconut and other trees was surrounded as Malay dwell-ings are by a high fence within which was another fence with his own dwelling and those of his wives on a neat sandy level under coco palms. His secretary a nice looking lad in red turban *baju* and *sarong* came out first and then the Datu Bandar a very pleasant able looking man with a cordial manner who shook hands and welcomed us. No notice had been given of our visit and this man who is reclaiming and bringing into good cultivation much of his land and who sets the example of working with his own hands was in red turban checked shirt and red *sarong*. Vulgarity is a disease of the West alone I think and this Oriental far from apolo-gising for his deshabillé took us up the difficult ladder which led into his house with as much ease as if he had been in his splendours.

I thoroughly liked his house, indeed I have seldom seen anything which appeared to me more fitting and tasteful. We stepped from the

---

* See Kulop Tunggal under Syed Abdul Rahman, p. 339.

ladder into a long corridor well matted. Then there was a doorway with a gold embroidered silk valance and a looped portière of white flowered silk or crêpe. This led into a small room very well proportioned with two similar doorways with portieres, one leading to a room which we did not see and the other to a bamboo or slotted gridiron platform which in a Malay house always leads to a smaller back house where cooking and etceteras are done and which seems given up to the women. There was a rich dim light in the room which was entirely of a dark red wood and there was only one long low window with turned bars of the same. There were 2 or 3 handsome cabinets with hangings of crimson and gold embroidery, and an ebony frame containing some Arabic writing hung above one doorway but they are very rigid Mohammedans and there was no 'likeness of anything in the heaven above or in the earth beneath or in the waters under the earth'. There was a draped table by one wall a couch and several chairs, and a round table covered with a fine woollen cloth of bright but cool yellow. The floor was covered with a reed mat and over this there were the most beautiful Oudh rugs in those mixtures of toned down rich colours which are so very beautiful. Richness and Harmony were characteristics of the room and it was distinctly Malay, one could not say that it reminded one of anything but of the fluted and coloured light streaming through rich stained glass.

The Datus brother and uncle came in the first a very handsome Hadji with a bright intelligent countenance. He had been eight years in Mecca studying the Koran under a renowned teacher and had spent several thousand dollars. 'We never go to Mecca to trade' he said 'we go for religious purposes only.' Mohammedanism is not among the dead faiths of the earth. These men looked superb in their red dresses and turbans. No head dress is as becoming as a turban and the sarong is beautiful. Their hospitality was very grateful. The wealthier Mohammedans though they never drink wine keep it for guests and they offered us champagne and on our refusing it they brought cows milk. Then they brought coffee of a delicious kind with a delicate aroma and not darker than tea of average strength. I never tasted coffee like it for excellence. It was made from coffee leaves. The Malays export the berry. A good many children stood about but we did not see any of the 'mean ones within the gates' though the Rajah gave us to understand that these children had three mothers. They had a good deal to say and did not leave their visitors to entertain them, though we were but 'Xtian dogs'. When Captain Shaw pressed on the Malays the total impropriety of shooting Chinamen as they were in the habit of doing, they said 'Why not shoot Chinamen they are only dogs, they have no religion?' The Datu Bandar sits on the Bench with the Resident and is a very useful magistrate, but the Datu Klana must confirm a capital sentence. Captain Murray behaved very badly to my thinking, in such a fine and easy way, clapping the Rajah on the back, humming snatches of songs, drumming on the table. If this is admissible with his own people he should adopt a dignified manner for his sovereigns sake to these native princes. I believe that he has become what he is and has sought exile in these wilds because Lady Gertrude Douglas went into a convent.

The gentlemen saw us to our buggies and we got back after dark. On Wednesday we did not do much. The Chinese of Serambang are under the control of three 'Capitans' [. . .] We went to pay complimentary visits for the new year to them with the Malay interpreter. We were received so kindly, wine and tea produced etc. Their houses were very rude with clay floors but they have nice carriages and their children were loaded with gold and diamonds. One had been here for 40 years another for 36 and they had made and lost and made fortunes. They get everything from China, and we need not hope to find among this strange shrewd people a market for our 'shoddy' and 'weighted cottons'. In one house a sweet little girl handed round the tea and cake and all even to babies who can hardly toddle across the floor came up and shook hands without shyness or forwardness. These children all wore crowns of red burned gold set with diamonds. When the girls are 12 years old they are shut up and never are seen by any man till the bridegroom lifts the veil at the marriage ceremony.

(*S.S. Rainbow Malacca Feb 1. 5 p.m.* I am once more in this steamer which was to have sailed at 4 but matsailed boats with cargoes of Chinese Malays fowls pineapples sugarcane etc keep coming off and we are not going to sail till 6.30. So like West Highland ways. The little steamer has long ago submerged her load line and is only about 8 inches out of the water, and still they load, and still the matsailed boats are coming off from the shore and the eight paddled boats with 2 red clothed men sitting on each thwart facing forwards and about 127 people mostly Chinese are huddled upon the little deck with goats and buffaloes and 40 coops of fowls and ducks the fowls and ducks cackling and quacking and the Chinese clattering. Such a Babel! 'Easy Ahead' shouts the Portuguese-Malay captain for she is only licensed to carry 100 and the water runs in at the scuppers as she rolls but 5 of the matsailed boats have hooked on. 'Run ahead full speed' – he vainly shouts – the Chinese are climbing up the stem over the bulwarks everywhere fairly boarding us and with about 150 souls and not a white man or a Xtian among them we sail away over the gaudy water into the gaudy sunset and beautiful sleepy tropical Malacca with its palm fringed shore and its colonial streets and Mt Ophir with its golden history and the good kind Lieut. Gov. and his family and the princely Stadthaus whose ancient rooms seemed almost like my property are passing into memories. There is 'no place to be' except a very small bridge on which is a small table on which the captain & I have had an excellent dinner with hen coops for seats and here I shall have to sleep. My ticket is in Chinese. In a Chinese steamer in which a lady is rarely seen Captain Shaw says that one is sure to be made very comfortable. What strange circumstances one finds oneself in when once one leaves the beaten tracks of travel.)

After this we i.e. Mr Hayward the Malay interpreter and I went into one of the large open markets full of tables in which gambling is carried on. People are being perpetually shaved at one end for a Chinaman has his head and face quite smooth and never shaves himself, the shaving the head being originally a sign of subjection to the Tartar conquerors. Tea is always being consumed, being kept warm in round baskets with lids wadded about 3 inches thick inside such as were sold some years ago in England under the name of 'Norwegian kitchens'. These markets have been crowded whenever I have seen them, and the interpreter said they were so all night. At a table sits a clothed croupier with piles of money before him and thronging round the table are as many half naked Chinamen as can contrive to see over each others' shoulders concentrated eager silent painfully in earnest for they stake all the gains of their hard labour at these tables. No one understands their method of gaming but there is a heavy brass [box] containing a single dice and they draw the cover slowly off this box amidst breathless silence. Gaming is illegal in Malacca and I have got one of these boxes which was confiscated there. In Sungei Ujong they are a source of revenue. They belong to these Chinese capitans and pay a licence fee to the government, 2 of $120 dollars a month and 2 of $50, showing how very large their gains must be. The Chinese work very hard and live on very little, but they are very poor now because owing to the great discoveries of tin in Australia its value has fallen nearly a half. They are wonderful people. I am quite coming round to the view of Sir Harry Parkes and others that China is destined to be the greatest of Eastern powers and a great colonising Empire. One Chinaman is worth at least 10 Japanese in force and tenacity.

I never can walk in a hot climate without being completely done up and I did not go out any more but wrote this letter to you. We had turtle soup not near so good as mock turtle for dinner, and turtle steak not near so good as veal which it somewhat resembles, sang Auld Lang Syne and went to bed. On Thursday we were up at 4 had breakfast and started punctually at 5 Captain Murray Miss Shaw and I in one buggy and Mr Hayward and the other Miss S. in the other. Horses had been sent on the night before and after changing them we went the next stage through most magnificent forest and jungle till they could no longer drag the buggies through the mud, and then 2 chairs and 3 saddle horses were waiting and 2 chairs for the 6 miles through the jungle. We rode along an infamous track, much of it knee deep in mud, through the glorious jungle but I found the ups and downs very trying on a sidesaddle and when we got through the worst part changed the pony for a chair. Outside the jungle there was something like English park and fox cover scenery varied by Malay campongs and groves of palms. Coming down one of the grassy hills on looking round I saw Captain Murrays big horse sitting on all fours on the slope and he sitting quietly on the top of it just as you would as if you had not come off! He is a bold but a very bad rider and his horses are always either falling or putting him over their heads.

At noon we reached the Lingei Police Station from which we had started in the sampan, and were received by a campong of police with fixed bayonets. We dined in the police station verandah, and as the launch had been obliged to leave just before because the water was falling we went down to Sampong in a sampan paddled by 4 men with paddles just like oval ended spades and with spade handles some of the policemen going down with us. There we found the launch and took leave of our eccentric but most kind and worthy host, who immediately turned up the river to dwell alone in his bungalow with his trusty dog his revolver and his rifle possibly to be murdered at last. As he disappeared into the wilds self exiled for the love of a woman, I could not help thinking how seldom a man's life is *permanently* either marred or blighted for such a cause. It was very calm and I read Trollopes Vicar of Bulhampton* till it grew dark when we had the splendid sight of a great tract of forest on fire close to the sea. We landed at Malacca at eight on a wooden pier accessible to launches at high water and 800 feet long. Several peons and 2 inspectors of police met us.

Our visit to Sungei Ujong has been the talk of the little foreign world of Malacca. It was thought very unsafe for the girls to go and some thought they would never get back. I liked getting to my solitary lair in the Stadthaus. The Shaws were most kind. A friendly welcome is very pleasant in this strange land. Captain Shaw says he can never forgive

---

* See *The Vicar of Bulhampton*, p. 344.

himself for not waiting for Captain Murray to write to arrange our transport and for sending us so hurriedly with so little food, but I would not have missed the Lingei River for a good deal. I never find travelling except on a good horse active enjoyment, but this glimpse of a new race, polity and order of things is very interesting and worth having. I wonder if you will like this letter? and if others will find this new world interesting?

ILB

Isabella's next letter covering her stay in Selangor no longer exists, but it is possible for us to read between the lines of *The Golden Chersonese* to guess what it contained. Principally, Isabella seems to have been offended by the aggressive and paranoid behaviour of the British Resident, William Bloomfield Douglas. In *The Golden Chersonese*, she wrote that his house had 'the appearance of an armed outpost', looking 'as if there were a need for holding down the population (which I am sure there isn't)'. One night 'as we sat in the verandah, maddened by mosquito bites, about 9:30 the bugle at the fort sounded the "alarm", which was followed in a few seconds by the drum beating "to quarters", and in less than five minutes every approach to the Residency was held by men with fixed bayonets'. Bird said she 'knew instinctively' the show was 'humbug', and sure enough, 'an orderly arrived with the note – "False alarm".' Then 'there was a fright of a different kind late at night, and the two made me so nervous that when the moonlight glinted two or three times on the bayonet of the sentry . . . I thought it was a Malay going to murder Mr. Douglas.' Certainly, she thought there was cause. Isabella was astounded by the arbitrary nature of the Resident's 'justice'; and on a riverboat she was horrified by his beating of a boatman. 'The Malays are a revengeful people,' she wrote. 'If any official of the British service were to knock them about . . . Well, some day – all I can say is, God help him.'

Open as these comments may seem, it appears that Isabella could have said more. She refrained because she feared libel. As she commented in a letter to John Murray, 'One may criticise as much as one likes when one criticises yellow or brown-skinned men but when people write on British officials and methods in any but the most eulogistic language they raise quite a storm.' Such comments imply that Isabella purposefully destroyed her Selangor letter. As a result, her clearest sentiments survive only through her 'official' correspondence printed below:

12 Walker St. Edinburgh Nov 16. 1882

Dear Mr Murray

I have sent the complete letter, of which you saw the greater part in type to the printer. The next is Sungei Ujong. The one which would naturally follow is on the 'protected' state of Selangor, but here I must ask you to help me by finding out through the Colonial Office *whether Mr Bloomfield Douglas, the Resident, has resigned, and whether his resignation has been accepted?* and next, though of much less importance to me, whether his son in law, Mr Daly,* still holds an official appointment in any part of the Malay Peninsula? Sir Benson Maxwell† wrote to me that he believes these persons have vacated their appointments, but his information is not always trustworthy.

At all events I am obliged to suppress a great part of my letter from Selangor. Mr Douglas is I think the most *fiendish* human being that I have ever seen. After close study I failed to find a redeeming point in his character. The mis-government of the state was gross and brutal – I saw scenes in which the Resident was the chief actor of the most brutal description, and heard more than I saw. It was a rule of fraud, hypocrisy, and violence. As the guest of the S.S.‡ government I 'ate salt' with this man, and would not under any circumstances put into print my opinion of him but *if he has resigned* I should not feel any hesitation in publishing some strictures on his administration, for they are not stronger than those which appeared in a recent Parliamentary paper from the pen of an official of the S.S. Government. If he has resigned (and I cannot see how he could hold office after that report was made) his resignation proves the reasonableness of any deprecatory remarks – if not, probably the whole letter which has certainly a degree of interest had better be suppressed.

Yours very Sincerely
ISABELLA L BISHOP

In response, John Murray assured Isabella that Douglas had been recalled. He did suggest, however, that she use caution. Isabella acquiesced: Douglas might prove 'a very ugly customer' and 'now that he has been compelled to resign I shall no longer feel it my duty to expose him'. Later she informed John Murray that she had 'avoided many personal references' to Douglas when writing about Selangor. 'In fact acting on the vulgar proverb "Never kick a man when he's down" I have let Mr Douglas off very easily.' Her journal letters then resume two weeks later with an account of her adventures in Perak.

British Residency, Larut. Malay Peninsula. At Mr Maxwells§
Assistant Resident Feb 13/79

'Great' Perak Letter
116 pages!!

My Own Pet
I came from Mr Justice Woods¶ at Penang yesterday in a gharry to the pier and their servant got a lumbering boat for me with an attap awning

---

* See Daniel Dominic Daly, p. 321.
† See Sir Peter Benson Maxwell, p. 334.
‡ State of Selangor.
§ See Sir William Edward Maxwell, p. 334.
¶ See Mr Justice Woods, p. 345.

and 5 Kling rowers who row with oars working in coils of rope. These oars have little hold on the water. The Strait was very calm and the fiery light of evening truly tropical. I went to Mrs Isemonger* Mr Maxwell's sister who I met at Mr Woods the day before. Her husband is police magistrate of Province Wellesley a most flourishing strip of land on the mainland ceded to England some years ago for an annual payment of $10000 to the Rajah of Quedoh.† It has rapidly filled up with Malays Chinese and Klings and grows sugarcane, tapioca, padi and coconuts. The shore is beautiful, a sandy beach a row of casuarinas of large size with grey feathery drooping foliage and thin coconut glades. A little jetty on which a Sikh policeman waited for me was a fitting landing and presently Mrs Isemonger came to meet me from her lovely bungalow under the palms on a bright green lawn with clumps of alamanda in full beauty.

Though it was getting dark Mrs I. took me to see the back country in a little trap but most of the drive was accomplished by the light of sheet lightening which was nearly incessant giving everything a weird unusual look. There are miles of coconut plantations with the trees in straight lines forming broad avenues which are very grand. Then cane and padi and then coconut plantations again. In coming back we saw numbers of Malay Campongs under the palms, each with a fire lighted underneath it and more fires in the wood for the water buffaloes with groups of these uncouth brutes gathered invariably on the leeward side so that the smoke may keep away the mosquitos. We dined and had a very pleasant evening. I like Mrs Isemonger very much. She is very gentle mannered, thoughtful, intelligent and studious and instead of being indolent like most women has really studied Malay and is translating a Malay book. She has strong opinions on public topics, specially on the politics of the Straits Settlements of which her father Sir Benson Maxwell was chief justice for some years. Mr Maxwell had promised to bring the 'Kinta' at 8 and it shows how pleasant the evening was that though I was very tired 8, 9, 10 and 11 came without our having exhausted our topics.

At 11.20 the 'Kinta' came up in the moonlight, a black shadow on a silver sea, roaring for a boat, but the surf was so heavy that it was some time before a boat could be got off and then Mr Maxwell whose voice precedes him and Mr Walker‡ landed bullying everybody as people often

---

* See Mrs Isemonger under E. E. Isemonger, p. 328.
† See Tunku Kudin, p. 330.
‡ See Captain R. S. F. Walker, p. 344.

do when they know they are delinquent. It was lovely, the shadows of palms on the dewy grass, the grace of the casuarinas, the shining water, the long drift of surf, the white moonlight. It was hard to get off and the surf broke into the boat but when once through it, the sea was like silver and the oars dripped fire and seen from the water the surf broke on the shore not in snow but in a long line of fire. The 'Kinta' is the steam launch of the Perak Government not near so fine as the 'Abdul Samat' but a quiet peaceful boat. There is a cabin in the bow with 2 couches on one of which the 2 sons of the exiled Sultan Abdullah of Perak[*] who are being brought up at Malacca were sleeping. I did not go below for some time as the heat was great.

Mr Maxwell is the Assistant Resident and magistrate of Perak, a very able man of 34, very bumptious & self reliant, very argumentative but really very pleasant, with a superabundance of energy. Captain Walker who has come here to take command of the Sikh troops for 6 months has been aide de camp to Sir William Robinson[†] and has rather too gushing a manner though he is very pleasant. The other passenger was Mr Innes[‡] (whose wife nearly lost her life lately in that horrible affair at Pangkor) Mrs Hill Burtons brother a man with a feeble despairing manner and vague unfocused eyes. He is superintendent of Lower Perak.

I did not sleep well because of the heat and rats and got up at 6 just as we entered the Larut river, one of the many rivers of this Peninsula which do not widen at their mouths, swiftly flowing, muddy, with a dense jungle and mangrove swamps and shores of shining slime at low water on which the crocodiles bask in the sun. But the tide was high and the river was brimming full, looking as if it must drown all the forest. It was a lonely silent land and densely green, and many an uprooted palm with its golden green plume and wealth of golden husked nuts came floating down on the rapid waters. Once we passed a small clearing where a few Chinese for the sake of gain were living in huts on the festering slime between the river and the jungle and again a police station on stilts, where 6 Malay policemen stood in a row on a stilted platform and saluted as we passed. Many a narrow creek well suited for murder over-arched with trees comes down into the Larut River. One might travel far up these in canoes and still be in the mangrove swamps and among crocodiles.

At 7 we came to a pier and a long shed 2 or 3 huts in a Dismal Swamp and some officialism white and partly so. Along the pier a small Chinese

[*] See Sultan Abdullah of Perak, p. 313.
[†] Sir William Cleaver Francis Robinson, p. 339.
[‡] See James Innes, p. 328.

steamer the 'Sri Sarawak' which trades usefully twice a week between this place Teluk Kartang and Penang was lying and we landed over her filthy deck on which filthy swine were wrangling for offal among half naked men almost as dirty. It was a dismal place on which we entered, a long shed with an office on either side but a great trade is done here in imports and nearly all the tin from the rich mines of Larut is exported from hence. While the others saw about business I waited in an empty office where was one chair a table much splotched with ink a mouldy ink stand a piece of an old almanac and an empty gin bottle. Looking out, cockle shells were piled against the wall, all along them there were ditches or creeks culling through profuse and almost loathsome vegetation and shining slime fat and iridescent swimming with loathsome living creatures under the fierce sun specially with small crabs with shells of a most brilliant but evanescent blue. The strong vegetable stench of this slime was overpowering.

After a time 3 gharries arrived. I have not seen their like before and no amount of practice in getting in and out of other vehicles would help one to the torturous process needed for getting in and out of these. They are two wheeled carts with a seat for 2 people and a board going across the front on which the driver sits when he is not running by his horse to threaten or drag it on, the whole with a projecting cover. The bottom is filled up with leaves grass and my small luggage and you put your feet on the drivers board. The gharries are driven by Klings with little clothing and are drawn by little rats of Sumatran ponies seldom 13 hands high with great energy. Mr Innes and I went in one Mr Maxwell and Mr Walker in another and Sultan Abdullahs boys in the 3rd. We soon met 3 great elephants one of enormous size rolling along, one of them with a man seated behind his great flopping ears. These were sent down for me, but even with my luggage I could not have used more than one.

We passed through a forlorn but beautiful looking Chinese village called Parmatang, masculine almost solely, where they were even building gharries, and selling all such Chinese things as Chinese coolies buy. Just the same there as everywhere. Yellow, lean, keen, industrious, saving, gambling, opium smoking, keeping the clan tie close, mysterious, forming no ties, keeping the main chance steadily in view, sober, mercenary, reliable, self-reliant, managing all their own matters even to a post office and money order office through which they constantly send home large sums to the interior of China, destined probably to dispute or share with us the empire of the East. They are supplanting our merchants quickly in Singapore and Penang, partly because they are astute enough to be honest. They are buying up the real property in Penang as fast as it falls into the market and they have already superseded every foreign merchant in Malacca. Except for the fortnightly P.&O. boat the whole mail goods and passenger traffic of the straits is in their hands and now I find them the miners mineowners traders and merchants of Perak numbering about 26000. It was their awful tribal fights in Larut continuing over 2 years and in which *several thousands* of lives were sacrificed which led to the British interference here as the country was being desolated and the rulers were powerless. When Mr George Campbell[*] to whose house I am going in Ceylon was Governor of Penang the steamers used to take from here to Penang 800 wounded men at a time and the Chinese merchants in Penang supplied the hostile tribes in Larut with ammunition and food the nominal object of strife being the possession of some of the largest tin mines.

How very little we know of the great problems of the east and how loud and boastful our ignorance is! I am daily more and more humiliated by our culpable ignorance, and by our ignorant assumptions of knowledge. We literally dont know enough to be able to ask intelligent questions of those who know a little more than ourselves and it is but *little* that any European can know of Oriental thought and feeling. We *cannot* know each other. I firmly believe that Disraeli is the only public man in England who from the accident of race knows anything of Oriental feeling at all. A great many things have come to my knowledge lately which show me how we cannot understand each other. Our Xtianity (even as we would wish it represented) our manners and our dress are simply loathsome to these Orientals as loathsome as the most degrading circumstances. This is a digression forced on me by the thought of our bumptious *ignorance* and *arrogant* pretensions to knowledge and government. I found that the people who have lived longest in the East and have the best right to speak are those who feel the most strongly the impossibility of knowing. For myself even when the barrier of language is broken down I look into the dark Oriental eye with no more understanding of its meaning than if it were the eye of a dog, and they look at us, as a very able Chinese barrister[†] told me, and see nothing in us but the incarnation of brute force allied to brute vice!

It was bright and hot, the glorious equable equatorial heat which I can bear quite well and when we got out of the mangrove swamp through which the road is causewayed, the usual foliage of the tropics was very fine and the trees were festooned with a large blue Thunbergia of great beauty. It is 7 miles from the landing at Teluk Kartang to Thaipeng where the

[*] See George W. Campbell, p. 319.
[†] Presumably Ng Choy, p. 320.

Residency is over completely level country but always drawing nearer to a beautiful wooded range the Hijan Mountains, which rise from the plain very picturesquely to a height of over 3000 feet with a most extraordinary *butte** called Gunong Pondok, a magnificent landmark for the whole region, and another mountain range of great beauty the highest peak of which Gunong Bubu is probably little under 6000 feet on the right. Shall I go through the pass of Buket Jugra I wonder and see the mysterious interior which lies beyond the dark blue-green ranges? We soon reached Permatang, another Chinese village of greater pretensions and population where are two very large 2 storied Malay houses in some disrepair where the wife or widow of the former Mentri of Larut† lives with a number of slaves. A quantity of mirthful looking slave girls were standing behind the window bars surreptitiously looking at us. In Perak 3/4 of the Malay people are slaves to the other 1/4 but it is their 'custom' and they dont wish it interfered with. I found Mr Innes a very dreary and unintelligible companion.

We got down at the House of Mr Wynne, government agent there, and something was said about breakfast which I was longing for but after I had had a bath and changed my dress, I found that we were to drive on another hour. Mr Maxwells abstemiousness and power of going without food are very uncomfortable for me. We drove on towards the mountains over whose cool summits cloud mists now and then drifted along an excellent road which at length entered a Chinese village more than a mile in length [. . .] and on the top of a steep isolated terraced little hill [was] the British Residency. Thaipeng is a thriving increasing place of 5000 people almost solely Chinese, although there is a Kling or Tamil population which keeps small shops, lends money, drives gharries and bullock carts, and washes clothes. This was the focus of the murderous warfare and the Chinese still require to be held with firm hands, as for instance they are not allowed to go out at night without passes and lanterns, or to belong to secret societies. They are tin miners except those who keep the shops which supply the miners and some of them are very rich. I think that the Mentri of Larut was deposed and exiled really for no other reason than that he failed to keep the Chinese in order. There are very few Malays here.

The Residency Hill is really too steep for the ascent of a vehicle but the plucky little pony and the Kling together pulled the gharry up the zigzags in a series of spasms, and I was glad to get out of the fierce sunshine into an airy house where there was some hope of breakfast.

---

* A term Isabella picked up in America, meaning an isolated hill with cliffs, often flat-topped.
† See Mantri of Larut, under James Woodford Wheeler Birch, p. 315.

The hill is planted with some miserable coffee with scanty yellow foliage. It has a magnificent view in one direction to the beautiful Hijan hills down which a waterfall dashes in a broad sheet of foam only half a mile off and which breeds a rampagious fresh breeze during a great part of the day, and on the other down on Thaipeng and other Chinese villages, on Chinese vegetable gardens exquisitely neat and most luxuriant, on pits formerly tin mines now full of muddy water and narrow muddy rivulets bearing the wash of the tin mines to the river Larut and all the weirdness and forlorness of an exhausted mining region and beyond this upon an extent of jungle the limit of which was beyond the limit of vision miles of treetops level as the ocean a deep monotonous green over which the cloud shadows sailed grandly.

The Residency is large and long only the upper story being uninhabited. A very deep verandah runs all round it approached by stairs at either end. Underneath are both rooms and quarters for the Sikh guards, several sentries carrying rifles with fixed bayonets and dressed in huge blue turbans scarlet tunics and white trousers patrol day and night. There are 450 of these men called Military Police but really soldiers and quite useless for police duty. Their joy would be in shooting and looting but they have no scent for crime. They are splendid looking men nearly all Sikhs and Afghans, with great moustaches and whiskers but they plait the long ends of their whiskers at the sides, and tuck the plaits under their turbans. When off duty they put on white turbans and robes which look as white as snow, and with their great height and superb features they look like Eastern princes. They have very good natured faces generally and are docile and peaceable though they have wars of words on theological matters, but they are very fond of money and being betrothed to little girls at home save nearly all their pay to buy land in India and settle down. The Chinese are very much afraid of them. One sees one Sikh driving 4 or 5 Chinese in front of him having knotted their pigtails together and holding the knot in his hand. They are commanded by Captain Swinburne* of the 80th foot of whom I have heard in Japan, China, Singapore and all along here as a most brilliant, fascinating and altogether misplaced person.

It is an odd house, consisting of a passage 30 feet wide and about as high in the highest part with a bow windowed front upon the immense verandah like the second saloon in the Iona. A red screen stands partly across this about the middle and the back part is used for dining and the front of sitting. My bedroom, bathroom and sitting room are on one side

---

* See Captain Paul Swinburne, p. 343.

and the room in which the Sultan Abdullahs boys sleep and on the other Mr Maxwells rooms and office as Mrs M. and the children are at home there is a bareness and poverty of ornament quite remarkable. There is a Chinese housemaid and a Malay butler, no pets of any kind, no super-fluities and a most abstemious table of 2 meals a day. Tea and bananas are brought at 7 and breakfast is nominally at 10 but in the 3 days that I have been here it has been at 11, 12, and 2. Dinner is at 7.30 but there is tea at 5. Mr. M. is very strong, and cares for little besides tea. Breakfast did not appear till 11.30! I had a nice quiet afternoon of writing to you and studying bluebooks.*

These boys of Sultan Abdullahs are the most amusing children I ever saw. They are 9 & 12 with irrepressible faces. They *never* cease speaking and are very playful and witty, but although a large sum is paid for their education at the house of an English schoolmaster in Malacca they speak atrocious pidgin English and never will speak Malay. They are never still for an instant, chattering, reading snatches from books, asking questions, turning somersaults, jumping on Mr Maxwells shoulders begging for dollars. They kept the house alive but today they have gone to Qualla Kangsa on my elephants on a visit to their relation the reigning (?) Rajah. I wonder what will become of them! Their father is in exile on the Seychelles, and though it was once thought that one of them might succeed the present Rajah, another Rajah is so popular with the Malays that it would be a pity to interfere with them.

In the evening Mr M. & I took a walk of over a mile down to the Treasury to thank Mr Marples the treasurer for having offered to be my host in case I arrived before Mr Maxwells return. I was glad I had not for Mr Marples was vulgar pretentious fat and greasy looking. Thaipeng was crowded and in the full swing of its evening money making. The night was very cool. My room looks towards the mountains and gets the breeze. In making my bed the Chinaman found a snake 4 feet long coiled under my folded duvet. There are 'trumpeter' beetles with bright green bodies and membranous transparent wings 4 inches across which made a noise loud enough for a body the size of a horse. Two were in the house and you could not hear any of us speak.

The next morning I got up at 6 and at 7 went with Mr Maxwell to see the hospital. It is mainly used for the Sikhs but there was one Chinaman there horribly mangled. He was stealing a boat on one of the creeks when an alligator got him and tore both legs, one arm and his back in such a way that it is wonderful that he lives. The doctor is a

* Government reports.

young Madrassee. The Sikhs are very troublesome owing to their different castes, and the impossibility of cooking for them consequently. I never saw such grand looking men. Breakfast was not till 12. After that Captain Swinburne and Mr Walker came and in the evening Captain S. walked with us to a clear mountain torrent which comes down among great boulders at the base of the mountains roaring through the glorious tropical vegetation as clear and cold as if it were a Highland stream dashing through the purple heather.

Mr Maxwell is very pleasant, physically and mentally strong with a cheery voice which precedes him, educated at Oxford and Lincoln's Inn, but brought up in the Straits Settlements of which his father Sir Benson Maxwell was Chief Justice. He is clever combative dogmatic, well read in several directions, self assertive self reliant arbitrary but I should think just, well read in poetry but neither poetic nor imaginative, one of those minds – light without colour – without tenderness or gentleness or self-indulgence, with a strong will but truly a gentleman and very easy to live with. He is Superintendent of Larut and Assistant Resident, Dictator in fact of Larut only subject to Mr Lows[*] interference. He is judge and can inflict the penalty of death only the reigning Rajahs signature being required to the death warrant. He rules the Chinese rigidly and hates them and I hear the hatred is returned. With his energy and strong will he succeeds in ruling everyone except Captain Swinburne who tenaciously asserts his responsibility to Mr Low only. He likes the Malays very much and I believe speaks their language as idiomatically as a native. He studies their literature superstitions and customs and has some very careful & valuable notes. He is very pleasant, likes talking and amuses me very much by his vehemence and quiet self-assertion. He is a very hard-working man. He has no softness, and I doubt whether he has any friends and he ignores the humanity virtues and feelings of people not born in his own social position. I imagine that he is hated by his European subordinates on this latter ground.

Captain Swinburne and Captain Walker dined here and we had a bit of plain roast mutton the first I have tasted for about 10 months. It was very nice. One becomes so tired of made dishes mainly fowls done up in about 20 different ways. Captain S. is a person who could not anywhere be overlooked a most aristocratic looking man of 40 tall and slender, very intellectual looking with a dash of acquired eccentricity of manner and tone a most incongruous element of the Perak crowd, a man who does not look severable from the doorsteps of a Pall Mall club.

---

[*] See Sir Hugh Low, p. 332.

His first address to me (stalking down the room) was 'The sooner you go away again the better – theres nothing to do nothing to see and nothing to learn'! He is 2nd son of Sir John Swinburne and a nephew of the Duke of Buckingham but was 39 before he got his captaincy! He is a very proud man but unlike Mr Maxwell, thoroughly appreciates the co-humanity of his inferiors. His temper is violent but he is just and is greatly beloved by the Sikhs and by the European inspectors who have only been induced not to resign in a body by his promising to come back at the end of his leave. The Rajah Muda* wanted him to use the Sikhs to catch a female runaway slave and on his refusal called him 'Dog of an infidel', and he drew himself up, saying 'You are a man of high birth in your country but I'm a man of high birth in mine, and so long as I bear Queen Victorias commission I refuse to accept insult – I take no future orders from your Highness' – nor has he. For a thorough man of the world I never heard such a brilliant talker, dashing over art, literature, politics, society, telling brilliant stories, never flagging, never caring the least what he says, and not 'regarding the equities of conversation'. I cant describe him better than by saying what Captain Shaw said 'When you see Paul Swinburne you'll see a man you'll not see twice in a life-time.' He gives a sad account of his part-cousin,† gifted, rich with all that life can offer within his grasp, but living for spirit drinking and opium, in which doubtless some of his poems have found their inspiration.

At this dinner of 4 there was noise enough for 20. Someone brought up the deadlock in Victoria which excited violent feeling for some reason not obvious. Captain Walker lost the gushing aide de camp manner which I had rather thought a veneer and his expression was literally black – Mr Maxwell fought for victory, and Captain Swinburne only to floor Mr Maxwell and having a little more knowledge he did it, but the row was deafening for both spoke at once and each attempted to outshout the other. I think that Captain S. and Mr Maxwell have a row every day but they like each other. Captain S. is aggravating. He begins upon some foible of Mr Maxwells, perhaps on his domineering manner with sarcasm mimicry and ridicule and having tormented him mercilessly without giving him time to reply he disappears saying 'Now my dear fellow its no use resenting it – you havent a friend in the world but me. You know if it were not for me, you'd be absolutely intolerable.' Mr Maxwell says that he (Captain S) is a genuine woman hater, but I have since found that this is not the case. How many strong characters are required to make up even the world that I know!

---

* See Raja Muda Yusef, p. 345.
† See Algernon Charles Swinburne, p. 342.

It is strange to be in a house in which there are no pets. Sometimes in the evening a wild animal called I think a lemur rushes through the house and out at the front verandah. I always fear to be startled by his tearing through my room in the depths of the night for here and elsewhere there are no bedroom doors, only screens beginning 18 inches from the ground.

Yesterday I got up and went out and up a hill which some Chinese have been clearing before sunrise. The tropic early morning is the loveliest time of the day. It is all rose colour and dew, and there is a delicious freshness about it. This was a lovely morning, the sun was so slow in coming above the eastern hill tops, and his rise was such a sudden glory, the teeming bird animal and insect world breaking in one moment in vociferous life, the tuneless morning hymns ascending without a discord. The sunsets are sometimes gaudily coloured but they are so brief that one has no time to enjoy them. They only make one long for the lingering gold and violet of more northern latitudes.

I have been very industrious here in writing to you and in reading up the very intricate and complicated affairs of these Malay States. I dont think we have done well. Lord Carnarvons[*] dispatches are wonders of grasp of affairs, cool judgement, honour, consideration and fair dealing, but the righteous ideas of the colonial office have been continually frustrated by the Governors of the Straits Settlements acting hastily under the influence of rumours born of ill informed panic and going too far to recede. As an instance of panic here is a telegram from Sir W. Jervoise[†] 'Send ships and reinforcements – the whole Malay Peninsula is rising.' Now the fact appears to have been that there were not 200 men in arms at any one time anywhere, and these were widely scattered and only armed with old fashioned muskets and against these we brought a European regiment several hundred gurkas mountain guns and two gunboats! As things now are I wish that we had pensioned off the Rajas and honestly annexed the 3 states. The Malays are really a very quiet people though they have got such a bad character. Most of the stories of piracy resolve themselves into the exaction of tribute by the river rajahs. Of course there are many bad characters who made their living by the disturbed state of things under feeble governments.

Today we have been in a gharry to Kamunting a Chinese mining town of 4000 people three miles from here in a very pretty ravine full of pitcher plants with purple cups and lids. I have no opportunity of

---

[*] See Carnarvon, 4th Earl, p. 319.
[†] See Sir William Francis Drummond Jervois, p. 329.

observing them but I am beginning to wonder whether they are partially carnivorous, for in the bottom of each cup there is a viscid secretion to which a whole mass of flies adheres. We went first to one of the largest tin mines belonging to a rich and very pleasant looking Chinaman who received and took us over it. It is like a large quarry with a number of small excavations in it which fill with water and are pumped by Chinese pumps worked by an endless chain but there are 2 powerful steam pumps here also. About 400 men were at work, lean yellow, leathery looking, swarming up out of the holes like ants in double columns, each one carrying a small bamboo tray holding about 3 lbs of stanniferous earth, which is deposited in a sluice and a great rush of water washes away the sand and leaves the stream tin as coarse as grains of giant blasting powder behind. The Chinese are wedded to these small baskets which involve a great waste of labour. They are paid by piece work and probably earn 1/6 a day. The road and other labours are worked by Klings who get 1/0 a day. The tin is smelted during the night in a very rude furnace with a most ingenious bellows and is then run into mounds of sand and re-appears as slabs weighing 54 lbs each. Its price has fallen from $109 to $56 in consequence of tin discoveries in Australia. This quantity pays $10.50 of export duty which is the chief source of revenue to the States of the Peninsula. Close to the smelting furnace there are long sheds with platforms along each side divided into as many beds as there are men each bed being merely a mat and a mosquito net. There are all the usual joss arrangements and time is measured by the burning of joss sticks. I saw several rain cloaks like those the Japanese wear only made of palm leaves. These and all other articles consumed by this large population are imported from China. They are far too thrifty to buy our worthless cottons and picks of inferior iron.

Then the Chinaman took us to some rooms he had built for a cool retreat to which in anticipation of our visit he had brought champagne, sherry and bitter beer! We failed to convince him that we preferred tea but he gave it to us with sweetmeats and coconut biscuits. He then insisted on taking our hired gharry with its scrubby pony and giving us his gharry with a fine Australian horse but Mr Maxwell says it is rather policy than courtesy as it gives him importance to be on friendly terms with the Resident. We drove on to Kamunting a Chinese town of about 3000 people with ditches and roads needing improvement and there visited a gambling saloon and I bought some Chinese purses. To see the peculiar expression of the Chinese face fully developed one needs to go to a gambling saloon. There is nothing specially shocking about it, being nothing more than an intensified love of gain seen without disguise.

Each coolie takes his pipe of opium when the days work is done and he always has what apparently no Chinaman can live without a teapot of tea kept always hot in a covered basket lined and very thickly wadded.

On our way back we called at a Sikh guard house and saw the 'child of the regiment' and then the magnificent Afghan sergeant took me to see his wife the woman of the regiment who is so rigidly secluded that even the Resident and the commanding officer have never seen her. She was a beautiful woman with an exquisite figure but loaded with jewellery. She wore a large nose jewel 7 rings of large size in each ear 4 necklaces and silver bangles on each arm from the wrist to the elbow besides some on her beautiful ankles. She had a baby boy in her arms clothed only in a silver circle and the father took him and showed him to me with great pride.

Qualla Kangsa — State of Perak. Ruler Rajah Muda Yusuf. Resident Hugh Low (absent.) Friday Feb. 14th. If I could accurately describe the circumstances of this journey and place you would perhaps think that 'of all my wild adventures past' this is the most singular. I can truly add 'This frantic feat will prove the last,' for in one week I hope to be in Penang and then to return home by conventional Ceylon. No more 'great' letters for you or revelations of new countries and their ways!

At 4.30 this morning Mr Maxwells energetic voice called me, and I got up feeling very tired, the unwanted dissipation of Captain Swinburne and Captain Walker having dined the night before and the racoon and the trumpeting beetle and the noise the guard made awaking me at 2 with a nightmare idea that the Sikhs had mutinied and that I should be murdered having caused me to have a very restless night. We had some bananas and chocolate and as day broke walked down the hill where I got into a little trap, drawn by a little Sumatra pony and was driven for 5 miles by Mr Gibbons, a worthy Australian miner who is road making in Larut, Mr Maxwell coming along on horseback. The 3 elephants which had been sent down to Matang from here to meet me the day I arrived not being wanted came up with Sultan Abdullahs boys and other elephants being telegraphed for it was found that the telegraph was broken. Mr M. had sent a messenger here for more elephants and was dismayed on getting to the place where the road became a quagmire which could not be crossed in the trap to meet the news that the elephants had gone away, so there was nothing but one elephant, which was carrying my baggage and was more than 2 hours behind. There was nothing else to be done but walk.

So Mr M. and I walked 4 miles, which I could not have done the half of had I not had my Bloomer dress on. The sunrise had been a splendid one, of crimson clouds which having turned grey screened the sun somewhat, and though so near the equator it was not too hot for walking. [. . .] The things along the track interested me very much from their beauty and variety. Today in the 25 miles I have counted 176 varieties of trees and shrubs, 53 trailers, 17 parasites, and 28 ferns close by the track. So high aloft as is the back of an elephant I saw more of the shrubs and parasitic ferns than I have yet done. There was an asplenium nidus (the birds nest fern) which had 47 perfect fronds radiating from a centre verging from the deepest green to the freshest pea green each frond being from 3 1/2 feet to 5 1/2! There was one orchid with hardly visible leaves which bore 6 crowded clusters of flowers close to the stem of the tree on which it grew each cluster being composed of a number of spikes of red coral tipped with pale green. Then were some very gorgeous erythrinas magnificent begonias and lilies many flowering shrubs a large trailer with blossoms of canary yellow, something like a convolvulus, and a universal trailer which blooms profusely, covering the ground and climbing over everything that is not high, a simple attractive flower a sort of orange salmon colour with a black centre. The ground is covered with the sensitive plant whose mimosa leaves are green above and brown underneath. It is one of the most prevalent beauties. Wonderful as is the *Drosera Rotemdifolia* I think that the sensitive plant is more so. Touch the leaves which are tripartite ever so lightly and as quick as lightening they fold up. Touch the centre 2 ever so lightly and stalk and leaves fall smitten. Touch the branch and every leaf closes and every stalk falls with a great energy and as rapidly as the twinkling of an eye. Walk over it and you seem to have blasted the earth with a fiery tread, for every trailing plant falls and the leaves closing show their brown backs, and in a second are burned and withered. One could experiment on it all day.

After walking nearly 4 miles about the most glorious sight I have ever seen since leaving home appeared. A turn brought us upon a small lake behind which the mountains rose with a wall enclosing the house and coconut groves of the dispossessed Mentri of Larut on the slope beyond the lake. That was an unimaginable sight. Though a lake no water was visible. From the water rose thousands and thousands of the leaves of the lotus peltate with wavy edges 18 inches in diameter quite round, cool looking under the torrid sun, intense green but with a blue bloom like that on a plum. Above them rose thousands of lotus flowers buds and seed vessels each one a thing of perfect beauty. The immense flowers varied from a deep rose crimson to a pink pale like that of a blush rose, some were just opening, others open, others wide open showing the crowded golden stamens and the golden disk in the centre. It was a most beautiful sight but there is no 'yellow lotus dust' in any stage of development[. It is an] emblem of purity, righteousness, immortality, and power, [and] even here where no proper sacredness attaches to it there is a kind of reverence for it as for a sacred thing. It looks a holy thing. I cannot imagine the glorious lotus bloom, less the glorious lotus leaf stared at, at Kew – still less an ornament in inane drawingrooms. I could have stayed there the whole day. From far off one sees the deep rose pink of those glorious blossoms, which carried me back to the great moats of the Castle of Yedo and to many an imposing altar in far off Japan from which already almost all disagreeable memories have faded.

Beyond this lake there is on the hill slope a most picturesque Malay campong, with very good houses and a mosque and passing through a gateway whose brick gate posts were still standing we entered the coco grove within the extensive wall which enclosed the house and appendages of the late Mentri of Larut who we have deported to the Seychelles for a supposed but never proved complicity in the murder of Mr Birch. The house is a very large one, of wood painted green and white with bold floral designs on a white ground round some of the circular windows and a very large porch (up a ladder of course) for followers to wait in. In a large shed there were 3 gharries, and behind the house a number of small houses for slaves and others. The family came up here yesterday on the elephants which Mr M. tried to borrow for me, but a number of girls and children mostly slaves probably were peeping through the window bars. Whatever I may think of the advantages of English rule, where it is established I often abhor our manner of acquisition, though in this case of Perak I believe that both the home authorities and Sir W. Jervoise acted for the best by the light they had which I fear was thick darkness. It would I think have been better to annex it and take the responsibility of a *nominal* as well as the many disadvantages of a real rule.

There was an empty house where I waited and Malays brought pierced coconuts, boiled buffalo milk and a great bouquet of lotuses with their seed vessels, out of which they took the seeds. Each seed in appearance and taste is like a hazelnut but in the very middle in an oval slit the future lotus plant is folded up a beautiful monocotyledon of intense green the one seed leaf being folded over a sheath. This is intensely bitter. I had not waited an hour before the elephant came up and was brought to the porch. Oh how hideous they are with their grey wrinkled hairless skins the huge ragged flappers which cover their ears, and with which they fan themselves ceaselessly, their small mean eyes, that hideous proboscis which coils itself round everything looking like a snake, the formless legs so like trunks of trees, the back with the steep slope down to the mean bare tail.

(A wah wah the most delightful of apes is hanging with its long lean arms round my neck and keeps taking my pen and dipping it in the ink. There are two of them and one is tempted to waste all ones time with them. This is such a little creature and is so grateful because I rescued it from a big ape which was beating it cruelly with a cane this morning. There is nothing that I should like so well to have as two of these half human creatures. The big one is exactly like Dr Candlish. I must give up writing for it has fallen asleep on my book and an elephant of enormous size, one of the 50 which were part of the regalia of the late sultan, is waiting to take me on a long jungle expedition.)

One has no idea what an elephant may do. Except themselves there is nothing grand about them. They have neither howdahs nor trappings. This elephant had several mats over its back covered with a piece of raw hide and on either side of its ridgy back bore a flat basket without a bottom filled with fresh twigs and leaves on which you sit with your feet hanging over the edge. These are held in their place by ropes of rattan and my Gladstone bag was tied on behind with the same. A noose of the same with a stirrup is for the driver to mount. He drives with a stick with a curved spike which if the elephant is bad is hooked into the great membranous flapper. There is a special elephant vocabulary which all the drivers speak. I scrambled into one of these baskets from the top of the porch and a young Malay lad into the other and the driver sat on the head with his legs behind the ears. Mr Maxwell assured me that he would not send me alone into a region without a European unless it was quite safe which I fully believed and so I started into the wilds.

Such riding is not comfortable. You get cramped and when you lean back on anything the rolling awkward motion is anything but pleasant, and you get cut under your knees by your feet hanging over the edge of the basket – Then the elephant had not been loaded 'with brains', and his pack was as troublesome as the straw shoes of the Japanese horses. It was always slipping forward and my enormous weight brought it down on my side so that I was always trying to wriggle myself up on the great ridge which was the elephants back bone and always failing and the man was always stopping and pulling the rattan ropes which bound the whole arrangement on and always failing to improve it. Before we had travelled two hours the great bulk of the elephant suddenly but gently subsided behind and then in front laying his huge forelegs out before him, and the men signed to me to get off which I did by getting upon his head and then letting myself down by a rattan rope round his neck, for even when 'kneeling' as they call it you need a good ladder for getting off and on. As I stood there it was noon and a nearly vertical sun streaming down from the deep blue sky.

It was strange this forest monster lying on the ground, and I the first European traveller in this region regarding the violence of which so much fuss has been made and 7 bluebooks have been written, quite unarmed, far in the interior with 2 Malays who could not speak a word of English. Strange too to be riding a beast one has only wondered at in a menagerie. I always thought that there was something splendid about elephant riding, a great howdah and trappings of cloth of gold but here though a man's dignity is estimated by the number of his elephants the equipments are mean and almost savage. When the thing had been put right the mahout climbed on the back and giving me 2 hands I scrambled up after which the creature raised itself quite gently from the ground. But the ride was 'a fearful jog' *if* a jog. The mahout went on leaving the animal to go a mile or more alone and he went into the jungle and began to rend and tear the trees, and then he went to a mud hole and drawing all the water out of it squirted it with a loud noise over himself and his riders covering my boots and skirt with mud and then when he came back to the track he several times stopped and seemed to stand on his head by stiffening his proboscis and leaning upon it and when I hit him with my umbrella he roared like a lion but with a louder roar than anything one could imagine. The boy was frightened and ran off to get the mahout and I was left alone with the elephant. I thought of you on a horse when one lets go the bridle and of you wondering what it will do. I wondered and always expected that it would lift me off with its trunk! There seemed to be many possible contingencies.

After the mahout was brought back I got off and the elephant was allowed to go and bathe himself in a river. He took plenty of water and threw it all over himself, and then he took a great deal more away with which to throw over himself as he went along the road. Thick though his hide looks a very small insect can draw blood and like the water buffalo he plasters himself with mud to protect his skin. Getting on again I rode for another hour or two but he crawled so and seemed about to lie down and the position on him was so fatiguing that I got off and walked [the] other two miles. He roared when ever he was asked to go faster sometimes with a roar of rage sometimes with one of angry remonstrance and sometimes with one of plaintive remonstrance. The mahout hardly ever rode on his head but walked behind him at last his pace became less than a mile an hour and though the driver tried to pull him along by a stick in his ear he would not go, and then the man got on his head just after which he made a great stumble and the man got off. Then I made signs that I would get off but the elephant refused to lie down and I had to let myself down his huge side till I could get my foot on the drivers shoulder. I did not get on again, but the man turned the animal into the jungle and brought my luggage on himself. Such was my first elephant ride! The boy who came with me told the people here that it was a wicked elephant, but on enquiring I found that the poor elephant was sick and tired to death.

(*Feb 16th* One might just as well live in a menagerie. I wondered on arriving to find 3 plates set for dinner knowing that there was no one here, and as soon as I sat down the magnificent turbaned Sikh butler brought in one large ape and the Malay servant brought in another and a *spahis* brought in a great retriever and tied it to my chair and the apes had their chutney and pineapple and eggs and bananas handed to them on Mintons china and the small ape sat on the table and constantly helped himself from my plate. Last night the tigers came very near the house roaring discontentedly. At 4 I woke hearing a loud noise below my window and looking out saw a wonderful scene. This house is on top of a hill covered with coconuts, and their glorious plumes were motionless against a sky blazing with stars. Four enormous elephants, one called the Royal Elephant 18 feet high were standing in a group at the door looking majestic, mahouts were flitting about with torches, – and Sikhs of great stature exaggerated by the fitful light, some in their beautiful white robes and others in their scarlet uniforms and dark turbans were grouped as onlookers. When I took down my dress to put on two lizards fell out of it – Now I have taken my fifth meal with no other companions than the apes who make me laugh with genuine laughter and the little wah wah the winsome little black ape lies on my knee all the time I write sometimes putting its long arms round my neck, and its ancient face against mine softly murmuring 'ouf ouf'. It is so good to get away from the 'wearing world' and live for a little under the coco palms in the unsophisticated society of apes and elephants. How Eka who will not stir without 'a white man' would hate my life here where there is not one for 25 miles! These apes would quite prevent one from being dull. They are always doing something new. One has just now taken a letter from an elastic and having opened it is pretending to read it. Another has jumped like a demon on the retrievers back and sitting astride is beating him with a ruler, a third having taken the cushions out of three chairs has laid them in a row and taking off the table cover has rolled it up for a pillow and is now lying down in an easy careless attitude, every now and then helping himself to a piece of pineapple. When they are angry they make a fearful noise, and if you hinder them from putting their hands in your plate they shriek with rage like children. They are frightfully jealous of the wah-wah and beat it and tease it whenever it is not with me. They take its food and when it screams with rage they laugh and show their white teeth. I never saw such ingenious teasing. Today at breakfast one was upsetting all the chairs in the room and I scolded it when it at once threw a banana at me. This wah wah has twice taken my pen out of my hand – it made that scrawl in the word pen. They cannot live out of the tropics or I would have a wah wah. I hear 'the roll of the British drum' and a bugle blast and a Sikh guard of honour in scarlet uniforms and blue turbans is winding round the base of the hill so I suppose the Resident is in sight, and that my companionship with apes alone is at an end. Mr Low arrived in the verandah just as I wrote that sentence, and I never saw such an amusing sight all the apes and the wah wah uttering piercing cries jumped at him till you could hardly see any of him for they were all hanging round him with their long arms welcoming him more warmly than most people would welcome their nearest relations after a long absence and the retriever went wild with joy. I don't wonder that people like the society of such simple loving creatures.)

I met many Malays on the road and 9 elephants in groups of 3 looking grand also several spahis looking superb. But it is a lonely region of forest and jungle, tiger elephant and rhinoceros haunted with only here and there some Malay cultivation of a rude kind banana tapioca and sugar not superior to Aino cultivation. It is very fine scenery very mountainous with one very fine pass beyond which rises a singular object an isolated limestone *butte* weather and ore stained with very brilliant colours full of inaccessible caves very high up with their entrances hung with stalactites the walls of perpendicular rock and the irregular summit forest covered. It is shaped like the Bass Rock but is probably 900 feet high and I did not see any place where its sides were not perpendicular. Ranges of high mountains rise all round and at the end of 10 hours travelling when the sun was low I looked down upon a broad and beautiful river with mountains on its other side a village on a promontory on its shores and above that a grassy hill covered with coco nuts with a small bungalow at its top which I knew must be the Residency from seeing the uniforms of the Spahi guard in front. There was a small bridge then a guardroom and some official houses on stilts and then I went up to the bungalow. [. . .]

A magnificent Oriental Butler received me and after I had had a delicious bath, dinner or what Assam called breakfast was served. I truly say served for nothing could be more elegant than the table equipments, linen China crystal flowers cooking. The Madrassee and a Malay waited and a Chinaman sat on the steps and pulled the punkah, while the apes sat on chairs and on the table. You can imagine how I liked it being free alike from the chatter and the strife of tongues. It all looked so harmonious, the glorious coco palms, the bright green grass, the sunset gold on the lake like river, the ranges of forest covered mountains ethereal in the purple light, the swarthy faces and scarlet uniforms of the *spahi* guard, the apes, the Argus pheasants – and odours rich and luscious floated in on airs like balm. Glories of the blazing tropics, untellable and incommunicable! I like Qualla Kangsa better than any place I have been at, and I like it specially because I know that the Resident rules Perak in the best interests of the people of Perak and with extreme kindness judiciously tempered with firmness.

I wrote to you till dinner at 7.30 when I wondered how I should arrange to go anywhere yesterday if no one spoke English but after dinner Mr Lows clerk a Singhalese came and arranged. He asked if I should be afraid of sleeping in the house alone but I was not especially when I saw that the Sikh guard was doubled at night and patrolled both the back and the front of the house. There are no doors or windows to shut, but I felt no fear for this splendid body of men enlisted in India for this special service is utterly reliable and trustworthy. Many of them wear medals for Indian Service but have re-enlisted because they are attached to the 'Imperial' service. One and all of them and all the swarthy motley crew which has inundated the Straits Settlements speak of 'the Empress'. 'Good Empress, good service' they say. [. . .]

I slept all night and awoke to another glorious day. I breakfasted with the apes, wrote to you and before 11 Mr Keyt the clerk came bringing an immense elephant as nice an animal as one would wish to have and Assam put pillows into the baskets and a good lunch. The elephant was such a monster that though he lay down I had to get upon his back by a good sized ladder. He was a well trained elephant, and did everything he was told, lying down and getting up, turning in no space, going 1/2 a mile in a river 9 feet deep, pulling down a tree when he was told to do it and holding up till we had safely passed under it a young tree which otherwise would have taken off our heads. I was sitting on the ground where there was hardly room enough for him to pass and yet he was so noble and gentle that I never thought of getting up though his great feet just touched me. He climbed up and down strangely steep places, and either lifted trees out of his way or took huge steps over them. He was told to pull down a banana for his dinner and he broke off the tough thick stem as if it had been a stick. Then he stripped the 8 foot leaves off and then holding the thick end of each leaf stalk under his huge foot he stripped the whole leaves on either side of the tendril with his trunk. Then with the dexterity of a monkey stripping a banana he stripped off the thick rind from the stem and revelled in the juices of the soft inside.

We rode for 7 hours in the forests up the left bank of the Perak River. Oh so beautiful! If I had had a horse and had been alone I should have liked it almost as well as Hawaii though the sun blazed like a furnace and the mercury could not have been less than 90°. I had several layers of thick cotton wadding wrung out in water under my hat. It was new to me, for there is a Malay population all along the river exclusively Malay – campongs in the coconut groves with durian nutmeg mango and other fruit trees shading the houses, and patches of padi, maize, cane in beautiful places. They lead the lotus life. Each house seemed to have all its inmates at home doing nothing chewing betel dreaming of nothing. The men only wear the sarong and a fez or handkerchief and the women only a sarong and another sarong unjoined round the upper part of their persons. The small children wear no clothes but silver ornaments. It was all so very beautiful savage life in all its simplicity. Yet in Perak 3/4 of the people are slaves to the remaining quarter! This is the native tropic life which I have never seen before i.e. life totally uninfluenced by European contact. Strange that these people should owe their religion, laws, customs to the Arabian prophet.

We went on for some hours and miles through all this beauty till we came on a campong under palms and nutmeg trees on a point above the beautiful river, and there the elephant knelt down and we got off and eat our lunch within the sweep of his trunk but he stood quite still except that he flapped his ears and occasionally squirted water over himself. A row of Malay men women and children sat on the grass and talked and laughed with Mr Keyt in Malay. One got me two nutmegs from a tree, they look a little like limes just turning yellow, but when one was split open in a bed of pure white the light brown nutmeg lay with the mace surrounding it lying on it in crimson streaks just like the veins upon a heart, such a beautiful thing, and it grows on such a beautiful tree with shining leaves. Here Mr Keyt said that they told him it was possible to ford the Perak and go back on the other side but then the mahout said that the elephant was a diver and that he would very likely dive just keeping his nostril above water and that though there was no danger of drowning we might get very wet. I said I did not mind this if there were really no risk so we all went down into the river and rode near the shore for fully 1/4 of a mile. I felt some trepidation at first – I did not feel that it would be nice to see the elephant disappear leaving only a pair of nostrils 2 yards ahead in the water but he behaved majestically, moving along with dignity though his feet sank deeply into the river bed and his huge bulk was submerged up to his eyes. Every second or two the end of his proboscis appeared above the water far ahead of him writhing and coiling like a hideous water snake. It was very beautiful, the clear shining river with the sun blazing down upon it, the lovely shores, the little sandy beaches and the great mountains with their varying shades of indigo. I did so wish that you could see me though I know that you would look apathetic and as if you saw an elephant moving along a tropical river every day!!!

When we began to turn in the direction of a diagonal crossing of the river, Mr Keyt said 'I'm going to take you to Kota Lama[*] – no European has ever been there – I've never been there myself or the Resident either.' Soon after when we were in the middle of the river he said 'A few months ago they would have been firing at us from both sides of the river.' It was very beautiful, the banks were steep and one saw Koto Lama quite a large campong in a palm grove with many durian trees. A good many people assembled on the bank some of the men with muskets and some with spears, but when the elephants scrambled up into the campong the people seemed quite friendly and I got down and climbed into a large house with a gridiron floor over which mats were laid in many parts. There were many women and children in it. They put a fine mat over a sack for me. Presently the room filled up with people till there were 50 seated in circles on the floor but some of the men were standing, one a thorough villain in appearance a Hadji in a dirty yellow turban and red sarong. All the other men wore sarongs only. The people looked much like savages and carried krises or parangs[†] and having been told that the Malays were disarmed I was surprised to see several muskets, a rifle and about 30 spears in the room. I bethought myself then of asking again the name of the place and when I heard it was Koto Lama I at once recognised it as the place which has the worst repute in the Malay Peninsula 'a nest of robbers and murderers' – 'the centre of disturbance and disaffection' etc. I then asked whose house it was and when I heard it was the Datu Sri Paduka Lila and that the woman next to me was

---

[*] See Kota Lama, p. 330.
[†] Malay daggers: large heavy knives.

widow of the Maharajah Lila,[*] who was executed for complicity in the murder of Mr Birch, I thought it was a little curious to be there. I bought a fine sleeping mat as a relic.

I have read several 'bluebooks' and have heard so much about the leading Rajahs and events that it was most interesting to me to see this place and these people. They sent a small monkey up a tree and he twisted off two coconuts and the milk was delicious. When I got on the elephant they took an entrance ladder from one of the houses and put it for me to get up with. Mr Low was very much displeased at first when he found that I had been there and said that Mr Keyt was ignorant and foolish 'but now that it has been done, he says that though he would not have taken the responsibility of letting a European go there that he is glad that I went as affording a proof such as he has not yet had of the complete pacification of the district', though he added that it would appear somewhat strange that the first visitor was a lady. He thinks that the visit and the friendliness shown by the people important enough to be the subject of a dispatch.

We came back by a very narrow and somewhat grown up elephant track on the side of the hill, through dense jungle in which we saw some very recent tiger tracks and then down to the lovely shore of the lovely river and got into a 'dug out', which is only an inch above the water and in which you have to sit without moving. A man crouches at the bow, but every motion of his paddle or pole just tips the edge of the boat under water and I thought it perilous. We landed at the little village of Qualla Kangsa in the golden glory of the sunset, in which the purple mountains were piled like Alps among the flaming clouds, and just along the river bank lay the Dragon Boat from which Mr Birch was murdered and in front of it a square bamboo floating bath through the side of which he was mortally wounded. On landing we met a very bright intelligent looking young Malay but a great dandy in white trousers, red sarong shorter than a kilt, black baju with gold buttons, gold watch guard and coloured fez with a keen and slightly scornful expression of face. He had a great many followers as all the Rajahs have. This is Rajah Dris[†] a Judge and next in succession to the Rajahship of Perak. He was not allowed to try the murderers of Mr Birch because he was supposed at the time to have abetted it, but Mr Low likes him very much and finds him a very valuable coadjutor. Mr Birch knew no Malay, was violent, drank and did some very high handed things. Mr Low says that Mr Douglas would be assassinated before he had been a week in Perak.

[*] See Maharaja Lela, p. 331.
[†] See Raja Dris under Raja Muda Yusef, p. 345.

Rajah Dris walked back with us and I heard him asking questions about me. The men of the village several of them being Hadjis were assembling for worship in the mosque lounging outside till the call to prayer came. This they do twice a day. Each man went into a floating bath and performed ablutions before worshipping. I then came home so entirely sleepy that after dinner I was obliged to go to bed. Sitting on an elephant is very tiring for ones spine for they crawl so slowly and one has nothing to lean against.

Feb 17th I was very glad that yesterday was Sunday for there was quiet and peace, which I needed after two days elephant riding. Mr Low arrived at 11 as I told you, the animals showing the greatest joy. We had breakfast at 12 and much talk. Mr Low is a man thoroughly esteemed and liked and is considered a most excellent administrator. He is 54 and has had 30 years experience in the East much of that time as police magistrate in Borneo. He is Mrs Pope Hennessey's father but has been for many years a widower. He does not like civilised men but is devoted to the Malays and to animals. He works 14 hours out of the 24 and is entirely devoted to quietly and patiently helping the Malays whose language he speaks like a native. His great desire is to train the Rajahs to rule Perak justly by themselves. He grudges every dollar spent on the English 'establishment' and lives in a two-roomed house. He speaks to Malays just as quietly and as respectfully as to English people and has completely won their confidence. He goes about unarmed and with only an unarmed orderly and the sentries on duty only carry canes during the day time. There is no proud bluster or humbug about him. Two thousand Malays lately migrated from Selangor into Perak to escape from Mr Douglas reign of terror. There is a very large native population now in Perak all along the river.

I had a very quiet afternoon and at sunset we went to see Rajah Dris who lives in a good house with European things in it which I dont like. He received us on the stairs very politely. His senior wife came in a heavy stupid looking woman daughter of the reigning prince. The room speedily filled up with female slaves and babies. There was a tablecloth on the table so very dirty. He gave us tea milk and preserved bananas, and when we went away sent a servant with a table lamp which he carried all the way.

A young man whom Mr Low was asked to take charge of and place in an appointment here was sunstricken 3 days ago with violent fever and delirium set in. No doctor exists in this Peninsula he overpowered 4 spahis who were taking care of him rushed about out of doors fell down faint was carried home died at 4 this morning and is to be buried in another hour in a little enclosure on a hill top where the grass grows very green round a number of white wooden crosses which mark the graves of the soldiers who fell here in 1876. This young man was of very good family, but was a thorough n'er do well and in his delirium was constantly imagining himself gambling and losing heavily. So truly sad!

We dined at 7.30 and afterwards while Mr Low smoked his pipe we had a great deal of talk about the native states. I told him all I had seen in Selangor* and he said that natives had often brought him similar stories but he had only partially believed them. The mercury was at 90° for several hours yesterday, fierce dry heat. It will be so for 3 months during which time there will only be casual showers. I have slept on a sleeping mat for 2 nights and find it cooler. Hot though it is the nights are quite cool enough for sleep. I did not sleep much last night however for so many rats and lizards ran about my room and the sentries challenged two people very loudly and tigers came so near the house as to scare the horses and poultry, and roared glumly in the neighbourhood for a long time, and at 4 I heard a messenger tell Mr Low that poor Mr St John was just dead. Mr Low begins his work in the verandah at 6 but does not breakfast till 12 or 1 so had my usual breakfast of banana and pineapple at 7 and my late breakfast at 8.30. I wish people would let one live on bananas. I am so thoroughly tired of fowls ducks and curry without vegetables varied by tinned soups and turtle eggs and steaks. Do you know that the Malay jungle fowls and the Sumatra Bantam fowls are supposed to be the originals of all the fowls in the world? The Malay jungle fowl is the counterpart of our common barndoor fowls. The glorious Argus pheasant of which Mr Low has 2 with 100 eyes on each feather and peacocks are natives of this state.

About 9 Captain Swinburne and Captain Walker of the Sikh regiment arrived and there was a great breakfast at 12 and the great ape was allowed to sit on the table and it eat sausages bananas pineapple chicken and curry and then seizing a large tumbler in which Captain Walker was drinking some champagne and soda water it drank a good deal before it would let the glass go. If drunkenness were not a human vice it would have been ludicrous to see this ape trying to seem sober, and to sit up, and then finding he could not staggering to a chair and trying to lie down very neatly resting his head on his hand and trying to look quite reasonable, but failing, and falling asleep. After that a Rajah came and asked me to go with him to his house and we walked down with his

---

* That is, what she had observed of the behaviour of the Resident, William Bloomfield Douglas.

train of followers and my Malay attendant. It was a very nice house but soon filled with people. Having no interpreter I could not tell whether the two women were his wives or sisters. He brought krises spears and parongs to show me, and they were all very jolly and made me pronounce the Malay names of things, and laughed heartily when I pronounced them badly. Since then there have been Rajahs and their followers and Malays all day in the verandah and on the steps, all received by Mr Low so courteously, and the Rajahs entertained with tea and cigars.

A short time ago the reigning prince who has not been turned into a cipher [as in Selangor] came in with a great train of followers, some only wearing sarongs, a grandson who he is devoted to and the deposed Sultan Abdullahs two sons the boys of whom I wrote before. This man Rajah Muda Yusuf seems much detested. He is said to have a very strong character to be grasping and to be a 'brute' but Mr Low gets on very well with him. Captain Swinburne says that it is absolutely true that 3 years ago he poured boiling water down the back of a runaway female slave, and then put a red ants nest upon it. He is an elderly man wearing a fez on a shaven head and a grey moustache. He has a fine forehead and a look of force, but the lower part of his face is coarse and sensual. He was fanning himself with his fez when I crossed the verandah and gave him a fan which he took without a gesture or word of thanks as if I were a Mohammedan woman. He and Mr Low talked business for an hour and then he left with his train of followers. All important business is transacted in what is called a Native Council. He said that the Datu at whose house I was on Sat. deserved hanging and should be hung!

Feb 18th Always glorious. One could not lead a more tropical life than this literally under the coco palms with apes baboons and elephants all about one and the mercury between 86° and 90°. Inland Perak is beautiful and the broad winding river gleams forever blue under the intense blue sky. 'Never wind blows loudly' but in the daytime a breeze rustles the palms. Gorgeous are birds butterflies and flowers, but often when the erythrina or the poinciana regia are strewing the ground with their flaming flowers I think with longing of the single fragile blossom of the trientalis Europeæ rising from its bed of moss and grass in beautiful Glen Cannich, of the crimson topped lichens, and the faint odour of primroses. If I am spared to return I think you and I must go there for a week. You would like it better now that you are studying botany. One might have a chance there of being 'cold to the bone'.

I did little yesterday but write to you identify some flowers by means of a book and waste my time with the apes till dinner at 7 after which we sat up sadly late like so many bachelors. Captain Swinburne improves on acquaintance, and he is a gentleman. I was to have gone early this morning the only steamer by which I could catch the mail of the 24th being a horribly dirty one which leaves Matang tonight a purely Chinese one but as Capt S. is also going Mr Low has arranged to send us to Penang in the steam launch *Kinta* on Friday which gives me two more days here and delivers me from 'knocking about' for 5 days in Penang or Province Wellesley. It is my last experience of the wilds. I am glad that Captain S. will be my fellow passenger to Ceylon. A steamer is the one place in which I am glad to have some one I know to walk with on deck and sit next to at meals. He says that Ceylon is much hotter than Perak.

At 5.30 the lamentable funeral of Mr St. John took place or rather at 6. Captain S. read the burial service out of my prayer book as it was too dark for them to see their own. Such a wretched termination at 21 of a career of dissipation it looked a rough oblong box – no one to be sorry. The Union Jack was thrown over the coffin which was carried by 6 Sikhs, Mr Low, Captain Swinburne, Rajah Dris and some followers, Sultan Abdullahs 2 boys who had nothing better to do followed, and the service was read by torchlight in the small enclosure where the soldiers graves are and when Mr Low came back the only remark made was 'Its best as it is – he'd only have gone from bad to worse.'

Today any length of time has been spent with the apes. I never saw such fascinating things. They look exactly like familiar demons. You see Mr Low walking in the verandah with these familiar spirits walking behind him with a stealthy tread. Anyone having them formerly would certainly have been burned as a witch. Now at the other end of this verandah Mr Low is transacting business with the Rajahs and a whole crowd of their followers are standing and lying about and Eblis the little ape is sitting on his shoulder with one arm round his neck and the big ape is sitting on the table opening letters while a third ape not a tame one is sitting on the rafters looking most unpleasant. The little ape often sits on my shoulder murmuring 'ouf ouf' which seems a noise expressive of affection and happiness. Besides that they say wah–wah in clear tones, and they scream with rage like children, but at sunrise as if to hail the sun they make a noise for some minutes which they never make again during the day very loud clear and musical as if made by human vocal organs like coo-coo-hooey, very cheerful and pleasant to hear. The forest resounded with it the morning I went up to Sungei Ujong.

At lunch they were both as usual sitting at table. Captain Walker is infatuated about the big ape who has rough jolly manners and likes fun and rough play. The butler was bringing me a cup of tea when this creature put out his long arm and threw the tea over the mat! He then took up a long glass of beer and began to drink it and when it was taken from him he took up the breast of a fricasseed chicken and threw it at the person who took it from him. He did every kind of ludicrous thing and then pulled everyone to go out with him as he always does at that hour and in a moment was at the top of a high tree leaping from branch to branch throwing himself down on coffee shrubs below swinging himself on a twig up again in a flash bounding leaping a picture of happiness strength and agility. The morning gathering of Rajahs and followers was there with Sikhs and Klings and I think that they thought Europeans very foolish to be amused so long with this display. These tame apes hate the Malays.

Meanwhile one of the followers was standing with a new animal held by a string 50 feet long one of the trained baboons which are used to get coconuts. He is hideous he stands on very high legs, but can walk quite erect like a man. He has a short curved tail sable coloured fur darkening down his back and a most repulsive face, very treacherous and ferocious looking. (You never saw such a sight. There are three black apes sitting under the roof in such a position that you only see their faces, and they are all leaning their chins on a beam, and with their grey beards are looking just like Dr Candlish.) He is called the dog-faced baboon. He is quite fierce but knows his keeper. If he were not kept chained he would go back to the jungle. He was sent up the tree but was very angry and shook his chain savagely. When he got up to the top he shook the branches, but none came off and then he chose a ripe nut, and twisted it round and round till its tenacious fibers gave way and then he threw it down. He chose every ripe nut on the trees and screwed each one off in the same way and came down in a very bad sulky temper. I never saw a worse faced brute.

You cannot imagine the interest it is to me to be able to study wild animals which are not in captivity and to see how very wise they are and how very like us. Last night there were 17 lizards in my room when I went to bed, but they are perfectly harmless and catch insects. About 11 last night a crowd hooting and yelling and beating clappers passed by in the darkness, and there was a sound of ravaging and rending caused by a herd of elephants having broken into the banana grounds. The natives have to watch their padi and other crops because no fence that they can put up is of any use against the monsters. Just now I saw Eblis and Mahmoud walking into my room and I soon went in to see what they were doing, and I found them lying one at each end of my bed each with his head on a pillow and there I have left them for Eblis is pining and is growing very weak, he cannot eat anything and Mr Low thinks he is sure to die.

Feb 19th The delightful ape was much worse while I was out yesterday and will certainly die. He can hardly hold anything in his cold feeble hands and he eats nothing. Mr Low looks completely miserable about him. The child looks such a human far away look just as you see in the eyes of people who have done with this world. I never would have one because its death would be far worse than the death of a dog – it is so very near of kin to us. The heat is very great today. There is less breeze, 91°. Heat may easily be borne in houses which are arranged for it, when as here and at Larut there are almost no mosquitoes, but when as soon as the heat of the day is over the mosquitoes begin life is really difficult and the strongest among the men who have been years out here suffer as much as I do. There is not a Malay in his mat hut or a Chinese in his crowded shed who has not his mosquito curtains. Last night a hideous and malignant insect of the bug species above an inch long appeared. The bite of this is nearly as bad as a hornets sting. The whole jungle contains wild beasts, specially the rhinoceros. Its horn is worth $15 but Rajah Muda says that there are certain horns marked in a peculiar way and that these can be sold to the Chinese for $500 for use as powder in medicine.

The whole population of this large state Mr Low estimates at about 45 000 Malays and 14 000 Chinese with a few Klings but now that things are settled Malays are coming in – 2000 have lately crossed in from Selangor they say to escape from the Resident.[*] I cannot think that these states have much future before them. Mohammedanism seems always antagonistic to progress and the large Chinese immigration does not do these countries any real good. It is strange to me that a people converted from Arabia and partly no doubt civilised from Arabia should not have constructed anything permanent. If they were swept away tomorrow in a single year not a trace of them would remain except their krises and spears. They have not been destroyed by wars or drink or diseases introduced by Europeans yet they must have gone on dwindling through a long course of years. One rarely sees women. They keep very much in their houses except when they work in the padi fields which are only clearings in the jungle.

Yesterday afternoon I had an expedition which I really liked, though

[*] William Bloomfield Douglas.

it ended rather badly but it seems impossible to describe it to those who have not seen the tropics. Captain Walker had been shooting on a lake of lotuses at some distance, and he asked me to go with him yesterday afternoon and we started at 3.30 with 2 Malays crossed the Perak in a dug-out and walked for a mile on the sandy, grassy shore which just there lies between the bright river and the jungle. Then we turned into the jungle and I waded through a stream up to my knees which when we came back was up to my waist. Then a very heavy shower came on and we were asked to climb into a Malay house of which the floor was entirely a gridiron. At least 3 families seemed to inhabit it and there were some very big men, but the women kept out of sight behind a mat screen. It was very forlorn. A young dog-faced baboon was chained there and under the house there was much dirt and rubbish among which fowls were picking. They brought us two young coconuts of which the milk was delicious. When the rain ceased we had some very rough walking and then got among the padi where the water was over ones ankles and in two places so unintelligibly hot that it was unpleasant to put ones feet into it. There were swarms of living creatures leaping in and out of the water some attaching themselves to one like leeches. I fell quite down in the water twice but one does not catch cold from getting wet here if one keeps in exercise then we came to a reedy ditch like stream in which there was a dug out with a great deal of water in it into which we all got and by careful balancing managed to keep its edges just above the water. The ditch opened into a reedy swamp where hideous pink water buffalo were enjoying themselves, and on the report of a gun they all tore away looking more like hippopotami than bovine quadrupeds. They are as ugly as a rhinoceros and when they are wet they are a bright salmon pink.

The swamp then became a lotus lake with thousands of these glorious things upon it. It seemed sacrilege almost to push tear and bruise them with our canoe. It was very beautiful but very sad and lonely, the forest coming to the verge of the lake with such an impenetrable wall of entangled trees and trailers that before setting ones feet on the shore space for them would have to be cut with a parong. And this extends all the way across the Peninsula! Mountains range above range all forest covered surround the lake and though the highest may not be over 6000 feet from their shape and from rising from nearly the sea level and from something in the grey sad atmosphere they looked fully 10000. Captain Walker got into the branches of a low tree which overhung the water to look out for teal and widgeons of which there were quantities, and meanwhile the Malays poled the canoe silently over and over the dreary lake in the dreary evening hoping to push up the birds. Any place more solitary and isolated one could hardly see – a most pathetic scene. It seemed to me to be growing darker and we went back for Captain W. and as he tried to get into the canoe the branch he trusted to snapped and he fell into the water up to his chin. Then the boat pole broke so that when we got back to the padi it was obvious that 'the dark' was coming 'at one stride' and I suggested that as we had 2 miles to walk and a river to cross at night perhaps Mr Low would be anxious especially as we should be late for dinner certainly but Captain W. thought not.

We had to wade all through the padi and it was quite dark when we got to the jungle in which the rain had made the footing most precarious. In darkness we waded through the river and along the bank of the Perak where the fireflies were flashing among the bushes in thousands, a most beautiful sight. When we arrived at the steep bank of the river where we had left the canoe there were two or three Malays who laughed and seemed very much pleased to see us and talked vociferously to our men, that is, vociferously for Malays who always speak low. It was a most difficult business getting down the steep slippery bank into the precarious canoe, and in the dark I sat down between the two gridirons in the water where I had to stay till we got over to the other side which took a long time against the stream.

When we had landed and were not very far from this house we met a Sikh sergeant very much excited. I dont know what tongue he spoke but I gathered from the repetition of the word Malaya that there was a great alarm at the Residency. Dont you know how all your pleasure is at once spoilt after you have been enjoying yourself when you find that people at home have been restless and uneasy and having endured these anxieties myself I was so very sorry. Captain Swinburne was leaning over the verandah quite angry and he said that Mr Low was out and very anxious. I was covered with mire and wet from head to foot. So I disappeared, and when we sat down to dinner I saw from Mr Lows silent gloomy manner than he had been really much annoyed, however before long he recovered and we had a very lively evening of conversation and discussion. Malay scouting parties had been sent in several directions, Rajah Dris was away with one and the Sikh force was all ready to do nobody knows what as there were no dogs. Captain Swinburne said that his fears did not go beyond the river which he says is dangerous to cross in the dark in a dug out, but Mr Low thought it *possible* that we might have been assailed by bad characters or that we might have been attacked by a tiger in the jungle and I might have been carried off being unable to climb a tree! Worse imaginings even I could not have had! But except for this I enjoyed the excursion very much. I have had much more of what I like at Qualla Kangsa. I dont really care for smooth easy travelling.

We had a very pleasant evening. Captain Swinburne improves on acquaintance and he has wonderful conversational powers. I think that Perak is fortunate in not having any English ladies. You have no idea of the total want of occupation for any but the best kind of women and they tattle and make mischief and create jealousies, and undermine civil servants with the view of pushing forward their husbands, and keep the little communities in constant hot water. There is not a European woman within a 12 hours journey of Qualla Kangsa and it is a happy thing. Today I am not doing anything as I am going to ride 18 miles to morrow on a man's saddle on my way back to Thaipeng. My luggage, with an accumulation of Malacca canes, mats, krises, tigers teeth and claws, and an elephants tusk go on an elephant, but I find elephant travelling tries my spine very much. The elephants are so slow. They must be used in the jungle as horses cannot get through the swampy ground but a lane has been opened through the jungle for 27 miles seaward from here on which a horse can go nicely.

Eblis is surely dying and like all animals has retired. He has gone into the roof where the untamed ape Sultan is supporting him hour after hour with his arm round him. This wild ape has been so gentle and good to Eblis ever since he became ill tending him as gently as a loving mother would though they are both he apes. This is like humanity for animals are usually cruel to sick ones.

You would *perhaps* like the spectacle just now. Two or 3 Rajahs are sitting and lying about up here and their numerous followers are clustered on the stairs. Mr Low never raises his voice to a native, and speaks to them as to Europeans. He is completely devoted to the interests of Perak and the natives look as if they liked him very much. They laugh so much with him, and are so completely at ease with him. He is only 54 but when he came here the Rajahs told him that they were 'glad that the Queen had sent an old gentleman'.

Residency Thaipeng. Larut. Perak. Feb 20th. On Wednesday I went out for a few minutes with Mr Low and when we came back he called Eblis from the roof but the poor child was too weak to come down the slope and began to cry feebly and the wild ape took him by one of his hands and put an arm round him and gently took him to where he could creep upon Mr Lows chair and then darted away, but all the daylight he was looking anxiously at Eblis through a hole in the roof and at 6 the next morning had so far conquered his timidity as to sit behind Mr Low on the window sill that he might watch his friend. Mr Low was miserable about the ape. He said he would give everything that it should live. He wrote to his daughter that he had never cared for anything in the world as for Eblis except for her. The little thing which only weighs about 20 ounces clung to him the whole time and kept putting out its feeble arms to him with a look of unspeakable affection on its poor pinched features murmuring ouf ouf. He poured drops of milk down its throat every ten minutes. I saw tears dropping from his eyes on it and I dont wonder, for such a bewitching human thing I never saw. He says if it recovers he shall never go away without it. If he put it down for one moment it screamed just like a baby and stretched out its thin hands.

I would give a great deal that it should get better for it is the one pleasure that the poor man has in the midst of his ceaseless toil. I never saw a kinder man (but caution and suspicion are his chief characteristics) he is always thinking of other people and is faultlessly generous and easy regarding his own concerns as for instance refusing to commit his servants to prison when they have robbed him saying 'poor things they know no better'. It is just the same with the apes. Mr Maxwell told me that Mr Low had made a very clear and careful copy of a long dispatch to Lord Carnarvon, when Mahmoud dipped his fingers in the ink and drew them over a whole page and he only took him in his arms saying 'Poor little creature you've given me a great deal of trouble but you know no better.' I wish one could know how things would be! I would have given up Ceylon which I dont care to go to at all. Mr Low has several times asked me to stay a month here and he said he had got so used to having me that he should miss me very much. He paid me a compliment which I shall preserve by writing it here – 'You've the pluck of six ordinary men, and you glide about the house and never speak at the wrong time – if men are visiting me they never know when to be quiet, but bother me in the middle of business.' This is very amusing for it would usually be said 'women never know when to be quiet'. Mr Maxwell says the same, that when men are here he can get nothing done 'for their clatter'.

I like Qualla Kangsa better than any place I have seen in my wanderings. It is 'the wilds'. There is rest there. Then the delightful apes are so much more pleasant than most people. Then there are birds and beasts of all kinds from elephants downwards. Then for a tropical place it is most beautiful and the Malay life is very interesting. Then the sight of mild & righteous rule which never leaves out of sight the training of the Malays to rule themselves is so constantly pleasing, and is all carried on under ones eyes. Mr Low would have sent me on elephants five days journey in the jungle with a Sikh guard, and up the river in the dragon boat for a few days. I am disgusted but I cannot live any longer without hearing that you are alive. If I had only known I might have led a wild life at Qualla Kangsa. I am sorrier to leave it than any place I have been at.

I got up at 5 and found Mr Low at his table nursing Eblis with Moloch the wild ape looking on. What a strange life it is for an Englishman to have no European within 25 miles, never to speak ones own tongue, and to have no companions but apes. I think that Rajah Dris will be able to reign righteously if Mr Low can stay another two years there. The sun was not risen when I went out. A horse with an ordinary English gentlemans saddle was there for me, and a Malay orderly with another, and the Royal Elephant for my luggage. It was absurd to see this huge animal lie down only to receive on his back my Gladstone bag roll and mats. Never again shall I see elephants rolling majestically along.

Feb 21st I have just got a telegram about the ape! I rode away wishing I were coming instead of going. It had all been so nice and the two days alone at first had been quite unique. I had 18 miles to ride. At first I did not like the English saddle, but it was easy to ride on, and I had a perfect little horse with a quick walk and an easy canter. Those were 'ways like ways'. I enjoyed that and believe now that with a good horse and a good saddle if I were in the Rocky Mts I could ride as I formerly did. People who knew anything about the Malay Peninsula would be surprised that a lady could ride through the jungle safely with only an unarmed Malay orderly.

There were no adventures. The sun pierced the mists and they all rolled away and when I reached the beautiful pass the apes were hooting their morning hymn and the forests rang with it and with the morning songs of birds. There were such glorious butterflies. [. . .] Through this pass a loud voiced stream of crystal water tumbles joyously – heard everywhere but seen only now and then foaming among granite boulders and resting in pools floored with golden sand. Gunong Pondok the limestone butte which is 1200 feet in height showed all his brilliancy of colour in the sunshine and Gunong Bubu one of the highest mountains in Perak showed his granite ridge above the forest. The lotus lake where I waited for the elephant on the way up was glorious a thousand rosy blossoms drinking in the sunshine, and a million classic leaves spreading their blue green shields above the water. I was sorry when I got over the bad road and found a gharry a covered two wheeled cart waiting for me but it was best as the sun was then high and fierce, and the risk of sun-stroke is great when one has not a pith helmet. I had 5 miles to drive then, and a beautiful Kling sat on the shaft with a Turkey red sarong on and a piece of Turkey cotton thrown gracefully on one shoulder. These Klings have a far less human expression than the apes, statuesque though they are. The hills behind Thaipeng looked cool and indigo coloured in the noon day heat and the waterfall, swelled by the rain of the night before was coming down in a sheet of foam.

But Thaipeng looked 'the wearing world' after beautiful silent Qualla Kangsa – the large shops with sign boards, the stalls in the streets, the tribal halls, the carts with a buffalo yoked singly for the spread of their huge horns is so great that 2 cannot be yoked together – the carts with 2 cinnamon coloured humped bullocks yoked together standing in trains at the shop doors, the gharries with their little Sumatra ponies, the crowds of Chinese coolies half naked, all the stir of Chinese industry. When I got in here I heard at once of a brutal murder committed by the Chinese the night before. A gang had waylaid a revenue officer in one of the narrow creeks and his hacked and mutilated body had drifted down here this morning. I took a bath and lay on my bed for three hours reading the papers up to Jan 17th quite a recent date. [. . .] It seems months since my hasty leaving of Singapore for Malacca yet it is only just five weeks! Only 2 months since I left Japan. Perhaps I shall be with you in 2 more if my journey is prosperous. I dont think you would know me for I am so stout that even my face is fatter and the tropic sun has burned me quite brown so that I might be taken for a Portuguese, and even my hair seems burned darker. The tropic sun does not produce on me the pain and swelling produced by the sun and wind of high latitudes, so I have not even worn a veil over my face.

P.&O. S.S. Malwa Feb 25. 1879 [. . .] We left at 5.30 and after a beautiful night anchored at Georgetown at 2 a.m. on Sat. but it was a most uncomfortable voyage. Mr Low had lent the Kinta to Captain Swinburne and me but Mrs Campbell a young widow a would-be lady and therefore very vulgar who had been on a visit to an official at Thaipeng asked for or rather demanded a passage for herself and baby. In addition she had an ayah and man. The cabin had 2 couches but she filled up most of mine with her luggage as well as the floor and the ayah slept there too and the man sat inside on the ladder so there were 5 human beings in this den, many mosquitoes and the mercury 87°. Then a whole bottle of milk was spilt and a phial of brandy and the child screamed continually during the night and at 2 the lady asked me to go and wake the gentlemen and get a teaspoonful of brandy to cure her sea-sickness and they laughed so tremendously that I scarcely dared to return with it. Then Capt Swinburne who is a professed woman and child hater was quite irrepressible and made his dislike so obvious and whenever the child cried he called to his servant 'Wring that brats neck,' the servant knowing no English! And at 2 when chocolate was brought and the child was kicking and roaring he called down to me 'Will you drink some chocolate to King Herods memory?' I came on deck before 3 thinking how much more interesting a sick wah-wah is than a peevish child.

Mr Maxwell who has 4 children did not behave much better and it was a great exertion for me by overdone courtesy and desperate attempts at conversation to conceal from her what they were doing. We had a very rough dinner on the top of the skylight by a ships lantern with about 8 Malays and natives of India tumbling over each other to wait on us. Everyone has so many followers in the East. Swinburne deliberately placed himself opposite to me to say 'I admire you more than any woman I know – you are a splendid traveller – you know exactly what you can do and cant do, you make every one bright and you glide about doing what few men would do without any fuss!' 'Yes' Mr Maxwell said 'Men fuss about everything – I should have been worried out of my life with arranging for a man, while you just quietly go about and you get over all difficulties without saying anything about it – You are a most splendid traveller. I suspected it from the day you landed with only a bag and roll!' I said it was the one talent on which I was usually compli-mented but I added without thinking 'But I am always despised at first' at which they never ceased to laugh, but it is quite true for 'my bodily presence is weak and my speech contemptible', and just because I 'make no fuss' I generally lose a day or two at first by people thinking that I cant do the thing I have come to do.

Captain S. gave the most characteristic account of his parting with the Sikh troops who were much attached to him because though he has a hasty temper he was always just and upright. He said 'These Orientals are such villains they knelt on the ground and embraced and kissed my feet.' We asked him what he said to them and he *says* he said 'You are a lot of unmitigated rascals – half of you deserve hanging but keep out of scrapes if you can till I come back, for I want to have the pleasure of hanging you myself.' But he really likes them and called after Captain Walker who remains as his substitute 'Now old man dont knock those fellows about.' The poor fellows whose tongue Captain S. speaks are in such terror at being at the mercy of an interpreter now and being in an irregular service they have little to protect them. Captain Walker showed all of us that he had a terrible temper. The Malays give sobriquets to all Europeans founded on physical or moral peculiarities. Captain S. they call 'the mad one' and 'the outspoken one' and Mr Maxwell 'the cat-eyed one' and 'the tiger cub'. Captain W. they had already called 'the black panther'.

When we anchored at 2 the Harbour Masters boat came off with a note from Mrs Isemonger Mr Maxwell's sister asking me to go to Province Wellesley, and at 6 the boat returned and took Mr Maxwell and me over there. It was so beautiful at sunrise with the interminable groves of palms and the long line of mournful casuarina trees above the sandy shore and the high hills of Penang on the other side of the narrow strait. We found Mrs I. away no one knew where, and we broke open the tea box and got some breakfast, but just as we were going away she appeared having been detained by the rain the night before. She is one of the nicest people that I have seen. We had a very pleasant morning though I was miserably tired and at 12 the boat came back and Mr Maxwell took me over to Georgetown. The six-oared gig which was one of the 'government facilities' took an hour in getting back against the tide in the blazing noonday sun. I drove in a gharry to Mr Woods where his clerk was waiting for me and drove me in his gharry the 3 miles to the foot of Penang hill. It is really very beautiful. It is a forest of coconuts under which are durian mangostein and other large trees while beautiful Malay Chinese and half caste houses lie in the deep fruitful shade. Showing how various are the races dwelling in peace under the shadow of our flag there were in that short distance a mosque a Hindoo temple a Siamese temple and a Chinese temple. [. . .]

Sunday seemed rather a long day as I could not be sufficiently alone. It was not possible to go to church. One has four miles of steep up hill which must be done either on a pony or in a chair carried by coolies on foot and then about 3 miles through coconut groves. I was disappointed at feeling less well at that high altitude and in the lower temperature than in the broiling heat of the lower regions. Perhaps equable heat is wholesome. [. . .]

On Monday morning the hill was so wrapped in cloud that the mail could not be signalled, however my luggage was taken down on the heads of coolies at 6. At 9.30 a telegram came that the mail was in and Mr Wood and I walked down the hill as I thought that would hurt me the least but the path is so steep that you cannot walk but must trot, & in the blazing heat we came down 4 miles in 1 hr 28 min! The hill is covered with nepenthes, pitcher plants or monkey cups, deep crimson, and all sorts of flowering trees shrubs and trailers among them the beautiful hoya carnosa one of the earliest flowers that I remember. I dont remember whether I told you that Mr Wood is the Chief Justice. Mr Hall his clerk met me with a gharry in which I drove to the Woods' town house where I changed my dress and had some food while Mr Hall got my ticket etc and then we drove to the pier where the last of the 'Government facilities' the Harbour Masters six-oared gig waited to bring me off here. Mrs Wood sent 2 large clusters of bananas for my use on the voyage. I hardly know how I shall live when I can no longer get them for they have formed the greater part of my food for 2 months and I *crave* for them. I never eat bread or butter and seldom taste tea or coffee or butchers meat!

I copy another paragraph from the Penang Gazette as I could not waste 1/0 in buying it. The colonial newspapers exercise the privilege of lying to the full. 'Miss Bird arrived from Larut early on Sat. morning in the Perak Government steam launch Kinta, attended by the Assistant Resident and the Commissioner of Police. Immediately on landing she proceeded to Penang Hill where she is the guest of Mr Justice Wood. We understand that her notes on the Residential System are already in the hands of the Administration at Singapore'!!!!

The costume and colour in Penang are wonderful. I admired the groups in front of the police court under the feathery shade of tamarind trees as much as anything I have seen – Orientalism in all its picturesqueness. This letter brings the series of 'great' letters to an end. I must now try to take rest having had none. Mr Cecil Smiths promise of 'Government Facilities' in the Malay Peninsula was nobly fulfilled, and the government officials everywhere were most attentive. I liked Perak, specially Qualla Kangsa and was generally interested throughout. I fear that you and the other readers of the Malay letters will like them far better than the Japan letters though they represented far more of painstaking and 'honest work'. It is getting too dark to see.

Your frugiferous bat
ILB

Although this would not be the last of Isabella Bird's 'great' journal letters to her sister, it is the last that appears to have survived. Within a year of Isabella's return to Scotland via Ceylon, Egypt and the Holy Land – including a four-day trek to the top of Mount Sinai – Henrietta caught a chill and came down with typhoid fever. She died five weeks later on June 5, 1880. Isabella was devastated. 'She was everything to me,' she wrote to John Murray, 'the inspiration of all my literary work – my best public, my home and fireside, my most intimate and congenial friend. . . . Beloved in life and mourned in death as few are mourned, there is not a memory of her which is not lovely, and this to me is at once the sting and the solace of her early removal.' To close friends such as Mary Macdiarmid and Ella Blackie, Isabella wrote that Henrietta 'was *my world*, present or absent, seldom absent from my thoughts'. She was 'the light, life, and inspiration of my life'. She was undoubtedly the most powerful influence on Isabella's writing, and without her, a certain vitality was gone. Her later letters have none of the power or freshness of those printed here.

That is not to say that Isabella stopped travelling. Although she paused briefly for her ill-starred marriage to her sister's doctor, John Bishop, when he, too, died she embarked on major journeys to Persia, Kurdistan, Morocco, India, Tibet, Japan, China and Korea. Even in her seventies, Isabella was inexhaustible: she rode a black stallion alone across the Atlas Mountains and camped out with the Berbers in 1901. When she died in an Edinburgh nursing home three years later, on October 7, 1904, her trunks were packed, corded, ready and waiting for her next journey to China.

Chronology

with special focus on the years covered by these letters

1831   October 15: Isabella Lucy Bird born at Boroughbridge Hall, North Yorkshire.

1832   Isabella's father, Edward Bird, appointed vicar of Maidenhead, Berkshire.

1833   Isabella's younger brother is born and dies at Maidenhead.

1834   Edward Bird appointed vicar of St. Alban's at Tattenhall, Cheshire. November 5: probable date of Henrietta Amelia Bird's birth.

1835   Isabella develops the first symptoms of her illness, which grants her extra care.

1842   Edward Bird forced to resign his living at Tattenhall because of the strictness of his views on Sunday labour. He is appointed to St Thomas's Church, Birmingham. The Birds take a house on Frederick's Road.

1847   Edward Bird stoned out of St Thomas's Church, largely because of his views on Sunday labour. He and Henrietta contract scarlet fever during an epidemic. Isabella and her mother, Dora, nurse them back to health. On recovery, Edward Bird resigns his post.

1848   The Birds take refuge with relatives in Eastbourne, then London, until Edward secures a living at the peaceable St Margaret's Church in Wyton, Huntingdonshire.

1849   Isabella's first pamphlet published, on the subject of free trade.

1850   Isabella undergoes an operation for the removal of a 'fibrous tumour' on her spine. The Birds spend their first summer in Scotland, in the hope of improving Isabella's health.

1852–3   Isabella suffers 'some sorrow', probably an unfortunate attachment.

1854   Isabella's father sends her to North America for her first major voyage. She visits Halifax, Prince Edward's Island, Boston, Cincinnati, Chicago, Toronto, Niagara, Montreal, Quebec and New York; then lingers in Boston for the season until her finances run out. Henrietta, now 20, stays at home.

1855   Isabella returns to Wyton after an absence of seven months. There she meets the travel writer John Milford, who introduces her to John Murray III. Autumn: Isabella writes up her experiences in North America for John Murray.

1856   *The Englishwoman in America* is published.

1857   Isabella's father sends her again to North America, where she remains for 11 months. She visits New York, Philadelphia, Washington, Boston, Albany, Niagara, Toronto, and Detroit; in the summer, various parts of Virginia, South Carolina,

Georgia, Illinois, Wisconsin, Minnesota and the Great Lakes. She meets Longfellow, Emerson and Thoreau in Massachusetts. She spends two 'seasons' in Boston with 'influential friends'.

1858   April 3: Isabella returns to Wyton. That night her father falls ill of influenza. He dies six weeks later aged 66 and is buried at Wyton. Isabella oversees the posthumous publication of *The Revival in America by an English Eye-Witness* by Edward Bird.

1859   *Aspects of Religion in the United States of America* published. Dora Bird takes her daughters to visit relatives in England, including Tunbridge Wells. Isabella then spends three weeks alone in Ireland investigating the 'Ulster Revival'. Autumn: Dora Bird moves with her daughters to Edinburgh, settling at 3 Castle Terrace.

1860   In Edinburgh, Isabella meets Anna Stoddart, who later becomes Isabella's first biographer. Summer: the Birds begin an annual pilgrimage to Oban and Mull. Isabella begins her emigration scheme for the Highland crofters.

1862–6 Isabella's crofters emigrate to Canada. Isabella and Henrietta publish articles in literary magazines and engage in acts of charity. Isabella possibly visits Canada for two months in 1866 to visit her crofters.

1866   May: Henrietta visits Tobermory on her own for several weeks, then returns to Edinburgh to nurse her mother. August 14: Dora Bird dies (also at the age of 66) and is buried in Dean's Cemetery, Edinburgh, where Henrietta and Isabella transfer their father's remains. Immediately after the funeral, the sisters separate for six months: Isabella to London, Farnham and Tunbridge Wells; Henrietta to Mull.

1867   February: Isabella and Henrietta reunite in Edinburgh, then spend the summer together at Oban and Tobermory, on the Isle of Mull. Winter: the sisters start working in Edinburgh to improve living conditions for the poor.

1869   *Notes on Old Edinburgh* by Isabella is published. The sisters spend the summer at Oban. When Henrietta leaves to visit friends in England, Isabella is prostrated by 'inflammation of the throat'. Henrietta does not return; Isabella is nursed by a new friend, Emily Clayton. Winter: the sisters choose to live in separate accommodation. Isabella moves in with Emily Clayton at 28 Rutland Square, while Henrietta remains at 3 Castle Terrace.

1870   Summer: Isabella stays with Emily in Edinburgh. Henrietta goes to Mull, where she adopts a little girl, Mary. Autumn: Isabella recovers sufficiently from her illness to journey on her own to Applecross, where she meets the travel writer Constance Gordon-Cumming. Winter: touring schools in the Highlands, while Henrietta enrolls in 'ladies' classes' at the University of Edinburgh.

1871   November: Isabella sets sail on the *St David* for a six-months cruise to New York, Maine, Italy, Algeria, Spain and Portugal. Henrietta stays in Edinburgh to study at the university.

1872   April: Isabella returns to Edinburgh. The sisters decide to give up the flat at 3 Castle Terrace. Henrietta moves to Tobermory; Isabella stays with Emily Clayton in Edinburgh. July 11: Isabella sets sail in the *Ben Nevis* for Australia. She arrives in

October, to stay two months. November 28: Isabella leaves Australia for New Zealand, where she stays one month.

1873   Jan 1: Isabella departs New Zealand for Hawaii, where she stays for seven months. August 6: Isabella departs Hawaii for San Francisco. Henrietta spends the summer travelling in Orkney, Shetland and Mull. September: Isabella arrives in Colorado, where she meets Jim Nugent (Rocky Mountain Jim). October: Henrietta pays for Mary, the girl she has adopted, to go to school in Edinburgh.

1874   January: Isabella returns to Edinburgh. The sisters rent a flat together at 17 Melville Street, where Isabella begins revising her Hawaii letters for publication. Spring: the sisters go together to Tobermory, where Isabella continues working on her book. Early June: Isabella departs on her own for London and Salisbury, leaving Henrietta at Tobermory. She sends her manuscript on Hawaii to John Murray, then leaves for Switzerland with Emily Clayton and Bessie Ker. Henrietta rents The Cottage in Tobermory for the first time. June 29: Jim Nugent is shot by Griff Evans in Estes Park, dying on September 7. Isabella returns soon after to Tobermory to see Henrietta. November: Isabella and Henrietta rent a flat together at 7 Atholl Crescent, Edinburgh.

1875   *The Hawaiian Archipelago* published, dedicated to Henrietta. Summer: Isabella and Henrietta visit Glen Affric, where Isabella pursues microscopic research on 'the lichens and cryptogams of the district'. July: they return to Tobermory. Isabella stays only a few weeks, leaving Henrietta for England to pay visits in Salisbury, Yorkshire, London and Tunbridge Wells. Autumn: Isabella alone in London, correcting proofs for Constance Gordon-Cumming's book on Fiji. November: Isabella rejoins Henrietta in Edinburgh and immediately succumbs to pleurodynia.

1876   April: Henrietta completes her Greek classes at the University of Edinburgh, and leaves for Tobermory, where she signs a five-year lease on The Cottage. Isabella remains in Edinburgh. July: Isabella goes to York, then joins Henrietta for a month in Iona, having refused to meet her at The Cottage in Tobermory, which she finds 'too relaxing'. September: the sisters return to Edinburgh, to 7 Atholl Crescent, where Isabella writes her articles on 'Australia Felix' for *The Leisure Hour*.

1877   Isabella and Henrietta help form a college for the training of medical missionaries in honour of David Livingstone. In so doing, they meet Dr John Bishop. When Henrietta falls ill, she calls in Dr Bishop rather than her regular doctor. He and Isabella begin to share evenings over a microscope. July: Isabella writes to John Murray that she is 'conditionally engaged'. Henrietta departs for Tobermory, Isabella for England. August: Isabella writes to John Murray that the engagement is dissolved. September: Isabella and John Bishop join Henrietta in Tobermory to 'heal the sick'. October: Isabella and Henrietta separate, with Henrietta staying in Tobermory. November: Isabella and Henrietta reunite at 7 Atholl Crescent, where Isabella writes up her Rocky Mountain letters. 'Australia Felix' published in instalments in *The Leisure Hour*.

1878   Isabella corresponds with Charles Darwin about where she should journey next. 'Letters from the Rocky Mountains' published in instalments in *The Leisure Hour*.

April: Isabella departs for Japan via North America, stopping in New York, Chicago, Salt Lake City and San Francisco. She then sails to Japan via Shanghai. Just before she leaves, Henrietta is stricken with illness. John Bishop promises to care for her while Isabella is away. December: Isabella leaves Tokyo for China. She arrives in Hong Kong in the middle of a fire.

1879   January: Isabella sets sail for Singapore via Saigon. She spends the next two months exploring the Protected Malay States before leaving in late February for Cairo via Ceylon. After an ill-fated pilgrimage to Sinai, she falls ill with typhoid fever and is sick the whole way home. May 27: Isabella rejoins Henrietta at The Cottage in Tobermory; Henrietta nurses her back to health. Isabella begins work on her book about Japan. October: *A Lady's Life in the Rocky Mountains* published by John Murray, dedicated to Henrietta. Both sisters leave Mull: Henrietta to Coates Crescent, Edinburgh, and Isabella to London. December: Isabella rejoins Henrietta in Edinburgh to finish manuscript on Japan, then leaves for London on her own.

1880   *Unbeaten Tracks in Japan* published while the sisters are apart. April 1: Henrietta leaves Edinburgh for Tobermory. April 20: Isabella returns to Edinburgh and learns that her sister is ill with typhoid. April 27: Isabella arrives in Tobermory to nurse Henrietta. April 30: John Bishop arrives in Tobermory to nurse Henrietta. June 5: Henrietta dies and is buried with her parents in Dean's Cemetery, Edinburgh. Isabella departs for Switzerland with Emily Clayton and the Kers. October 1: Isabella returns alone to The Cottage in Tobermory. December: Isabella leaves Tobermory for 28 Rutland Square, Edinburgh, to stay with Emily Clayton. While there, she accepts John Bishop's proposal of marriage.

1881   March 8: Isabella marries John Bishop in deepest mourning at Barton House, Warwickshire. They spend a brief honeymoon at Malvern, then return to their new home at 12 Walker Street, Edinburgh. Isabella spends the summer alone at Tobermory. Early September: Isabella returns to Edinburgh. The King of Hawaii confers on her the Hawaiian Literary Order of Kapiolani. October: Isabella meets Queen Victoria during a state visit to the Edinburgh Infirmary. She returns alone to The Cottage in Tobermory for six weeks. November: John Bishop falls ill after operating on a Swedish sailor in the erisypelas ward of the Edinburgh Infirmary. Isabella rushes to his side. They journey together to England. Isabella publishes *Hymns and Poems of the Late Henrietta A. Bird*.

1882   January: Bishop recovers sufficiently to return to work in Edinburgh; Isabella falls ill with carbuncles on her spine, requiring constant attention. April: Isabella travels alone to Tobermory for two weeks, then rejoins Bishop briefly in Edinburgh. May: Isabella travels alone to Italy, where she meets Emily Clayton and the Kers. She spends most of the summer with them on the Continent, returning to Edinburgh to see Bishop briefly in late July. August: Isabella goes alone to The Cottage in Tobermory for a month, returning to Edinburgh in September. By early December, both Bishop and Isabella are seriously ill, Isabella with a 'spinal attack'.

1883   *The Golden Chersonese* published, dedicated to Henrietta. April: Isabella travels alone to Tobermory and Bishop recovers. June: Isabella leaves Tobermory for London, where she is joined by Bishop. Together, they go to Canturbury and Devonshire.

July 18: Bishop has become so ill that they have to stop at Clifton for several weeks, then carry on to nearby relatives. Bishop remains seriously ill. Early December: they move to London where Bishop is diagnosed with pernicious anaemia.

1884–5 Isabella takes her husband to health spas in England and on the Continent, hoping to improve his health. They also spend some time together in Tobermory. Bishop grows continually worse.

1886 January 3: in Cannes, Bishop undergoes a transfusion (before the typing of blood) by Sir Joseph Lister. March 6: Bishop dies; cause of death is listed as pernicious anaemia. He is buried in Cannes; later his remains are transferred to the Bird family tomb in Dean's Cemetery, Edinburgh. 'A Pilgrimage to Sinai' published in instalments in *The Leisure Hour*. 'The Visitation of Mountain Jim' published in *Phantasms of the Living*. The editors prove Isabella could not have seen Jim's ghost. Isabella, undismayed, tells John Murray and Anna Stoddart varying stories about the visitation at this time.

1887 Prostrate with 'spinal attacks', Isabella moves to London to be near St Mary's Hospital, Paddington. November: she buys a house in Maida Vale.

1888 Isabella sells her house in Maida Vale, along with her Eastern curios, and gives her books to the University of Edinburgh. She spends the following months visiting friends. She also takes a brief trip to Northern Ireland, after promising John Murray that she will 'incite no riots'.

1889 Isabella departs for India and Tibet to establish hospitals in honour of Henrietta and her husband.

1890 Isabella travels across Persia, Armenia and Turkey, from the Persian Gulf to the Black Sea, before returning to London. Ultimately, she is gone for two full years.

1891 April: Isabella visits the House of Commons to speak on 'the Armenian Question' several times. She dines with Gladstone, the Prime Minister, and corresponds with Lord Curzon. *Journeys in Persia and Kurdistan* published.

1892 Isabella is elected the first female fellow of the Royal Geographical Society. She becomes a fellow of the Scottish Royal Geographical Society at the same time. She is also elected an honorary fellow of the Oriental Society of Pekin. John Murray III dies; John Murray IV becomes her publisher.

1893 *Heathen Claims and Christian Duty* published. Isabella is presented to Queen Victoria as an eminent traveller, and enrolls in photography classes in London.

1894 *Among the Tibetans* published. January: Isabella departs for the Far East via North America to visit Japan, Korea, China, Manchuria and Vladivostok, taking hundreds of photographs on her journey.

1895 She returns to China and Korea, spends the summer in Japan, then goes once more to China and Korea.

1896 Isabella takes a boat up the Yangtze, then returns to Korea and Japan.

1897 March: Isabella arrives in London, after an absence of three years and two months.

1898   *Korea and Her Neighbours* published.

1899   *The Yangtze Valley and Beyond* published.

1900   *Chinese Pictures* published. April: While staying at The Cottage in Tobermory, Isabella falls down the cliffside and injures herself. She gives up The Cottage because she can no longer manage the hill. She buys a house at 140 Lexham Gardens, Kensington, in London.

1901   Isabella visits Morocco, where she travels alone through the desert. She stays six months. 'Notes on Morocco' published in *The Monthly Review*.

1903   Isabella, seriously ill with spinal tumours, moves back to Edinburgh, to 16 Melville Street. She has been diagnosed with advanced heart disease and thrombosis.

1904   October 7: Isabella dies, one week short of her 73rd birthday. She is buried with her family in Dean's Cemetery.

Notes on People and Places

Isabella Bird's letters teach an important lesson in personal history: figures and events that loom large on the horizon of an individual life are rarely those recorded by scholars. Many of the people who flit across the tapestry of Isabella's daily life have long since slipped into oblivion. Others are known today largely because of her books. At the same time, Isabella travelled at an important period of colonial history, and she met a number of prominent individuals. These alphabetically arranged notes attempt to identify and briefly describe those figures whose mark endures. Cross-references to other entries are indicated by an asterisk.

Sultan Abdullah of Perak played a prominent role in the murder of James Birch,★ Resident of the Malay state of Perak, in 1875, sparking the brief but fiery Perak War. In 1873, Abdullah had negotiated the Pangkor Engagement with Sir Andrew Clarke, then Governor of the Straits Settlements, in which Abdullah promised to make over the revenues from Larut (part of Perak) for ten years to Tan Kim Ching, a Chinese merchant, and to William Henry Read, a senior unofficial member in the Legislative Council in Singapore. In exchange, the British government promised to pay Abdullah's debts and promote him to sultan. Clarke arbitrated, but from the beginning the intent was to pension off Abdullah in favour of the Raja Ismail, who was seen as more pro-British. Unfortunately for Clarke, Ismail boycotted the conference, and the Pangkor Engagement was signed in 1874 by Abdullah without Ismail. This treaty, which made Abdullah sultan, was the first to establish a British Resident in the Malay States; in this case, Perak. The British Resident's advice was to be taken on all matters not concerning Malay custom or religion, making the Resident ruler in practice if not in law. This system might have worked, had not the Resident, James Birch, taken it on himself to curb Abdullah's spending, which quickly changed Abdullah's mind about the treaty's benefits. In retaliation, Abdullah had Birch assassinated in Pasir Selak by the Maharaja Lela.★ A short war and longer trial ensued. In the end, Abdullah was exiled to the Seychelles and the Maharaja Lela was hanged. At the time of Isabella's visit in 1879, Abdullah's mother had just sent his two small sons to the new Resident, Sir Hugh Low,★ so that the British government might provide for their education. Eventually, Sir Andrew Clark gained permission from the Colonial Office for Abdullah to return to Singapore to join his sons, which he did in 1894.

The Alexanders (called the 'Chalmers' in *A Lady's Life in the Rocky Mountains*) were the family with whom Isabella first stayed in Colorado. The letters from this period appear to have been lost, but we know from Isabella's published account that she found them rough. Having come from Illinois for their health nine years before, the family lived in a dugout on the north bank of the Big Thompson River, with a crude bridge across the water and a derelict sawmill. Isabella depicts the Alexanders as cheerless, grasping folk. In addition to the parents, 'the family consists of a grown-up son, a shiftless, melancholy youth; a girl of sixteen, a sour, repellent-looking creature with as much manners as a pig; and three hard, unchild-like younger children. By the whole family all courtesy and gentleness of act or speech seem regarded as "works of the flesh", if not of "the devil".' Possibly Isabella destroyed this letter, like those from New Zealand, because she was unhappy with her stay.

Sher Ali, Emir of Afghanistan from 1863 to 1879, was a leading figure in Britain's Great Game. Initially friendly toward British interests, Ali allied with Russia in its attempts to extend power into Central Asia, leading to the outbreak of the second Afghan War. Ultimately, Sher Ali's forces were defeated by the British and he fled the country. He died in exile in 1879 while Isabella was in Hong Kong, to be succeeded by his pro-British nephew, Abdar-Rahman Khan.

Princess Alice, born in 1843, was the third of Queen Victoria's nine children. At eighteen, Princess Alice had married Prince Louis of Hesse (later Grand Duke Louis XIV), and became known thereafter as Princess Louise. Her seven children included a daughter, Alix, who became the wife of Nicholas II, Russia's last czar. The first of Queen Victoria's children to die, Princess Alice succumbed to diphtheria in 1878.

James Allen, irrepressible amateur poet and plagiarist, appears as 'Mr Lyman' (the lie man) in *A Lady's Life in the Rocky Mountains*. 'A slangy, assured fellow of twenty,' as Isabella describes him, Allen had fallen ill at theological college and travelled to Colorado to recover. Allen's insatiable appetite was a sore point in the lean winter months at Estes Park, as was his 'dishonourable conduct regarding private papers'. He had a habit of not only copying but stealing them. Interestingly enough, in 1874 when Jim Nugent★ was shot, Allen became the administrator of Jim's estate. From court records, it seems that Allen tried to make off with Jim's money and most of his possessions, but the court secretary held him accountable. Allen does appear to have appropriated Jim's papers, however. Their whereabouts have never been traced, which is unfortunate, as Jim and Isabella corresponded until Jim's death on September 7, 1874.

Altnacraig was the Highland home of Professor Stuart Blackie★ and his wife Ella, completed in the autumn of 1866. It stood above the Sound of Kerrera, and was a place of great festivities, as the Blackies enjoyed entertaining their friends. Henrietta and Isabella visited often, beginning in 1867. While Isabella chatted with Ella, Henrietta and the professor wrote poems to one another about the surrounding landscape.

Samuel and *Mary Austin* were members of the elite expatriate community of Hilo, Hawaii, intimately connected with its missionary world. Arriving from Buffalo, New York, in 1853, Sam Austin was initially appointed police magistrate of Hilo, but he rose to become Circuit Court Judge within two years. He specialised in cases of morality involving both Hawaiians and the growing community of white settlers. In addition, Austin founded Onomea, one of the first sugar plantations on the Big Island, seven miles north of Hilo.

James Balfour was a leading member of Victoria's Legislative Assembly from 1866 to 1869, and from 1874 until his death in 1913. Born in Scotland in the same year as Isabella, Balfour emigrated to Melbourne at the age of twenty-two and quickly achieved prominence as a director of companies, newspaper proprietor and advocate of Victoria's Presbyterian Church. At the time of Isabella's visit, Balfour had just returned from an extended European tour undertaken to recuperate from an eye injury. He was participating in the Royal Commission on Charitable Institutions and was active in the church. He returned to office in 1874.

The *Ben Nevis* was the steamer on which Isabella set sail from Liverpool for Australia's Port Philip Harbour on July 11, 1872. Captain McPetrie seems to have been its master. Isabella was deathly ill on this voyage, and so characterised the experiences as being tainted by 'loud quarrels, noisy complaints and a dirty stewardess'. It took her several months to recover.

Christian Bertelmann, whom Isabella met briefly on her way to Hanalei, became one of Kauai's most famous lepers. In order to avoid isolation on Molokai, Bertelmann disguised himself as an old woman and was smuggled into Japan, hoping to find a cure. Unsuccessful, Bertelmann returned to Kauai, where his family kept him hidden by day in a secret room. At night he saddled his horse and rode round the island, playing ghostly melodies on his flute, until he died in 1895.

Bessie. See Elizabeth Ker.

Bessie Twinker was the mare bought by Isabella shortly after her arrival in Hilo to ride around the Big Island. As with Isabella's other horses, such as Birdie★ and Johnny Smoker, Bessie Twinker became an important character in the travel narratives Isabella published after her return home; in this case, *The Hawaiian Archipelago*.

Louis Courtier Biggs, colonial chaplain in Malacca at the time of Isabella's visit, was the author of *Hymns Ancient and Modern, for use in the services of the church* (1867) and *English Hymnology* (1873).

James Woodford Wheeler Birch, the first British Resident of Perak, was murdered at Pasir Salak in November 1875, sparking what has come to be known as the Perak War. Although Birch had been posted to Perak as an advisor, not a governor, through the Pangkor Engagement in 1874, he was hungry for real power and decided to whip Perak into shape by modernising the revenue system and abolishing slavery and debt bondage. In particular, Birch decided to to curb the personal extravagance of the Sultan Abdullah,★ who was squandering Perak's tax revenue upon himself. Birch's ideals may have been good, but his diplomacy was lacking. As Isabella wrote, 'Mr Birch knew no Malay, was violent, drank and did some very high handed things.' As a result, Sultan Abdullah sent a secret deputation to complain to the British Governor about Birch's behaviour in May 1875, but Governor Sir William Jervois★ sided with Birch. Tension mounted until July when Sultan Abdullah called the leading Malay chiefs to a meeting. Abdullah had decided that Birch must go, and if peaceful methods failed, it would be up to the Maharaja Lela★ to kill him. With the exception of Raja Muda Yusef,★ the senior chiefs agreed. Meanwhile, Jervois, like Birch not blessed with powers of diplomacy, threatened to dissolve the sultanate if Abdullah did not comply with Birch's demands to rule the state. A few weeks later, Birch followed Jervois' threats by forcing Abdullah to sign proclamations about a new revenue system that Abdullah had publicly opposed. In so doing, Birch humiliated Abdullah, and the crisis point was reached. Birch decided to post notices about the new revenue system himself in villages around Perak, but when he arrived in Pasir Salak, he was speared and then hacked to death in a bath house on the orders of the Maharaja Lela. After a brief war, and a longer trial, the Maharaja Lela was hanged, along with two followers, and his office abolished. For their complicity in Birch's murder, Sultan Abdullah, the Mantri of Larut, the Laksamana and the Shah Bandar were exiled to the Seychelles. (Other chiefs implicated in the plot were pardoned.) Sultan Abdullah was succeeded by Raja Muda Yusef, and James Birch by Sir Hugh Low.★ Today, a granite monument stands by the riverbank where Birch fell: 'Here at the fort of Datok Maharaja Lela the Honourable J.W. Birch, First British Resident of Perak, was killed in the performance of his duty on 2nd November 1875.'

Harriet Bird, who lived in London, was a first cousin of Isabella and Henrietta Bird. She died shortly after Isabella's husband, John Bishop,★ in 1886. Harriet was the daughter of either Henry or George Merttins Bird, both of whom served in India. The latter is most likely: when George Merttins Bird died in early manhood, his widow took her two children with her to live at Taplow Hill, the seat of Isabella's grandfather. Isabella spent most of her early years at Taplow, where she would have had the opportunity to become close friends with this cousin.

Birdie was the bay Indian pony 'with legs of iron, fast, enduring, gentle, and wise' that Isabella rode through the mountains of Colorado, beginning on October 20, 1873. So sagacious was the horse that she became a bona fide character in Isabella's story when the traveller wrote up her adventures in *A Lady's Life in the Rocky Mountains*.

Dr John Bishop was known in later life as 'Mr Bird', perpetually overshadowed by his wife's accomplishments. Born in Sheffield in 1841, Bishop had come to Edinburgh to study medicine in 1866, gaining his M.D. seven years later with a thesis that won a gold medal. He became fellow of the Royal College of Surgeons in 1876 and of the Royal College of Physicians in 1879. While still a studious young man in his early thirties, Bishop had met Henrietta, and through her, Isabella, who had just published *The Hawaiian Archipelago*. The doctor and the writer shared a passion for microscopes, and their friendship led Bishop to propose in the summer of 1877. Isabella seems to have accepted initially but later declined. When she did marry him in 1881, soon after the death of Henrietta, it seems to have been more a matter of loneliness than love. Bishop was 40, Isabella, 50, and she treated the wedding like a funeral, dressing in black. As she wrote to a friend on the eve of the event, 'I feel marriage a tremendous step to take without her and *with* her I could never have endured a third.' Bishop died five years later, in 1886.

Professor John Stuart Blackie and *Ella*, his wife, were close friends of the Birds in Scotland. 'The Pro', as he was called, was Chair of Greek at the University of Edinburgh. A charismatic teacher and prolific writer, he espoused the cause of educational reform and Gaelic studies, and almost single-handedly raised the £12,000 needed to endow Edinburgh's Chair of Celtic Literature. The author of *Lays and Legends of Ancient Greece* (1857) and *Mursa Burschicosa* (1869), he nonetheless found time to tutor Henrietta in Greek and seems to have formed a special bond with her. Ella Blackie was closer to Isabella.

Notes on People and Places

Mrs Brigham appears as 'Mrs Dexter' in *The Hawaiian Archipelago*. According to Isabella's published work, it was the illness of Mrs Brigham's son that compelled Isabella to land with them in Hawaii, despite her original plan to go straight from New Zealand to California. In her letters, however, Mrs Brigham appears not to have a son; instead, she has a husband who is piloting a steamer between the islands.

Sir James Brooke, Raja of Sarawak from 1841 to 1868, arrived in Singapore in 1839 intent on furthering European settlement in 'this Eden of the Eastern Wave'. Learning that the chief minister of the Sultan of Brunei, Pangiran Mura Hassim, was warring with rebel Sea Dyak tribes in Borneo, Brooke crushed the rebellion and was rewarded with Sarawak. This embarrassed the British government, which feared Dutch retaliation in response to Brooke's encroachment on its 'sphere of interest'; but Brooke's title to Sarawak delighted Singapore merchants. Brooke then spent several years exploring the interior of Sarawak; partially suppressing the practices of headhunting and piracy; and establishing a secure government. In 1845 Brooke's survival seemed tenuous when his patron, Pangiran Mura Hassim, and all his brothers were assassinated in a palace plot by the Sultan of Brunei. But Brooke, with powerful diplomatic skills, managed to convince the Sultan to cede him Sarawak in perpetuity, as well as the tiny island of Labuan.

John Buchanan (known as 'Mr Buchan' in *A Lady's Life in the Rocky Mountains*) became a permanent resident of Estes Park in 1874 by marrying the niece of Griff Evans,★ Mary Jane Roberts. This young lady seems to have attracted more notice than just Buchanan's: that same year, on her birthday, Jim Nugent★ named Mary's Lake in Estes Park in her honour. Roberts had arrived in the valley in June 1873, so she is probably the niece mentioned by Isabella in her letters.

Richard Hale Budd, described by Isabella as '1st commissioner of education and chief inspector of schools', was educated at Rugby under Thomas Arnold and at St John's College, Cambridge. He then emigrated to Australia in 1840 to become a sheep farmer. Farming proved unsuitable for his constitution, so Budd turned to private tutoring and eventually established his own school in Melbourne in 1849. When this, too, failed during the Gold Rush of 1854, Budd became an inspector of schools. His rise was steady but sure, and by 1872, when Isabella arrived, Budd had been Inspector General for nearly a decade. Just after her departure, however, the Secular Education Act of 1872 replaced his post. He spent his retirement teaching the classics to young ladies until his death in 1909.

Lady Angela Burdett Coutts was Sarawak's financier during the time that Sir James Brooke was alive. Burdett Coutts, a multimillionaire by the age of twenty-three, was one of the most influential philanthropists of the Victorian age. She lavished her inherited fortune on the underprivileged, building homes for abandoned women and prostitutes, and churches for the poor. Her ties to James Brooke had begun when they were children in Bath. In the 1850s and 1860s, Brooke sent Burdett Coutts flowers and verses, and in exchange she funded his kingdom – but they never married. In his will of 1862, Brooke had even left her Sarawak. Burdett Coutts publicly accepted this trust 'for and on account of the Government of Great Britain', using her leverage with Gladstone (over dinner) to have the first British Council appointed to the region in 1864. But shortly thereafter, James Brooke began to neglect her. Burdett Coutts told Brooke she no longer wanted his kingdom, and he made a new will that established his nephew, Charles Johnson Brooke, as his heir when he died in 1868. Their relationship is chronicled in *Rajah Brooke & Baroness Burdett Coutts: consisting of the letters from Sir James Brooke, first white rajah of Sarawak, to Miss Angela (afterwards Baroness) Burdett Coutts* (1935).

Bishop John Shaw Burdon came to China with the Church Missionary Society.* Originally posted to Zhejiang, Burdon moved to Beijing after the third Opium War in April 1862 to take up the post of Vicar to the British Embassy. In addition, he taught English at the Translation Bureau in Beijing under the Qing Foreign Ministry. He rented a house in the city centre to spread the gospel and set up a primary school. Twelve years later, Burdon was promoted to Bishop of the South China Diocese and took up his post in Hong Kong. During Isabella's tour of the Far East in 1878, she seems to have met the Burdons at Yokohama and during her stay in Hong Kong; later, in Scotland in 1882, Bishop Burdon and his wife stayed with Isabella in Edinburgh and Tobermory; and Isabella stayed with them again when she returned to Hong Kong in 1895. Until his death, John Shaw Burdon was the voice of the Anglican Church in South China.

William Byers arrived in Denver during the Gold Rush of 1859 with the express purpose of starting a newspaper. The result was *The Rocky Mountain News*, still the region's principal journal after more than a century. Byers used the *News* to promote Colorado as the country's most amazing territory. He publicised agricultural experiments, offered free seeds to anyone stopping by his office, gave away guidebooks, and eventually became not only Denver's premier newspaperman but president of its Chamber of Commerce. Had it not been for a widely publicised extra-marital affair, Byers might well have held political office. Instead, he became Grand High Priest of the Masons' Grand Chapter of Colorado.

Dr Adam Cairns, the churchman, was known in Australia for his fiery sermons against the 'wild passion' of Melbourne theatres and 'the witchery of female loveliness'. He believed in a literal interpretation of the Bible and was a profound Sabbatarian (i.e. someone who believes that no work should be performed on Sunday). In the 1850s, well before Isabella's visit, Cairns was instrumental in healing the schism in Melbourne's Presbyterian Church and creating a new body called the Presbyterian Church of Victoria. He was also active in recruiting clergymen from Scotland to preach in Victoria.

Mr Cameron ('the fiend'). Very little information on Cameron survives, aside from what Isabella tells us in her letters. From these we may deduce that Cameron knew Isabella's father in Birmingham, where Edward Bird was curate before moving to Wyton in Huntingdonshire in 1848. He seems to have shared the Bird family's radical Sabbatarian views that no work should be done on Sunday. We also know that Cameron, like the Birds, travelled in Scotland, perhaps for the same reason – an affection for the Scottish Presbyterian Church. Isabella mentions meeting Cameron's wife in Oban, where the Birds did not travel till the 1860s. She also comments that Mrs Cameron had 'reason' to dislike her but does not say why. Was Cameron the man who caused Isabella to suffer 'some sorrow, over which she brooded in the early fifties'? Was he the man who broke her heart? A definitive record of his identity is yet to be found. In 1874, James Balfour★ invited a Dr Andrew Cameron of Melbourne to edit a Presbyterian paper of his devising. Given the close ties Isabella witnessed between Cameron and Balfour, this may well be the gentleman concerned. Another possibility is James Cameron, a Presbyterian clergyman who emigrated from Scotland in 1853 – but to New South Wales. Many details of James Cameron's life dovetail with Isabella's description, and he had ties to Victoria's Presbyterian Church. (He even took his sickly wife and children home to Scotland in the 1860s – just in time to visit Oban to meet the Birds?) James Cameron, however, lived in Sydney, so any similarities are probably coincidental. As for 'the fiend', the phrase appears twice more in Isabella's correspondence, in comments she made in Colorado a few months later when she was struggling with her feelings for Jim Nugent.★ After the gunslinger expressed his passion for her at Estes Park, Isabella wrote to her sister, 'Thus again that hideous whisky fiend crosses my path.' Does this mean the difficulty with Cameron was that he drank? Or maybe he was 'fiendish' simply because he broke her heart? As Isabella wrote to Ella Blackie in 1879 when *A Lady's Life in the Rocky Mountains* was published, 'Don't let anybody think that I was in love with Mountain Jim for I have never been in love but once.' Perhaps Mr Cameron was the man.

George W. Campbell, whom Isabella proposed to visit in Ceylon, had been Acting Lieutenant Governor of Penang under Governor Sir Harry Ord. Although Colonel A.E.H. Anson had been appointed Penang's Lieutenant Governor in 1871, Campbell held his place throughout the early 1870s until Anson was ready to take up his post.

Robert Smith Candlish, Doctor of Divinity, joined with Thomas Chalmers★ in establishing the Free Church of Scotland. He was the author of *The Fatherhood of God* (1865) and *The Gospel of Forgiveness* (posthumous, 1878). His church in Edinburgh was located near the Bird family's flat at 3 Castle Terrace, where Henrietta and Isabella lived in the 1860s while their mother was still alive. Isabella published a brief sketch of his life in the March 1881 issue of *The Catholic Presbyterian Magazine*.

Carnarvon, 4th Earl, Henry Howard Molyneux Herbert, British statesman, tried to establish self-government in a handful of British overseas possessions. Under-secretary for the colonies in 1858–9, Lord Carnarvon served as Colonial Secretary in 1866–7 and 1874–8. He adamantly opposed the attempts made by Sir William Jervois★ and James Birch★ to annex the Malay States, and also resisted Australia's attempt to acquire New Guinea because the colonies refused to bear the expense. Earlier, he had overseen the passage of the British North American Act in 1867, which gave Canada its dominion status. He tried to do the same for South Africa in 1875 but failed. Perhaps most importantly, it was Lord Carnarvon who met secretly with Charles Stewart Parnell in 1885 to discuss the possibility of Irish Home Rule. Although he was unable to find a settlement acceptable to both Parnell and the British Prime Minister, he himself seems to have favoured making Ireland a self-governing province within a federated United Kingdom.

Thomas Chalmers formed the Free Church of Scotland in 1843, when 451 ministers walked out of the established church. A remarkable preacher, fund raiser, and advocate for the poor,

Chalmers served as an inspiration to Dr Adam Cairns,★ the leading Australian Free Churchman at the time of Isabella's visit.

Chalmers Manse in Melbourne was named after Thomas Chalmers.★

The *Chiefton*, along with the *Clansman* and the *Clydesdale*, was a steamer run by the Hutcheson Brothers off the north of Scotland. After Isabella began publishing articles in *The Leisure Hour*, *Good Words* and *The Family Treasury* in the early 1860s, she was given a free pass (for life) on these steamers as the Hutchesons' tribute to her literary gifts. Whether or not this family was related to the Hutcheson who rented the Birds their flat at Castle Terrace is unclear.

Ng Choy, the first Chinese to practise law in the British system, was born in Singapore and educated at St Paul's College, Hong Kong, and Lincoln's Inn. He was also the first Chinese to become a magistrate and to serve on Hong Kong's Legislative Council, to which he was appointed in 1880 by Sir John Pope-Hennessy.★ These years in Hong Kong were difficult for Ng Choy: in his youth he had become dangerously indebted through land speculation schemes, and he was only saved from financial ruin through his mother-in-law's generosity. Ng Choy resigned his seat on the Legislative Council in 1883 when his tenure expired, and he moved with his wife's family to Tientsin, where he joined the Chinese Imperial Service as legal advisor and interpreter. Over the next thirty years, Ng Choy became a powerful force in the Beijing-based administrations of the last Qing emperor and the new republic. Under his official name Wu Ting-fang, he became Minister of Foreign Affairs and Minister of Justice, as well as Foreign Minister to Spain, Peru, Mexico, Cuba and twice to the United States. Choy's years in America are chronicled in his book *America through the Spectacles of an Oriental Diplomat* (1914).

The Church Missionary Society was founded in 1799 by evangelical clergy as the Society for Missions in Africa and the East. It was to grow into one of the largest and most influential missions of the nineteenth century. Stressing biblical faith, personal conversion and piety, the Society employed in its heyday more than 1,300 missionaries, 375 local clergy and 1,000 local agents. It generated an annual income equivalent to £20 million and each year produced over half a million periodicals, many books and thousands of leaflets. (Isabella's *Heathen Claims and Christian Duty*, for example, was published by the organisation in 1893.) Converting the Chinese was of particular interest. After trying to penetrate the mainland for two decades without success, missionaries from every society were admitted to five ports in 1842 by the Treaty of Nanking that concluded the first Opium War. An anonymous gift of £7,000 enabled the Society to send two ministers, George Smith and Thomas McClatchie, in 1844. Five years later, George Smith became the first Bishop of Victoria, Hong Kong, with religious jurisdiction over China. When Isabella visited Canton in 1879, the Church Missionary Society's China Mission was well established.

Emily Clayton met Isabella when her mother, Dora Bird, sickened and died in 1866. Emily had nursed Dora through her last illness, and with the Kers (Elizabeth and Isabella) became Isabella Bird's closest friend. Stoddart describes Clayton as 'a woman of exceptionally bright intelligence' who was made extremely anxious by Isabella's adventures. She was sure Isabella was physically unfit, and would remonstrate with her when she returned to Scotland. Isabella laughingly called her 'Mother Hen'.

Reverend Titus Coan and *Fidelia*, his wife, settled on the Big Island in 1836, where they instigated a major religious revival that drew thousands of rural Hawaiians to Hilo in the late 1830s and early 1840s. Titus Coan's subsequent memoirs, *Life in Hawaii: An Autobiographical Sketch of Mission Life and Labors*, was a foundation work for all travellers to Hawaii at the turn of the century.

Captain James Cook, navigator and explorer with the Royal Navy, is most famous for his expeditions to the Pacific Ocean. He received his first commission in 1768 from the Royal Society to convey a team of scientists to Tahiti to observe the transit of the planet Venus across the sun. That done, in 1769 Cook was to find the so-called 'Terra Australis', or southern landmass. Striking south and southwest from Polynesia, Cook found and charted all of New Zealand, then crossed the Tasman Sea for Australia, surveying as he went. After stopping in Jakarta for supplies, he returned to Britain, where he was promoted to commander and presented to King George III. His next expeditions, in 1772 and 1775, enabled him to complete the first east–west circumnavigation in high latitudes. He charted Tonga and Easter Island; discovered New Caledonia and the South Sandwich Islands (now Hawaii). For these efforts, Cook was elected a Fellow of the Royal Society. In 1779, searching for the Northwest Passage, he was forced to land for repairs on what is now called the Big Island. His crew clashed with the Hawaiians, and in a brief fracas on the beach at Kelakekua, Cook was slain. A monument, the only bit of land in Hawaii owned by the British crown, today marks the place.

Daniel Dominic Daly was the nephew of Sir Dominic Daly, Governor of South Australia (1861–8). In the 1860s, he had been a surveyor accompanying Gryan's Expedition of 1869 to Palmerston (now Darwin). There, the young Daly met and married Harriet Douglas, eldest daughter of Captain William Bloomfield Douglas,★ first officially appointed Government Resident to Palmerston. When Douglas was forced to resign in 1873, Daly and his wife accompanied the family, first to Singapore and later to Selangor in Malaya, where Douglas made Daly his second-in-command, in charge of the Public Works, Survey and Lands Department. When Douglas was again forced to resign in 1882 because of corruption and mismanagement, Daly likewise resigned but quickly obtained employment with the North Borneo Company. Returning tit for tat, Daly hired Douglas, but both men were soon forced once more to resign because of corruption. Daly's wife, Harriet, seems to have been made of stronger metal: she recorded her experiences in Australia in *Digging, Squatting and Pioneer Life* (1887) and for years wrote a column from London for the *Sydney Morning Herald*.

Charles Darwin, naturalist, evolutionary theorist and author of *On the Origin of Species by Means of Natural Selection* (1859) and *The Descent of Man* (1871), corresponded with Isabella in 1877 when she wrote to ask for advice on whether she should journey to the Andes or to the mountains of northern Japan. Darwin, like Isabella, was an author published by John Murray, who seems to have put them in touch. Darwin had expertise in travelling through South America: his theories of natural selection had been developed during the five-year voyage of the HMS *Beagle*, which surveyed the east and west coasts of that continent before

321

sailing to the Pacific islands. (These experiences are chronicled in his *Journal of Researches into the Geology and Natural History of the Various Countries Visited by H.M.S. Beagle* in 1839 and *Zoology of the Voyage of H.M.S. Beagle* in 1843.) Although Darwin had enjoyed South America – braving his way through armed political rebellions, riding with the gauchos in Argentina and exploring the Andes himself – he did not consider the terrain suitable for a woman. His advice helped persuade Isabella that she would be better off going to Hokkaido.

Mr and *Mrs Dewy* are described by Isabella in *A Lady's Life in the Rocky Mountains* as 'a very intelligent and high-minded American couple . . . whose character, culture, and society I should value anywhere'. They were drawn to the Rocky Mountains because of Mr Dewy's 'pulmonary disease', presumably tuberculosis. They went riding with Isabella and read aloud to each other at night. They do not appear to have been permanent residents but rather travellers like herself.

Frederick Victor Dickins, pioneer of Japanese studies, was born in Manchester in 1838. After being educated in Paris, Dickins took his medical degree at London University. His first job was as a medical officer on a steamer bound for Australia; and in 1862 he joined the Royal Navy as a surgeon. Attached to the HMS *Euryalis*, Dickins was stationed in the East Indies and China before arriving in Japan, where he resigned his commission. He explained to Ernest Satow that he had 'fallen in love with things Japanese in the early '60s', and in 1865 he produced the first scholarly translations of Japanese literature into English. He was also the first scholar in any language to write about the printmaker Hokusai. Abandoning his medical career, Dickins returned to London to study law at the Middle Temple. He was admitted to the bar, married, and returned to Japan in 1871, where he lived for the next eight years. Dickins wrote, with Stanley Lane-Poole, *The Life of Sir Harry Parkes*★ (1894), as well as *Primitive and Medieval Japanese Texts* (1906). With Satow, he was a founding member of the Asiatic Society of Japan.

Benjamin Disraeli, British statesman and novelist, was twice Prime Minister, in 1868 and again between 1874 and 1880. In his twenties, Disraeli had toured the Near East, returning to London in 1832 to enter politics. One goal among many was to model the British Empire to a degree after Turkey's. Whether or not he succeeded, Disraeli's approach to imperialism was decidedly 'oriental' by the standards of the time: purchasing the Suez Canal in 1875; naming Victoria 'Empress of India' in 1876; and protecting Turkey in the Russo-Turkish Wars. Such actions, combined with Disraeli's Jewish heritage, prompted many Victorians to believe, like Isabella, that 'Disraeli is the only public man in England who knows anything of Oriental feeling at all.' This led him to be loved and hated in almost equal measures. After the Conservatives were defeated in the general election of 1880, Disraeli retired to his home at Hughendon to finish his last novel, *Endymion*, shortly before he died in April 1881. Soon after he was buried in the family vault, Queen Victoria came to lay a wreath upon his grave. Among Disraeli's many novels were *The Wondrous Tale of Alroy* (1833); *Coningsby; or the New Generation* (1844); *Sybil; or the Two Nations* (1845); and *Tancred, or the New Crusade* (1847).

Gustave Doré, French printmaker, was the premier book illustrator of the late nineteenth century. Employing more than forty woodcutters in his studio, he produced over ninety illustrated books, including the *Oeuvres de Rabelais*, the *Contes Drolatiques* of Balzac, and the *Inferno* of Dante. He also painted grand historical canvases in the manner of Delacroix. Isabella would have known him best for his woodcuts for her favourite book, Milton's *Paradise Lost*.

Captain William Bloomfield Douglas, a career officer with the British Colonial Service, had entered the Royal Navy at the age of twenty to serve during the first Opium War. He resigned a few months later, in 1842, to fight pirates in Sarawak with Sir James Brooke,★ a relative by marriage, and thereafter joined the Colonial Office. Ultimately Douglas was to serve as an administrator in China, Australia and Singapore before being appointed Resident of Selangor in 1876 by Governor William Jervois.★ He held this post until 1882, when he was forced to resign to avoid an investigation into corruption, incompetence and financial mismanagement. (Douglas had also been forced to resign his post at Darwin, Australia in 1873. There, he had squandered money; ignored official instructions; quarrelled with his subordinates; failed to control a gold rush; and was suspected of irregularities concerning his own investments. He also had to be warned about his drinking.) In Selangor, Douglas kept away from the local population in a heavily guarded residency, and was continually on the lookout for assassination attempts. He brutally executed a number of criminals at the scenes of their crimes, and more than once he handed the reins of government to his son-in-law, D.D. Daly,★ who seems to have been possessed of a vicious temper. On the bright side, however, it was Douglas's idea to shift Selangor's capital from Klang to Kuala Lumpur before he joined the British North Borneo Company.

Nathaniel Dunlop was an influential Glasgow shipping magnate and author of *An Analysis of Foundered and Missing Ships* (1882). Isabella approached him in the early 1860s to arrange for crofters from the Western Highlands to emigrate to Canada. Dunlop wrote that Isabella 'astonished me by her energy and her capacity in making arrangements for the conveyance of the emigrants'. He agreed to help, and Isabella placed all her emigrants on his ships between 1862 and 1866, when the illness she suffered after her mother's death forced her to abandon the scheme.

Dunraven, 4th Earl, Windham Thomas Wyndham-Quin, was the master of 40,000 acres in Ireland and Wales in the 1870s. Irish-born and Oxford-educated, Lord Dunraven had a passion for adventure. Just out of university, he had become a war correspondent in Abyssinia for the *Daily Telegraph*, and during the Franco-Prussian War he had reported from the front. Soon afterwards, the Earl accompanied Henry Morton Stanley★ on his search for Dr Livingstone★ in Africa, where he developed a taste for big-game hunting that led him to Colorado in 1868. Five years later, for a sum rumoured to be between $5,000 and $10,000, he purchased Estes Park from Griff Evans★ as his private game reserve, where he hunted with Buffalo Bill. For the purpose of this story, Dunraven is most significant for the part he played in the murder of Jim Nugent.★ The American trapper had opposed the Earl's purchase of Estes Park and refused to sell his own claim, which straddled the only way into the park. Eventually Jim refused to let Lord Dunraven or his associates travel through the pass without a fight. Tensions ran high, and Griff Evans shot Jim on June 29, 1874, at the provocation of one of Dunraven's agents, William Haigh.★ Though Dunraven was not present during the gunfight, in the public eye he was held responsible for Jim's death. He nonetheless retained Estes Park as a private hunting lodge until 1907, when he sold it to F.O. Stanley of Newton, Massachusetts, for $75,000.

Mr Dykes was possibly Charles Dyte, the original representative for Ballarat East, who had just been voted out of office at the time of Isabella's visit. Parliamentary records from the 1860s indicate that Dyte and Balfour worked closely together, proposing legislation in common and voting alike. Possibly Isabella met or heard about Mr Dyte from the Balfours or Cairns, whose company she shared in Melbourne. It is also possible, of course, that Mr Dykes was a different man.

The Edinburgh Medical Missionary Society, founded in 1841, is the oldest mission in the western hemisphere devoted to healing the sick. It was also the favourite charity of Isabella and Henrietta Bird, and John Bishop,★ who were active in promoting its interests in Scotland. In her later years, Isabella established hospitals around the world to Henrietta's and John's memory through the EMMS. In particular, she wished to establish one in Nazareth, to fulfil John Bishop's dying wish. Although Isabella failed, the EMMS had actually owned and operated a hospital in Nazareth since 1861. In the nineteenth century, the EMMS also established missions in India, Nepal, China and Southern Africa.

Sam Edwards was the partner of Griff Evans★ at Estes Park. In *A Lady's Life in the Rocky Mountains*, Isabella described Sam Edwards as 'tall, thin, and condemnatory looking; keen, industrious, saving, grave, a teetotaller, grieved for all reasons at Evans's follies, and rather grudging; as naturally unpopular as Evans is popular; a "decent man", who, with his industrious wife, will certainly make money as fast as Evans loses it'. Apparently a veteran of the Union Army during the Civil War, he told Isabella stories of his march through Georgia with General William T. Sherman, who famously burned nearly every city in his wake between Atlanta and the sea in order to ensure victory for President Lincoln.

Reverend Ernest John Eitel quickly became one of the nineteenth century's most noted sinologists after arriving in China with the London Missionary Society★ in 1865. He was the author of *Three Lectures on Buddhism* (1871); *Feng-Shui; or, the Rudiments of Natural Science in China* (1873); *A Chinese Dictionary in the Cantonese Dialect* (1877); *A Handbook of Chinese Buddhism* (1881); and *Europe in China: The History of Hongkong from the beginning to the year 1882* (1883). Both teacher and preacher, Eitel was Hong Kong's Inspector of Schools between the years 1878 and 1897.

Emily. See Emily Clayton.

Queen Emma was the wife of King Kamehameha IV of Hawaii, also known as Alexander Liholiho. Although she was of royal Hawaiian blood, Emma had been adopted at birth by an English doctor and his half-English wife, and raised in the Church of England. As queen, Emma, together with her husband, established the Anglican Church of Hawaii. In return, Queen Victoria became the godmother of their only child, Albert, who died in 1862, just a year before King Liholiho's death and the ascension of Kamehameha V to the throne. In 1874, on the death of King Lunalilo,★ Emma campaigned for the throne herself. She was narrowly defeated in a popular election by David Kalakaua.

Griff Evans, originally from Wales, started 'squatting' in Estes Park in 1867 with his wife, Jane, and their first three children. By the time Isabella visited in 1873, Evans had turned Estes' two log cabins into a profitable hotel where he entertained guests, while his wife and children resided in nearby Denver. Isabella described Griff Evans as 'hospitable, careless, reckless, jolly, social, convivial, peppery, good natured, "nobody's enemy but his own" . . . He is a splendid shot, an expert and successful hunter, a bold mountaineer, a good rider, a capital cook, and a generally "jolly fellow".' The only trouble was that Evans drank, and when intoxicated his temper was hot. Ultimately, this combination proved fatal for Jim Nugent,★ otherwise known as Rocky Mountain Jim. Evans shot him on June 29, 1874, shortly after Isabella's departure, in what seems to have been a quarrel over the purchase of Estes Park by Lord Dunraven.★ Jim's cabin in Muggins Gulch straddled the only way in or out of the park, and Jim refused to sell. On the day in question, Jim was riding his horse past Evans's lodge when William Haigh★ called out to Evans that 'Jim's on the shoot!' Evans, who was asleep inside and possibly drunk, woke up with a start, grabbed his rifle and came out firing a round of buckshot called 'blue whistlers'. Rather than hitting Jim directly, the buckshot ricocheted off a nearby wagon wheel and came to lodge at the back of Jim's skull. Jim hung on for two months, calling Evans a murderer in the *Fort Collins Standard*. Evans was arrested but acquitted on the grounds of self defence. He later became the proprietor of the St Vrain Hotel in Longmount.

General Ulysses S. Grant, commander of the Union Army during the Civil War, was elected the eighteenth president of the United States in 1869. His supporters hoped he would end the turmoil that had marked the tenure of Andrew Johnson, who had taken office without election on Lincoln's assassination, and faced the nation's first impeachment trial. Instead, Grant was criticised for simony and corruption, particularly after he was seen with two known gold speculators, Jay Gould and James Fisk. The re-election campaign in 1872 to which Isabella refers was fierce, and the outcome was by no means certain.

Archdeacon John Henry Gray had lived twenty-three years in China when he decided to return to England, 'the land of our nativity', in 1875, seemingly to find a wife. Author of *China, a History of the Laws, Manners and Customs of the People* (1878) and *A Journey Round the World in the Years 1875–1876–1877* (1879), Gray was perhaps most famous for his travel narrative, *Walks in Canton* (1875), to which Isabella refers in *The Golden Chersonese*. Gray returned with his new bride to Canton in 1877, but they stayed for little more than a year, chronicled in Mrs Gray's own book, *Fourteen Months in Canton* (1880). The pair departed in 1878, a few months before Isabella's arrival.

William Lowthian Green was no average vulcanologist. Just before the publication of his study of Mauna Loa in 1875 – *Vestiges of the Molten Globe, as exhibited in the figure of the earth, volcanic action, and physiography* – the British-born Green abandoned science for politics to become Minister of Foreign Affairs (later Minister of Finance) under King David Kalakaua. Over the next fifteen years, Green played a major role in Hawaiian politics. He was a member of the all-white Hawaiian League that forced Kalakaua to sign the 'bayonet constitution' in 1887, which gave voting rights to non-citizens by raising the income and property requirements. Under this document, Hawaiian islanders were effectively disenfranchised and Pearl Harbor was granted to the United States government. The Hawaiian

League further forced Kalakaua to adopt Green as his premier, thereby making Green the most powerful man in Hawaii.

Dr Thomas Guthrie was a prominent social advocate in Scotland and a close friend of the Birds. For forty years, he campaigned tirelessly for improved working-class housing, temperance and schools for the poor. In 1847 he published his most influential work, *Plea for Ragged Schools, or Prevention is Better than Cure.* Then, with the help of the *Edinburgh Review* and *Sunday Magazine*, he raised enough money to start a series of these 'ragged schools', where children were fed, clothed and given vocational training. Isabella wrote an article on his schools in *The Leisure Hour* in 1861. Guthrie died in 1873, while Isabella was in Hawaii.

William Haigh, the 'luxurious Englishman' who appears as 'Mr Fodder' in *A Lady's Life in the Rocky Mountains*, acted as the agent of Lord Dunraven★ in acquiring the property of Estes Park. In the process, he quarrelled with Jim Nugent,★ who refused to sell his land in Muggins Gulch, and Haigh seems to have instigated the trapper's murder at Griff Evans's★ hands. That day, Haigh was sitting outside the lodge at Estes Park when he saw Jim riding up with his dog. He yelled inside to Evans that Jim was 'on the shoot', adjuring Evans to get his gun. According to newspaper accounts, Haigh even told Evans to 'give him the other barrel' after the first shot had missed. This second shot, which lodged in Jim's brain, proved fatal. For her part, Isabella was tormented by the knowledge that Haigh and Jim had first met each other through her agency, when she introduced them at Namaqua as she boarded her stagecoach. In *A Lady's Life in the Rocky Mountains*, Isabella writes that the last thing she saw in Colorado was the two men shaking hands.

Dr Charles Handfield Jones was a physician at St Mary's Hospital in London in 1872 and the author of the influential article 'On the Morbid Changes in the Mucous Membrane of the Stomach'. A specialist in neuralgia, Handfield Jones was consulted by Isabella specifically with regards to her nervous condition, and it was he who recommended her journey to Australia.

Dr William Hanna was a leader of the Free Church of Scotland in Edinburgh in the 1860s, where he developed a close relationship with the Birds. In her biography of Isabella, Anna Stoddart comments that she 'owed much' to Dr Hanna, 'and warmly acknowledged his help in the things of the Spirit. He could divine her perplexities almost before she admitted them, and his courageous treatment of the Life of lives . . . made his faith a fortification of her own.' This 'Life of lives' was Thomas Chalmers,★ the founder of the Free Church and Hanna's father-in-law, whose biographer he had become in 1847. In addition to the *Life of Chalmers*, Hanna was also known for *The Passion Week* (1866) and *Letters of Thomas Erskine of Linlathan* (1877). He was a frequent contributor to *The Sunday Magazine* and *Good Words*. He died shortly after Isabella's return from Japan, in 1882.

Mr Hayward, Superintendant of Police in Sungei Ujong, is described by Isabella in *The Golden Chersonese* as 'the first European to come up here'. Hayward had 'acted as guide to the troops during the war, and afterwards disarmed the population'.

Colonel Heath, an officer in the Confederate Army and amateur sculptor, aroused Isabella's ire partly because of her distaste for the Confederacy at large. The Bird family was closely related by blood to William Wilberforce 'the Liberator', who in 1807 had succeeded in making British involvement with the American slave trade illegal. Confirmed abolitionists, the Birds supported the Union during the Civil War, and would be unlikely to regard any Confederate with affection.

Reverend A. Henry is described by Isabella in *The Golden Chersonese* as an American missionary who had preached, in 1881 alone, '190 times in Chinese, and 5 times in English; held 52 Bible class meetings, and 13 communion services; baptized 45 adults and 8 children; travelled on mission work by boat 2540 miles, by chair 80 miles, and on foot 670 miles; visited 280 different towns and villages, and distributed 14,000 books. His life is a happy combination of American energy and Christian zeal.'

Sir Stephen Hill, Governor of Newfoundland from 1869 to 1876, served as Governor of the Gold Coast (1851–4), Sierra Leone (1854–62), and the Leeward Islands and Antigua (1863–9) before moving to North America. He had strongly supported confederation with Canada, and was disappointed when the election of 1869 gave the anti-confederates a majority in Newfoundland's legislature. In fact, so convinced was Hill that Newfoundland had no future without a confederacy that he even went so far as to demand that the Colonial Office impose it forcibly. The Queen declined, and Hill retired. He moved to London in 1876. His daughter married the colonial administrator Captain E.W. Shaw.★

Sir Joseph Dalton Hooker, botanist, explorer and friend of Charles Darwin,★ travelled extensively in the Middle East, India, the United States and the South Pacific, visiting Borneo, New Zealand, Antarctica and the Himalayas. Hooker spent his travels sketching, journalising and collecting plants to bring home for the Royal Botanic Gardens at Kew, where he was assistant director (1855–65) and director (1865–85). Hooker was the author of *The Botany of the Antarctic Voyage of H.M. Discovery* (1844–60); *Rhododendrons of Sikkim Himalya* (1849); *Handbook of New Zealand Flora* (1864); *The Flora of British India* (1872–97); and *Journal of a Tour in Morocco and the Great Atlas* (1878). His last major botanical expedition was to the Rocky Mountains in 1877. In correspondence at this time, he gave Isabella advice on her travels in Asia as she advised his in Colorado.

Alexander Hunt was the fourth territorial Governor of Colorado serving from 1867 to 1869. He had moved from California to Cherry Creek, Colorado, during the Gold Rush after losing all his money in the Wall Street Panic of 1857. As judge of the territory's Vigilante Committee, he had cleansed the community of undesirables by hanging them. Hunt's executions were rewarded with a presidential appointment as United States Marshal, and later he was appointed as Governor of the Colorado Territory. Hunt's administration was dominated by conflicts between the white settlers and Native Americans, principally the Utes.★ By 1867 tensions were running so high that Central City started offering cash for Ute scalps, and many settlers feared for their lives. To broker peace, Hunt brought Ute chiefs and President Andrew Johnson together in Denver in 1868; but Johnson reneged on his land deal, thereby infuriating the Utes.★ Travelling from camp to camp to talk to Ute chiefs, Hunt defused the situation only to discover on his return to Denver that he had been relieved of his duties by newly elected President Ulysses S. Grant,★ who wanted to establish a close friend, Edward McCook, in the office. As Isabella shows, in 1873 Hunt was still considered by many to be the rightful governor, and he used his power to help develop the Denver Pacific Railroad and the Kansas Pacific Railroad. He died in 1894 and is buried in the Congressional Cemetery in Washington, DC.

Dr Francis Blake Hutchinson and *Alice*, his wife, lived with their four children and Swiss hired girl near the mouth of the Big Thompson Canyon at the time of Isabella's visit. In *A Lady's Life in the Rocky Mountains*, Isabella calls them 'the Hughes'. The son of a London physician in a large practice, Dr Hutchinson had emigrated to Colorado in the hopes of curing some 'pulmonary disease'. However, neither the doctor nor his wife seems to have had much sense, and Isabella comments that they 'were cheated in land, goods, oxen, everything, and, to the discredit of the settlers, seemed to be regarded as fair game'. Shortly after Isabella's departure, Alice died giving birth to their fifth child. Francis then married the Swiss nanny, Emma Herzogg, and decamped with the whole family for Hawaii (this last at Isabella's advice). There, he was appointed port physician as well as physician of the Insane Asylum in Honolulu, where the family lived until 1882. They then emigrated to New Zealand, where Dr Hutchinson was licensed as a Lay Preacher in the Anglican Church; and again to Switzerland, where he died in 1910, aged seventy-two.

James Innes served in Sarawak before taking up the post of Collector of Revenue and Magistrate in Selangor, which made him the second-in-command of Captain William Bloomfield Douglas★ at Kuala Langat. Although Douglas preferred to entrust duties to his son-in-law, D.D. Daly,★ Innes kept his post from 1876 to 1878 and again from 1880 to 1882, when he resigned. These years have been chronicled by James's wife, Emily Innes, in *The Chersonese with the Gilding Off* (1886), in which the couple emerge as rather sensitive and officious, inclined to blame the Colonial Office for leaking roofs and unfavourable foreign exchange. In return, the Colonial Office reported that James Innes was 'a disreputable officer', expressing doubt about his claims that he had no choice but to reign because he had refused to condone wrong behaviour. According to Innes, Captain Douglas had mismanaged the land office and permitted wholesale corruption by his inferiors. While this was true, Innes went too far when he attempted to implicate Sir Hugh Low,★ accusing him of abetting the practice of slavery in Perak when Low was actually trying to abolish it. When Innes's threats for compensation achieved no results, his wife wrote her book. Nominally shaped as a rebuttal to the romanticism of Isabella's *Golden Chersonese*, it was in fact a last-ditch attempt to wrest a pension for James from the Colonial Office. It didn't succeed.

E.E. Isemonger, Police Magistrate of Province Wellesley at the time of Isabella's visit, had entered the junior ranks of the Civil Service in 1856, specialising in audit work. He was transferred to the Straits Settlements in 1867 where he slowly rose through the ranks. Roughly the same age as Sir William Maxwell,★ Isemonger evidently married Maxwell's sister, the daughter of Sir Peter Benson Maxwell.★ He retired in 1891 as Resident Councillor of Malacca.

William Jackson was organist and choir master at Exeter Cathedral from 1777 until his death in 1803. Best known for *Twelve Songs* (1755) and *Twelve Canzonets for Two Voices* (1770), Jackson also composed a setting for 'Te Deum Laudamus', or 'We Praise Thee, O God', that achieved immense popularity in the Victorian church. An amateur painter, Jackson was friends with Thomas Gainsborough; and he wrote books such as *Thirty Letters on Various Subjects* (1782), *Observations on the Present State of Music in London* (1791), and an autobiography, *The Four Ages* (1798).

Jardine, Matheson & Co., founded in 1832 by British merchants William Jardine and James Matheson, was initially engaged in the opium trade. Today, it has the longest continuous history of any western business connected with China. By 1879, when Isabella visited Hong Kong, Jardines' interests included wharves, warehouses, cotton mills, mining, and a newly opened ice factory. The company had just established the first railroad in China – from Shanghai to Wuhan – and the first inter-office telegraphs. Later, in the 1890s, Jardine's started the Star Ferry Company and Hongkong Land, which reclaimed wetlands in Victoria Harbour to create the Central Business District. Its subsidiaries were based all over Asia, and its interests protected by British diplomats like Sir Harry Parkes.*

Sir William Francis Drummond Jervois served as Governor of the Straits Settlements in 1875–7. Born in 1821, Jervois had been educated at Gosport and Woolwich military academies prior to being commissioned in the Royal Engineers. He was a career officer with the British Empire, serving in South Africa, Bermuda, India, Hong Kong and Canada before his appointment to the governorship of the Straits Settlements in 1875. Unfortunately, such breadth of experience did little to make Jervois diplomatic, and he spent his time in Malaya engaged in a tug-of-war between the British Government, the British Residents and the Malay Rajas. Most of all, Jervois wanted to enforce direct government by the three British Residents established in Selangor, Perak and Sungei Ujong, thereby annexing Malaya in practice if not in law. Such actions horrified the Earl of Carnarvon,* particularly when they led to the murder of James Birch* in 1875 and the ensuing Perak War. Jervois's attempts to suppress the rebellion were clumsy and expensive, though ultimately successful. To Lord Carnarvon, he sought to justify his actions by arguing that he had encouraged Birch to seize power in Perak in order to carry out the unwritten intentions of the Pangkor Engagement. Carnarvon responded by calling a halt to further expansion in the Malay States and prohibiting any form of direct rule. Jervois's appointment was terminated in 1877 and he was transferred to a defence advisory position for the governments of Australia, New Zealand and their neighbouring islands. After a few unfruitful years, Jervois was named Governor of South Australia and later Governor of New Zealand. He died in 1897.

Mr Kavanagh ('Mr Kavan' in Isabella's book) was a miner and deer hunter. His name seems to have been more properly spelt 'Cavanaugh', as a man of that name is listed as a resident of Estes Park at the time of Isabella's visit. In fact, on November 23, 1873, when Isabella was snowbound with Mr Kavanagh in Evans's cabin, the *Denver Tribune* ran an article that 'Cavanaugh, of Estes Park, killed two deer, and broke the leg of a third one, at one shot.'

Elizabeth Ker (Bessie), who became Isabella's executrix, played a crucial role in preserving letters, manuscripts and photos of the traveller. Unfortunately, Bessie's letters to John

Murray V show that she often felt overwhelmed by her duty and sometimes lost important documents, such as Isabella's letters about her pilgrimage to Sinai. On September 19, 1912, Bessie deposited a trunk with the Murrays containing letters and other *objets d'art* that had belonged to Isabella. Similar shipments were sent to the Royal Geographical Society, the Scottish Geographical Society, and Christie's. What happened to Henrietta's letters, diaries and sketches – loaned to Anna Stoddart in 1904 to provide material for her biography – is unknown. Possibly they remained with Bessie's papers until her death in 1915, and were then disposed of by Bessie's executrix, Robina.★

William Keswick and *Francis Bulkeley Johnson* were powerful members of the trading firm Jardine, Matheson & Co.★ In 1879, at the time of Isabella's visit, William Keswick was forty-five. The great-nephew of the firm's founder, he had arrived in China in 1855, been a partner since 1862, and opened Jardine's first Japanese branch in 1859. (This, incidentally, was not only the first Japanese office for Jardine's but for any western business, as Keswick had acquired Lot. No. 1 in the first Yokohama land sale of 1859.) A man of vision, Keswick was entranced by the era's technological progress and the possibilities it offered. Bulkeley Johnson wrote in 1877 of 'negotiations Keswick was making with Edison for the patent rights in the Far East of the light bulb'. Bulkeley Johnson was not impressed, and in due course he retired. Keswick stayed on, overseeing Jardine's business first in Hong Kong and later in London, where he became a Conservative MP in 1898. Keswick died in his sleep in 1912. Both men served on Hong Kong's Legislative Council.

Miss Kingsley is often identified by Bird scholars as the explorer Mary Kingsley, who achieved fame in the 1890s with her travels in West Africa, but is actually Mary's cousin, Rose. (In 1873 Mary Kingsley was a little girl of eleven who had never been to Colorado.) Eldest daughter of the evangelical writer Charles Kingsley, Rose had travelled to the territory in November 1871 to join her brother Maurice, who was treasurer of the Colorado Springs Company, started by General William Jackson Palmer.★ In 1874 Rose Kingsley published an account of her travels, *South by west, or winter in the Rocky Mountains and spring in Mexico*, which included columns that had originally appeared in *Out West*.

Colonel Kittridge appears to have been yet another Civil War veteran from the Union Army who had travelled to Colorado for his health in the 1870s. On Kittridge's advice, Isabella stayed briefly with his wife at their cabin at Oil Creek, describing it as 'very small and lonely, and the life a hard grind for an educated and refined woman' in *A Lady's Life in the Rocky Mountains*.

Kota Lama, the village where Isabella was taken by Mr Keyt, had found its place on the imperial map through the murder of Major H.L. Hawkins, leader of a search party to capture the Maharaja Lela★ after the murder of James Birch★ in 1875. Hawkins was speared in a surprise attack on January 4, 1876, while his staff and escort were busy disarming the Malays. No one else was hurt. Isabella appears to have confused this village with Pasir Salak, where Birch himself was killed.

Tunku Kudin was the Sultan of Kedah at the time of Isabella's visit; she mistakenly refers to him as the 'Rajah of Quedoh'. Today, Kudin is remembered principally for his complaint in 1896, after the establishment of the Federated Malay States, that 'my country has been bought and sold like a buffalo'.

Maharaja Lela, one of Perak's eight major chiefs, became famous shortly before Isabella's visit to Malaya as the assassin of the first British Resident, James Birch.★ The Maharaja had not been present at the signing of the Pangkor Engagement that established Birch as Resident of Perak, and he had never agreed to its terms. Moreover, as the traditional role of the Maharaja Lela was to execute anyone who infringed loyalty in Perak, it made sense that he was the other chiefs' choice as assassin when they decided that Birch must go. As a result, in September 1875 Lela built a bamboo stockade around his house in Pasir Selak. When Birch sent envoys demanding that Lela pull it down, he reportedly replied, 'You can go back and tell Mr Birch to get all the troops he can from England and I will fight.' In November, when Birch travelled from village to village posting notices to enforce the collection of revenues, the Maharaja Lela seized his opportunity. Having deputed the actual posting of notices in Lela's village of Pasir Selak to his interpreter, Birch went down to the bathhouse for a swim, guarded by a Sikh sentry. While Birch bathed, a fracas broke out around the interpreter. Eight men killed the subaltern while the Sikh sentry speared Birch through the bathhouse walls. When Birch's body surfaced in the river, another man hacked at it until the corpse sank to the bottom. The Maharaja Lela then provided his followers with a huge feast of buffalo meat; sent the women and children into the jungle; and prepared for the oncoming war. Initially Lela rebuffed the British, but within a week his stockade was destroyed and Pasir Selak burnt to the ground. Although Lela and his followers were never apprehended, he surrendered to the Maharaja Johore in July 1876 in order to restore peace to Perak. He was tried and hanged for his complicity on January 20, 1877.

George Henry Lewes, editor, author and literary critic, is remembered today principally for his alliance with Mary Ann Evans (alias George Eliot), one of Isabella's favourite novelists. Author of *Comte's Philosophy of the Sciences* (1853), *Life and Works of Goethe* (1855) and *The Physiology of Common Life* (1859), Lewes was a frequent contributor to journals like *The Leader* and was for many years the editor of *The Fortnightly Review*. Unable to marry Evans because he was already married to a woman who had abandoned him, Lewes lived with her as husband and wife until his death in 1878.

J. Elsom Liller, a native of Chester, emigrated to Colorado Springs in 1872 at the writer Charles Kingsley's behest in order to become the first editor of *Out West*. It was in this journal that Isabella published her famous account of ascending Long's Peak with Jim Nugent.★ Overall, however, this little magazine was not a success, and its founder, General William Jackson Palmer,★ shut it down in 1873 and reopened it as the *Colorado Springs Gazette*. Liller, widely disliked for his crusade against whisky in the territory, did not fare much better. He died of an overdose of laudanum in 1875.

David Livingstone, Scottish missionary and explorer, played a major role in defining nineteenth-century European attitudes about Africa. Joining the London Missionary Society★ in 1838, Livingstone set sail for South Africa in 1840 and arrived in Cape Town the following year. Over the next three decades, Livingstone established a reputation as a dedicated Christian, fearless explorer and committed abolitionist. He assisted in the discovery of Lake Ngami in 1849, for which he was awarded a gold medal by the Royal Geographical Society; and he explored the region around the Zambezi River in the 1850s, when he discovered and named the Victoria Falls in 1855. After publishing *Missionary*

331

Travels and Researches in South Africa in 1857, and *Narrative of an Expedition to the Zambesi and Its Tributaries* in 1865, Livingstone began his quest to discover the source of the Nile. En route Livingstone placed Lake Mweru and Lake Bangweulu on European maps, but the source of the Nile itself eluded him. He pressed on into the interior, further than any European had gone before. By this point his health was imperilled, and it was a sick and failing man that Henry Morton Stanley★ found in Ujiji on the shores of Lake Tanganyika in 1871. Stanley's entreaties to Livingstone to return to England and give up his quest failed. Discovering the Nile's source had become for Livingstone an *idée fixe*, and he died trying, at Chitambo, in what is now Zambia, in 1873. Like all readers, Isabella seems to have been quite taken by Livingstone's heroism. In 1876 she was active in establishing the National Livingstone Memorial in Edinburgh – a college for the training of medical missionaries and nurses to help the poor in Africa. In the late 1870s Isabella had also gone to John Murray's in London to read Livingstone's journals in manuscript, which had been published as *The Last Journals of David Livingstone* in 1874.

The London Missionary Society was founded in 1795, largely as a result of the deeds of William Carey. In 1792 Carey had been inspired by his own pamphlet *An Enquiry into the Obligations of Christians to Use Means for the Conversion of Heathens* to establish a Baptist Society for Propagating the Gospel Among the Heathens. He sailed with a fellow missionary for India; their work attracted much attention in religious circles, leading to the creation of the LMS. Although its first efforts failed disastrously (a ship of missionaries sailing to Tahiti in 1799 was captured by pirates not once but twice), the LMS did spearhead the introduction of the Anglican Church into South Africa, Madagascar, India and the islands of the South Pacific. With regards to China, the LMS entered with the other missions in 1842, after the Treaty of Nanking, placing missions in Shanghai, Amoy and Hong Kong. Others were established after the third Opium War ended in 1860. The last missions the LMS started in China were in Canton and Beijing; the delay was caused by these cities' open hostility against the British, which was no longer as evident by the time Isabella visited in 1878.

Sir Hugh Low began his diplomatic career under Sir James Brooke★ in Sarawak in the 1840s, where he spent an uneventful thirty years as a civil servant on the small island of Labuan. (Sir John Pope-Hennessy,★ Governor of Hong Kong, also served on Labuan, where he met and married Low's half-Malay daughter, Kitty.) Such a long time in a small place meant that Low was a 'throwaway officer' – a man who had never managed to advance – when he was assigned to Perak in 1877, two years after the murder of James Birch★ and about a year and a half before Isabella's arrival. Perak brought out all of Low's talents – his fluency in Malay, his finesse as a diplomat – and for the next twelve years Low overcame immense political and personal odds to emerge as the Malay States' foremost administrator. He created a state council that included all the leading Malay, Chinese and British dignitaries; paid off the state's staggering debt in less than six years; developed a communications infrastructure that opened up Perak to the outside world; and encouraged the process of slavery to atrophy by dictating that everyone born in the state was born free. Likewise, Low's approach to environmental conservation was farsighted: Perak was the first Malay state to issue laws governing water supplies, forestry and wildlife. He also introduced the cultivation of rubber trees to the Peninsula, which was ultimately to transform its trade. By the time he retired in 1889, Perak was at peace with a thriving economy that attracted thousands of immigrants. For his services, Low was knighted and granted a generous pension that enabled him to spend his remaining years in Italy. He died in Alassio in 1905.

King William Charles Lunalilo was Hawaii's first elected but shortest-lived monarch, reigning for only twelve months between 1873 and 1874. Handsome, well educated and just, Lunalilo enjoyed overwhelming popularity with the Hawaiian people, but his short reign was plagued by American carpetbagging and the growing scourge of leprosy that was wiping out the native Hawaiian Islanders. Lunalilo succumbed to depression and alcoholism, and died in his Waikiki home, aged thirty-nine. In *The Hawaiian Archipelago*, Isabella calls Lunalilo 'the equal of Queen Victoria'.

Lieutenant Governor Rufus Lyman was the son of Sarah and David Lyman, the first missionaries to arrive in Hilo, in 1832. Rufus Lyman had previously worked as an overseer on the Onomea Plantation run by Samuel Austin;★ later he married into the Hawaiian-Chinese community of Hilo, enabling him to unite these groups with his own circle of affluent white missionaries. His parents were the proprietors of the Hilo Boarding School, referred to as Father Lyman's Industrial Training School in Isabella's letters.

Reverend Lorenzo Lyons was one of the first missionaries to arrive on what is now called the Big Island. Isabella describes him as a courageous preacher who had to make his way down from the cliffs into the hidden valleys by swinging from tree to tree with ropes.

Sir James MacBain, an elder of Chalmers Church and a prominent member of the Legislative Assembly, represented the district of Wimmera at the time of Isabella's visit to Australia. In 1853 he had emigrated in Brunel's *Great Britain* to work in the Melbourne branch of the Bank of New South Wales. Four years later, he became managing partner of Richard Gibbs & Co., which was purchased by the Australian Mortgage (Mercantile) Land and Finance Company in 1865. MacBain was retained as chairman and managing director for the next twenty-five years. An ardent Presbyterian and politician, MacBain used his power for the common good. When he died of hepatitis in 1892, the funeral procession was two miles long and a public monument was erected in his honour.

Mrs Mair was possibly Catherine Lyons Mair, wife of Lieutenant-Colonel William Mair, who commanded a volunteer rifle force in St Kilda at the time of Isabella's visit. (He was promoted to the Melbourne district just after she left.) William Mair had arrived in Australia in 1842 as a police escort of two hundred convicts. His gentrification reflects Victoria's own.

Mary (later Mrs Macdiarmid) was the little girl Henrietta adopted in Tobermory in 1870. Anna Stoddart describes her as a 'lonely and sensitive' child who repaid Henrietta with devoted affection. Henrietta taught her to read, then paid for her education at an excellent boarding school in Edinburgh. She called her 'my child', and Mary called Henrietta the 'mother of my spirit'. Presumably Mary helped to fill the gap left by Dora Bird's death and Isabella's travels.

Archduke Ferdinand Maximilian of Austria was Emperor of Mexico from 1864 to 1867, at the behest of Napoleon III. His empire was a failure from the start, as most of the country supported a rebel faction led by Benito Juárez. When affairs in France compelled Napoleon III to withdraw his troops in 1867, Juárez used the opportunity to lay seige to Querétaro, where Maximilian and most of his forces were based. Ultimately, Maximilian was captured and shot. It is to these events that Isabella refers in her account of the young Prussian tutor, Waldemar Müller.★ There is also a famous painting by Edouard Manet of Maximilian's execution.

Sir Peter Benson Maxwell was Recorder of Singapore and Chief Justice of the Straits Settlements (1867–71). He retired after fifteen years' service in Malaya, just before official British intervention. Author of *Whom Shall We Hang?* (1855), *An Introduction to the Duties of Magistrates and Justices of the Peace* (1871) and the pamphlet *On the Interpretation of Statutes* (1886), Maxwell was perhaps most noted in the colonial service for his study *Our Malay Conquests* (1878). This last attacked British intervention in the Straits Settlements, its methods and objectives at a time when Maxwell's son, William,★ was one of the empire's most noted administrators. In short, Maxwell did not believe the British had any right to extend themselves further into Malaya.

Sir William Edward Maxwell, son of Sir Peter Benson Maxwell,★ was a formidable autocrat who carried out policies in office that openly discriminated against the Chinese. Assistant Resident of Larut at the time of Isabella's visit, Maxwell 'ruled rigidly' and was 'virtually a dictator', she wrote. Since he did not speak Chinese, he was forced to conduct business with the immigrant population through translators who he himself recognised as prejudiced and untrustworthy. Not that Maxwell treated even his own kind gently. According to the historian John Gullick, one of Maxwell's British officers equated visiting the Resident to entering the headmaster's study at school: 'One expected to be swished . . . I never had the nerve to say more than "Yes, Sir," and "No, Sir".' From Larut, Maxwell rose to become Colonial Secretary of the Straits Settlements in Singapore, and might have become Governor had it not been for his rival, Sir Frank Swettenham, who possessed more diplomatic finesse. In 1895, after his proposal for a federation of Malay States was defeated in favour of one by Swettenham, Maxwell departed to become Governor of the Gold Coast. He died two years later.

Messageries Maritimes was founded in Marseilles in 1851 as a shipping carrier company. First called Messageries Nationales, then Messageries Impériales, it became Messageries Maritimes in 1871. Initially, the company operated routes only in the Middle East, but as a reward for carrying troops to the Crimean War, the Emperor bestowed on the young shipping company the steamers needed for a transatlantic line running between Bordeaux and Brazil. This enabled Messageries to grow rapidly, serving the Pacific Ocean and the South China Sea as well as the Mediterranean, the Black Sea, the Red Sea, the Atlantic and the Indian Ocean. With the invention of the aeroplane in the twentieth century, however, and two world wars that claimed over half its fleet, Messageries saw a decline in its fortunes. In 1977 it merged with the Compagnie Générale Transatlantique to become the Compagnie Générale Maritime.

Missionary Enterprises in the South Sea Islands, published in 1837, chronicled John Williams's experiences with the London Missionary Society★ in the Solomon Islands, New Caledonia, Samoa and Vanuatu before he was slaughtered at the age of forty-three on a beach on the island of Erromanga in 1839. Williams's untimely death established him as a Christian martyr who had given his life to save the souls of the Polynesians, and his book *Missionary Enterprises* became a bestseller. It had been written in 1821 in New South Wales, Australia, where Williams had gone in the hopes of improving his wife's health (she too was a missionary with the Society). The book was illustrated by George Baxter with engravings of the islands where he had preached, and it is to these images that Isabella refers. The full title was *A Narrative of Missionary Enterprises in the South Sea Islands, with remarks upon the natural history of the islands, origin, language, traditions and usages of the inhabitants* (1837).

Mohawk was Isabella's horse in the 1850s when her father was curate of Wyton in Huntingdonshire. There, Isabella acquired a reputation as a fearless rider who could mount any horse, even those no woman had ridden before.

Waldemar Müller, musician and schoolteacher, was born in Brandenburg on April 15, 1846. He told Isabella that he spent his late teens serving Archduke Ferdinand Maximilian in his efforts to become emperor of Mexico, claiming to have been wounded at the final battle of Querétaro in 1867. Whether or not this is true, he was wounded in San Diego in 1870 by Cave Johnson Couts, for allegedly assaulting one of his daughters. Müller was tutor to Couts' children at their home, Rancho Guajome. Nominating himself a 'one-man prosecutor, jury and executioner', according to Lyle Annable in 'The Life and Times of Cave Johnson Couts', the irascible Couts 'unloaded two charges of birdshot' into Müller. He survived and left town. A year later, Müller arrived in Honolulu from San Francisco. He briefly taught music and languages at Punahoa School, then became private tutor to the Sinclair children at Makaweli, where he stayed for the next four years. Leaving teaching to become a planter, Müller moved to Koloa to grow arrowroot in 1876, then to the Big Island where he grew coffee and canned pineapple commercially. In 1885 he married a Hawaiian woman, with whom he had ten children. Müller died in Kona on October 25, 1924.

Commander Patrick James Murray, Resident of Sungei Ujong (1875–80), died shortly after Isabella's departure. Isabella described him in *The Golden Chersonese* as a 'jack-of-all-trades', who was 'Superintendant of Police, Chancellor of the Exchequer, Surveyor of Taxes, Board of Trade, Board of Works, and I know not what besides. In fact *he is the Government*.' More personally, Isabella said that Murray was 'a man about thirty-eight, a naval officer, and an enterprising African traveller'. He was 'hasty when vexed, but thoroughly kind-hearted; very blunt, very undignified, never happy out of the wilds'. During the Perak War, Murray had been Acting Resident of Sungei Ujong, appointed by Sir Andrew Clarke, and when it was over he was faced with the difficult task of disarming the Malays and deciding who had supported the British and who had not. Such a task in another man's hands might have created many enemies, but Murray made himself invaluable to the people of Sungei Ujong by dispensing medicine and curing a multitude of physical maladies. Unfortunately, when Murray himself fell ill, there was no one to treat him. In *The Chersonese with the Gilding Off*, Emily Innes★ attributed his death to sunstroke. More likely Murray succumbed to a sudden attack of malaria. In 1881, he was posthumously awarded a medal for service to the British Empire.

Jim Nugent (also known as *Rocky Mountain Jim*) was described by Isabella in *A Lady's Life in the Rocky Mountains* as 'a shocking figure'. When she first saw him, he was rigged out in 'old trousers made of deer hide, held on by an old scarf . . . a leather shirt, with three or four ragged unbuttoned waistcoats over it; an old smashed wideawake, from under which his tawny ringlets hung; and with his one eye, his one long spur, his knife in his belt, his revolver in his waistcoat pocket, his saddle covered with an old beaver skin, from which the paws hung down; his camping blankets behind him, his rifle laid across the saddle in front of him and his axe, canteen, and other gear hanging to the horn, he was as awful looking a ruffian as one could see'. Jim was apparently fond of telling tall tales to uphold this image. As George Kingsley, the doctor who attended him in his last illness, recalled, he was known as 'the Mountainous One' because of 'the extraordinary altitude of his lies'. He convinced Isabella that he was the cast-out son of a noble Irish family; to others, he claimed to be a disgraced schoolteacher or a defrocked Catholic priest. Whatever the truth, he was shot by Griff Evans★ on June 29, 1874, because of a land dispute, and died in Fort Collins two months later, on September 7, 1874. The most extensive (if unreliable) account of his character is given by Isabella in *A Lady's Life in the Rocky Mountains*.

Admiral Otter of the Government Naval Survey Service lived just outside Oban, across the sound from Tobermory, in a great manor house, according to Anna Stoddart. His wife worked with Isabella and Henrietta in relieving the suffering of the poor, helping Isabella mobilise crofters for her emigration scheme to Canada.

General William Jackson Palmer, founder of the Denver and Rio Grande Railway, several newspapers and many other business ventures, made his home in Glen Eyrie, Colorado. A graduate of West Point and a veteran of the Union Army during the Civil War, Palmer established an empire of land, coal and mineral companies that led to the flourishing of some Colorado towns and the demise of others. Among the cities he established were Colorado Springs, Durango, Palmer Lake, South Pueblo and Alamosa. He retired a multi-millionaire in 1901.

Miss Park ('Miss Karpe' in *The Hawaiian Archipelago*) is described by Isabella as 'the typical American travelling lady, who is encountered everywhere from the Andes to the Pyramids, tireless, with indomitable energy'. She accompanies Isabella on her first ascent of the volcano Kilauea, chronicled in a letter that has now been lost. One thing is clear, however: Isabella and Miss Park did not get along. In the published account, only the pseudonym – Karpe – expresses Isabella's true feelings about this woman, who was sickly, jealous and prone to complain.

Sir Harry Parkes, British representative in Japan from 1865 to 1883, was called by Ernest Satow 'the bugbear of the Japanese public'. He had initially gone to the Far East in 1841 at the age of thirteen, following his two sisters to Macao. He never looked back. He was by turns interpreter, soldier and diplomat, even becoming a prisoner in the Opium War of 1860, when he faced torture in Beijing and was threatened with death. These experiences made Parkes a hero in London, and in 1865 as a reward the British crown placed him in a 'tutelary' position towards the Japanese government. It was here that Isabella met Parkes: he hosted her in the British Legation in Tokyo. Isabella became fond of Parkes, but the Japanese didn't: they found his style of diplomacy autocratic and his favouring of British merchants offensive. As a result, his presence in Japan became increasingly tense, and in 1883 he was transferred to Beijing by the Colonial Office. In China, however, Parkes was plagued by memories of being a prisoner of war – the only other time he had seen the capital city – and found it hard to adjust. His wife died in 1880 in Edinburgh, around the same time as Henrietta Bird. This dual loss brought Sir Harry and Isabella together in Scotland, and solid-ified a friendship that lasted until the diplomat's death in March 1885, at the height of the Anglo-Russian conflict over China. *Unbeaten Tracks in Japan* is dedicated to the Parkes.

Rear Admiral Sir William Edward Parry, British arctic explorer, accompanied Sir John Ross in 1818 in an expedition to find the Northwest Passage. His own later attempts are chron-icled in *Journal of a Voyage for the Discovery of a Northwest Passage from the Atlantic to the Pacific* (1821) and *Narrative of an Attempt to Reach the North Pole* (1828). Parry did in fact discover the passage's entrance, and he attempted to access the Pole by sledge from Spitsbergen, but he was forced to turn back by his exploring party's exhaustion. Presumably Isabella com-pared her own writing with Parry's as a means of highlighting her wintry (and watery) exploits during her Atlantic crossing in 1872.

Peninsula & Oriental Steam Navigation Company (also known as P&O) was founded in London in 1822 as a means of linking Great Britain with the Iberian Peninsula. During the Portuguese and then the Spanish civil wars of the early 1830s, P&O steamers ran guns and carried troops for the legitimate heirs to both thrones. During peacetime, the company brought giraffes from Africa for the London zoo; traded in silk and indigo; and signed the first commercial contract for carrying mail by sea. After expanding to Egypt in 1840, P&O steamers revolutionised passenger traffic: two-thirds of its customers were civil servants, but it also carried missionaries, bankers, industrialists and world travellers to destinations as far-flung as India and Ceylon. It suffered a minor setback in the 1870s after failing to recog-nise the strategic importance of the Suez Canal, but Isabella Bird's letters indicate that the company quickly recovered by extensive economising. P&O remained Britain's premier shipping company until the Second World War, when it lost 182 ships, thereafter to be replaced by air as the preferred mode of transportation. Today, the company still exists, spe-cialising in containers, ferries, tankers and luxury cruise ships.

John Dietz Perry, Missouri industrialist, came to Colorado in 1870 as president of the Kansas Pacific Railroad, chartered by the Territory of Kansas to connect it to Denver. Wealthy and well established socially in St Louis, Perry was charmed by the Colorado landscape and began acquiring lands in the West Plum Creek area in 1872. Since Perry married twice and had six children, it is unclear which 'Miss Perry' provided Isabella with such hospitality on her visit to Perry Park. The brother Isabella mentions was probably Charles, who was living there year-round in 1873 to oversee the buildings' construction. The Perry family kept Perry Park for thirty years, despite being bedevilled for two decades about their land rights. (Some of the titles had been in Charles's name, and he died in 1876 with no heirs.) The family eventually sold Perry Park in 1903.

Sir John Pope-Hennessy was deeply unpopular with the Victorian public because of his efforts to secure equal status for his subjects, wherever he was posted. Governor of Labuan

(1867–71), the Gold Coast (1872–3), the Bahamas (1873–4), and the Windward Islands (1875–6), Pope-Hennessy was a man ahead of his time. He incurred the wrath of white planters in Barbados by trying to pass legislation against the harsh treatment of slaves. He outlawed flogging and encouraged black labourers to emigrate to other islands, providing 'tickets of leave'. A proponent of prison reform, Pope-Hennessy also insisted that black prisoners were ill treated, and in Barbados in 1876 he released as many as 39 prisoners in one day, proclaiming their innocence. Lastly, he proposed a federation of the Windward Islands that would have further deprived white planters of their power. The result was predictable: riots were common, a special police force was sworn in, and the military was called out. To restore order, the Colonial Office recalled Pope-Hennessy in 1876 and transferred him to Hong Kong, where he served as Governor from 1877 to 1882. In Hong Kong, Pope-Hennessy followed similar policies that met with equal ill will. One of his first actions, in 1877, was to cancel the exclusive rights of Europeans to build in the centre of Victoria. He gave the Chinese more educational facilities, protected their cemeteries, abolished the public flogging of Chinese criminals, and proposed the first typhoon anchorage to protect the boat population in the bay. Junior posts in the government service were opened to the Chinese by competitive examination, and he gave the Chinese population British citizenship by local ordinance. Finally, in 1880 Pope-Hennessy appointed the first Chinese lawyer, Ng Choy,★ to Hong Kong's Legislative Council in order to establish a precedent of Chinese self-government. Liberal by today's standards, in his own time Pope-Hennessy was censored by the Colonial Office, shunned by his peers, and ultimately forced to step down from the governorship of Hong Kong and gazetted to Mauritius, where he incited yet more controversy through his proposals for humanitarian reform. Suspended in 1886, Pope-Hennessy was reinstated as Governor of Mauritius the following year. He was forced to retire from this office in 1889, and died within two years. His grandson, the writer James Pope-Hennessy, described Sir John as an 'enigmatic and emotional' figure whose career was marked by his 'humanitarian beliefs, volatile judgments and autocratic behaviour' in every region he administered.

Mrs Proudie, wife of the Bishop of Barchester in *Barchester Towers* (1857), was the creation of the Victorian novelist Anthony Trollope. A profound Sabbatarian who henpecks her husband, Mrs Proudie was to become one of Trollope's most memorable characters. So popular was the 'woman bishop' as a 'type' that she reappeared in several other novels in his Barsetshire series.

Fanny Puckle seems to have been one of Isabella's closest friends from Wyton, where Edward Bird was curate from 1848 to 1858. Wyton, located on the Ouse, full of walks and drives, was in many ways an idyllic place, and the two women apparently developed a special closeness. When exactly Fanny married her second husband, *Fred Puckle*, and emigrated to Australia is unclear: possibly some time in the mid-1850s, as their eldest child was born in 1858. In Isabella's article 'Australia Felix', Fred appears as the jovial 'Mr Hale', who had emigrated to Melbourne to seek his fortune some twenty-five years earlier, in 1847. Presumably he had returned to England in the 1850s, when he and Fanny met. Isabella describes the couple as comfortable, prosperous and devout, teaching Sunday School and raising a family of four children.

Syed Abdul Rahman was the Dato Klana, or 'referee Rajah', of Sungei Ujong at the time of Isabella's visit. Rahman's succession in 1873 had not been popular among the chiefs of the region. Since his father was an Arab, he was regarded as an outsider, despite his status as the nephew of the previous Dato Klana, who had died without an heir. As a result, Rahman had to struggle for power with his second-in-command, the Dato Bandar, then Kulop Tunggal, for the first fifteen years of his reign until the British exiled Tunggal to Singapore. Thereafter, his reign went well and he was perceived as a kind and just ruler. He was on cordial terms with both the Chinese and the British in Sungei Ujong, having spent a number of years in the polyglot community of Malacca.

Father Giovanni Timoleone Raimondi, who had arrived in China in 1860 after the third Opium War, was named Bishop of Victoria by Pope Gregory XVI in 1874. Raimondi held this post until he died at the Mission House in Glenealy in 1894.

Mary Waterhouse Rice and *William Hyde Rice* possessed a deep concern for the people of Kauai, both Hawaiian and foreign, and they worked tirelessly on their behalf. William Rice was both rancher and legislator, serving as the last Governor of Kauai. His mother, Mary Sophie Rice, became one of the *grand dames* of Kauai along with Mrs Eliza Sinclair.★

Ring, Jim Nugent's★ dog, was the best hunting hound in Colorado according to Isabella Bird. In *A Lady's Life in the Rocky Mountains*, she writes that he had 'the body and legs of a collie, but with a head approaching that of a mastiff, a noble face with a wistful human expression, and the most truthful eyes I ever saw in an animal'.

Robina, a close friend of Henrietta and Isabella at the time these letters were written, seems to have had a yen for misadventure, eventually embroiling herself in an unspecified scandal from which Ella Blackie★ had to extract her. What exactly Robina did is unclear, but when Isabella returned to Edinburgh in 1874, she curtailed their friendship. Later, in 1915, when Isabella's executrix Elizabeth Ker★ died, a 'Robina Elizabeth Gildea or Martin' was given the duty of disposing of her private papers, including all those still in her possession from Isabella Bird. If this is the same irresponsible Robina, it might further explain the disappearance of many of Isabella's letters.

Sir William Cleaver Francis Robinson came to Malaya in 1877 after serving as an administrator in Montserrat (1862–6) and Lieutenant Governor of Prince Edward Island (1873–4). Somewhere he had learned to govern by proxy, as he spent his eighteen months as Governor of the Straits Settlements entrenched in his gleaming mansion in Penang. Robinson fared slightly better as Governor of South Australia (1883–9) and Hong Kong (1891–8). In this last post, he increased the unofficial membership of the executive council to two, one of whom was to be Chinese; he ended the practice of holding government office and relevant commercial interests at the same time; and he tried to diminish the influence of Jardine's.★ Robinson left office in Hong Kong in January 1898, six months before the acquisition of the New Territories.

Captain John Ross was a manager of the Princeville Plantation, started in 1855 as a coffee farm by Robert Wylie, Hawaii's foreign minister. Ross had apparently settled in the area around 1870, when he became postmaster of Hanalei. By 1875, Ross had assisted in Princeville's transition from coffee to sugar, helping to plant the cane and establish a mill, which he owned. But sugar farming at Princeville proved a struggle. In 1877 Ross sold his shares of the property and purchased the nearby Kilauea Plantation, then a cattle ranch, with his partner E.P. Adams. Together, Ross and Adams turned Kilauea into a successful sugar plantation, building a three-mile railroad to assist with shipment and delivery. It eventually ran from Ross's mill down to Kahili, enabling the two men to organise the still-extant Kilauea Sugar Plantation Company.

John Ruskin, English writer, critic and artist, championed the nineteenth-century Gothic Revival Movement. When Isabella wrote to the Blackies★ from California mentioning Ruskin, they had just returned from Italy, so it is likely that their comments to her had focused on Ruskin's Italiana, such as *The Stones of Venice* (1851). Ruskin is also famous for his connections to the Pre-Raphaelite Brotherhood; his loss of a libel action brought against him by the American painter James McNeill Whistler; his creation of the artisan society, the Company of St George; and his books *Modern Painters* (1843–60), *The Seven Lamps of Architecture* (1849), *Fors Clavigera* (1871–84), and the autobiography, *Praeterita* (1885–89). This last was left incomplete on his death in January 1900.

St Thomas's Church was the parish church where Edward Bird preached in Birmingham from 1842 to 1848. In her biography, Anna Stoddart describes it as 'a large, gloomy church, built in the worst possible taste', in a grandiloquent neoclassical style. It was from this church that Edward Bird was cast out for his radical Sabbatarian views.

Colonel John McAllister Schofield and *Brevet Brigadier General B.S. Alexander* went to the Hawaiian Islands in 1873 to survey the kingdom for the American government. During Isabella's stay, they accompanied Lunalilo★ to Hilo to see if its port – then called Byron's Bay – might serve their purpose of establishing a naval station on the islands. Their report to President Grant,★ kept secret for twenty years, suggested instead that Pearl Harbor on Oahu would make an ideal base and should be acquired by the U.S. government by any means necessary. Lunalilo died before he could be swayed, but Schofield and Alexander had more luck with the next king, David Kalakaua. In 1887, Schofield convinced Kalakaua to sign the 'bayonet constitution', so called because Kalakaua thought he would be executed if he refused, that disenfranchised the native Hawaiians and granted the United States exclusive rights to Pearl Harbor. They then took the young king on a tour to San Francisco, where he died of pneumonia in the royal suite of the Sheraton Palace in 1891.

Luther Severance Jr was the son of a retired congressman and United States Commissioner to the Sandwich Islands of the same name, who died in Maine in 1854 after serving for three years in Oahu. After their father's death, Luther and his brother Henry moved to Honolulu, where they established the first large rice plantation in the Hawaiian islands. In 1867 Henry returned to San Francisco and Luther moved to Hilo, where he was appointed sheriff, postmaster and customs collector by King Kamehameha V. His wife, Lucinda Clark Severance, was the sister of Mary Austin,★ which explains the close ties Isabella witnessed between the two families.

340

Captain E. W. Shaw, Lieutenant Governor of Malacca, was an Irish naval officer who had been private secretary to Sir Stephen Hill★ (and married his daughter) when Hill was Governor of the Leeward Islands and Antigua in 1863–9. In Malacca, Shaw was well liked by both Malay and Chinese citizens, and performed efficiently during the Sungei Ujong troubles of 1874. He died suddenly at his post in 1879, five weeks after Isabella's departure.

Captain William Beach Sigley was a Civil War veteran from the Union Army who moved with his wife to Longmount from Chicago in 1871 in pursuit of better health. On arrival, the Sigleys found the two-story St Vrain Hotel under construction. They became its managers and were sole operators from 1872. The hotel was a favoured stopping place for travellers journeying to and from Estes Park, and Sigley was a bluff, hearty host. When he retired in 1874, the hotel was purchased by Griff Evans,★ presumably as a replacement for the lodge in Estes Park he had sold to Lord Dunraven.★ The St Vrain Hotel was destroyed by fire in 1879.

Elizabeth McHutchison Sinclair, whose story Isabella relates, was one of Kauai's most prominent foreign settlers, buying the island of Niihau for $10,000 from King Kamehameha V in 1863, as well as 22,000 acres of the Makaweli lands for $15,000 from Princess Victoria Kamamalu in 1865. The Sinclair clan operating these lands at the time of Isabella's visit included the matriarch Eliza Sinclair; her eldest son Francis, who managed Niihau; her invalid son James; her eldest daughter Helen Robinson, who had abandoned an abusive husband in New Zealand, taking her son Aubrey with her; her widowed daughter Jean Gay with her stepson, three sons and two daughters; and her youngest daughter Annie, who had recently married Kauai settler Valdemar Knudsen. (Isabella mistakenly relates that Helen Robinson was widowed, which is most likely the story that the Sinclairs told.) Today, the Robinson family still operates these lands, and Niihau remains 'the forbidden island'.

Sam Slick, an irreverent Yankee clock peddler, was the creation of Canadian author Thomas Chandler Haliburton. He first appeared in the satirical *Clockmaker* in 1836, passing down-to-earth judgement on pioneer life and manners. *The Clockmaker* sold so well that Haliburton issued it in three separate series, then continued the misadventures in *Sam Slick's Wise Saws and Modern Instances, or What He Said, Did, and Invented* (1853) and *Sam Slick in Texas, or the Piney Woods Tavern* (1857). In the mid-nineteenth century, Sam Slick was the prototype of the plain-talking, fast-dealing American backwoodsman.

Mr Smith of Canton. A number of Smiths worked for Jardine, Matheson & Co.,★ making it difficult to determine which Mr Smith Isabella means. James Warley Smith, for example, was a tea-taster in Canton; James Adam Smith worked first in Canton, then founded the Manila-based firm Smith, Bell & Co., which contracted for Jardines; Herbert Smith was a partner in the late 1890s; John Abel Smith had been instrumental in founding Jardines in the 1830s and 1840s. As Jardines was a family-run company, many descendants of John Abel Smith worked in China in the nineteenth century. Alternatively, Isabella could be referring to Arthur Smith, a Jardine's employee and author of *Chinese Characteristics* (1894). It is even possible that Isabella's Mr Smith was the son of the Rev. George Smith, first Anglican bishop of Hong Kong, as she mentions that his brother was a rector in Canton.

Sir Cecil Clementi Smith, then Colonial Secretary of Singapore, suggested that Isabella visit the Malay States during her visit in 1879. Smith had spent much of his previous service in Hong Kong, as Colonial Treasurer (1871–8) and Registrar General (1864–78). After his time in Singapore, Smith was made Colonial Secretary of Ceylon in 1885 and Governor of the Straits Settlements in 1887. So popular was his tenure that the Chinese community petitioned Queen Victoria for his continuance when he left Singapore in 1893. It was, however, because of Smith that Pahang was mistakenly added in 1887 to the states of Perak, Selangor and Sungei Ujong as a British protectorate. Angry at this loss of power, the Pahang rajas revolted in 1891, murdering British settlers in a rebellion lasting several years. This rebellion was quashed after Smith's departure in 1895 when its leader, Bahaman of Semantan, surrendered in exchange for amnesty. In the meantime, Smith had advocated a closer grouping of the protected states under a more centralised government, a plan carried out in 1896 after his retirement.

Dr James Smith of Koloa was the principle western doctor on Kauai when Isabella visited in 1873; most foreign visitors to the island boarded at his house. His son, Jared – or Young Smith, as Isabella calls him – succeeded James as Kauai's government physician in the 1890s. Jared was murdered in 1897 by friends of a young girl he had diagnosed with leprosy – a diagnosis that condemned her to transport to Molokai.

Sir Henry Morton Stanley, correspondent for the *New York Herald*, achieved fame with his rescue of the Scottish explorer David Livingstone,* whom he found dying in Ujiji on Lake Tanganyika in 1871. His account, *How I Found Livingstone*, was published in 1872. Stanley was awarded the gold medal of the Royal Geographical Society and was later knighted by Queen Victoria for his service to the empire. Many English readers like Isabella, however, found Stanley to be little more than a disagreeable Yankee newspaperman. Joseph Conrad mocked him with a short vignette in *Heart of Darkness*.

Sir Thomas Grainger Stewart, professor at the University of Edinburgh and contributor to the intellectual journal *The Athenaeum*, was Isabella's principle physician. Knighted by Queen Victoria in 1894, Grainger Stewart remained one of Isabella's closest confidants until his death in 1900.

John Bird Sumner and *Charles Richard Sumner* were second cousins to the Birds on their father's side. The first was probably the 'Quiet Uncle John' to whom Isabella refers in her Rocky Mountain letters; he became Archbishop of Canterbury in 1848. Neither Isabella's father, Edward Bird, though one of ten children, nor her mother, Dora Lawson, had a brother John. The generation gap between Isabella and the archbishop made it all the more likely that she would call him 'uncle' rather than 'cousin'. His brother, Charles Richard Sumner, was made Bishop of Winchester in 1827.

Algernon Charles Swinburne was the author of *Atalanta in Calydon* (1865), *Poems and Ballads* (first series, 1866; second series, 1878), *Ave Atque Vale* (1867–8), and *Essays and Studies* (1875). While a student at Balliol College, Oxford, in the 1850s, Swinburne had met the Pre-Raphaelite painters William Morris, Edward Burne-Jones and Dante Gabriel Rossetti. He had been attracted to their brotherhood, which stressed the need for artists to rebel.

The result in Swinburne's writing was a poetic invention marked by what Victorian critics called 'feverish carnality': poems dealing not merely with beauty but with bestiality, enshrining 'unnamable' topics in melodic verse. In 1879, Swinburne's health collapsed as a result of his alcoholism and sado-masochistic tendencies. He was rescued and restored to health by the artist Theodore Watts-Dunton, becoming in turn a figure of respectability with intensely conservative views. He died in 1909 in Putney.

Captain Paul Swinburne, described by Isabella as the '2nd son of Sir John Swinburne and a nephew of the Duke of Buckingham', became Perak's police superintendant on January 29, 1877, just nine days after the Maharaja Lela★ was hanged for the murder of James Birch.★ Swinburne had been a member of the 80th Regiment, and was released by the War Office explicitly to take up this post. He served only one year before being relieved by Captain R.S.F. Walker.★ More notably, Swinburne was the cousin of the English poet Algernon Charles Swinburne.★

Tung-Wah Hospital for the Chinese sick and dying was opened in 1869, following a scandal about conditions in the Kwong Fuk Che Temple that revealed the total lack of medical care for Chinese patients in Hong Kong. Originally a repository for ancestral tablets of Chinese who died away from their family homes on the mainland, the Kwong Fuk Che Temple provided a place for people to die without bringing bad luck to their homes. Conditions in this 'death house' were horrific, with no medical facilities and minimal levels of care. An investigation followed by publication of a highly critical report prompted several members of the Chinese community to set up the Tung-Wah Hospital and establish a management board. This became an unofficial but powerful platform for the expression of Chinese interests in the nineteenth and twentieth centuries. At the time of Isabella's stay, in 1879, the Tung-Wah Hospital Board was, in fact, the only means by which the Chinese elite could get themselves heard by the British government.

The Ute people are the oldest continuous residents of Colorado, having displaced the Anasazi, or 'ancient ones', who had made their homes in the region's sandstone caves. To the east and northeast of the Utes were once the Arapahos, Cheyennes, Commanches, Sioux and Pawnees. To the south were Apaches and Navajos. In other words, the Utes were surrounded by enemies on all sides, which forced them to form small hunter-gatherer clusters in isolated pockets in the Rocky Mountains. With the introduction of horses in the early nineteenth century, the Utes unified into a band of warriors, engaging in a series of 'Indian wars' between 1864 and 1870 with white settlers. Today, the tribe's remaining 1,800 members live in a reservation in Southwest Colorado around the Sleeping Ute Mountain. Said to bear a haunting resemblance to a Ute warrior lying on his back, with his headdress stretching out over to the land, this mountain is sacred to the Ute people, who have slept in its shadows 'from the beginning'. The state of Utah bears their name.

Father Damien de Veuster left Honolulu for Molokai in May 1873, while Isabella was in the Hawaiian islands. The Belgian missionary priest was concerned that the lepers on Molokai were being deprived of the consolations of religion in their enforced isolation. Choosing to immolate himself there without orders from his society – the Sacred Hearts of Jesus and Mary – and acting contrary to the advice of the Catholic Church, Father Damien took on

343

the spiritual and physical responsibility for Hawaii's lepers. In April 1889, Father Damien himself died from the disease.

The Vicar of Bulhampton, published in 1870, outlines Anthony Trollope's conception of English virtue. Its luckless heroine, Carry Brattle, is seduced then abandoned by her lover in London. Meanwhile, her brother Sam is falsely accused of murdering a farmer in the village of Bulhampton. It is up to the local vicar to uncover the real murderers and to reconcile Brattle senior with his son and daughter. A side plot that deals with the Nonconformist Church would have been of particular interest to Isabella.

Captain R.S.F. Walker relieved Paul Swinburne★ as commander of the Perak Police during Isabella's stay. Unlike Swinburne, who retained the position for little over a year, Walker kept it for nearly seventeen, from 1879 to 1896. An ex-Army officer, Walker sought to model his police force after the military, giving special preference to Sikhs. (He even went so far as to rename his force the '1st Battalion Perak Sikhs'.) Under Walker's control, the force numbered over 900 men by 1896 when it was renamed the Malay States Guides with Walker at the helm. In 1900, Walker, now Lieutenant-Colonel, became Acting Resident of Perak when Sir Frank Swettenham was on leave. Isabella noted that Walker had a 'terrible temper' and was called by the Malays 'the black panther'.

Dr Charles Hinckley Wetmore was Hilo's first western doctor, having arrived there as a missionary in 1849. Together, he and his wife served the medical needs of the growing foreign population in East Hawaii, setting up a seaman's hospital and a drugstore on the waterfront. His daughter Frances became the island's first female physician.

John Greenleaf Whittier, American poet and one of the founders of the Republican Party, is best known for his narrative poem 'Snowbound, A Winter Idyll'. Based on Whittier's fond memories from his childhood in Haverhill, Massachusetts, 'Snowbound' is representative of his sincere, moralistic yet emotional style.

Samuel Wilberforce, son of the famous abolitionist William Wilberforce, and a relative of Isabella Bird, served in succession as Bishop of Oxford; chaplain to the House of Lords; and lord high almoner to Queen Victoria. In 1869 he was named Bishop of Winchester, a post he used to initiate a movement to modernise the language of the King James Bible. Before this project could be completed, however, Wilberforce was killed tragically, falling from his horse near Leatherhead in Surrey on July 19, 1873, while Isabella was in Hawaii.

Prince William – better known as Kaiser Wilhelm II – was the grandson of Queen Victoria, a family relationship that led London newspapers to publicise his youthful indiscretions in Prussia in the early 1870s. The eldest son of Frederick III and Victoria's eldest daughter, Vicky, William early on shaped a reputation for himself as impulsive and impolitic. As emperor, William's attempts to make Germany the greatest naval, colonial and commercial power in the world led to the outbreak of the first World War. He was forced to abdicate in 1918, and spent the rest of his life in retirement in Holland. He died there during the Second World War, in 1941.

Bishop Alfred Willis arrived in Honolulu in 1872 to minister to the Anglican community on Oahu at the request of Queen Emma. While there, he established numerous churches and schools, and had among his pupils a young Sun Yat-Sen, who later led the 1911 revolution in China. Willis was an open advocate of Hawaiian self-government, and published numerous articles exposing American attempts to annex the islands. In 1902, when the annexation did in fact occur, Willis fled to Tonga, fearing that his life might be taken by supporters of the new government. He stayed in Tonga for the next 18 years, translating hymns and the Bible. He died while on a visit to England in 1921.

Mr Justice Woods was probably a relation of Robert Carr Woods, who had died four years before Isabella's visit to Malaya. Sailing to Singapore via Bombay in 1844, Woods had become the first editor of the *Straits Times*, and was prominent among those who opposed Sir James Brooke★ in his acquisition of Sarawak. While in Malaya, Woods qualified as a lawyer and practised with the Straits Settlements' Supreme Court, being called to the bar at Gray's Inn in 1873. Two years later, Woods was Acting Puisne Judge when he died suddenly at the age of fifty-nine. Among his clients, his death was felt perhaps most powerfully by the Mantri of Larut, who was afterwards exiled to the Seychelles for his role in the murder of James Birch.★

Raja Muda Yusef, Raja Dris. In her *History of Malaysia*, Mary Turnbull describes Raja Yusef as 'a difficult man, grasping and unpopular among the Malays, old fashioned in his thinking and with little understanding of the outside world', whereas his son-in-law, the Raja Dris (later Sultan Idris), was 'intelligent and adaptable, appreciating the need for change and modernisation' while still preserving the traditional culture of the Malays. In his time in Perak, Sir Hugh Low★ worked closely with both men to restore order, pay off the state's debt, and reestablish confidence in the British residential system after the murder of its first Resident, James Birch.★ Low was outlasted in Perak by Idris, who spoke powerfully of the Pangkor Engagement at a 1903 conference on British rule in Malaya, reminding all present that they were meant to advise, not to govern the Malay states. Idris himself must have known that this had never been the case. Perhaps for this reason he sent his son, the Raja Alang Iskander, to Balliol College, Oxford, so that Iskander might have a better chance of claiming his birthright as ruler, in practice as well as name, when he succeeded Idris as sultan of Perak.

Bibliography

In addition to the published works below, I have utilised the Isabella Bird papers in the John Stuart Blackie Collection of the National Library of Scotland, and in the Luther Severance Collection of the Lyman House Memorial Museum in Hilo, Hawaii. I have also explored the relevant holdings of the National Archives of Scotland; the National Library of Ireland; the British Library; the Bodleian Library; the Library of Congress; the Denver Public Library; the University of Hawaii Library at Manoa; the Firestone Library of Princeton University; and the print and photographic archives of the Royal Geographical Society in London. Most significant, of course, was the extensive Isabella Bird Collection owned by John Murray, from which the majority of these letters are taken. Without the patient assistance of Virginia Murray, the archivist, this edition would never have been completed.

I. BOOKS AND ARTICLES BY ISABELLA BIRD

The Englishwoman in America, London: John Murray, 1856

The Revival in America by an English Eye-Witness [by Edward Bird], edited and introduced by Isabella Bird, London: Seeley, 1858

Aspects of Religion in the United States of America, London: Sampson Low, 1859

'A Visit to Dr. Guthrie's Edinburgh Ragged Schools', *The Leisure Hour* 10 (1861): 247–251

Notes on Old Edinburgh, Edinburgh: Edmonston & Douglas, 1869

The Hawaiian Archipelago: Six Months Among the Palm Groves, Coral Reefs, and Volcanoes of the Sandwich Islands, London: John Murray, 1875

'Australia Felix: Impressions of Victoria', *The Leisure Hour* 26 (1877): 39–44; 87–92; 149–152; 183–186; 218–220; 249–251; 314–318; 413–416; 469–472

'Letters from the Rocky Mountains', *The Leisure Hour* 27 (1878): 24–28; 61–62; 72–76; 110–111; 136–141; 215–221; 280–285; 360–365; 471–475; 501–508; 615–619; 634–637; 669–671; 693–696; 740–743; 781–784; 795–797

A Lady's Life in the Rocky Mountains, London: John Murray, 1879

Unbeaten Tracks in Japan: A Record of Travels in the Interior, Including Visits to the Aborigines of Yezo and the Shrines of Nikkó and Isé, 2 vols, London: John Murray, 1880

Hymns and Poems of the Late Henrietta A. Bird. With Biographical Sketch of the Author [by John Stuart Blackie], edited by Isabella Bird, Edinburgh: James Taylor, 1881

The Golden Chersonese and the Way Thither, London: John Murray, 1883

'The Visitation of Mountain Jim', *Phantasms of the Living*, eds. Edmund Gurney, Frederick Myers and Frank Podmore, 2 vols, London: Rooms of the Society for Psychical Research, 1886, vol. 1: 531–532

'A Pilgrimage to Sinai', *The Leisure Hour* 35 (1886): 15–20; 94–98; 173–178; 233–238; 314–317

'Under Chloroform', *Murray's Magazine* 3 (1887): 327–330

Bibliography

Journeys in Persia and Kurdistan, Including a Summer in the Upper Karun Region and a Visit to the Nestorian Rajans, 2 vols, London: John Murray, 1891

'A Journey through Lesser Tibet', *The Scottish Geographical Magazine* (1892): 513–528

Heathen Claims and Christian Duty, London: Church Missionary Society, 1893

'Among the Tibetans', *The Leisure Hour* 42 (1893): 238–244; 306–312; 380–386; 450–456

Among the Tibetans, London: Religious Tract Society, 1894

Korea and Her Neighbours. A Narrative of Travel, with an Account of the Recent Vicissitudes and Present Position of the Country, London: John Murray, 1898

The Yangtze Valley and Beyond: An Account of Journeys in China, Chiefly in the Province of Sze Chuan and Among the Man-Tze of the Somo Territory, London: John Murray, 1899

Chinese Pictures. Notes on Photographs Made in China, London: Cassell & Co, 1900

'Notes on Morocco', *Monthly Review* 5 (1901): 89–102

This Grand Beyond: The Travels of Isabella Bird Bishop, edited and introduced by Cecily Palser Havely, London: Century Publishing, 1984

II. BOOKS AND ARTICLES ABOUT ISABELLA BIRD

Anon, 'Snapshots in the Far East: Interview with Isabella Bird Bishop', *Wide World Magazine* (1899): 17–21

Anon, 'The Art of Travelling: An Interview with Mrs. J.F. Bishop', *Climate Magazine* 1.4 (1900): 117–122

Anon, 'Mrs. Bishop', *Edinburgh Medical Journal* XVI (1904): 383

Barr, Pat, *A Curious Life for a Lady: The Story of Isabella Bird*, London: John Murray, 1970

Birkett, Dea, 'The Loves of Isabella Bird Bishop', *Blackwood's Magazine* 314 (1973): 385–395

Chappell, Jennie, 'Isabella Bird Bishop', *Women of Worth*, London: S.W. Partridge & Co, 1908, 59–90

Checkland, Olive, *Isabella Bird and 'A Woman's Right to Do What She Can Do Well'*, Aberdeen: Scottish Cultural Society, 1996

Dunning, Harold, *The Life of Rocky Mountain Jim*, Boulder: Johnson Publishing, 1967

Grainger Stewart, Agnes, 'Some Recollections of Isabella Bishop', *Blackwood's Magazine* 176 (1904): 698–704

Gullick, John, 'Isabella Bird's Visit to Malaya', *Journal of the Malaysian Branch of the Royal Asiatic Society* 52.1 (1979): 113–119

——'Isabella Bird: "Escape from Civilisation" in Malaya', *Adventurous Women in Southeast Asia: Six Lives*, ed. J. Gullick, Kuala Lumpur: Oxford University Press, 1995: 196–245

Horsley, Reginald, *Isabella Bird, the Famous Traveller*, London: 1912

Jardine, Evelyn, *Women of Devotion and Courage: No. 4, Isabella Bird*, London: Cassell & Co, 1957

Kaye, Evelyn, *Amazing Traveler: Isabella Bird*, Boulder, Colorado: Blue Penguin Press, 1994

Middleton, Dorothy, 'A Lady's Life in the Rocky Mountains', *The Cornhill Magazine* 994 (1952): 274–300

——'Isabella Bird Bishop, 1831–1904', *Victorian Lady Travellers*, New York: Dutton, 1965: 19–53

Morgan, Susan, 'The Company as the Country: On the Malay Peninsula with Isabella Bird and Emily Innes', *Place Matters: Gendered Geography in Victorian Women's Travel Books about Southeast Asia*, New Brunswick: Rutgers University Press, 1996, 135–175

Bibliography

Murphy, Dervla, 'The Loves of Isabella Bird Bishop', *Blackwood's Magazine* 314 (1973): 385–395

Pickering, John, 'Isabella Bird's Desperado: The Life and Death of Rocky Mountain Jim', *This Blue Hollow: Estes Park, the Early Years, 1859–1915*, Niwot, Colorado: University of Colorado Press, 1999, 53–80

Sprague, Marshall, 'Love in the Park', *A Gallery of Dudes*, Boston: Little, Brown & Co, 1967, 119–146

Stoddart, Anna, *The Life of Isabella Bird (Mrs. Bishop)*, London: John Murray, 1906

Williams, C, *The Adventures of a Lady Traveller: The Story of Isabella Bird Bishop*, London: Sunday School Union, 1909

II. OTHER SOURCES CONSULTED

A. Victorian Writing about Countries Visited by Isabella

Innes, Emily, *The Chersonese with the Gilding Off*, 2 vols, London: R. Bentley & Son, 1885

Kingsley, George, *Notes on Sport and Travel*, London: Macmillan, 1900

Kingsley, Rose, *South by west, or winter in the Rocky Mountains and spring in Mexico*, London: W. Isbister, 1874

Kipling, Rudyard, *Kipling's Japan: Collected Writings*, ed. H. Cortazzi and G. Webb, London: Athlone Press, 1988

Landor, A. Henry Savage, *Alone with the Hairy Ainu; or, 3,800 Miles on a Pack Saddle in Yezo and the Kurile Islands*, London: John Murray, 1891

Maxwell, Sir Peter Benson, *Our Malay Conquests*, London: P.S. King, 1878

McNair, John Frederick, *Perak and the Malays*, London: Tinsley Brothers, 1878

Twain, Mark, *Letters from Hawaii*, Boston: Houghton Mifflin, 1866

B. Critical Studies

Aitken, Maria, *A Girdle Round the Earth*, London: Constable, 1987

Allen, Alexandra, *Travelling Ladies*, London: Jupiter Books, 1980

Birkett, Dea, *Spinsters Abroad: Victorian Lady Explorers*, Oxford: Basil Blackwell, 1989

Blunt, Alison, *Travel, Gender and Imperialism*, New York: Guilford Press, 1994

Callaway, Helen, *Gender, Culture, and Empire*, London: Macmillan, 1987

Choudhuri, Nupur, and Strobel, Margaret, eds, *Western Women and Imperialism: Complicity and Resistance*, Bloomington: Indiana University Press, 1992

David, Deirdre, *Rule Britannia: Women, Empire and Victorian Writing*, Ithaca: Cornell University Press, 1995

Donaldson, Laura, *Decolonizing Feminisms: Race, Gender and Empire-Building*, Chapel Hill: University of North Carolina Press, 1992

Foley, Timothy, ed., *Gender and Colonialism*, Galway: Galway University Press, 1995

Frederick, Bonnie, and McLeod, Susan, eds, *Women and the Journey: The Female Travel Experience*, Pullman: Washington State University Press, 1993

Gilbert, Sandra, and Gubar, Susan, *The Madwoman in the Attic: The Woman Writer and the Nineteenth-Century Literary Imagination*, New Haven: Yale University Press, 1984

Gullick, John, 'Syers and the Selangor Police, 1875–97', *Journal of the Malaysian Branch of the Royal Asiatic Society* 51 (1978): 1–55

Grewal, Inderpal, *Home and Harem: Nation, Gender, Empire and the Cultures of Travel*, London: Leicester University Press, 1996

Haley, Bruce, *The Healthy Body and Victorian Culture*, Cambridge, MA: Harvard University Press, 1978

Hamalian, Leo, *Ladies on the Loose: Women Travellers of the 18th and 19th Centuries*, South Yarmouth: John Curley & Associates, 1981

Hammerton, James, *Emigrant Gentlewomen*, London: Croom Helm, 1979

Jayawandena, Kumari, *The White Woman's Other Burden: Women and South Asia During British Rule*, London: Routledge, 1995

Kaplan, Caren, and Grewal, Inderpal, *Scattered Hegemonies: Postmodernity and Transnational Feminist Practices*, Minneapolis: University of Minnesota Press, 1994

Keay, John, *Eccentric Travellers*, Los Angeles: Jeremy P. Tarcher, 1982

Keay, Julia, *With Passport and Parasol: The Adventures of Seven Victorian Ladies*, London: BBC Books, 1989

Kranidis, Rita, *The Victorian Spinster and Colonial Emigration*, New York: St. Martin's Press, 1999

——(ed.) *Imperial Objects: Essays on Victorian Women's Emigration and the Unauthorized Imperial Experience*, London: Macmillan, 1997

Lewis, Reina, *Gendering Orientalism*, London: Routledge, 1996

Macleod, Ray, and Milton, Lewis, *Disease, Medicine and Empire*, London: Routledge, 1988

McClintock, Anne, *Imperial Leather: Race, Gender and Sexuality in Colonial Conquest*, London: Routledge, 1995

——*Maids, Maps and Mines: Gender and Imperialism*, Minneapolis: University of Minnesota Press, 1993

Melman, Billie, *Women's Orients*, London: Macmillan, 1992

Mills, Sara, *Discourses of Difference: An Analysis of Women's Travel Writing and Colonialism*, London: Routledge, 1991

Pratt, Mary Louise, *Imperial Eyes: Travel Writing and Transculturation*, London: Routledge, 1992

Rittenhouse, Mary, *Seven Women Explorers*, New York: Lippincott, 1964

Robinson, Jane, *Wayward Women: A Guide to Women Travellers*, Oxford: Oxford University Press, 1990

Russell, Mary, *The Blessings of a Good Thick Skirt: Women Travellers and Their World*, London: Flamingo, 1994

Showalter, Elaine, *A Literature of Their Own, from Charlotte Brontë to Doris Lessing*, London: Virago, 1982

——*Sexual Anarchy: Gender and Culture at the Fin-de-Siècle*, London: Virago, 1992

——*The Female Malady: Women, Madness and English Culture, 1830–1980*, London: Virago, 1987

Spivak, Gayatri, 'Imperialism and Sexual Difference', *Oxford Literary Review* 8 (1986): 225–40

Tabor, Margaret, *Pioneer Women*, London: Macmillan,1930, 4 vols

Trollope, Joanna, *Britannia's Daughters: Women of the British Empire*, London: Hutchinson, 1983

349

Acknowledgements

I would like to thank Virginia Murray, Grant McIntyre, Gail Pirkis, Caroline Westmore and Drusilla Calvert at John Murray publishers; John Murray VII, for the story about the tricycle; my supervisor, Nick Shrimpton, and my examiners, John Kelly and John MacKenzie, at Oxford; my partner Martin Stein, for finding Isabella's photograph in Hawaii; as well as the staff of the Bodleian Library; the British Library; the Royal Geographical Society; the National Library of Scotland; the Scottish Records Office; the National Library of Ireland; the Library of Congress; the Denver Public Library; the University of Hawaii Library; and the Lyman House Memorial Museum in Hilo, where Sherise Kana'e was of particular help. Nor would this endeavour have been possible without the generosity of the Rhodes Trust, which funded my initial trips to Japan and Malaysia; and the Naval Academy Research Council, whose grants enabled me to visit Hawaii, England and Scotland in search of unpublished material while I was an assistant professor there, from 1998 to 2001. More personally, I would like to dedicate my work on this volume to my own sisters Elizabeth and Juliet. Please accept my heartfelt thanks.

Finally, I would like to thank John Murray for permission to reproduce all the unpublished letters of Isabella Bird, and the National Library of Scotland for allowing reproduction of four letters from their collection: Hawaii letter from Hennie, 1873 (MS 2642 ff 19); The Sea to Ella Blackie, 1872 (MS 2630 f 187); Japan to Ella Blackie, 1 May 1878 (MS 2633 ff 16); Japan to Ella Blackie, 12 August 1878 (MS 2633 ff 22).

Index

Abdullah, Sultan of Perak, 270
  sons, 270, 271, 275, 293, 294, 313
Abdulrahman, Syed (Dato Klana), 245, 248, 264, 339
Afghans, in Malay Peninsula, 274, 280
Aino, 205
Aitkens and Tilburns, 50
Akaroa (New Zealand), 93
Albany (USA), IB's travels to, 308
Albion (steamer), 40
Alexander, Brevet Brigadier General B.G., 59, 105, 340
Alexander, Mrs (of Hawaii), 139–40
Alexanders (of Colorado), 167, 313
Algeria, IB's travels to, 31, 309
Ali, Sher, 211–12, 314
Alice, Princess, 211, 314
Allen, James (of Colorado), 184, 185, 186, 187, 190–1, 192–3, 314
  greed, 188, 190–1
Alma (Colorado), 162
Altnacraig (Scotland), 204, 314
America
  IB's opinion of, 79
  IB's travels to, 31, 143–99, 203, 204, 307–8, 309, 310, 312
  see also Colorado; Hawaii
Americans
  IB's opinion of, 67, 84, 126–7, 171, 190
  language, Colorado expressions, 144
animals
  Colorado, 147, 157, 172, 179, 195
  Hawaii, 72
  Malaya, 249, 253–4, 278, 285, 292, 295; alligators, 249, 250, 260; apes, 260, 283, 285–6, 292, 294–5, 295–6, 299–300; baboons, 295; buffaloes, 246, 297; rhinoceros, 249, 296; snakes, 249, 275; tigers, 244–5, 249, 251, 285, 292
  see also elephant riding; elephants; horseback riding
Arapaho, 163
Arkansas Divide (Colorado), 151–2
Armenia, IB's travels to, 311
Austin, Mary, 57, 61, 72, 106, 107, 110, 314
Austin, Samuel, 57(n), 58, 111, 314
Australia, 16, 33–55, 309
  IB's impression, 37, 38, 39, 40, 43
  publication of adventures, 203

Babu the Hadji, 244, 248, 252, 253, 257
  and the alligator, 250, 251
Balfour, James, 36, 314

Balfour, Mrs, 49
Banks Peninsula (New Zealand), 93
Barr, Pat, 7(n), 8, 9(n), 11(n)
Bear Canyon (Colorado), 171
Ben Nevis (steamer), 33, 35, 309, 315
Bergens Park (Colorado), 156, 157
Bertelmann, Christian, 101, 315
Bessie see Ker, Elizabeth 'Bessie'
'Bessie Twinker' (IB's horse), 65–6, 67–8, 106–7, 315
  in foal, 167
Big Island (Hawaii), 56–8, 61, 66, 69, 70–3, 75, 77–9, 84, 105–7, 110–25, 127–9, 130, 132–4, 136, 137
Big Thompson Canyon (Colorado), 194, 198
Biggs, Louis Courtier, 239–40, 241, 242, 315
Biggs, Mrs, 241, 242
Birch, James Woodford Wheeler, 315
  character, 290
  murder of, 245, 282, 290
Bird, Dora (IB's mother), 3, 8, 307, 308
Bird, Edward (IB's father), 3, 7–8, 17, 122(n), 307–8
  The Revival in America by an English Eye-Witness, 308
Bird, Harriet, 103, 215, 316
Bird, Henrietta
  biographical details, 3, 14, 307–10
  adopted child see Macdiarmid, Mary
  character and abilities, 9–10, 12
  education, 308, 309
  health, 203
  Hymns and Poems of the Late Henrietta A. Bird, 310
  IB's comments on, 99–100, 154, 178, 180, 185, 189, 203–4, 289
  IB's reaction to her death, 14–15
  letters, 8, 9, 140–2
  relationship with IB, 7–14, 140–1, 305–6
  travels, 9, 10, 141–2
Bird, Isabella
  biographical details: 3–4, 307–12; education, 4; honours, 2, 310, 311; relics, 2–3; wedding, 14–15
  abilities and interests: animals see animals; artistic interests, 4, 65; charity work, 4, 308; cooking, 58, 62, 65, 188, see also food; foreign and current affairs, 21, 22, 52–3, 211–12, 258, 272, 278, 282, 311; Highland crofters' emigration scheme, 4, 308; horseback riding see horseback riding; literary interests,

4; medical matters, 134, 165, 172, 187, 252 (see also hospitals); microscopes, 4, 16, 19, 203; organ playing, 189, 190; photography, 2, 21, 312; religion, 3, 52–3, 95–6, 162, 167, see also Christians and Christianity; scientific interests, 4, 203; travelling, reasons for, 4–7, 163, 203
  characteristics: 4; class consciousness, 17; dislike of heat, 171; fears, 22–3, 157, 261, 280 (of libel, 267; of water, 109, 128); 'free leggism', 177, 180, 194; men as chosen companions, 113, 124, 192
  health: 4–7; between travels, 203; carbunculosis, 6; drinking, 6(n), 33; in Japan, 204–5; reasons for ill-health, 5–6, 81, 128; use of bromide, 6, 145, 147, 173
  relationships: 3; aunts, 3–4; parents, 7–8; with Empire, 20–3; with Henrietta, 7–14, 140–1, 305–6; personal comments from IB, 99–100, 110, 154, 178, 180, 185, 189, 203–4, 289; with men, 14–20, 32, see also Bishop, Dr John; Cameron, Mr; Heath, Colonel; Lunalilo, William Charles, King of Hawaii; Nugent, Jim; Ross, Captain; Wilson, Mr; religious connections, 3
  writings: first article, 4; IB on travel writing, 154, 163; letters: comparison with published work, 13; organization of, 2; religious writing, 4; Among the Tibetans, 312; Aspects of Religion in the United States of America, 308; 'Australia Felix', 13–14, 309, 310; Chinese Pictures, 21, 312; The Englishwoman in America, 307; The Golden Chersonese, 5, 13, 22, 267, 311; Good Words, IB's contributions, 4, 129, 154, 183; The Hawaiian Archipelago, 5, 12–13, 13–14, 56, 309; Heathen Claims and Christian Duty, 312; Journeys in Persia and Kurdistan, 311; Korea and Her Neighbours, 312; A Lady's Life in the Rocky Mountains, 5, 13(n), 18(n), 19(n), 143, 199, 310; The Leisure Hour, IB's contributions, 4, 203, 309, 310, 311; 'Letters from the Rocky Mountains', 310; 'Long's Peak' (article for Out West), 189, 192; 'Notes on Morocco', 312;

351

Bird, Isabella, writings (cont.)
  Notes on Old Edinburgh, 4(n), 308; 'A
    Pilgrimage to Sinai', 311; Unbeaten
    Tracks in Japan, 5, 13–14, 310;
    'Under Chloroform: A
    Psychological Fragment', 5(n); 'A
    Visit to Dr. Guthrie's Edinburgh
    Ragged Schools', 4(n); 'The
    Visitations of Mountain Jim'
    (Phantasms of the Living), 20(n), 199,
    311; The Yangtse Valley and Beyond,
    312
'Birdie' ('Bird') (IB's horse), 147, 149,
  150, 151–2, 155, 156, 170, 171,
  179, 181, 183, 195–6, 316
birds
  Australia, 48
  Colorado, mountain-eagle, 195
  Malaya, 249, 292, 297
Birkett, Dea, 10(n)
Birmingham (England), 36, 62
  St Thomas' Church, 3, 42, 307
Bishop, John (husband of IB), 2–3,
  14–15, 16, 17–18, 19, 309–10, 311,
  316
Black Canyon (Colorado), 176
Black Rock (Australia), 53
Blackie, Ella, 316
  comments by IB on, 155, 192
  editing of IB's letters, 2
  letter from HB, 8(n), 9, 140–2
  letters from IB, 6(n), 9(n), 15(n), 18,
    31, 199, 203–5, 306
  letters to IB, 230
Blackie, Professor John Stuart, 9, 10(n),
  183, 204, 316
  see also John Stuart Blackie Collection
boats
  Canton, 213, 233
  in IB's journey in Malay Peninsula,
    252–3
  night travel, 253–4
  Singapore, 238
  see also steamers
Boston (USA), IB's travels to, 308
Boulder (Colorado), 170, 171
Brigham, Captain, 90
Brigham, Mrs, 56, 89, 90, 92, 105, 177,
  317
Brighton (Australia), 37
Britain and the British, IB on, 161–2,
  205, 212, 242, 272, 278, 279, 282
British Residents, Malay Peninsula, 258
Brooke, Sir James, Raja of Sarawak, 238,
  317
Browning, Robert, 21
Buchanan, John, 164, 174, 317
  in Estes Park with IB, 177, 181, 182,
    183–4, 187, 189
  IB's opinion of, 193
Budd, Richard Hale, 36, 38, 317
Budd, Mrs, 36, 52
Burdett Coutts, Lady Angela, 238, 317
Burdon, Bishop John Shaw, 208–9, 210,
  212, 229, 233, 234, 318
Burdon, Mrs, 209, 210, 232
Burtelmann see Bertelmann, Christian
Byers, William, 144, 147–8, 318

Cairns, Dr Adam, 36, 49, 50, 318
Cairns, Mrs, 36, 49
Cairo, 310
Cameron, Mr 'the fiend', 15, 33, 35, 50,
  51, 52, 53–4, 130, 318
Cameron, Mrs, 35, 52, 53
Campbell, George W., 272, 319
Campbell, Mr (Mrs Mair's brother-in-
  law), 51
Campbell, Mrs (young widow), 302-3
Camperdown (Victoria, Australia), 47, 48
Canada, IB in, 308
Candlish, Robert Smith, 155–6, 159–60,
  187, 283, 295, 319
Canton, 212-13, 214, 223–8
  bridal procession, 227
  executions, 220–2
  godowns, 212
  'joss houses', 213, 223
  legal process, 218–20
  shops, 214, 226–7
  see also China
Carnarvon, 4th Earl (Henry Howard
  Molyneux Herbert), 278, 319
Ceylon, 310
Chalmers family, 230
Chalmers, Miss, 230
Checkland, Olive, 4(n), 5, 6(n), 15
Cheyenne, 149
Chicago (USA), 204, 310
Chiefton (steamer), 38, 320
Chillingworth, Mr, 69–70, 87, 128
China
  IB's travels to, 206–34, 310, 312
  literary examinations, 224–5
  opium in, 211, 228
  see also Canton; Hong Kong
Chinese
  comparison with Japanese, 210, 212,
    214
  IB on, 210–11, 212, 265, 271–2
  in Malay Peninsula, 258, 263, 264,
    271–2, 273, 279–80
  treatment by foreigners, 211
Chinese New Year, Malacca, 246–7
Choy, Ng (Wu Ting-fang), 233, 320
Christians and Christianity
  in China, 211, 212, 224, 232, 233, 234
  the Church in Australia, 52-3
  Singapore, 237
  see also religion
Church Missionary Society, 234, 320
Clayton, Emily, 308, 309, 310, 320
  letters to IB, 138, 172, 181, 182, 187,
    230
  mentioned in IB's letters, 37, 56, 164,
    166, 172(n), 181, 185, 187
Clear Creek (Toughcuss Canyon)
  (Colorado), 167, 168–9, 170
Clifford, Hugh, 23
climate see weather
Coan, Miss, 58, 66
Coan, Titus and Fidelia, 58, 127, 152,
  230, 321
Colorado, 16, 143–99, 309
  benefits for IB, 154
  consumptives in, 153–4
  description, 146, 152, 156, 157,

  158–9, 160–1, 167–8, 171, 180–1,
    195
  IB's reputation in, 197
  letters from, 143–99
  publication of adventures, 203
  railroad, 167
Colorado City (Colorado), 152
Colorado Springs (Colorado), 153
Cook, Captain James, 69, 130, 321
Cope, Mr, 235, 236, 237, 238
Coutts see Burdett Coutts
Craik, Bob, 161
Curzon, Lord, 311

Daly, Daniel Dominic, 268, 321
Damon, Mr, 93, 94, 100
Daniels, Judge, 69, 79, 85, 87
Darwin, Charles, 203, 235, 310, 321
Davies, Mr, 131, 137
Davies, Mrs, 131
Deer Valley (Colorado), 162
Denver (Colorado), 144(& n), 147, 148
Denver Stage Road, 161
Detroit (USA), IB's travels to, 308
Dewy, Mr, 145, 164, 165–6, 173, 322
Dewy, Mrs, 144, 145, 164, 165, 322
Dickins, Frederick Victor, 234, 235, 322
Disraeli, Benjamin, 71, 208, 272, 322
Doré, Gustave, 195, 322
Douglas, Lady Gertrude, 264
Douglas, Captain William Bloomfield,
  237, 290, 291, 292(n), 323
  IB on, 22, 267, 268
dress
  Canton, 211, 226
  Hawaii, 63, 64
  Malay Peninsula, 243–4, 246–8, 252
Dris, Raja, 290, 291, 294, 298
Dunedin (New Zealand), 56
Dunlop, Nathaniel, 35, 184, 185, 323
Dunraven, 4th Earl (Windham Thomas
  Wyndham-Quin), 161, 323
Dykes, Mr, 36, 324

earthquakes, Hawaii, 110, 119, 134
Edinburgh, 11, 34, 49, 155–6, 163, 185,
  306, 308, 309, 310, 311, 312
Edinburgh Medical Missionary Society,
  212, 309, 324
Edmondston and Douglas (publishers),
  129
Edwards, Captain, 210, 232
Edwards, Mrs Sam, 163, 164
Edwards, Sam, 164–5, 181, 194, 196, 324
Edwina (steamer), 41–2
Egypt, 310
Eitel, Reverend Ernest John, 234, 324
Eldort (German sailor), 108
elephant riding, 283–5, 287–8, 291
elephants, in Malay Peninsula, 249, 254,
  280, 281, 282-3
  swimming, 288–9
Ellis (bailiff), 119, 124
Emerson, Ralph Waldo, 308
'Emily' see Clayton, Emily
Emma, Queen of Hawaii, 137, 138, 324
Estes Park (Colorado), 19, 143, 154, 164,
  165

Index

description, 176–7, 185
IB leaves, 193
IB returns to, 198
IB's letters from, 172-93
Europe, IB's travels to, 310, 311
Evans, Griff, 143, 144(*n*), 154, 164, 165, 166, 197, 325
drinking, 172
IB's money and, 172(*n*), 193
and murder of Jim Nugent, 199, 309
Evans, Jane, 144(& *n*), 147
Evans, Jinny, 147, 149, 163

Fairplay (Colorado), 162
Fall River Canyon (Colorado), 175, 178–9
'the fiend' *see* Cameron, Mr 'the fiend'
food
bananas, IB's liking for, 292, 305
Canton, 228
in Estes Park, 175, 176, 179, 184, 187, 190
Hawaii, 73, 137
Malay Peninsula, 255–6, 257, 265, 276, 282, 305
see also Bird, Isabella, abilities and interests, cooking
Fountain River (Colorado), 155, 156, 157
French Mail Steamer, 235
Friendly Islands, Sinclairs in, 94

Garden of the Gods (Colorado), 155
Gay, Aubrey, 104
Gay, Eliza, 95, 104
Gay, George, 97
Geelong (Victoria, Australia), 47
Georgetown (Colorado), 166, 168, 169
Georgetown (Penang, Malay Peninsula), 302, 304
Georgia (USA), IB's travels to, 308
Gladstone, William, 21, 311
Glazer, Mr, 165, 172, 197
Glen Affric (Scotland), 309
Glen Eyrie (Scotland), 152, 155
'Golden Chersonese', 253
Golden City (Colorado), 165, 166, 167, 170
Golt, Dr (of Hangchow), 230
Good Words, contributions by IB, 4, 129, 154, 183
Gordon-Cumming, Constance, 16(*n*), 308, 309
Grant, General Ulysses S., 45, 325
Gray, Archdeacon John Henry, 222, 325
Great Gorge of Manitou (Colorado), 154
Great Lakes (USA), IB's travels to, 308
Great Platte Canyon (Colorado), 143, 147, 159, 161
Green Lake (Colorado), 168–9
Green, William Lowthian Green, 105, 111, 112-24, 139, 325
character, 113, 124
Greenwell, Dora, 129, 131
Greenwell, Mr, 129, 131
Gunong Bubu (Malay Peninsula), 301
Gunong Pondok (Malay Peninsula), 273, 301

Guthrie, Thomas, 4, 55, 91, 105, 180, 326

Haigh, William, 198, 199, 326
Halemanu, 76, 83
Hall, Charley, 119, 131
daughters, 131
Hall, Mr, 305
Halls Gulch (Colorado), 159, 162, 164
Hanalei Valley (Kauai, Hawaii), visit to, 101–2
Hananui (Halemanu's son), 74, 78, 82
Hanapeipei Falls (Kauai, Hawaii), visit to, 96–8
Hanapeipei River (Kauai, Hawaii), 92
Handfield Jones, Dr Charles, 34, 39, 326
Hanna, Dr William, 183, 186, 326
Hawaii, 16, 56–142, 309
advantages, 126
climate, 71–2, 89, 106, 126, 129–30, 134
disadvantages, 126–7
earthquakes, 110, 119, 134
IB's costs in, 139
IB's nostalgia for, 156, 157, 288
lava flows, 107, 109
mountain sickness, 122-3
olivines (crystals), 107, 109
pali climbing, 76, 81, 82-3
politics and government, 60, 63, 67
population, 72, 126–7, 132
publication of IB's papers on, 183, 203
volcanoes, 106, 111, 114–16, 117–18, 120–2
way of life, 72, 73, 74
see also volcanoes
Hawaii, king of *see* Lunalilo, William Charles, King of Hawaii
Hayward, Mr, 253, 259, 262, 326
alligator shooting, 249, 251
as IB's escort, 248, 249, 252, 258, 265, 266
Heath, Colonel, 16, 144, 145, 146, 327
Henry, Mrs, 215
Henry, Reverend A., 215, 230, 327
Hijan Mountains (Malay Peninsula), 273, 274
Hill, Sir Stephen, 241, 327
Hilo (Big Island, Hawaii), 56, 57, 58, 106, 107, 110–11
Hokkaido (Japan), 204–5, 205(*n*)
Hokodate Island (Hokkaido, Japan), 204–5, 205(*n*)
Hong Kong (China), 206–10, 310
description, 207–8, 209–10, 228–9, 233–4
fire, 208–9, 230–1, 310
harbour, 211
IB's fame in, 233
see also China
Honolulu (Oahu, Hawaii), 88, 104, 138
Hooker, Sir Joseph Dalton, 234, 327
horseback riding, hunting wild bullocks in Hawaii, 134–5
horseback riding, IB
Australia, 48
bloomer suit, 59, 67, 70, 75, 80, 96, 137, 144

Colorado, 168, 169, 176, 181, 186
Hawaii, 59–60, 61, 84–5, 97, 103, 110, 132; Hawaiian native saddle, 70; lassoing, 134–5; on volcano, 118, 123
Malay Peninsula, 301
side-saddle, 147, 149, 169
therapeutic effects, 126, 128, 134, 136, 140
horses, 48, 65–6, 67–8, 72-3, 76, 106–7, 112, 124, 147, 149, 150, 151–2, 155, 156, 167, 170, 171, 179, 181, 183, 195–6
see also 'Bessie Twinker'; 'Birdie' ('Bird'); 'Johnny Smoker'; 'Mohawk'; Waimanu horses
hospitals
established by IB, 311
Thaipeng, 275
Tung-Wah (Tun-Wah) Hospital for the Chinese Sick and Dying, Hong Kong, 229, 233
House of Commons, IB's visit, 311
houseboats, Canton, 213, 223
Hualalai (Big Island, Hawaii), 128–9, 132, 133–4, 136
Hunt, Alexander, 144, 148, 149, 327
Hutchinson, Alice, 145, 177, 198, 328
Hutchinson, Dr Francis Blake, 145, 194, 197, 328

Iao Valley (Maui, Hawaii), 183
Idaho Springs (Colorado), 168
Illinois (USA), IB's travels to, 308
India, IB's travels to, 311
Innes, Emily, 23
Innes, James, 270, 271, 273, 328
insects
Hawaiian, cockroaches, 80
Malayan, 275, 296; ants, 259–60; crickets, 260; fireflies, 261; termites, 260
Iona (Scotland), 309
Ireland, IB's travels to, 308, 311
Ise (Japan), 205
Isemonger, E. E., 269, 328
Isemonger, Mrs, 304
Islam
in Malay Peninsula, 244, 263, 296; Hadjis, 241
Island Harbour, Maine (USA), 31
Isle of Mull (Scotland), 8, 308, 309
Italy, IB's travels to, 31, 309, 311

Jackson, William, 230, 329
Japan, IB's travels to, 204–5, 310, 312
Japanese
comparison with Chinese, 210, 212
IB on, 210–11, 252
Jardine, Matheson & Co., 213, 329
Jenny (schooner), 89–90
Jervois, Sir W. William Francis Drummond, 278, 282, 329
Jim ('Rocky Mountain Jim') *see* Nugent, Jim
John Murray Archives, 2(*n*)
John Stuart Blackie Collection, 2(*n*)
'Johnny Smoker' (horse), 106, 112, 124

353

Johnson, Francis Bulkeley, 206, 222, 330
Johnson, Mrs (of Hawaii), 92, 101, 102-3
Jones, Mrs Cosmo, 261
junks, Canton, 213, 223

Kaiwiki (Big Island, Hawaii), 66
Kamunting (Malay Peninsula), 278, 279
Kapalapala (Big Island, Hawaii), 123
Kauai (Hawaii), 89–104, 106
   landscape, 97, 100–1, 103
Kavanagh, Mr, 144, 164, 329
   cooking, 183, 188
   with IB in Estes Park, 174, 177, 180,
      184, 186, 187
   IB's opinion of, 189, 193
   on Mr Nugent, 192
Kawaihae (Big Island, Hawaii), 69, 127,
   128, 137
Kealakekua Bay (Big Island, Hawaii), 69,
   130, 137
Keilambete (Australia), 46
Ker, Elizabeth 'Bessie', 35(*n*), 141, 185,
   309, 310, 329
   letter to John Murray IV, 2(*n*)
   letters to IB, 138, 172, 182, 185, 230
   mentioned in IB's letters, 37, 99, 110,
      113–14, 164, 166, 172, 181, 185
Ker family, 56, 88, 91, 128, 141, 166
Keswick, William, 206, 330
Keyt, Mr, 287, 288, 289, 290
Kilauea (Big Island, Hawaii), 69, 114–17
Kilauea (steamer), 66, 68, 79, 87, 104,
   128, 130, 137
Kin Kiang (steamer), 220, 230
Kingsley, George, 18
Kingsley, Rose, 148, 330
Kinta (steam launch), 269–70, 294, 302
Kittridge, Colonel, 157, 330
Klings (Muslim settlers), 237, 302
Kohala hills (Hawaii), 71
Koloa (Kauai), 89, 90–1
Kona (Big Island, Hawaii), 69, 127–30
Korea, IB's travels to, 312
Kota Lama (Malay Peninsula), 289, 330
Krull, Mr, 103, 104
Kuala Kangsar (Qualla Kangsa), 280–99,
   300–1
Kuala Linghie (Qualla Linghie), 249, 266,
   267
Kudin, Tunku, Sultan of Kedah, 269, 330
Kyoto (Japan), 205

Lahaina (Maui, Hawaii), 87–8
Larut (Malay Peninsula), 268, 270–1
Larut River (Malay Peninsula), 270, 274
legal process
   Canton, 218–20
   Hong Kong, 231–2
   Perak, 293
   Sungei Ujong, Malay Peninsula, 258–9
Leisure Hour, The, IB's contributions, 4,
   203, 309, 310, 311
Lela, Maharaja, 289–90, 331
leprosy, IB's interest, 88, 124
Lewes, George Henry, 228, 331
Lihue (Kauai, Hawaii), 99
Liller, J. Elsom, 150, 153, 154, 155, 162,
   331

Liller, Mrs, 153, 155
Linghie River (Malay Peninsula), 251,
   261
Livingstone, David, 203, 309, 331
London (England), IB in, 21, 307, 309,
   310, 311, 312
London Missionary Society, 234, 332
Longfellow, Henry Wadworth, 308
Longmount (Colorado), 144, 171, 172,
   180, 197
Long's Peak (Colorado), 163, 168, 175,
   176, 183
Low, Sir Hugh, 276, 290, 292, 293, 296,
   301, 332
   affection for his apes, 286, 296,
      299–300
   on IB, 300
   and IB's excursion, 298
   IB's opinion on, 291, 299, 300, 333
Lunalilo, William Charles, King of
   Hawaii, 15, 58–9, 60, 62–4, 65, 310,
   333
   IB's opinion of, 59, 66–7
   poem written for IB, 67
   ride with IB, 67–8
Lyman, Lt Governer Rufus, 58, 59, 65,
   333
Lyons, Reverend Lorenzo, 72, 85, 127,
   333

Macao passage, 230
MacBain, Sir James, 49, 50, 333
MacBain, Mrs, 49, 51
Macdiarmid, Mary, 55, 61, 117, 142,
   308, 309, 333
   letters from HB, 14(*n*), 306
McGinn's Gulch (Colorado), 173, 174,
   180, 182, 195
Mackinzie, Mr and Mrs, 35
McPetrie, Captain, 50
Maine (USA), 31
Mair, Mrs, 51, 333
Makaueli (Kauai, Hawaii), 92
Malacca, 237, 239–40, 242–3, 264–5, 266
   Chinese in, 272
   Dutch Stadthaus, 240, 246, 266
Malacca Straits, 235, 236
Malay Peninsula, 235–306, 297–8, 310
   British Residents, 22–3, 258
   gharries, 271
   IB's luggage from, 299
Malay villages, 250–1, 252
Malays, 243–4
   IB on, 252, 278
Manchuria, IB's travels to, 312
Manitou (Colorado), 154–6
Marquesas Islands, Sinclairs in, 94
Mary *see* Macdiarmid, Mary
Maui (Hawaii), 87–8, 105, 106, 183
Mauna Kea (Big Island, Hawaii), 71, 86,
   105, 113, 119, 134
Mauna Loa (Big Island, Hawaii), 69, 110,
   125, 133
   IB's ascent, 111–24
   Mokuaweoweo (crater), 118, 120, 125,
      133
Maximilian, Archduke Ferdinand, 95,
   333

Maxwell, Sir Peter Benson, 23, 268, 276,
   334
Maxwell, Sir William Edward, 268, 269,
   270, 271, 276, 279, 280, 334
   home life, 275
   IB's opinion of, 22, 273, 277, 303
   nickname, 304
   opinion of IB, 300, 303
Melbourne (Australia), 40, 47, 52-5
   Chalmers Manse, 33–8
Mentri of Larut, 273, 281, 282
Meyer, Mr, 96–7
Middleton, Dorothy, 4(*n*), 21(*n*)
Milford, John, 307
Milton, John, *Paradise Lost*, IB's
   comments, 123–4
Minnesota (USA), IB's travels to, 308
*Missionary Enterprises in the South Sea
   Islands*, 243, 334
'Mohawk' (horse), 48, 335
Moir, Dr, 34, 35–6
Mokuaweoweo crater *see* Mauna Loa
Molokai (Hawaii), 88, 124
Monthly Review, The, 312
Monument Park (Colorado), 152
Morocco, IB's travels, 312
Mortlake (Victoria, Australia), 45–7,
   125
Mount Shadwell, Mortlake (Victoria,
   Australia), 38–45
'Mountain Jim' *see* Nugent, Jim
Muda Yusef, Raja *see* Yusef, Raja Muda
Mull (Scotland), 8, 308, 309
Müller, Waldemar, 91, 95–6, 97, 335
Murray, Commander Patrick James, 250,
   251, 253–4, 256, 264, 266, 335
   cabin in hills, IB's visit, 259–60
   description, 257–8
Murray, Hallam, correspondence with
   AS, 2(*n*), 20(*n*)
Murray, John III
   IB's manuscript sent to, 309
   letters from IB, 13(*n*), 14(*n*), 15(*n*),
      17(*n*), 21(*n*), 22(*n*), 23(*n*), 267, 310
   and visitation of Mountain Jim, 311
   death, 311
Murray, John IV
   correspondence with AS, 2(*n*), 20(*n*)
   as IB's publisher, 311
   letters from IB, 7(*n*)
   see also John Murray Archives
Muslims *see* Islam

Naamhoi prison (Canton), 215–18
Namaqua (Colorado), 198
Native Americans *see* Arapaho;
   Cheyenne; Ute
Nawiliwili (Kauai, Hawaii), 104
Nelson, Mrs William, 230
Nevada (steamer), 56
New York (USA), IB's travels to, 31, 308,
   309, 310
New Zealand, 16, 56, 168, 309
   Sinclair family in, 93–4
Niagara (USA), IB's travels to, 308
night travelling, 102, 253–4
Niihau (Hawaii), 93, 94
North, Marianne, 21

Nugent, 'Rocky Mountain' Jim, 16,
18–20, 143, 172, 175, 184, 186,
309, 336
   confesses attachment to IB, 175–6, 182
   correction of IB's article, 192-3
   description, 143, 144–5, 174, 178–9,
   182, 186, 192-3
   drinking, 176, 182, 193
   final parting from IB, 198–9
   gift from IB, 165
   IB's dream about, 178
   IB's feelings for, 180, 182, 185, 193,
   199
   on Mr Powers, 146
   murder, 199
   note from IB, 179

Oahu (Hawaii), 58, 104, 138
Oban (Scotland), 308
Onomea (Big Island, Hawaii), 61, 106
Oriental Society of Pekin, IB elected as
   honorary fellow, 311
Orkney (Scotland), HB in, 141, 309
Otter, Admiral, 36, 336
Out West (Colorado monthly), 154, 189

Palmer, General William Jackson, 155, 336
Palmer, Major, 232
Paris, Miss, 131
Paris, Mr, 130, 131
Park, Miss, 57, 68, 73, 336
Parkes, Lady, 205
Parkes, Sir Harry, 205, 222, 229, 230,
   232, 265, 336
Parmatang (Chinese village, Larut, Malay
   Peninsula), 271
Parry, Rear Admiral Sir William Edward,
   32, 337
Pearl River, 230
penal system *see* legal process
Penang Gazette, 305
Penang (Malay Peninsula), 304, 305
   Chinese in, 271–2
Perak (Malay Peninsula), 245, 291, 293
   Chinese in, 272
   IB on, 282, 288
   population, 296
Perak River (Malay Peninsula), 288
Perak (Malay Peninsula), IB in, 268–301
Permatang Pasir (Sungei Ujong, Malay
   Peninsula), 250, 273
Perry, John Dietz, 151, 337
Perry, Miss, 151
Perry Park (Colorado), 151
Persia, IB's travels to, 311
Philadelphia (USA), IB's travels to, 308
Pickering, James, 18–19
Pikes Peak (Colorado), 154, 155, 157,
   158
'Pincher' (dog), 129, 155, 191
plant life
   Colorado, trees, 156, 157
   Hawaii, 64–5, 85, 129, 130; ti leaves,
   74
   Malay Peninsula, 278–9, 281–2, 288
Pope-Hennessy, Sir John (Governor of
   Hong Kong), 22, 208, 229, 232,
   233, 234, 337

Pope-Hennessy, Mrs, 232, 291
Portugal, IB's travels to, 31, 309
Power, Mr, 143, 144, 145–6, 148, 173
prisons
   Hong Kong, 229, 231–2
   Naamhoi, 215–18
Province Wellesley (Malay Peninsula),
   269, 304
Puckle, Fanny, 33, 38, 39, 40–1, 43–4,
   46, 47, 48, 338
Puckle, Fred, 39, 41, 42, 43, 44, 46, 47,
   48
Puna (Big Island, Hawaii), 106, 107

Qualla Kangsa (Kuala Kangsar, Malaya),
   280–99, 300–1
Qualla Linghie (Kuala Linghie, Malaya),
   249, 266, 267

railroad
   Colorado, 167
   IB's journey in America, 204
   Rio Grande Railway, 149–50
Raimondi, Bishop Giovanni Timoleone,
   234, 339
Rainbow (Steamer), 237–8, 264
   engineer, 238–9
Reid, Mr, 113, 117, 123
Reid, Mrs, 111
religion
   in America, 162, 167
   importance to IB, 3
   Sinclairs in Hawaii, 95–6
   see also Christians and Christianity,
   Islam
Rice, Mary Waterhouse, 99, 100, 101,
   103, 139, 339
Rice, William Hyde, 99, 100, 137, 339
riding *see* elephant riding; horseback
   riding
'Ring' (Jim Nugent's dog), 174, 339
river voyages
   China, 230
   Malay Peninsula, 250, 270, 290
   see also 'Kinta' (steam launch); sea
   voyages
Roberts, Mary (niece of Mrs Evans),
   147–8
Robina (friend of IB), 32, 140, 339
Robinson, Mrs (of Hawaii), 95, 96, 97,
   104, 139
Robinson, Sir William Cleaver Francis,
   237, 240, 339
'Rocky Mountain Jim' *see* Nugent, Jim
Rodinot, Mrs, 69, 70, 79, 85, 87
Ross, Captain John, 15, 102, 103, 339
Royal Geographical Society, 1, 21, 311
Rumbow Hills (Malay Peninsula), 249
Ruskin, John, 204, 340

Saigon, 310
St David (steamer), 31, 309
St John, Mr, 291–2, 294
St Kilda (Australia), 130
St Thomas' Church, Birmingham, 3, 42,
   307, 340
St Vrain valley (Colorado), 172-3, 196
Salt Lake City (USA), 204, 310

Sampong (Malay Peninsula), 266
San Francisco (USA), 143, 203, 204, 309,
   310
Sandwich Islands *see* Hawaii
Schofield, Colonel John McAllister, 59,
   340
Scotstown (Victoria, Australia), 49
Scottish Royal Geographical Society, IB
   elected as fellow, 311
sea voyages, 31–2, 56, 68–9, 87–8,
   89–90, 104, 206–7, 210–11, 235,
   236–7, 239
   see also river voyages
Selangor (Malay Peninsula), 267, 291,
   292, 296
Sempang (Malay Peninsula), 248–9, 250
Semple, Miss, 93
Serambang (Malay Peninsula), 256, 261,
   264
Severance, Helen, 107, 108
Severance, Lucinda, 62, 68, 107, 108,
   109, 111, 112, 132, 139
   letter from Cumming, 16(*n*)
   letters from IB, 7, 20
Severance, Luther Jr, 58, 59, 62, 107,
   108, 109, 111, 340
Shanghai (China), 310
Shaw, Captain E. W. (Lieut. Governor of
   Malacca), 239, 240, 241, 242, 244,
   245, 248, 263, 265, 266–7, 341
Shaw daughters, 241, 244, 251–2, 255,
   259, 262, 266
Shaw, Mrs, 241–2, 245, 246, 247
Shetland (Scotland), HB in, 141, 309
ships *see* steamers
Sigley, Captain William Beach, 145, 341
Sigley, Mrs, 197
Sikhs
   in Hong Kong, 208, 211, 231
   in Malay Peninsula, 274, 275–6, 277,
   285, 286, 287, 303–4
Sinai, 310, 311
Sinclair family of Kauai, 90, 91, 93–6,
   97
Sinclair, Elizabeth McHutchison, 90(*n*),
   93, 94–5, 96, 341
Sinclair, Mr, 92, 94, 104
Singapore
   Chinese in, 271
   description, 235–6
   IB's travels to, 310
   St Andrew's Cathedral, 237
'Slick, Sam', 160, 251, 341
Smith, Sir Cecil Clementi, 236–7, 305
Smith, Dr James, 89, 90–1, 99, 342
   daughters, 100, 104, 137
Smith, Jared ('young Smith'), 90
Smith, Mr, of Canton, 213, 224, 230,
   341
Smith, Mrs (Hong Kong), 232
Snowden, Chief Justice (Hong Kong),
   232, 233, 234
Society Islands, Sinclairs in, 94
Society for Psychical Research, 20(*n*),
   199
South Carolina (USA), IB's travels to,
   308
South Park (Colorado), 160, 162, 166

Spain, IB's travels to, 31, 309
spas
  IB's visits, 311
  see also springs
Spencer, Captain, 67
Spencer, Frank, 69, 70, 72–3, 83–4, 85, 86, 110–11, 127–8
Spencer, Miss, 80, 110, 113
Spencer, Mrs, 127
Spencers Ranch, Waimea, 70, 75, 105
springs
  Colorado, medicinal springs, 155
  Hawaii, warm springs, 108–9
  see also spas
Sri Sarawak (steamer), 271
Stanley, Sir Henry Morton, 106, 342
steamers
  Albion, 40
  Ben Nevis, 33, 35, 309, 315
  Chiefton, 38, 320
  Edwina, 41–2
  French Mail Steamer, 235
  Kilauea, 66, 68, 79, 87, 104, 128, 130, 137
  Kin Kiang, 220, 230
  Messageries Maritimes, 207, 334
  Nevada, 56
  P. & O. steamers, 207
  Rainbow, 237–8, 264
  St David, 31, 309
  Sri Sarawak, 271
  see also boats
Stewart, Sir Thomas Grainger, 34, 342
Stoddart, Anna
  on HB, 8, 10
  The Life of Isabella Bird (Mrs Bishop), 2, 4(*n*), 6(*n*), 8(*n*), 9(*n*), 10(*n*), 11(*n*), 12(*n*), 13(*n*), 14(*n*), 15(*n*), 20
  meets IB, 308
  publication of false anecdotes, 2(*n*)
  and visitation of 'Rocky Mountain Jim', 311
Sumner, Charles Richard, 45, 342
Sumner, John Bird, 45, 189, 342
Sunday Magazine, The, 4
Sungei Ujong (Malay Peninsula), 244, 245, 248, 250, 256–64
  British Residency, 256–7
  gaming in, 265
Swinburne, Algernon Charles, 277(*n*), 342
Swinburne, Captain Paul, 274, 280, 292, 293, 302, 342
  description, 274, 276–7, 299, 303
  on IB, 303
  and IB's excursion, 298
  nickname, 304
Switzerland, IB's travels to, 310

Tahiti, Sinclairs in, 94
Taluk Kartang (Malay Peninsula), 272
Tarryall Creek (Colorado), 158
Tchang (steamer), 230
Thaipeng (Malay Peninsula), 273, 274–5, 302
Thompson, Mr, 60, 62, 67, 111, 139
Thompson, Mrs, 58
Thompson River (Colorado), 179
Thoreau, Henry David, 308
Tibet, IB's travels to, 311
Tobermory (Scotland), 182, 192, 308, 309, 310, 311, 312
Toronto (Canada), IB's travels to, 308
Toughcuss Canyon *see* Clear Creek
Trollope, Anthony
  'Mrs Proudie', 229
  Vicar of Bulhampton, 266
Tung-Wah (Tun-Wah) Hospital for the Chinese Sick and Dying, Hong Kong, 233
Tunggal, Kunlop (Dato Bandar), 262–4
Turkey, IB's travels to, 311
Turkey Creek Canyon (Colorado), 163

Ulupalakua (Big Island, Hawaii), 105, 137
United States *see* America
Ute, 148, 149, 163, 343
Ute Pass, 154

Van Warmers, Mr, 144, 149
Veuster, Father Damien de, 124, 138, 139, 343
Victoria (Australia), 36–55, 136
Victoria (Hong Kong, China), 233–4
Victoria, Queen, 310, 312
Virginia (USA), IB's travels to, 308
Vladivostock, IB's travels to, 312
volcanoes
  Hawaii, 106, 111, 114–16, 117–18, 120–2, 124
  see also Kilauea; Mauna Loa

Wailua Falls (Kauai, Hawaii), 103
Wailuki Valley (Maui, Hawaii), 105, 106, 183
Waimanu horses, 72-3, 76
Waimanu valley (Big Island, Hawaii), 73, 75, 77–9
Waimea (Big Island, Hawaii), 70–2, 84, 105, 124–5
Waimea Canyon (Kauai, Hawaii), 99
Waipio Valley (Big Island, Hawaii), 72–3
Waipoo Falls (Kauai, Hawaii), 99
Wakatipu Lake (New Zealand), 136
Walker, Captain R. S. F., 271, 276, 280, 292, 294, 344

excursion with IB, 297–9
  IB's opinion of, 269–70, 277, 304
  nickname, 304
Walker, Mr, 130
Wall, Mr, 132-5
  character, 134
Wall, Mrs, 132, 133, 136–7
  mother, 133
Waller, Mr, 144, 145, 164
  horse belonging to, 180, 183
Wanganui (New Zealand), 93
Warrnambool (Australia), 42
Washington (USA), IB's travels to, 308
weather
  Australia, 38, 39, 44–6, 46–7, 54, 125, 136
  Colorado, 150, 166–7, 174–5, 195
  Hawaii, 71–2, 89, 106, 126, 129–30, 134
  Hong Kong, 233
  Malay Peninsula, tropical sunsets, 238, 261, 278, 290
  Singapore, 236
Wetmore, Dr Charles Hinckley, 58, 59–60, 107, 111, 112, 344
Whittier, John Greenleaf, 150(*n*), 344
Wilberforce, Bishop Samuel, 138, 179
Wilhelm II, Kaiser, 344
Williams, John, *Missionary Enterprises in the South Sea Islands*, 243
Willis, Bishop (from Honolulu), 69, 70, 131, 138, 345
Willis, Mrs, 138, 139
Wilson, Mr (from Waimea), 83, 84, 85, 86, 105, 111, 112, 127, 129
  proposals to IB, 15, 17, 86, 125–6
Wisconsin (USA), IB's travels to, 308
women
  in Canton, 223–4
  in Colorado, 189
  English, in Malay Peninsula, 299
  in Hawaii, 77
  IB's opinions on, 166, 192
Woods, Mr Justice, 268, 304–5, 345
Woods, Mrs, 305
words
  coined by IB: 'dil', 34; nangarenes, 35; quank, 91
  'larrikin' (Australian invention), 48
Wyton (Huntingdonshire, England), 307, 308

Yakoob Khan, 211–12
Yangtse River (China), IB's travels to, 312
Yarra River (Australia), 37
Yezo *see* Hokkaido
Yusef, Raja Muda, 277, 280, 293, 294, 345